How to pass

ECDL

We work with leading authors to develop the
strongest educational materials in computing,
bringing cutting-edge thinking and best
learning practice to a global market.

Under a range of well-known imprints, including
Prentice Hall, we craft high quality print and
electronic publications which help readers to understand
and apply their content, whether studying or at work.

To find out more about the complete range of our
publishing, please visit us on the World Wide Web at:
www.pearsoned.co.uk

How to pass **ECDL**

For Microsoft® Office 2000

Paul Holden and Brendan Munnelly

Approved
Courseware
Syllabus
Version 4.0

PEARSON
Prentice
Hall

Harlow, England • London • New York • Boston • San Francisco • Toronto
Sydney • Tokyo • Singapore • Hong Kong • Seoul • Taipei • New Delhi
Cape Town • Madrid • Mexico City • Amsterdam • Munich • Paris • Milan

PEARSON EDUCATION LIMITED
Edinburgh Gate
Harlow CM20 2JE
Tel: +44 (0)1279 623623
Fax: +44 (0)1279 431059

Website: www.pearsoned.co.uk

First published in Great Britain in 2004

© Pearson Education Ltd 2004

The rights of Paul Holden and Brendan Munnelly to be identified as the Authors of this Work have been asserted by them in accordance with the Copyright, Designs and Patents Act 1988.

ISBN 0 131 13012 9

British Library Cataloguing in Publication Data
A CIP catalogue record for this book can be obtained from the British Library

'European Computer Driving Licence' and ECDL and Stars device are registered trade marks of The European Computer Driving Licence Foundation Limited in Ireland and other countries. Pearson Education Ltd is an independent entity from The European Computer Driving Licence Foundation Limited, and not affiliated with The European Computer Driving Licence Foundation Limited in any manner. *How to Pass ECDL for Microsoft® Office 2000* may be used in assisting students to prepare for the ECDL. Neither The European Computer Driving Licence Foundation Limited nor Pearson Education Ltd warrants that the use of this coursebook will ensure passing the ECDL. Use of the ECDL-F Approved Courseware Logo on this product signifies that it has been independently reviewed and approved by ECDL-F as complying with the following standards:

Acceptable coverage of all courseware content related to the ECDL.

This courseware material does not guarantee that the end user will pass the ECDL. Any and all assessment items and/or performance based exercises contained in this coursebook relate solely to this product and do not constitute or imply certification by The European Driving Licence Foundation in respect of any ECDL examination. For details on sitting ECDL examinations in your country please contact your country's National ECDL/ICDL designated Licensee or visit The European Computer Driving Licence Foundation Limited web site at http://www.ecdl.com.

Candidates using this courseware material should have a valid ECDL/ICDL Skills Card. Without such a Skills Card, no ECDL/ICDL Examinations can be taken and no ECDL/ICDL certificate, nor any other form of recognition, can be given to the candidate.

ECDL/ICDL Skills Cards may be obtained from any Approved ECDL/ICDL Test Centre or from your country's National ECDL/ICDL designated Licensee.

References to the European Computer Driving Licence (ECDL) include the International Computer Driving Licence (ICDL). ECDL Foundation Syllabus Version 4.0 is published as the official syllabus for use within the European Computer Driving Licence (ECDL) and International Computer Driving Licence (ICDL) certification programme.

All product and company names are ™ or ® trademarks of their respective owners.

The screenshots in this book are reprinted by permission from Microsoft Corporation.

10 9 8 7 6 5 4 3 2
08 07 06 05 04

Typeset by Pantek Arts Ltd, Maidstone, Kent
Printed and bound in Great Britain by Ashford Colour Press Ltd, Gosport, Hants

The Publishers' policy is to use paper manufactured from sustainable forests.

contents

Introduction vii

Introduction

About ECDL

ECDL, or the European Computer Driving Licence, is an internationally recognized qualification in end-user computer skills. It gives employers and job seekers a standard against which they can measure competence – not in theory, but in practice. Its seven modules cover the areas most frequently required in today's business environment.

In addition to its application in business, the ECDL has a wider social and cultural purpose. With the proliferation of computers into every aspect of modern life, there is a danger that society will break into two groups – those who have access to computer power, and those who do not: the information 'haves', and the information 'have nots'. The seven modules of ECDL are not difficult, but they do equip anyone who passes them to participate actively and fully in the Information Society.

For more information about ECDL, visit these websites: www.ecdl.com and www.ecdl.co.uk.

About this book

This book covers the entire ECDL Syllabus Version 4.0. The syllabus is not product-specific. You can use any hardware or software to perform the tasks in the ECDL tests. All the examples in this book are based on PCs, and on Microsoft software, as follows:

- Microsoft® Windows 2000
- Microsoft® Word 2000
- Microsoft® Excel 2000
- Microsoft® Access 2000
- Microsoft® PowerPoint 2000
- Internet Explorer 6.0
- Outlook Express 6.0

If you use other hardware or software, you can apply the principles discussed in this book, but the details of operation may differ.

Good luck with your ECDL studies and tests.

1

Basic concepts of Information Technology

After tools and machines, computers were the third in a line of useful devices that humans invented to help them to do the otherwise difficult or impossible. Modern computers can perform a very wide range of tasks, one after the other, or even all at the same time. And while tools and machines work directly with physical objects, computers work with something more fuzzy: *information*.

In this module you will learn about the main hardware elements in a modern computer: the central processing unit (CPU), the memory (RAM) and the disk drive. You will also meet a number of other devices – such as modems, scanners and digital cameras – that are increasingly considered normal parts of a computer system, whether in the home, school or workplace.

A computer *is* hardware, but it *does* software. Software determines how the computer behaves – the particular task it performs at any given time. In this module you will discover the difference between operating system software such as Microsoft® Windows, and application software such as word processing, spreadsheet and database programs.

Computer networks and the Internet, usage of computers across a range of sectors from healthcare to manufacturing, issues surrounding hacking and viruses, compliance with data protection principles, and an awareness of some health and environmental concerns – these topics complete this introductory module. Welcome to the world of Information Technology. Now it's your world.

1.1 Tools, machines, computers

Learning goals	At the end of this lesson you should be able to:

- distinguish between tools and machines;
- list features of computers that set them apart from either tools or machines;
- state the units in which information storage is expressed in computers.

New terms	At the end of this lesson you should be able to explain the following terms:
Tool	An instrument operated by muscular strength that enables the user to perform a useful but otherwise difficult or impossible task.
Machine	A device that is powered all or mostly by a source other than human effort.
Computer	A general-purpose, programmable device that can process and store information.
Hardware	Hardware is the term used to describe the physical parts of a computer system.
Software	Software is the term used to describe the instructions that cause the computer system to behave in a given way.

Computers: our latest invention

Humans invented computers only after we invented two other kinds of things first: *tools* and *machines*. You can think of the computer as the third in a line of useful devices that were created to help do the otherwise difficult or impossible.

You don't need to think too hard to suggest examples of tools: saws, screwdrivers, scissors, clocks, weighing scales, bicycles and tin openers all spring to mind.

Machines are an advance on tools in that they are powered by some form of energy other than human effort. Our first machines were powered by animals, wind and running water. More recent examples of everyday machines include gas cookers, electric radios and petrol-engined cars.

How computers are different

Two basic differences set *computers* apart from the tools and machines that went before them:

- **Multi-purpose**: Modern computers can perform a very broad range of tasks, one after the other, or even all at the same time. In technical terms, computers are said to be programmable. Programs (sets of instructions) make computers behave in specific ways: to act as word processors or to control electricity-generating stations.

- **Information processing**: While tools and machines work directly with physical objects, computers work with something more fuzzy: information. Information is the result of drawing things, counting things, measuring things, and keeping diaries or logs of things.

Information and how it's measured

In computing, information is measured in terms of how much storage space it occupies. A bit is the smallest unit of information that a computer can store and process. It can have one of two possible states: on (indicating 1) or off (indicating 0). Four bits of information storage can represent any of 16 different values – for example, 16 different colours or sounds.

Eights bits add up to one byte. A kilobyte (KB) is a thousand bytes, a megabyte (MB) is one million, and a gigabyte (GB) is one thousand million.

Tools: the chimp, the banana and the stick

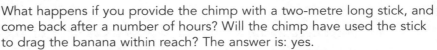

Imagine a chimpanzee in a cage and, about two metres outside the cage, a tasty banana lying invitingly on the ground. The chimp sees the banana, wants it, but cannot reach it.

What happens if you provide the chimp with a two-metre long stick, and come back after a number of hours? Will the chimp have used the stick to drag the banana within reach? The answer is: yes.

Experiments have shown that most chimps learn to use the stick as a tool. In the wild, chimps have been seen using sharp-edged stones to crack open seeds and nuts, sticks to prise termites out of the ground, leaves as toilet paper and handkerchiefs, and twigs as toothbrushes.

For thousands of years we humans have used tools: spades to turn the soil, bows and arrows to hunt animals, and, more recently, saws, screwdrivers, scissors, clocks, weighing scales, bicycles and tin openers.

A tool is an instrument that enables us to channel or focus our muscle power so that we can do the otherwise difficult or impossible.

The stick provided to the caged chimp does not make the chimp stronger or more agile. It does, however, make the chimp less hungry. Tools are useful. That's why we invented them. Tools have two major limitations, however. They usually have just a single purpose, and they require human effort to work.

Machines: the wind in our sails

After we invented tools, we began to invent things that set us apart from chimpanzees and cleverer animals: we invented machines. A machine is an instrument that is powered all or mostly by a source other than human effort.

Horses were trained to pull ploughs, and dogs and reindeers to tow sleighs. We harnessed the wind to propel ships across lakes and oceans, and to turn millstones for grinding wheat into flour. The energy in rivers we used to turn water wheels that powered weaving looms. More recently we have learned to harness hydrocarbon fuels – coal, oil and gas – to power machines and to generate electricity that, in turn, powers other machines. Gas cookers are machines, as are electric radios and petrol-engined cars.

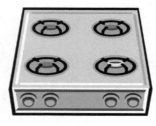

Because machines harness the energy of Nature, they can perform actions we could never do with our muscles: machines can lift and pull huge weights, spin thousands of times a second, and create very high temperatures in furnaces and very low ones in freezers. Following the machine came the automatic machine: a machine that works on its own. Microwave ovens and washing machines are automatic: you can start them, set them a time to finish their task, and go and do something else while they get on with it. Another example is the thermostat in a central heating system: it 'knows' when it's time to switch on and, when it 'senses' that the temperature is correct, it can switch itself off again. Automatically.

 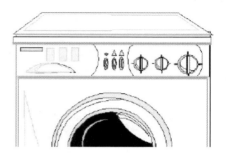

While machines do not require human effort to operate, they share with tools the limitation that they can usually perform just a single type of task.

Computers: the multi-purpose information processor

The tool, then the machine, followed by the automatic machine – and finally the computer. The last is just the latest in a line of things we humans have created to help us perform useful tasks. The idea of tools is simple enough; even chimps can understand them. You can probably use lots of machines without thinking too much about what you are doing: CD players, hairdryers, and so on. There may even be a few machines that you can take apart and put back together again. But computers?

Two basic differences set computers apart from the tools and machines that went before them:

■ **Multi-purpose**: Over a few hours you can use the same computer as a typewriter, a graphic design studio, a sound and video editing suite, a financial accounts tracker, an e-mail sender and an Internet browser. No tool or machine can perform such a wide range of tasks, one after the other. Modern computers can even do all the above at the same time!

How does a computer know which task to perform? The answer is that we give it instructions. These instructions are called programs. Programs make computers behave in specific ways: to act as word processors or to control electricity-generating stations. Computers are said to be programmable.

Word 2000   Excel 2000   Access 2000   Powerpoint 2000   Internet Explorer

Above you can see five icons, little images that represent applications. You use Microsoft® Word for word processing (see ECDL Module 3), Microsoft® Excel to work with numbers (Module 4) Microsoft® Access for databases (Module 5), Microsoft® PowerPoint for presentations (Module 6), and Internet Explorer for surfing the Web (Module 7).

- **Information processing**: While tools and machines work directly with physical objects, computers work with something more fuzzy: information. You can think of information as a kind of picture of the world rather than the world itself. In a hospital, for example, tools and machines are used directly on patients, but computers are used to record and process information about those patients.

Let's look more deeply at what information is, and then explore how we measure it.

Information: our picture of the world

Information is the result of drawing things, counting things, measuring things, and keeping diaries or logs of things. The 'things' could be the number of sheep in a flock, the colour of a child's eyes, the size of a field, the length of time since the last drought, or the intensity of an earthquake.

From earliest times, people have created information, and then communicated that information to others. We can send information across distances, by passing a note to the person sitting beside us, or by sending a postcard halfway around the world. Information can also travel across time: manuscripts in a museum can tell us tell us how people lived long ago, and future generations may watch our movies and read our newspapers.

> SCHOOL REPORT ON PUPIL
>
> SCHOOL YEAR 2001/02
>
> School... *Holy Child B.N.S.*
> Pupil... *Andrew Munnelly* Class... *V*
> No. of attendances... *169 days*
> Conduct... *Very good*
> Social Development... *Very good*

Information, although a slightly fuzzy concept, is stored in a physical way. It might be written in ink on paper (a school report), carved on a tree trunk (lovers' initials), recorded on a computer disk (health records) or chiselled on stone (an epitaph). These are all examples of information and information storage media.

How long is a piece of information?

Length we measure in metres, volume in litres, and weight in grams. But how do we measure information? You have probably experienced times when you had too little information to make a decision, and others when you were overloaded with information. But can you imagine saying that yesterday you had precisely one-quarter of the information you have today, or that tomorrow you will have 27 times as much?

In computing at least, the answer is: yes. Computerised information is measured by the amount of space it fills. If one file takes up twice the space of another inside a computer, then it contains exactly twice as much information. It's that simple. Don't confuse the quantity of information with its value. More is not always better. And all information, whatever its amount, can be inaccurate or misleading or downright false.

Computers: down to just two numbers

Computers can store only a single type of information: numbers. In fact, even the smartest computers understand just two numbers: 0 and 1. Everything – *everything* – entered into a computer is first converted into a string of 0s and 1s, and all forms of computer output – including text on the page, graphics on the screen, music, even telephone conversations – have to be converted into their final form from the 0s and 1s.

Computers do more than store information; they also process it. In simple terms, a computer accepts the input of information, processes it in some way, and then produces output. The input might be a mathematical problem, the supplier invoices for the month, a search for a good restaurant in Sydney, or the temperature of a furnace. The output might be the answer to the mathematical problem, the cheques to pay the invoices, the name and address of the restaurant, or the instructions to shut the control valves on the fuel supply.

In the middle – inside the computer's brain – the numbers are added together in various ways and combinations, according to the computer's program. The only magic is the fact that these calculations take place at a rate of millions per second – and, of course, the human ingenuity in the computer programmer.

Everything we see computers doing today – and we see them doing a lot – they are doing because they can process information and then store the results of their processing. However, this principle is masked by one outstanding fact: what computers do may be simple, but they do an incredible amount of it, quickly and reliably.

What colour is an information bit?

A bit is the smallest unit of information that a computer can store and process. You can think of a bit as a light bulb that has only two possible states: on (indicating 1) or off (indicating 0). As you can imagine, very little information can be stored in a single bit.

Let's explore the idea of computer bits by relating them to the numbers of colours that can be displayed on a computer's screen. Your screen is made up of about 480,000 little squares called pixels, each one of which can show a different colour. Behind each of these individual pixels is an amount of information storage, measured in bits.

- **1-bit colour**: How many colours can be stored in a single bit? Just two. When the bit is on (1), the dot on your screen looks white. When it's off (0), the dot looks black. A black-and-white screen, therefore, can get by with just a single bit of information behind each screen pixel.

- **2-bit colour**: Let's double the number of bits per screen pixel to two. Now each pixel can have any of the following states:

    00, 01, 10, 11

    That's four possible combinations. Each pixel can now display one of four colours at a single time: for example, white, light grey, dark grey and black.

- **4-bit colour**: Moving along, let's increase the number of bits per screen pixel to four. How many possible combinations of four numbers are there? Here's the answer. Count them:

    0000 0001 0010 0011 0100 0101 0110 0111 1000 1001 1010 1011 1100 1101 1110 1111

As you can see, four bits of information storage for each screen pixel make it possible for your screen to show any of 16 different colours.

In summary, the more bits that are available to each pixel, the greater the range of colours that the pixel can display. Each additional bit doubles the number of colour possibilities. In mathematical terms, an X-bit colour computer screen can show 2^X different colours.

Modern computer screens typically have what is called 24-bit colour, which means that their individual pixels can display any one of 16.8 million colours at one time. This is rather more than a person with average eyesight can distinguish.

What is the sound of an information bit?

As with computers and colours, so too with computers and sound. Today's computers usually have speakers attached through which you can play back music and other sound files that are stored inside the computer. Let's consider the possibilities.

- **1-bit sound**: What would this be like? Just two options are possible: no sound (represented by 0) and a single-tone beep (represented by 1).

- **2-bit sound**: This gives you four possibilities: no sound, or any one of three different tones. An improvement, but still a long way short of the capability to reproduce music or the human voice.

- **4-bit sound**: Getting better. You can now enjoy silence or any of 15 different notes.

The more bits of information storage that are available to your loudspeakers, the greater the range of notes that the speakers can reproduce. Today's computers typically have 64-bit sound capability, more than enough for even the most demanding music enthusiast

What about text? Eight bits (256 possible values) are required to store all the letters of the alphabet in lower- and uppercase format, plus all the numbers, punctuation marks and special symbols found on a computer keyboard.

From bits to bytes, kilobytes, megabytes and gigabytes

A bit, however, is an impractically small unit. When computer people talk about information, they use the term bytes, where eights bits add up to one byte.

In the metric system, we place the prefix *kilo* or *mega* before a unit when we mean a thousand times or a million times – for example, a kilometre or a megahertz. A *kilobyte* (KB) is simply a thousand bytes, and a *megabyte* (MB) is a million bytes. Prefixes you may not have met before are *giga*, meaning one thousand million and *tera* meaning a million million. These give us the *gigabyte* (GB) (a billion bytes) and the *terabyte* (TB) (a trillion bytes).

Whenever you see the term megabyte, just think of eight million little boxes of information, each one holding a 0 or 1. (That's right, eight million, not one million, because each byte contains eight bits.) The table below lists some typical computer files with their approximate size.

Computer file	File size (approx.)
A short e-mail	10 KB
A one-page word processed letter	20 KB
A colour image	60 KB
A web page	100 KB
A database of 1,000 names and addresses	800 KB
A 3-minute song	3 MB
A 60-minute video with sound	350 MB

Hardware and software

Computer systems consist of two very different types of elements: *hardware* and *software*.

- Hardware includes all the physical things that you can touch, feel, weigh, and, on rare occasions, kick. You will learn more about hardware in Lessons 1.2 and 1.3.

- Software is the intangible information component – the instructions, or programs that tell the hardware how to behave. Software is described in detail in Lesson 1.4.

Computers: smaller, faster, cheaper

The entire history of commercial computers occupies just the last 30 or 40 years.

In the 1960s, a commercial computer occupied a large air-conditioned room; it needed a team of specialists to operate it; it consumed vast amounts of electricity; and it frequently broke down.

Today's computers are typically much smaller and faster: what previously took up a full room fits into a small box. They can store more information; they consume less power; and they have become far easier to operate.

To give you some idea of the speed of advance, the first personal computers (PCs) were launched in 1979, with a clock speed (don't worry about it – it's just how we measure the speed of computers) of about 5 megahertz (MHz). Today, if you go out to buy a new PC, it is unlikely that you will be offered anything less than 2GHz – 400 times as fast. Similar progress has been made in the other main measure of computer power – storage capacity.

You don't need to understand how this has been achieved, and you don't need to know all the details. However, you should be aware of the speed of progress and the main ways in which it is measured. So, if you go out to buy a computer, you will at least know what questions to ask, and will understand the answers.

Every year, computers are becoming smaller, faster, cheaper, more reliable and easier to use. They are being used in all sorts of situations where it would previously have been impossible to use them: not only in business and government, but also in education, entertainment, health care, sport, art and design. You see computers in homes, clubs and restaurants; you don't see them (but they are there) in car engines, in bank ATMs (automatic teller machines), in supermarket checkouts, in washing machines, in telephone systems, in video recorders. You are probably wearing one at this moment, on your wrist, buried inside your watch.

You're surrounded.

But you're not under threat: computers are the latest in a long line of tools and machines. They are designed by people to meet people's needs; they are operated by people. People turn them on. People turn them off.

People like you.

The ECDL is designed to take the fear out of computing, to give you the knowledge and the skills you need to use this technology. With this book, you will learn about the most common PC applications. You won't learn everything: it is not necessary to know everything – it's not even possible. What this book aims to do is to teach you enough – enough to perform most of the tasks that most people do most of the time, and to give you enough confidence to tackle the unknown, and to learn from experience.

Conclusion

A computer is a multi-purpose machine that processes information. A program is a set of instructions that make computers behave in specific ways. Computerized information is measured by the amount of space it fills. Its basic unit is the bit. A byte is eight bits, a kilobyte (KB) is a thousand bytes, and a megabyte (MB) is a million of them. Hardware includes the physical components of a computer. Software is the instructions that tell the hardware how to behave.

1.2

Two memories and a brain

Learning goals	At the end of this lesson you should be able to:

- describe the role of the CPU in a computer, and state how its performance is measured;
- describe the role of RAM, ROM and the disk drive in a computer, and state how their capacity is measured;
- describe how RAM, ROM and the hard disk differ from one another in terms of size, duration of storage, and physical construction.

New terms	At the end of this lesson you should be able to explain the following terms:
Central Processing Unit (CPU)	The CPU is the brains of a computer. It is in the CPU that most calculations take place, and the CPU speed largely determines the speed of the computer.
Random Access Memory (RAM)	RAM is the computer's working memory, and an important factor in determining a computer's speed. RAM is volatile: as soon as power is turned off, whatever data was in RAM is lost.
Read Only Memory (ROM)	Computers typically contain a small amount of ROM that holds small programs for starting up the computer. Unlike RAM, ROM cannot be written to, and is not volatile.
Hard Disk	A spinning magnetic disk on which computer data can be stored. Typical storage capacities range from a few to a few tens of gigabytes.

Computers: why some are better than others

What characteristics set one computer apart from another? In this lesson you will focus on the three critical elements of hardware in a modern computer: the central processing unit (CPU), the main memory (RAM), and the disk drive, often referred to as the hard disk.

CPU: the computer's brain

The *central processing unit (CPU)* is the 'brains' of the computer. Its speed, measured in gigahertz (GHz), is one of the two main factors that determine the overall speed of the computer. A typical modern PC has a processing speed of 2 GHz or greater.

Main memory (RAM)

Random Access Memory (RAM) is a temporary storage area where the computer holds the instructions and data that it is currently working on.

RAM is volatile – its contents are erased if the power supply is cut off. Memory capacity is measured in bytes. A typical modern PC has a RAM size of 256 or 512 MB (million bytes). The amount of RAM in a computer is the second factor that affects its overall speed of operation.

System memory (ROM)

Read only memory (ROM) is another kind of memory. Its role is to store the computer's own programs, particularly the instructions necessary to start the computer. Everyday computer users are unlikely to be concerned about ROM – they cannot write to it.

Hard disk

The *hard disk* is a third and a permanent kind of memory. It is different from both RAM and ROM in the following ways:

- **Storage method:** Disks record information magnetically, in much the same way as music tapes or videotapes. In RAM and ROM, information is stored electronically.

- **Slower speed:** The writing and reading of information involves the mechanical movement of a read/write head over a fast-spinning disk. This makes hard disks slower than RAM or ROM.

- **More fragile:** The presence of moving parts means that hard disks are more likely to malfunction than non-moving RAM or ROM.

The brain: yours and your computer's

The brain or engine of a computer goes under a number of names: central processing unit (CPU), processor or, simply, chip. The length of time it takes a computer to perform a task depends critically on the speed of the CPU. Processor speed is measured in gigahertz (GHz). The bigger the number, the faster the processor, and the more calculations it can perform per second. Processor chips are made by companies such as Intel, AMD and Cyrix. Intel's range of Pentium processors are probably the most widely used in Personal Computers (PCs).

The processor speed is often included in the name of the computer. You are unlikely to be offered a PC with a processor speed of less than 2 GHz.

The two most important components of a CPU are the following:

- **Arithmetic Logic Unit (ALU)**: As its name suggests, this performs arithmetic computations, such as addition and multiplication, and logical (decision-making) operations, such as comparisons between values.

- **Control unit**: This extracts instructions from the computer's memory, and then decodes and executes those instructions. As directed by the instructions it reads, the control unit can produce signals to control other parts of the computer. For example, it can transfer data between memory and the ALU, and tell the ALU to perform certain operations on that data.

Short-term memory: yours

Human short-term memory has two characteristics:

- **Limited size**: Only so much information can he held in short-term memory before it fills up. Most of us can store no more than about seven items at one time – the names of seven playing cards, for example, or a seven-digit number.

- **Limited duration**: Information stays in our short-term memories for only 20 seconds or so, and then it's gone.

Short-term memory: your computer's (RAM)

A computer's short-term memory is also limited in size, and after a short time, its contents are lost. In technical terms, it is said to be volatile. The computer's short-term memory is known as Random Access Memory or RAM. Here it holds the program that it is currently performing, the information that it is currently processing, and the interim results of its calculations.

The 'R' in RAM is its main advantage. It can be accessed randomly, which means that the computer can get at any piece of data directly – it does not have to look through the storage area from the start until it finds the piece of interest. This makes it fast.

RAM is measured in bytes. Today's computers typically have 256 or 512 MB of RAM. (This is twice as much as you would have been offered for the same price last year, and probably half as much as you will be offered this time next year.) In general, the more RAM the better.

- More memory means that your computer can perform single tasks more quickly, because it can handle larger 'chunks' of information at a time.

- More memory means that your computer can perform multiple tasks at one time without a noticeable drop in performance. For example, you could enter numbers in a spreadsheet, download a file from the Internet, and print out a word processed report – all at the same time.

It is relatively easy to upgrade the memory on your computer by buying additional memory chips. They are inexpensive and easy to install. Depending on what you are using your computer for, additional memory can make a huge difference to its performance. (Don't, however, attempt to install additional memory without expert guidance.)

Long-term memory: yours

Your first day at school, your phone number, and the capital of France – these are examples of the kind of information that you store in your long-term memory. Human long-term memory has two characteristics:

- **Potentially unlimited size**: No one has ever been known to 'use up' their long-term memory.

- **Potentially unlimited duration**: Information in long-term memory can last a lifetime.

Long-term memory: your computer's

A computer's long-term memory is its disk drive, often referred to as the *hard disk*. Some computers may have more than one such drive. Computer disk drives differ from RAM:

- **Huge storage capacity**: Like RAM, hard disk capacity is measured in bytes, but is it much, much larger than that of RAM. A new computer today will typically come with a 80–120 GB disk drive – that's 80–120 billion bytes.

Let's consider this slowly. 120,000,000,000 bytes. The 32 volumes of *Encyclopaedia Brittanica* contain approximately 44,000,000 words, or approximately 220,000,000 characters (bytes). A 120 GB disk could hold that text almost 156 times, yet it only weighs about 1 kg, and takes up less space than one of the encyclopaedia's volumes. Disk drive size does not significantly affect a computer's speed of operation. But along with processor speed and RAM size, it is the third performance measure you should consider when buying a computer.

- **Non-volatile storage**: Information stays on a hard disk permanently. It is not lost when you switch off the computer.

Computer RAM and disk drives also have important physical differences:

- First, disks record information magnetically, in much the same way as music tapes or video tapes. They are not volatile: once the information is recorded, it remains on the disk until it is changed or deleted.

- Second, the process of getting information onto a disk or retrieving information from a disk involves mechanical movement. The disk revolves at a constant high speed, and a read/write head moves in and out just above the surface of the disk. Moving parts eventually wear out and, as a result, disks are more likely to malfunction than non-moving RAM. The moving parts also introduce delays into the processes of reading and writing, whereas reading from RAM is almost instantaneous.

From short- to long-term memory: studying and saving

In humans, the transfer of information from short- to long-term memory is usually called learning or studying. In computers, the act of saving a file copies the information it contains from volatile RAM to permanent storage on the disk drive.

It is a good idea to save your files at regular intervals. Remember that the computer works on your data in RAM, which is volatile. If there is a power cut, or if someone accidentally unplugs your PC, everything you have done since you last saved will be lost. Virtually every Windows-based application has a pull-down **File** menu, that offers the **Save** command as a menu option.

ROM: the other type of RAM

Don't confuse RAM with another kind of memory that you may occasionally hear of: *ROM (Read-Only Memory)*. This is where the computer stores its low-level programs, particularly the instructions necessary to start the computer. ROM differs from RAM in two ways:

- First, it is not changed after the computer is assembled (you can read it, but not write to it), and

- Second, its contents remain unchanged even when the power is turned off.

Conclusion

The CPU (processor), RAM and the hard disk are the three critical hardware components of a computer. The first is the brains of the computer, where the decisions are made. The second is where the computer stores the information it is currently working on and the instructions it is currently following. And the third is its permanent and very large storage area. Another storage area, named ROM, holds the computer's start-up instructions.

1.3

Information in, information out

Learning goals	At the end of this lesson you should be able to:

- list the main peripheral devices found on modern computers, and describe their functions;
- list the main types of removable storage for computer data;
- list the main types of computers, and describe them in terms of power, cost and typical usage.

New terms	At the end of this lesson you should be able to explain the following terms:
Floppy Diskette	A small magnetic disk that can be removed from the computer. A diskette typically holds 1.4 MB of information.
Zip Drive	A disk drive that can be built-in or attached to a computer that reads and writes high-capacity, removable magnetic disks, known as Zip disks.
CD-ROM	A disk that typically stores about 650 MB of data. Standard CD-ROMs can be written to only once. CD-RW disks can be written to multiple times.
DVD	Similar to a CD-ROM but with a much larger storage capacity – up to 3.7 GB.
Magnetic Tape	Commonly used for keeping backup copies of large volumes of data, these are too slow for normal everyday use, because their content cannot be accessed randomly.
Multimedia	The use of computers to present text, graphics, video, animation and sound in an integrated manner. Hardware elements include scanners, sound cards, loudspeakers and microphones.

Out of the box: the essentials

The system unit – usually a beige or grey box – of a computer houses the processor, the memory, the hard disk, and the electronics to control all the other components.

Everything outside the grey box is peripheral, which is why all the other objects are called peripherals. In most computer systems, the three essential peripherals are the keyboard and mouse (used for input), and the screen (used for output).

Out of the box: optional extras

There are a number of other devices that, although they are not essential, are normal parts of the system in the home, school or office. These are a printer, a modem, and loudspeakers. Some others – scanners, digital cameras, microphones – would have been considered exotic a couple of years ago, but are increasingly considered 'normal'.

Removable storage

A wide range of removable storage devices are available that can be used to transfer information easily from one computer to another, or used as security backups in case of loss, damage or theft of the computer.

These include *diskettes, Zip disks, CD-ROMs, CD-RWs, DVDs, magnetic tape cartridges*, and external hard disks.

Computer types

Computers fall into a number of different categories, although the dividing line between the categories is not always clear. At the top end are mainframes, next come network computers, then ordinary PCs and laptops, and finally and most recently, personal digital assistants or PDAs.

The computer keyboard

A keyboard is a set of typewriter-like keys that enables you to do two types of things:

■ **Enter information**: For example, when you type a letter in a word processor you are using the keyboard to enter information.

■ **Issue instructions**: You can also use your keyboard to tell your computer to perform certain actions. For example, the computer may ask you if you want to save a file and offer the following choice: press **Y** to save the file or **N** to discard it.

Keys on a computer keyboard are of three types:

■ **Alphanumeric keys**: Letters and numbers.

■ **Punctuation keys**: Comma, full stop, semicolon, and so on.

■ **Special keys**: **Function** keys, **control** keys, **arrow** keys, **Caps Lock** key, and so on.

Screen/Monitor/VDU

Also called the monitor (because you use it to monitor what is going on in the computer) or the visual display unit (VDU), the screen looks somewhat like a television. Most programs are designed in such a way that you appear to enter input directly from the keyboard onto the screen.

In fact, the information is passed to the CPU, and the CPU shows you what it has received by displaying it on the screen. Most programs also give you continuous feedback on their progress, and display their output on the screen.

Mouse

The mouse is the tool you use to move the pointer around the screen. The underside of the mouse houses a ball, and, as you move the mouse over your desk, this ball detects the movements, and converts them into movements of the pointer. Move the mouse left, the pointer moves left; right, and the pointer moves right; push the mouse away from you, and the pointer moves up the screen; pull it towards you, the pointer moves down. After a very short time it becomes second nature.

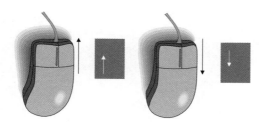

Note that the ball only moves (and therefore the pointer only moves) when the underside of the mouse is in contact with the desk. So you can move the pointer a long distance in one direction by making a series of short moves in that direction with the mouse, each time lifting the mouse so that the return journey does not affect the position of the pointer.

The mouse has two or three buttons on top: these are used to signal to the computer that the pointer has arrived where you want to go. You press one of the buttons once (called a click), or twice in quick succession (called a double-click).

The mouse (or whatever pointing device you use – see the next section, Other pointing devices) makes operation of the computer easy, and even intuitive, but it is seldom absolutely necessary. Most programs allow you to move the pointer around the screen and choose your options using special keys or combinations of keys on the keyboard. Some users prefer this: it means they can do all their work from the keyboard – they don't have to switch back and forth between the keyboard and the mouse.

Other pointing devices

Mice are by far the most common pointing devices, but there are others.

- **Trackballs**: These are like upside-down mice: you move the pointer by manipulating a ball in a special housing with your fingers. Trackballs are useful in situations where desk space is limited.

- **Joysticks and games controllers**: These fulfil the same function as the mouse or trackball, but are designed specially for games and simulation.

- **Touchpads**: Most portable computers have a device built into the keyboard for moving the pointer, either in the form of a miniature joystick, or a pressure-sensitive touchpad that detects movements of your finger.

- **Light pens**: These are pen-shaped devices that, when placed close to the screen, can be used both to draw and to control icons or choices shown on the screen.

- **Touch screens**: You will often see these in public information kiosks: the user simply touches the screen at the point of interest in order to exercise a choice from the options displayed.

- **Graphics tablets**: These are flat surfaces that detect the movement of a plastic stylus (pen) across them. They are typically used for art and design applications, but smaller versions are becoming common in 'pocket', 'hand-held' or 'palmtop' computers. These devices (known as Personal Digital Assistants, or PDAs) are too small to allow typing.

Printers

There are several kinds of printer on the market: the two most common are:

- **Laser printers**: These use a technology similar to that used in photocopying to transfer the image of a page onto paper. The image is 'drawn' under instruction from the computer.

- **Inkjet printers**: These have a moving 'pen' (the write head) that holds an ink cartridge. This moves back and forth over the page and, under computer control, ejects a minute quantity of ink at the precise point where it is required on the page.

You will occasionally come across a third category of printer: impact printers. These work like a typewriter: they hammer out the required characters onto the page through an ink-impregnated (or carbon-covered) ribbon. There are several kinds, using slightly different techniques for making the marks on the paper: dot matrix printers, daisy wheel printers, and line printers. Nowadays their use is confined to specialist applications (printing receipts from cash registers, printing the time of arrival on a ticket in a car park), or high-volume printouts that do not use graphics (tax forms, electricity bills).

Plotters are used in specialist applications, such as producing architectural or engineering drawings. Most of them are designed to produce large drawings accurately. They are relatively expensive.

How to choose a printer

Some of the factors you should consider when buying a printer are:

- **Speed of output**: Most laser printers can print 8 or 12 pages a minute. This speed may depend on what you are printing: graphics, or text pages with a variety of different fonts, tend to be slower. If you need a faster printer, be prepared to pay a lot more.

  Inkjet printers are generally a lot slower than laser printers, but their speed doesn't depend on what you are printing. The quality of the print tends to vary, because they rely on a moving write head.

- **Colour**: If you want colour output, you have to buy a colour printer. It's that simple. Colour laser printers are expensive; colour inkjet printers are only slightly more expensive than black-and-white printers.

  Some colour printers use three different inks or toners to produce their output, some four. Some use a combined three- or four-colour cartridge, some a separate cartridge for each colour. Your choice depends on what you are using the printer for. If you are only occasionally using colour output, make sure you have a separate black cartridge: the density of the black printout from a black cartridge is much higher than that from a combination of colours. If you get a combined four-colour cartridge, you will be throwing out the almost-full colour inks just because you have run out of black.

- **Cost of consumables**: The initial cost of the printer is only one of the cost factors that you need to consider: ink cartridges (for inkjet printers) and toner cartridges (for laser printers) have to be replaced regularly, and it is worthwhile calculating the cost per page of output before making your final decision.

Modem

A modem is used to connect your computer to the telephone network, so that you can send e-mail, or use the Internet. Most computers sold today include a modem already installed in the system unit, but they can also be obtained as external devices that are connected to the computer by a cable. Most modems can enable your computer to function as a fax machine (although, unless you have a scanner, you are limited to sending text-only faxes). See Lesson 1.5 for more details.

Multimedia

Computers can manipulate any kind of data that can be converted into numbers, including music, pictures, animated drawings, video and speech. A range of applications has grown up around this capability, in which text, video and sound are mixed to deliver instruction, information or entertainment. These applications are called *multimedia* applications, and a computer that can run them is often called a multimedia computer. Most computers nowadays can run these applications. However, if this is your main interest, you may want to consider a computer with a larger screen, and more advanced sound generation and video display capabilities. In addition, a number of specialized peripherals are available.

Scanner

Think of a scanner as the first half of a photocopier – it copies a photograph, drawing or page of text into the computer, where you can use a program to manipulate it, or print it out (like the second half of the photocopier). You can use the scanner to include a drawing or photograph in a newsletter, or use Optical Character Recognition (OCR) software to decipher the text, and use all or part of it in a word-processing document (without having to re-type it).

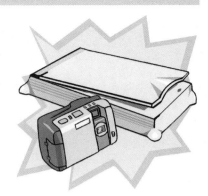

Digital camera

A digital camera works exactly like a standard camera, except that it does not use photographic film – the images are recorded digitally in the camera's memory. From there, you can transfer them to your computer and subsequently print them out, use graphics software to edit them, archive them for posterity, or e-mail them to your friends.

Loudspeakers

Loudspeakers are standard equipment on almost all new computers. They are used to play music and other sounds.

Sound cards

Again, your system unit almost certainly includes a sound card, which is used to control all the audio output (music, speech, etc.). However, if the quality of music output is important to you, you may want to upgrade from the sound card supplied as standard equipment.

Microphone

Many software applications can be controlled by speech commands. These are spoken into a microphone.

Looking after your hardware

Modern computers are robust and reliable: once they start working, they tend to go on working. But remember that they are sensitive instruments, and avoid testing their tolerance.

DO give your computer room to breathe: it has to have access to fresh air so that the fan can keep the electronics cool.

DON'T block the air vents by stacking books or magazines or (worse) draping clothes over the back of the computer.

DO keep the computer dry. Excessive moisture can play havoc with electric circuitry.

DON'T eat or drink while using your computer: crumbs can clog up your keyboard. A spilt cup of coffee can wreck your computer and (probably worse) cause the loss of all the files stored on the computer.

DO keep your computer free of dust: you will notice that it tends to attract dust. Clean the air vents occasionally, and use an anti-static wipe on the screen.

DON'T expose your computer to extremes of temperature.

DO shut down the computer in an orderly fashion, by systematically closing the applications you have opened.

DON'T just switch it off or pull the plug from the socket.

DO keep diskettes away from the screen: the strong magnetic field generated by the screen may erase or change some of the data.

DON'T move the system unit while the computer is in operation – you risk damaging the hard disk drive.

When something goes wrong

You are more likely to be a computer user than a computer engineer. Therefore respect your PC as a delicate instrument – if it seems to be malfunctioning, don't try to fix it. You risk destroying it or electrocuting yourself. Always call a person qualified to deal with the problem.

Information you can take with you

Hard disk drives are built in to the computer, and are not (generally) transferred between computers. There is, however, a wide range of removable storage devices that can be used to transfer data easily from one computer to another, or used as security backups in case of loss, damage or theft of the computer. These include diskettes, Zip disks, CD-ROMs, CD-RWs, DVDs, magnetic tape cartridges and external hard disks.

Diskettes (floppy disks)

Until quite recently, the floppy disk or diskette was the most commonly used medium for transferring information between computers. If you wanted to take a document from your office computer to your home computer, you simply copied the document to the diskette, and brought it home in your pocket. You passed files to your work colleagues in a similar way. Diskettes were also the principal way of loading programs onto a computer. The term floppy came from an earlier time when diskettes were, in fact, floppy. Since the late 1980s, however, diskettes use a hard plastic shell with a sliding metal cover. The most common type of diskette holds 1.4 MB.

Zip disks

The entire text of this book fits onto a single diskette, but not its graphics. As computer files began to include more and more images, and audio, animation and video elements, floppies were no longer an option for file transfer or backup storage. High-capacity removable diskettes began to find favour. Some use magnetic technology, some laser technology. Among the most popular such devices is the Zip disk, which uses a Zip drive from the Iomega Corporation. It provides storage of 100 MB, 250 MB or 750 MB.

CD-ROM

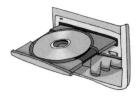

The letters CD-ROM stand for Compact Disk Read-Only Memory. A CD-ROM looks like a music CD, and in fact CD readers in computers are almost all capable of playing music CDs. The move from diskette to CD-ROM as the favoured medium for distributing software has taken place mainly because of the size of modern software applications: they need more storage space. (More space is required because the programs have added functionality, because they are more graphic in design, and because they may include other multimedia elements.) A single CD-ROM can hold as much information as 460 diskettes – about 650 MB.

CD-ROM drives (the part of the computer that reads CD-ROMs) are now offered as standard on all new computers. The only performance measure to watch out for is the speed of the drive, always quoted as a multiple of the normal music CD-player speed: nowadays, 36× speed or 40× speed CD-ROM drives are normal.

To record information on a CD, you need a CD writer (or 'burner'). Information is encoded on the surface of CDs as tiny holes, which are detected by a laser beam.

CD-RW

A limitation of standard CD-ROMs is that, while that can be read as often as necessary, they can be written to only once. A newer type of CD-ROM is the CD-ReWritable disk or CD-RW. You can work with CD-RW drives and disks just as you would with floppy diskettes or hard disks by writing data to them multiple times.

DVD

CD-ROMs are now being overtaken by DVDs (Digital Versatile Disks), which look similar, but have a great deal more storage capacity – up to 3.9 gigabytes or GB.

Most modern PCs come with a drive that can read CD-ROMS, CD-RWs and DVDs.

Magnetic tape (data cartridges)

Magnetic tape – usually in cassettes not unlike music cassettes – is commonly used for keeping backup copies of large volumes of data. It is less useful in normal everyday use, because it cannot be accessed randomly: the computer has to read it through from the beginning to find the part of interest.

External hard disk

These are disk drives that are similar to regular, internal drives in all but one respect: they are removable. Such drives can range in storage capacity up to 180 GB. A disadvantage is that they are more prone to damage, due to their internal moving parts.

Medium	Typical capacity	Typical cost of medium (July 2003)
Hard disk (Fixed)	80 to 120 GB	£80 to £220
Diskette	1.4 MB	Less than £1
CD	650 MB	Less than £10
DVD	3.9 GB	£20 to £30
Zip	750 MB	Less than £20
Tape	4 to 100 GB	£20 to £70

Computers: more than one type

Computers fall into a number of different categories, although the dividing line between the categories is not always clear.

At one end of the spectrum are mainframes. These are big, expensive machines, typically used by large corporations, governmental organizations and scientific research establishments. They are expected to run continuously, 24 hours a day, 365 days a year. They are capable of processing huge numbers of transactions, and performing extremely complex calculations.

At the other end of the spectrum are the computers most of us are familiar with – the PC (personal computer), formerly known as the microcomputer. Today, PCs can be bought for less than £1,000. PCs come in various shapes and sizes. Desktop computers are the most common form of PCs: they generally include a system unit, a screen and a keyboard, as separate components. Laptop or notebook computers are more portable: the screen is a flat liquid crystal display (LCD), which forms a lid hinged to cover the keyboard and system unit. Laptops are somewhat more expensive than desktop PCs.

Somewhere in the middle of the range are network computers. Because they play an essential role in administering and protecting the security of often very large computer networks, they offer greater processing power, storage capacity and reliability than PCs. Prices begin in the £5,000–10,000 range.

The personal digital assistant or PDA is a hand-held device that combines some or all of the functions of a computer, mobile phone, fax sender, web browser, e-mail client and personal organizer. Unlike laptops, most PDAs use a stylus rather than a keyboard for input, and incorporate handwriting recognition features. Some PDAs also boast voice recognition capabilities. PDAs are also called palmtops, hand-held computers and pocket computers. Expect to pay at least £300 for a reasonably high-performance PDA. PDAs are used mainly by mobile staff, such as travelling sales representatives.

Devices for input, for output, and for both

One way of categorizing items of computer hardware is to ask: is this device for inputting information or for outputting it? Clearly, a microphone is an input device, and a loudspeaker is an output device. Another input device is a digital camera, while printers are output devices.

A keyboard is an input device: you use it to enter information and commands to the computer. But what about the monitor? Monitors are usually output devices, but a touchscreen monitor is both an input *and* an output device. So too is a modem. Disk drives can also be considered as both input and output devices.

Conclusion

The basic PC consists of a system unit, a screen and a keyboard. Virtually all PCs include a pointing device – most commonly a mouse. Other items that are almost essential are a printer, and a modem for connecting the computer to the telephone network. Most PCs sold today are equipped for multimedia: they include loudspeakers, sound cards and microphones. To capture images, drawings, or photographs and include them in newsletters, project reports or e-mails, you need a scanner or a digital camera. Look after your computer, so that it gives a long life of good service.

14.

Software: the two kinds

Learning goals   At the end of this lesson you should be able to:

- distinguish between system software and application software;
- describe the process of software development;
- discuss software licensing and the different types of licence.

New terms   At the end of this lesson you should be able to explain the following terms:

Software	The programs (sets of instructions) that determine how the computer behaves.
System Software (Operating System)	Software that performs such tasks as recognizing input from the keyboard and mouse, sending output to the screen, communicating with printers and other peripherals, and keeping track of files.
Application Software	Programs that do real work for users. For example, word processors, spreadsheets and database management systems.
Licensed Software	Software that may be used only when the relevant user organization or individual has purchased the right to do so under certain conditions.
Shareware	Software that is typically available free of charge, but the author usually requests that you pay a small fee if you like the program and use it regularly. Registered users can receive service assistance and updates.
Freeware	Copyrighted software given away without charge by the author. Typically, the author allows people to use the software, but not sell it.

What is software?

A computer is hardware, but it does software. *Software* determines how the computer behaves – the particular problems it solves at any given time.

About system software

Also known as the Operating System (OS), *system software* controls the computer itself. All other programs depend on the operating system to communicate with and control the hardware.

On PCs, the most common example of system software is Microsoft Windows. When you add a new piece of hardware to your system, you might have to load a special piece of software called a driver to enable the operating system to control the hardware.

About application software

Application software is software that addresses a 'real world' problem – it does something that you or I want done. When you have completed your ECDL, you will be able to use several application programs: word processing, spreadsheets, electronic mail, and so on.

How software is made

Software development requires a cycle of research, analysis, development and testing, involving the following types of people:

- **Systems analysts**: These are the 'architects' that study the real-world processes that the software is intended to support, and produce the design for the software.

- **Programmers**: These are the 'builders' that translate the design into a working program. They write instructions that tell the computer what to do in order to accomplish the task for which the system is intended.

Software testing is almost never comprehensive, so that errors and problems sometimes occur (bugs).

Software copyright

Software belongs to the authors, and, in general, copying it is illegal. It's piracy. Software copyright takes three main forms:

- **Licensed software** must be purchased and used only under specified conditions.

- **Shareware** is typically available without charge, but a small payment must be made if it is used regularly. Registered users typically receive service assistance and updates.

- **Freeware** is software that, although copyrighted, is given away without charge by its author.

Software

Software is the intangible side of computing: it is the generic name given to all the programs – the sets of instructions – that determine how the computer behaves. We distinguish between two kinds of software: system software and application software.

- **System software** is concerned with the computer itself – what devices it can control, how it manages files and storage, and how it deals with exceptional conditions.

- **Application software** is concerned with the world outside the computer – the world of business, entertainment or education.

Application software

There is a saying that 'People don't buy a shovel, they buy a hole in the ground'. Similarly, you don't really want a computer: you want the ability to write and edit letters, prepare household or business accounts, and perhaps obtain information from the Internet for a homework project or business plan. Programs that enable you to perform such useful actions are called *application programs* or, simply, *applications*.

At the end of this ECDL course you will be able to use the applications listed in the following table.

ECDL module	Application type	Example
3	Word processor	Microsoft Word
4	Spreadsheet	Microsoft Excel
5	Database	Microsoft Access
6	Presentation	Microsoft PowerPoint
7	Web and E-mail	Microsoft Internet Explorer and Outlook Express

Some application programs, for example Microsoft Word and Internet Explorer, are very common, and many computers are sold with them already installed. Another common type of application is desktop publishing (DTP) software. The term DTP describes the process of combining text and graphics on a PC screen to produce documents such as newsletters, brochures, books, and so on. Some popular DTP applications include Microsoft Publisher, QuarkXPress and Adobe PageMaker.

Other applications are developed for more specialized tasks. An architect might use a sophisticated drawing application to design houses; a submarine builder might purchase a piece of project management software to help keep track of the thousands of components. In Lesson 1.7 you will look in more detail at the types of applications in daily use in areas such as business, administration, education, manufacturing and healthcare.

System software

A computer needs more than just application programs. It also needs *system software*, otherwise known as the *operating system* (OS). Here are the more important asks performed by an OS:

- **Hardware management:** The OS works directly with your computer's hardware. It recognizes key presses, tracks mouse movements and clicks, and sends output to the monitor. The parts of the OS that control hardware devices are called *drivers*. Many drivers, such as the keyboard driver, come with the OS. For printers, scanners and other peripheral devices, you typically need to install a new driver when you connect the device to your computer.

- **File management:** The OS manages the storage of information in memory and on your hard disk drive. It enables you to create and name new files, open existing ones, organize files into folders, and copy files between different folders and storage devices.

- **Application management:** The OS controls the running of all application programs on the computer. A modern OS such as Microsoft Windows supports *multitasking*: it can run many application programs at the same time.

  Examples of operating systems include the various versions of Microsoft Windows (such as Windows 98, Windows 2000 and Windows XP), Apple MacOS, Linux, and SunOS.

Graphical user interface

Modern operating systems and application programs present their features through what is called a *graphical user interface* or *GUI* (pronounced gooey). The main elements are as follows:

- **Windows:** Rectangular, moveable, and resizable areas of the computer screen. Different windows can show the contents of different files, or display information about different hardware resources. In the example below you can see two windows. The top one shows the disk drives on the computer, and the lower shows a text file.

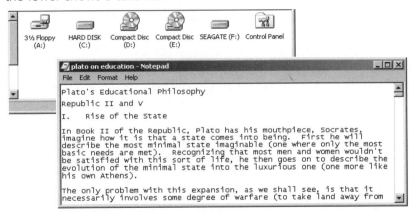

- **Icons:** These are small images that, when clicked with the mouse button, can instruct the computer to perform particular actions. An icon's appearance should indicate its purpose. Clicking on the print icon below, for example, tells the computer that you want to print the currently open file.

- **Pull-down Menus:** These are lists of commands that you can issue to the computer. When you click a menu's name, the commands on that menu are displayed on your screen. You can then click the particular command that you require.

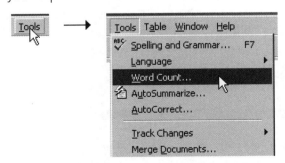

How software is made

The development of any software system involves a cycle of research, analysis, development and testing, involving the following types of people:

■ **Systems analysts**: They study the business processes that the software is intended to support, and produce the design for the software. They decide what the software should do (but not necessarily how it should do it). You can think of the systems analyst as the software architect. Systems analysts are focused on the needs of the users and the application area.

■ **Programmers**: They translate the design into a working program. They write instructions that tell the computer what to do in order to accomplish the task for which the system is intended. You can think of the programmer as the software builder. Programmers are focused on the computer, its capabilities and its limitations.

Software copyright

In general, software is licensed rather than sold. When you buy a software package, you don't own the software: you gain the right to use it under specified conditions. Most *end-user licence agreements* allow you to run the program on only one machine and to make copies of the software only for backup purposes.

In general, software is easy to duplicate, so it is easy for unscrupulous people to make unauthorized copies: don't do it. It's piracy; it's illegal; and it deprives an individual developer or a company of their rightful income, which they need to produce the next version of that piece of software, or the next application that you will want to use.

Don't accept software from dubious sources, whether in person, by mail order, or over the Internet. You are responsible for the legality of the software that you use.

Some software, called freeware, is distributed without charge: you find it on disks given away with magazines, or you can download it from the Internet. Again, you should be clear about the terms of use: in most cases, you can use it, but you may not, for example, sell it for profit, change it in any way, or label it as if it was your own product.

Other software is called shareware. It is widely distributed in much the same way as freeware. You can try it out, but if you decide to use it you are expected to send a licence fee to the developer. In some cases, this is based on honour; in other cases, the shareware version will not function after a time period (typically 30 days), or certain functions are disabled in some way. When you register with the developer and send the licence fee, you are given a fully working copy of the software, or a password to unlock the disabled functions.

Licensed software typically requires a unique, identifying code known as a Product ID to be entered when it is installed. If you buy a physical copy of the software, the ID is usually located on the user guide, licence agreement or packaging materials. If you purchase the software over the Internet, the Product ID is typically sent to you in an e-mail message. After the software has been installed, you can usually see the Product ID on the window that is displayed when you choose the **Help | About** command.

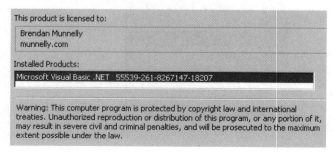

This product is licensed to:

Brendan Munnelly
munnelly.com

Installed Products:

Microsoft Visual Basic .NET   55539-261-8267147-18207

Warning: This computer program is protected by copyright law and international treaties. Unauthorized reproduction or distribution of this program, or any portion of it, may result in severe civil and criminal penalties, and will be prosecuted to the maximum extent possible under the law.

Software versions

Software developers don't like saying that they have finished an application – they prefer to say that they have brought it to a certain point in its development so that it can be sold to the public. But as soon as the first version of a software application is released, you can be sure that the developers are already busy working on the next version.

Most developers use a numbering system to identify software versions. Version 1.0 becomes version 1.0.1, 1.0.2, and so on; then version 1.1.0, 1.1.1, and so on; then version 1.2, 1.3, then 2.0, and so on.

As with Product IDs, you can usually see an application's version number in the window that is displayed when you choose the **Help | About** command. In this example for Adobe Acrobat you can see that the version number is 5.0.5.

Problems with software

Software – even the smallest piece of application software – is complex. It is difficult to test thoroughly, because it is difficult to imagine every possible input in every possible combination. Sometimes mistakes are made, or unusual circumstances are not adequately catered for by the designers or programmers.

When the software produces incorrect or unexpected results, it is said to have a bug. Bugs can range from minor irritations, where, for example, the screen displays are inconsistent, through significant errors, such as incorrect totals on invoices, to total collapse.

Too many applications can slow down your PC

Be aware that when you run a number of different applications at one time, such as Microsoft Word, Excel, PowerPoint, a computer game, and an e-mail application, the applications will run more slowly together than if they were run individually. In short, running multiple applications at the same time slows down your PC's performance.

Data

Data is another intangible in a computer system, but it is not generally built by the software developer. It's built by users – people like you. So to write a letter, you need a keyboard, a screen and a printer (hardware), and you need a word-processing program (software). The letter itself, and the name and address of the recipient, are data.

Data is held on a computer system in files. Files are organized into directories (otherwise known as folders). Files and directories are given names, so that you can find them and recognize them when you need them, and so that the operating system can find them and work on them when it needs to. In Lesson 1.8 you will learn how to protect your data files against damage, loss or theft.

Conclusion

Application software are programs such as word processors that perform useful tasks. System software (the operating system) is software that controls the computer itself. Commercial licensed software must be purchased and used only under specified conditions. Software belongs to its authors and, in general, copying it is illegal. Software is developed by systems analysts and programmers in a process that involves detailed research, analysis, program development and testing. Testing is almost never comprehensive, so errors and problems (bugs) sometimes occur.

Computer networks

Learning goals   At the end of this lesson you should be able to:

- list the main advantages of computer networks;
- list some disadvantages of computer networks;
- distinguish between LANs and WANs;
- describe a client–server network;
- explain the purpose of a modem, and know how data transfer speed is expressed;
- explain the following telecommunications terms: PSTN, ISDN and ADSL.

New terms   At the end of this lesson you should be able to explain the following terms:

Computer Network	Two or more computers that are connected together by some means to provide their users with such services as printer-sharing, file-sharing and e-mail.
Local Area Network (LAN)	A network that connects computers located within a small area.
Wide Area Network (WAN)	A network that connects computers over a wide area, typically across international boundaries.
Client–Server Network	A network architecture in which each computer is either a client or a server. Clients tend to be ordinary PCs that rely on a server to complete a particular task. Servers are more powerful computers that 'serve up' files or applications to the clients.
Modem	A device that converts outgoing digital signals used in a computer into analogue signals, so that they can be carried over the telephone network, and converts incoming analogue signals into digital form.
Data Transfer Rate	The speed at which a modem or other device can move information. Expressed in bits per second (bps). Modern modems operate at 56 kbps.
ADSL	A technology that can provide very fast data transfer over the traditional analogue-based telephone system.

Networks and groupwork

A *computer network* is the result of joining two or more computers together. In computer networks, as in other areas, the whole can be more than the sum of the parts.

Networks open up new computing possibilities: sharing of printers and other hardware resources, of files, and of applications. They also make possible e-mail, the exchange of messages between users of computers that are connected to a common network. Networks enable groupwork, a type of collaborative effort that would otherwise be impossible.

LANs, WANS and client-server networks

Networks can be categorized by their size. For example, LANs (*Local Area Networks*) connect computers in a single room, building or group of adjoining buildings, while WANs (*Wide Area Networks*) connect computers at locations within the same or different countries.

Another ways of looking at a network is in terms of the roles played by different computers attached to it. One of the more widely used is the *client-server* architecture, in which some computers act as clients and a smaller number act as servers. The Internet is an example of a client-server network.

Modems

Networks that connect computers in geographically distant locations use the telephone system as a channel of communication. The telephone system was originally developed to reproduce and carry the sound of the human voice in the form of analogue signals, and is unsuitable for carrying the digital signals used by computers.

Hence the need for *modems*: devices that enable computers to exchange information over the telephone system. Modem speeds or *data transfer rates* are measured in bits per second.

PSTN, ISDN and ADSL

These are three important terms in telecommunications. The first and second refer to two very different types of physical cables and the exchanges that connect them. PSTN is the older-style, human-voice carrying system. ISDN is the newer digital system, created specifically to carry computer-style digital signals.

ADSL, in contrast, refers to a method of transferring data at very high speeds through the traditional, analogue PSTN telephone system. It is proving so successful that some who upgraded to ISDN are moving back to a combination of PSTN and ADSL.

Computer networking: from individual to groupworking

When your computer is connected to other computers – whether they are in the same building or on the other side of the world – it is part of a computer network. You can still use it to do your own work as usual, but several new possibilities open up:

- **Sharing hardware**: In a stand-alone world, people can print only if a printer is attached directly to their computer. By connecting one or more printers to a computer network, everyone whose computer is also attached to the same network can print their documents.

  Printer-sharing means that everyone can print (although not at the same time) without everyone having an individual printer. The same is true of other hardware devices, such as modems and scanners.

- **Sharing files**: On a stand-alone computer, you can work with all the files stored on your computer's hard disk. On a network-connected computer, you may be able to work with files stored on other people's computers too.

  Rather than have network users rummaging through each other's hard disks, information that is needed by everyone in a particular department (in accounts, for example, or in a warehouse) is usually stored on a single, powerful, permanently switched-on computer called a file server.

Word 2000

- **Application sharing**: Rather than install an application such as Microsoft Word on each individual computer, the software can instead run on a central server. Network licensing of software applications, sometimes called per seat pricing, is generally cheaper than multiple stand-alone licensing.

- **Exchanging electronic messages (e-mail)**: Meetings, telephone conversations, letters and memos – typically, these are the ways in which people in an organization communicate with one another.

  Computer networks make possible another form of communication called electronic mail, or e-mail for short. This is the exchange of messages between users of computers that are connected to a common network.

  In computer networks, as in other areas, the whole can be more than the sum of the parts. Network users can participate in a kind of co-operative work that would otherwise be impossible: groupwork or workgroup computing. For example, one person can write the first draft of a business report, another can edit it, a third can lay it out, while a fourth can contribute a drawing or a scanned photograph.

Networks: is there a downside?

Networking is not without its risks and disadvantages:

- You have to take your turn in the queue for printers and other devices that are shared over the network.

- You might feel less in control when you are sharing documents, databases and information with other users of your network. For documents with multiple authors and editors, you might need to put in place a document change and tracking system.

- Networks can be technically complex. Not every company has the required expertise in-house to keep things running smoothly and fix them when they go wrong – and bringing in outside help can be expensive.

  So, even for relatively small networks, the cost of ownership in terms of money and hassle can be quite high in comparison to a collection of stand-alone PCs.

LANs and WANs

Networks come in two sizes: big and small:

- **LAN**: A Local Area Network or LAN connects the computers in a single room, building or group of adjoining buildings.

- **WAN**: Large corporations operate computer networks that connect offices at locations within the same or different countries. These are called Wide Area Networks or WANs.

In reality, most networks are bigger than LANs but smaller than WANs. But, for some reason, no one has thought up a name for them.

Computer networks can be open to everyone or restricted to a chosen few. An example of a private access network is one operated by a company or government agency for its own personnel only. An example of a public access network is the Internet.

Networks: clients and servers

Networks come in different arrangements. Or, in technical language, different network architectures. One of the more widely used is the client-server architecture, in which some computers act as clients and a smaller number act as servers:

- **Server**: This is a computer that contains files or applications that it 'serves up' to the clients on request. Servers tend to be large, powerful, permanently switched-on computers.

- **Client**: Typically, a client computer is an ordinary desktop or mobile PC that relies on a server to complete particular tasks. It might request some information from the server, for example, or even use a software application that is installed on the server machine.

The Internet is an example of a client–server network.

Networks and the telephone system

How do the computers in a network actually connect with one another? Well, in a LAN it's relatively simple: the computers (and printers and other devices) are connected together with a special cable. However, in a WAN, that isn't an option. It would be quite impractical to run network cables from one side of the country to another, or from one continent to the next.

The solution is that WANs use cables already in place – the cables of the national and international telephone system (the Public Switched Telephone Network or PSTN). They also use all the other technology of the telephone network – satellites, microwaves, optic fibres, and so on. This has advantages, and one major disadvantage too:

- **Advantages**: It's already in place (so there is no need to run WAN cables across rivers and over mountains), and its connection points are never far away (the phone system reaches into every workplace and virtually every home).

- **Disadvantage**: Computer signals (the ones that travel around inside a computer) are a different 'shape' from the signals accepted by the phone system (ones resulting from the sound of the human voice). Computer signals are digital; voice signals are analogue.

A digital signal consists of one of two possible states only, each state representing a 0 or a 1. Analogue signals, which mimic the sound of the human voice and music, can vary continuously between an upper and lower value.

Modems: what do they do? and how quickly?

Connecting a computer to the PSTN presents a problem: *a signal shape* problem. To solve this problem, we need a device than can do two jobs. Which job it does at any particular time depends on the direction of the information transfer:

- **Outgoing information**: When your computer sends data (such as an e-mail) down the phone line, the device must 'shape' the signal – convert it from computer-shape to phone-shape (digital to analogue).

- **Incoming information**: When you receive data (such as a file from a distant computer), the device must 'deshape' the signal – reconvert it back from phone-shape to its original computer-shape (analogue to digital).

Another, rather poetic, word for the act of shaping anything in this way is modulation. A device that shapes (*modu*lates) and deshapes (*demo*dulates) a signal is called – guess what? – a modem.

Most modern computers have built-in modems. To connect such a computer to the telephone system, you plug the phone line into the socket at the back of the computer.

In modems, the speed at which information can be transferred is everything. How can you tell how fast a particular modem is? The answer is provided by the modem's data transfer rate, as expressed in bits per second or bps. Most modems today can transfer data at around 56 kbps (kilobits per second, or thousands of bits per second).

From PSTN to ISDN

In recent years telephone companies have been building exchanges and laying cables that handle digital rather than analogue signals. For computer users, this has opened up an alternative to using modems and the normal telephone network (PSTN). The most widely used such service goes under the name of the Integrated Services Digital Network or ISDN.

ISDN's early users were businesses that needed frequent high-volume communication with other offices. This service was simply too expensive for low-volume users. This is beginning to change – the cost of ISDN is now within the reach of small businesses and home users. ISDN gives access to two 64 kbps channels; these can be used separately or combined to exchange data at 128 kbps.

You do need a special 'box' to connect a computer to an ISDN line. This box is sometimes referred to as a 'digital modem', even though, as you now know, such a term is contradictory. Its true title is a terminal adapter.

Staying with PSTN: ADSL

Just when analogue-based telephone lines and exchanges were set to become a thing of the past, along came the Asymmetric Digital Subscriber Line or ADSL. This is a new technology that allows very high data transfers rates over the older, analogue-style PSTN. ADSL can move data at rates of up to 9 mbps when receiving data (known as the downstream rate) and up to 640 kbps when sending data (known as the upstream rate). The relatively low upstream rate is not a problem for most of us, because it is a lot faster than we can type.

ADSL requires a special ADSL modem often called a cable modem. The term ADSL is misleading. It does not really refer to the line, which is the same line that you can use to make ordinary voice phone calls, but to the modems that convert the PSTN line into a high-speed data pipe. Such rates transform the existing PSTN from one limited to voice, text and low-resolution graphics into a powerful, ubiquitous system capable of bringing multimedia, including full motion video, to everyone's homes.

You don't need a computer or an Internet connection to exchange short text messages with friends and colleagues – you can use your mobile phone's Short Messaging Service (SMS). SMS messages may be up to 160 characters in length, which is usually long enough to tell your friends where you'll meet them, or what time you'll be home.

SMS or texting has been hugely successful, particularly with young people, and a sub-language of phrases and abbreviation has grown up around it.

CUL8R	see you later	BFN	bye for now
BTW	by the way	NRN	no reply necessary
PCM	please call me	B4	before

You can also use text messages to exchange ringtones and small graphics such as logos and icons.

Conclusion

Computer networking enables users to share resources such as hardware, applications and data files, and to exchange electronic messages or e-mails. This kind of co-operative work over a network is known as workgroup computing, or groupwork. Networks may cover a small area (LANs) or a larger region (WANs). WANs typically use the telephone system (the PSTN) to establish connections between distant computer users. This requires the use of a modem. Telephone companies increasingly offer ISDN and ADSL services for high-speed computer communications.

1.6

The Internet and e-commerce

Learning goals

At the end of this lesson you should be able to:

- list the main features of the Internet;
- say why the Internet is most useful for e-mail;
- distinguish between client-server and web-based e-mail;
- describe the web and state the two purposes of HTML;
- list some advantages and disadvantages of e-commerce;
- list some advantages and disadvantages of teleworking.

New terms

At the end of this lesson you should be able to explain the following terms:

Internet	The Internet is a worldwide network of interconnected networks.
World Wide Web	The range of documents published on the Internet in a format that enables them to be displayed using a web browser.
Web Browser	A program that enables you to display web pages and follow links from one web page to another.
Search Engine	A program that searches the World Wide Web for documents that match your criteria.
E-commerce	Business conducted over a network or the Internet. The products and services offered may or may not be available in digital form.
Teleworking	Performing work from home or any location that is not the conventional workplace, using computers and Internet technology.

Introducing the Internet

The *Internet* – everyone's talking about it. It may even be one of the main reasons you decided to learn about computers. If you connect to the Internet, you can:

- Send electronic mail to other Internet users (e-mail).

- Display information stored on computers all around the world (the web).

- Purchase products and service online (e-commerce).

You can think of the Internet as a rich resource that you can use for research, news, entertainment, education, information, sports, current affairs, shopping and art. The Internet is sometimes known as the Information Superhighway or, more simply, the Net.

E-mail: the two kinds

The most popular use of the Net is for exchanging e-mail. Two kinds of e-mail are possible. The first is called client–server e-mail; the second is known as web-based e-mail.

Popular e-mail client applications include Microsoft Outlook Express, Microsoft Outlook and Qualcomm Eudora. The two most widely-used such web-based e-mail services are provided by Microsoft Hotmail and Yahoo! Mail.

Surfing the web

The term *World Wide Web* or web is used to describe a file sharing service that operates over the Internet. Each web page on the web has a unique address known as a Uniform Resource Locator or URL.

Web pages are in a format called HTML, which stands for HyperText Markup Language. HTML is used for two purposes: page formatting and hyperlinking.

A *search engine* is a website that trawls the Internet looking for documents that contain information of interest.

Doing business online: e-commerce

Businesses around the world are beginning to use the Internet as a way of developing their markets, a move known as *e-commerce*. Examples of the kinds of things that people can use the Internet for include buying airline and rail tickets, checking bank statements, booking concert tickets and topping up mobile phone credit.

Moreover, the Internet can change the way you shop: you can shop 365 days a year, 24 hours a day, compare prices from different suppliers, and communicate with other buyers to get their views on quality and suitability.

Millions of people have access to the Internet; hundreds of thousands of computers are permanently connected to it – computers owned by governments, universities, companies, retailers, voluntary organizations and private individuals. What exactly is it? Here are five main points that you need to know:

- **A network of networks**: The Internet is a network, but not of individual computers. It's a network of networks. And each attached network has its own collection of individual computer users.

- **The two servers**: Every network attached to the Net has at least two servers: a mail server that manages the exchange of e-mail messages between its users and the rest of the Net, and a file server for hosting web pages and other files that the network makes available to other Net users.

- **A common protocol**: In international diplomacy, the word protocol describes an agreed way for people from different countries and cultures to meet and communicate. In networking, protocol means the rules governing communication between computers of different types, models, ages and sizes.

  TCP/IP (you don't need to know what the term means) is the Internet's protocol. Actually, the 'I' in TCP/IP stands for Internet.

- **The Net is the road, not the traffic**: Don't confuse a network with the kinds of services that can be operated over a network. A network makes possible a number of activities; but on its own it does nothing at all. You can think of a network as like a railway track; it is not much use without trains (such as e-mail) running over it.

  When we talk about an e-mail network, for example, we mean a network running software that provides an e-mail service. E-mail is not the network: take away the e-mail and the network is still there.

  Internet-based services have their own protocols that run on top of TCP/IP. The e-mail protocol is known as SMTP, and the web protocol is called HTTP.

- **The role of the ISP**: Unless you have your own mail server and file server computers, and a few other important and expensive items of hardware and software, you cannot connect to the Internet directly. Remember that the Net is a network of networks, not a network of individual computers such as an ordinary PC.

  Most people who connect to the Net do so through an Internet Service Provider, an organization that operates a network of the type that can connect to the Net. Most ISPs do not charge for their services, so that the only cost of Internet access is that of making a local telephone call to your ISP.

E-mail and the Internet

Even the smallest network of two users can support the exchange of e-mail messages. For a number of reasons, however, the Internet has become the world's most popular network for carrying e-mail:

- The network is already in place: there is no need to create a new physical network connecting all the people you want to communicate with.

- It has a huge population of already-connected users: the chances are high that the person you want to communicate with has an Internet connection.

- It is designed so that there is no single point of failure: if one computer on the network breaks down, or one phone line fails, the message is routed a different way to avoid the problem.

- It uses common standards: messages sent from one computer system in one country can be received and interpreted correctly by a different computer system in a different country.

Internet e-mail: the two kinds

The Internet supports not just one but two kinds of e-mail. The first is called client–server e-mail; the second is known as web-based e-mail:

- **Client–server e-mail**: In this approach, e-mail messages that you write are stored on your PC, and are then sent over the Net to their recipient. Conversely, to read your incoming e-mails, you first transfer them from the Net to your computer. This is called downloading your e-mail.

  Popular e-mail client applications include Microsoft Outlook Express, Microsoft Outlook and Qualcomm Eudora.

- **Web-based e-mail**: In this arrangement, your e-mail messages, whether incoming or outgoing, are always stored on the Net. No messages are kept on your PC. The two most widely-used such services are provided by Microsoft Hotmail and Yahoo! Mail.

  Each has its advantages. With client-server e-mail, you can write new messages and read previously received ones without being connected to the Net. The disadvantage is that you typically need to use the same PC every time you want to use e-mail. With web-based e-mail, you cannot work with e-mail unless you are online to the Net, but you can do so from any Net-connected computer, anywhere in the world.

The World Wide Web and the Internet

The term World Wide Web or web is used to describe a file sharing service that operates over the Internet. The file servers are called web servers, and the files they make available are known as web pages. A client software application that sends requests to a web server to access web pages is called a web browser. The most widely used web browsers are Microsoft Internet Explorer, Netscape Navigator and Opera.

Each web page on the web has a unique address known as a Uniform Resource Locator or URL. This contains the name of the web server, and includes (or implies) the name of a particular web page on that web server.

HTML and the web

Web pages are in a format called HTML, which stands for HyperText Markup Language. HTML is used for two purposes:

- **Design**: HTML controls the appearance of a web page, including the size, style, colour and positioning of text, and the insertion of images, audio, video and animated elements.

- **Hyperlinking**: HTML enables web pages to be linked together, irrespective of where they are physically located, so that a visitor can follow the links from web page to web page.

  This enables you to pursue a research topic from the general to the specific, from detail to the big picture, from graphic to text, from text to sound. These links are called hyperlinks, and files constructed with hyperlinks are called hypertext, or hypermedia if graphics, sound and video are involved.

Internet search engines

Faced with the huge amount of information on the web, how can web surfers hope to locate individual items of interest to them? The answer is to use a so-called search engine.

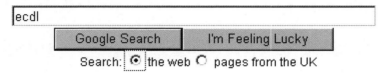

A search engine is a program that allows you to enter a word or phrase, searches for instances of it, and then displays (returns) a list of web pages that match your entered word or phrase. A popular search engine is www.google.com.

You can use search engines to find the share price of a company, flight times from Rome to Athens, comparisons of different brands of vacuum cleaner, the correct spelling of a word in German, the prognosis for a medical condition, tonight's TV listing ... it's all there – somewhere.

Intranets and extranets

The word intranet looks like a misspelling, but it's not. An intranet is similar to the Internet in all but two features:

- **Private access**: Intranets are run by companies and other organizations as private networks for the benefit of their own personnel. In contrast, the Internet is open to the general public.

- **Network not inter-network**: A few intranets may be inter-networks, but the vast majority are simple networks, and most are humble LANs. The Internet is an inter-network, and a huge one at that.

An intranet takes its name from the fact that it uses the same protocols as the public-access Internet: TCP/IP for basic network connectivity, SMTP for e-mail, and HTTP for file sharing. For this reason, the same type of server and client software can be used with intranets as on the Internet.

What's an extranet? There are times when you want some people to come and visit some parts of your intranet – for example, authorized suppliers and key customers. An intranet that allows restricted access from the outside is known as an extranet. Extranets have wide application in the area of supply chain management.

E-commerce and the Internet

Businesses around the world are beginning to use the Internet as a way of developing their markets. This move of business to the Internet is known as e-commerce (or electronic commerce). Here are a few examples of the kinds of things that people can use the Internet for:

- Buy airline and rail tickets.

- Check bank statements.

- Book concert tickets.

- Top up mobile phone credit.

When you are making a trip, you can plan your itinerary, find the cheapest flights, look at alternative hotels and compare their facilities and prices, check out special offers, look at maps, and check event listings. You can book flights, hire cars, hotel or guest-house accommodation, concerts, sporting events, even meals in your favourite restaurant.

Moreover, the Internet can change the way you shop. You can:

- Shop 365 days a year, 24 hours a day.

- Compare prices from different suppliers.

- Buy direct from the manufacturer, or from a supplier anywhere in the world.

- Communicate with other buyers to get their views on quality and suitability.

On the downside, you can't touch and feel the goods before you buy them, and not everybody feels secure about giving out personal details and a credit card number over the Internet. Online consumers also need the reassurance that they can return unsatisfactory or incorrect goods.

Finally, in the physical world, shopping can be an opportunity for social interaction and a way of keeping in touch with the local community. Online shopping does not offer these opportunities.

Teleworking and the Internet

We no longer have computers at home just for fun. The Net makes it possible for people to work from home or to *telework*. What are the tools of your trade? A computer? Access to the Internet? Printers, scanner, telephones? Well, you can have all of these at home, and be just as productive as you are at the office. Here are a few advantages of teleworking:

- You don't have to commute.

- You are not distracted by office politics or other people interrupting you.

- You can set your schedules to suit your home life better.

- Your employer benefits from reduced office space requirements, and can also attract quality staff from a wider pool.

But there can be disadvantages too:

- Some find teleworking quite isolating. They miss the interaction with colleagues, and, from the employer's perspective, teamwork and loyalty to the organization can suffer.

Many people have established professional design studios and desktop publishing businesses at home using PCs. Others have managed to use their PCs to offer desktop video or sound editing comparable to that offered by expensive and sophisticated dedicated equipment. Book-keepers, accountants, journalists, writers and database designers are also able to work from home nowadays, thanks to the PC and its connectivity.

Conclusion

The Internet is a worldwide network of interconnected networks. It is by far the most common medium for e-mail, and also provides the infrastructure for the World Wide Web. The web is a vast array of files – including text, image, sound and video files – that that can be accessed with a web browser. A search engine is a web page that allows you to locate web pages that contain information of interest. The Internet is enabling many businesses to reach new markets and offer new services to customers around the world. This is known as e-commerce.

17

What computers are used for

Learning goals   At the end of this lesson you should be able to:

- identify situations where a computer might be more appropriate than a person for carrying out a task – and where not;
- list some applications of computers in the following areas: government, healthcare, education, business administration, the manufacturing industry and retailing;
- describe the adoption of computers in the following sectors: airlines, banks and insurance companies.

New terms   At the end of this lesson you should be able to explain the following terms:

Information Society   A progression from earlier agricultural and industrial eras. Incomes and wealth now depend critically on information processing and ownership.

Information Rich/Poor   A division between those who have access to computers and know how to use them, and those that have not and do not.

It's a computerized world

Computers and related technologies are touching our lives from the time the electronic alarm clock wakes us up to the time we use the remote control to turn off the television at night. Computers control the cycles in your washing machine, the delivery of money through an automatic teller machine, and the supply of fuel to a car engine. Almost anywhere you see something happening 'automatically', there is a computer at its heart, monitoring the outside world and responding to it.

In this lesson you learn about the increasing applications of Information Technology to a number of key areas of work and life.

Computers: what are they good at?

Computers are useful where there are large volumes of data to be maintained, analysed, stored and filtered, or where complex or repetitive calculations have to be performed.

But, equally, it is important to recognize that computers are not suitable for every task: some are better left to human judgement and action.

Work and life in an Information Society

Farmer, factory worker, and now information worker: these three terms sum up the career history of human life. In our *Information Society*, emphasis has been transferred from brawn to brain. Value, wealth and income now depend critically on our ability to capture, analyse, process and distribute information.

The idea of the ECDL – and of this book – is to enable you to use some of the tools necessary for active participation in the Information Society.

However, you already have the most important tools, and you know how to use them: your natural intelligence, your critical faculties, the ability to judge whether or not something makes sense. No amount of technology can replace these.

Information Technology: what is it?

The term Information Technology (IT) covers all forms of technology that are used to create, store, transfer and process information in its various forms – such as numbers, text, images, sound, and video. IT includes hardware and software, networking and telecommunications.

The term is often used in the context of a business or other organization (as in 'I work in the IT Department') or in the context of society generally (as in 'IT is changing the way we live').

Information Technology: here, there and everywhere

In our modern economy many of the goods we consume and the services we use would not be available without computers.

- In the Age of Agriculture, most of the work, and most of the value, related to food production. A single measure, the amount of land ownership, set the rich apart from the poor.

- In the Industrial Age, the availability of food was almost taken for granted. Value, wealth and incomes depended more on manufactured goods.

- In the Digital Age, the Computer Age, or the Information Age (take your pick), the balance has shifted towards service occupations in which information, knowledge and intelligence play the key role. The emphasis has been transferred from brawn to brain. Our society can justifiably be called an *Information Society* because value in our society comes from information.

In 1800, a list of society's 100 wealthiest persons would have been dominated by land owners. A hundred years later, owners of factories that made physical goods, and of railways and ships that transported them, would have joined the list.

Nowadays, those involved in information-based activities are to the fore: owners of information copyright (whether in software, music, films or books), makers of equipment that processes information (computer hardware), and providers of information distribution systems (telecommunications, and the electronic and print media). Even those who do not work directly in an Information Technology sector use and rely on computers in their everyday work. As the following topics show, we are all *knowledge workers* now.

Computers in government

Governments need to manage very large bodies of information, including:

- **Registers of births, marriages and deaths**: In most EU countries such records are now in electronic rather than in paper-based form. As a result, information requested by the public can be provided more easily and quickly.

- **Tax and social welfare records**: In a modern state, it would be almost impossible to maintain these records in a usable condition without computers.

- **Census of population data**: Economists and social researchers can perform statistical analyses of computer-based records with minimal effort, the better to anticipate and provide for social changes.

- **Voting registers**: This is another area that benefits from the convenience of storage, ease of updating and speed of retrieval associated with computerized record-keeping.

- **Vechical registers**: As with voter records, the use of computers for holding details of motor vehicles may bring advantages for the state and citizens alike.

Increasingly, government agencies are exploiting the Internet to enable members of the public to enter and update information directly. For example, businesses can file tax returns online, and all citizens can view information on available health, social and other services. This application of computers allied with communication is called e-government.

Computers in healthcare

Healthcare is increasingly dependent on computers in every aspect of its operations. Its chief uses are as follows:

- **Patient records systems**: Modern hospital administration is a heavily computerized activity. It includes scheduling expensive and scarce equipment, drawing up rosters, and making appointments for patients.

  In addition, computers are used for monitoring patients' conditions and alerting staff when abnormalities arise. Computers also allow doctors to keep comprehensive patient records, and to conduct research into the effectiveness of different treatments.

- **Diagnostic instruments and surgical equipment**: Like wristwatches, pocket calculators and washing machines, modern medical equipment typically contains built-in or embedded processor chips that add to the range of functions it can perform.

- **Ambulance control systems**: Planning the most effective ambulance deployment, tracking their current location, and scheduling regular pickups – all these operations can be achieved with the aid of computers.

- **Medical research**: Most modern drugs are designed with the aid of computers, and manufactured under computer control. The Human Genome Project, which promises major breakthroughs in the treatment of genetic disorders, would be impossible without powerful, number-crunching computers.

- **Online service provision**: Computers and communications technology are being combined to deliver health services to remote regions: the patient can connect to a major centre (or a centre of specialist expertise) for diagnosis and, in some cases, for treatment. This development is expected to yield significant cost savings and better treatment for patients in the coming years.

Computers in education

When you hear about young people using computers in schools, you may think they are doing something very technical, like programming or electronics. They seldom are. In schools, the main uses of computers include:

- **Student registration and timetabling systems**: As with a government agency or hospital, the administration of a school or college is greatly simplified by the use of computerized record-keeping.

- **Computer-based training (CBT)**: A huge and growing variety of CD-based educational software presents traditional school subjects in a structured and entertaining way. Computers enable each student to progress at his or her own pace – the computer will repeat lessons as often as necessary, without losing patience!

  In some science subjects, computers can be used to simulate experiments that are either dangerous or expensive.

- **Homework help**: Students can surf the Internet to retrieve information from libraries, universities, government agencies, voluntary bodies, news organizations and other sources. They can communicate with students in other countries, and co-operate with them on research projects.

  Having gathered the required information, students can then use computers to write, edit and design their homework projects. School newsletters and posters can also be created cheaply and quickly.

- **E-learning**: In a knowledge-base economy, learning is a lifelong process. So-called e-learning courses offered over the Internet are growing in popularity, because they can be pursued with minimal disruption to work routine or family commitments. As with CBT, students can set their own pace, and monitor their performance. Students can also use e-mail to correspond with tutors and other people following the same course. Sometimes e-learning is integrated with elements of classroom-based or instructor-led training – a combination known as blended training. E-learning does not always work well, however. Some students progress better with face-to-face human interaction.

Computers in business and administration

Most business organizations depend on computers to:

- Keep accounts.

- Prepare invoices, statements and various financial reports.

- Maintain records of customers and suppliers.

- Hold details of stock.

- Calculate payroll.

- Write and edit letters, memos and reports, and design sales presentations.

- Communicate with other companies.

- Collect market intelligence.

- Collaborate with partner organizations in joint activities.

Computers are also used in more complex and specialist processes such as resource planning, scheduling, analysis and forecasting.

Computers in airlines, banking and insurance

Three of the business sectors that were among the first to adopt computers continue to apply them in new ways:

- **Airlines**: Seat reservation systems have relied for decades on computers for their operation. Virtually every airline today offers Internet-based booking systems. Indeed, with some airlines, this is the only way you can reserve your seat.

  The cost savings from removing the travel agent from the booking process are, in theory at least, passed on to the consumer in the form of lower fares.

- **Banking**: Like airlines, banks have long depended on computers for information storage and processing. They too are exploiting the reach of the Internet to provide direct, online services to their clients. The result is fewer high street branches.

- **Insurance claims processing**: It was their ability to perform mathematical calculations quickly and accurately that made computers an essential business tool for the insurance sector. As the range of insurance-related products grows in range and complexity, so too does the reliance on computers.

Computers in the manufacturing industry

In the manufacturing industry, the range of applications includes all of the usual administrative functions, and a whole lot more besides. Modern automated manufacturing plants rely on computers to:

- Collect orders from customers.

- Issue bills of materials (BoMs) according to the customer's specifications.

- Order the necessary materials automatically from the relevant suppliers (having first checked that they can deliver on time).

- Schedule the plant and personnel necessary for satisfying the customer's order.

- Control machine tools in manufacturing the required product.

- Monitor raw material usage and finished product quality.

In addition, computers can help in determining the optimum stock levels of existing products, and in the design and development of new ones.

Computers in retailing

The retailer's relationship with technology has progressed a long way from the installation of the first mechanical cash registers. Four main applications of computers in retailing are as follows:

- **Electronic point of sale (EPOS)**: In supermarkets, and increasingly in smaller shops, computers are used at the checkout to scan the bar codes on your purchases, and to calculate your bill.

- **Stock replenishment**: In many stores, the information on your purchases is passed immediately from the till to the warehouse, and orders for replacement stock are generated automatically when stock falls below a given point. Instructions can also be generated for the personnel responsible for stacking the shelves, so that the products are always available.

This technology help the store keep its stock to the minimum necessary to satisfy its customers, so that money is not tied up unnecessarily in stock and storage space.

- **Real-time pricing**: Using a central computer system at store, regional or national level, managers can amend product prices, perhaps several times during a single day, to reflect stock levels or perhaps competition from rival outlets.

- **Customer loyalty schemes**: Some stores issue cards that retain a record of an individual customer's purchases over time. In return for modest discounts, store owners gain a valuable database of the public's buying patterns and habits.

Information Technology: for better or worse?

Some find this proliferation of computers disturbing. Is there no aspect of our lives that is untouched by computers, and is this always and necessarily a good thing? Are computers replacing people, creating unemployment? Perhaps computers are being used to manipulate and control us? And are all computer-assisted services and all computer-manufactured goods better than their predecessors? These questions don't have clear-cut answers.

In the world of art, there are also difficulties: does computer-generated 'art' deserve the name? Can a computer write poetry, make paintings, compose music? And should we judge these 'creations' by the same criteria that we judge work made by humans? As we said, these questions do not have clear-cut answers. But it is worth thinking about them, because they are becoming increasingly relevant to everyday life.

Is every possible application of computers necessarily a good one? Are all computer-manufactured goods and computer-assisted services better than their predecessors? The following table lists some possible uses of computers. Which ones would *you* be happy or unhappy with?

	Possible application of Information Technology
1.	Calculate interest on your bank saving account?
2.	Decide whether you should be approved for a bank loan?
3.	Administer parking fines?
4.	Use a computer as a judge in a traffic court?
5.	Store X-rays or other medical records?
6.	Analyse an X-ray or other medical test and prescribe treatment?

Here are two general rules about which tasks are better performed by computers or are better left to humans:

- **Where computers are useful:** Where large amounts of information need to be stored, where stored information needs to be retrieved and updated quickly and easily, and where complex or repetitive calculations have to be performed on information.

- **Where computers are not useful:** Where decisions need to be made that require human judgement based on human values.

Remember that the information on any computer or on the Internet was created and input by someone, somewhere. And that 'someone' could be biased, misguided, prejudiced or just plain wrong.

Information rich and information poor

It has been said that if work was such a good thing, the rich would have kept more of it to themselves. But wealth and poverty can be measured in a number of different ways, not all of them financial: in health, for example, and in family and free time.

Computerization brings with it the danger that society will be divided into those who have access to computers and know how to use them (the *information rich*), and those that have no access to computers or don't know how to use them (the *information poor*).

The ECDL will equip you with the skills to participate in the Information Society.

However, you already have the most important skills, and you know how to use them: your natural intelligence, your critical faculties, the ability to judge whether or not something makes sense. No amount of technology can replace these, and you should never be blinded by technological wizardry so that you doubt these innate talents.

Conclusion

In our Information Society, wealth and incomes depend increasingly on the ability to create, process and distribute information in all its various forms. Computers are widely used in government, business, financial services, manufacturing, healthcare and education. While computers can store large amounts of information, retrieve selected information easily and perform complex calculation quickly, those tasks that require human judgement are better left to humans to perform.

1.8

Keeping your information safe

Learning goals	At the end of this lesson you should be able to:

- describe how to protect data from unauthorized access, loss, damage or theft;
- say what a computer virus is, and list a number of sources of possible virus infection;
- state the principles of anti-virus protection;
- state the principles of data copyright;
- state the principles of data protection and the main provisions of the EU Data Protection Directive.

New terms	At the end of this lesson you should be able to explain the following terms:
Backups	Copies of software or files on a second storage medium, such as disk or tape, as a precaution in case the first medium fails.
Username	A name that identifies a particular user to a computer network. Usernames are typically assigned by the network administrator.
Password	A confidential combination of letters and/or numbers that guarantees that no one else can access a computer, network or file in your name.
Access Rights	A system of making available or unavailable certain commands and/or information to users based on their role within an organization.
Computer Virus	A program that is loaded onto a computer without the user's knowledge and that damages software or data files in some way. Most viruses have the ability to replicate themselves.
Data Protection	The concept that information relating to individuals (personal data), collected and used by organizations, is subject to certain regulations.

Information Technology: two words

What pictures are conjured up by the term 'Information Technology'? Perhaps an image of a computer, or of a physical device such as a printer or scanner? But technology is only one half of IT; the other is information. In fact, information or data is often the most valuable part of a computer system, because it is the least easily replaced.

For that reason, you should learn the necessary steps for protecting your data against loss, damage – or theft.

Frequent file saves and backup copies

It is good practice to save your work at regular intervals while you are working. This prevents data loss resulting from a power cut, or if someone accidentally unplugs your PC.

To protect against loss or damage to files on your computer's hard disk, make regular *backup* copies of all your data files on floppy diskette or other removable medium, and store them safely at home or at another location.

Apply usernames, passwords and access rights

Enforcing a system of *usernames* and *passwords* is a common method for protecting information that is held on a single computer or on multi-user computer networks.

Organizations often apply different computer network *access rights* to different individual users or categories of users. Whenever a user logs into the network, the system checks their access rights and displays or hides certain commands or data accordingly.

Protect against computer viruses

Computer viruses are destructive programs that attack your files, and are designed to transfer easily and stealthily from one computer to another. Ensure that you install reputable anti-virus software on your computer that will automatically scan your disks, and detect and remove (disinfect) any viruses found.

Comply with data protection laws

Anyone who maintains databases of personal information must comply with the responsibilities imposed by the EU Data Protection Directive. Among its requirements are that information must be collected for specified and explicit purposes, and that it must be relevant, accurate and up-to-date.

Save your files as you work with them

Save your files at regular intervals while you are working. Clicking the **File | Save** command saves your file by copying it from RAM to your hard disk drive. If there is a power cut, or if someone accidentally unplugs your PC, everything you have done since you last saved will be lost. It is a good discipline to save after every paragraph of text, or after you have done any complex operation.

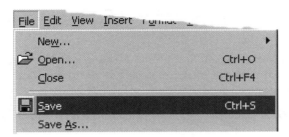

The **Save** button

Virtually every Windows-based application has a pull-down **File** menu that offers the **Save** command as a menu option. Choosing this **File | Save** command saves your file by placing a copy of it on your hard disk drive. Some applications also offer a toolbar with a range of clickable buttons that include a button for saving your current work. Clicking the **Save** button on the toolbar has the same effect as choosing the **File | Save** command.

Keep backup copies of your files

Files on your PC or any other computer can be lost or destroyed accidentally. The hard disk may develop problems, or the whole workplace may be destroyed by fire.

You can protect yourself against these nightmare scenarios by keeping backup copies of all your data files on floppy diskette, Zip disk, CD or other removable medium, and storing them safely at home or at another location. That way, even in the worst situation, you can be up and running very quickly after a disaster.

Apply usernames and passwords

Enforcing a system of usernames and passwords is a common method for protecting information that is held on a single computer or on multi-user computer networks.

- **Username:** Your username identifies you to the computer or network that you are accessing. It answers the question: 'Who are you?' On computer networks your username is usually assigned to you by the system administrator. Your username is not necessarily confidential.

- **Password:** This answers the question: 'Are you really who you say you are?' Your confidential password is your guarantee that no one else can access a computer, network or file in your name. On most systems you are free to choose your own password and change it as often as you wish. In fact, it is a good idea to amend your password regularly.

  Choose a password that is not too obvious – if it is easy to guess, its purpose may be defeated. However, choose a password that is easy to remember. If you forget it, you may not be able to get at your own data, and if you write it down, it may be discovered and used by someone else. The best passwords include both numbers and letters, so that unauthorized persons will find them less easy to guess.

The act of entering a username and a password is usually called accessing or logging in. In the example below, notice how your username is displayed on screen after you type it. As you type your password, however, the screen masks the characters behind a line of asterisks – just in case some inquisitive person is looking over your shoulder.

Usernames and passwords can be used to protect:

- **Single computers**: Most operating systems allow you to set up a username and password, so that only you or another person who knows this information can use the computer.

- **Specific files**: Some applications such as Microsoft Word allow you to apply a password to an individual file. You can even set up two passwords: one for anyone who wants only to open and read the file, and a second for anyone who wants to amend or delete the file in any way.

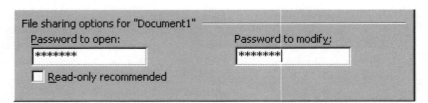

- **Computer networks**: Usernames and passwords are most commonly found on computer networks, including the biggest network of them all, the Internet.

Good passwords	Bad passwords
banana39	johnsmith
tul54ip	tuesday
3tomorrow4	computer

Assign appropriate access rights to network users

In multi-user computer networks used within organizations, the network administrator typically assigns different access rights to different individual users or categories of users. Whenever a user logs into the network, the system checks their access rights and displays or hides certain commands or data accordingly. Here are a few examples:

- **Financial accounts**: Staff in the purchasing department may be able to view and enter purchase orders, while only the manager may be able to amend or cancel previously entered orders. Higher-level accounts tasks relating to the nominal ledger or budgets may be restricted to one or a few senior accounts personnel.

- **Stock control**: All staff may be able to book materials in and out of the warehouse, while only managers may have the ability to adjust or write off quantities, and revalue stock.

- **Hospital records**: Administrative staff may be able to view all patient records, and to book future appointments. But only medical personnel would have the ability to prescribe medicines and vary their dosage over time.

Protect against viruses

Computer viruses are destructive programs that attack your files, and are designed to transfer easily and stealthily from one computer to another. Their effects can vary in severity:

- **Minor irritation**: Where a message is displayed on your screen, but no files are damaged.

- **Inconvenience**: Where one or more files are affected.

- **Total disaster**: Where the entire hard disk is rendered unusable.

Viruses are spread through files downloaded from the Internet, through files attached to e-mails, and through the exchange of infected diskettes. Protect your computer from virus infections by taking the following simple precautions:

- Never open an e-mail attachment unless you know what is in the attached file. Perhaps surprisingly, you are more likely to receive viruses from people you know than from strangers. Some viruses replicate by e-mailing themselves to e-mail addresses they find in your list of e-mail contacts.

- Be careful when opening an e-mail from an unrecognized source. Plain-text e-mails cannot contain a virus, but HTML-format e-mails do carry a possible virus hazard.

- Never download a file from the Internet unless you are satisfied that it comes from a reputable source.

- Use the most recent virus-scanning software to check every diskette and CD offered to you, whatever its source. Even reputable companies have been known to spread viruses unknowingly by distributing infected disks.

Prevention is better than cure: set up your anti-virus software so that it will automatically scan your disks (hard drive and diskette), and detect and remove (disinfect) any viruses found. Anti-virus software does not guarantee that your computer will never be infected, but it does reduce your vulnerability greatly. Also obtain regular program updates from your anti-virus software supplier.

Guard against loss or theft of portable devices

Portable laptop computers, PDAs, and mobile phones are increasingly used by workers in every sector, and by students and young people too. As their usage expands, so too does the risk of loss or theft. Replacing a missing or stolen device can be financially costly, but money is not the only cost.

If you have not set a PIN code on a mobile phone, all text messages and contact details stored in the phone are accessible to the thief. For PDAs and laptops the security issues are even greater: confidential files and access passwords for logging onto public or private company networks may be compromised.

Control access to paper-based information

Whatever the dangers of intrusion or unauthorized access to a computer system, remember that once you commit data to paper, it becomes vulnerable to different kinds of security risks.

If your data is of a sensitive nature, plan and implement a security policy for paper-based information such as computer printouts and faxes.

Protect the workplace

It's important also to secure the physical environment where your computers are located. You and your colleagues need to be aware of the potential risks from visitors, both invited and uninvited. Most organizations operate a visitor sign-in and pass system.

Your security is only as strong as its weakest point. Staff members, including teleworkers, need to be aware of their responsibilities in the area of security – take the time to develop simple reporting procedures that everyone can follow in the event of a suspected breach of security, whether physical or electronic.

Protect against power failure

Not all security breaches arise from malice. Think of the damage that a sudden power cut could do to your organization: unsaved data files, lost network connections. You might consider investing in an uninterruptible power supply (UPS). This is a device that protects your PC against total power cuts as well as sudden surges or drops in supply voltage.

Other people's data: respect data copyright

Not all the data you work with on a computer may be yours. Some may be the property of others. Remember that computer data carries the same copyright rights and responsibilities as printed works or musical compositions: someone created it, and that person owns it.

If you download information – whether text, graphics, audio or video – from the Internet or obtain it from diskettes or other media, you may not have the right to include it in your own publications without the consent of the author or creator.

Comply with data protection regulations and principles

We all appear in numerous databases: banks, insurance companies, educational institutions, employers and governments all hold files full of personal information. Our date of birth, address and marital status, our incomes, credit and educational records, our health, criminal and bill-paying histories are all known by various institutions. This information is sometimes general, sometimes specific. It may be sensitive and, in the wrong hands, damaging or dangerous.

Marketing departments are willing to pay large sums of money for name and address databases of specific categories of people. This enables them to target products and services at precise sectors of the population.

It follows that the collection, maintenance and protection of information is a serious responsibility. Wrong or misleading information could lead to a person being refused a mortgage, a job, an overseas work visa or medical insurance. It could ruin their life. Holding personal information thus demands sensitivity and respect. This is reflected in the *data protection* laws.

The EU Data Protection Directive

All EU countries either have already adopted laws to give effect to this EU Directive or will shortly do so. The Directive requires that all computer-based data be:

- processed fairly and lawfully;

- collected for specified and explicit purposes;

- adequate, relevant and not excessive;

- accurate and up-to-date where necessary;

- maintained in a form that means that the data subject (that is, the person about whom the data is gathered) cannot be identified once their identification is no longer necessary;

- protected against accidental or malicious disclosure or access – in particular when the data is transferred over a computer network;

- not transferred from within the EU to a non-EU state that does not have similar data protection measures in place.

It is quite common for data to be gathered about Internet users – this enables online businesses to target their marketing more effectively. Such information is also subject to the rules on data protection. The EU Directive sets out the information that must be provided to web users when such details are collected, including the identity of the collecting body, the purposes for which the data is intended, the likely recipients of the data, and the right to access the information and correct it if it is inaccurate. Each EU Member State must ensure that controllers of information respect the above rules.

Conclusion

Data files are probably the most valuable and irreplaceable elements of your computer system. Protect your data by saving frequently, making regular backup copies and installing anti-virus software. A good security system should protect both computerized and paper-based files. Computer data carries the same copyright rights and responsibilities as printed materials. The EU Data Protection Directive imposes specific responsibilities on anyone who maintains databases of personal information.

19

Looking after number one

Learning goals   At the end of this lesson you should be able to:

- describe some of the hazards associated with using a computer;
- describe sensible computing practices;
- list some ways in which you can minimize the negative impact on the environment of computer usage.

New terms   At the end of this lesson you should be able to explain the following terms:

Repetitive Strain Injury	Damage to tendons, nerves, muscles and other soft body tissues resulting from repeated physical movements.
Ergonomics	The application of scientific information concerning humans to the design of objects, systems and environment for human use.
ENERGY STAR	Developed by the US government, an internationally recognized energy efficiency standard for computers and other equipment.

While using a computer is generally safe, there are a number of hazards, and all of them are avoidable. Most of them – in particular *repetitive strain injury* and eyestrain – arise only if you use the computer for long periods without a break. Others arise from bad posture or inappropriate positioning of equipment. Cabling and electricity overload also present a potential source of accidents.

Avoid repetitive strain injury (RSI)

If you do any physical activity for a long time without a break, you risk straining or injuring yourself. Using a keyboard or mouse for a prolonged period can lead to the computer user's equivalent of tennis elbow. It can affect the fingers, hands, wrists, elbows or even the back. Avoid repetitive strain injury by:

■ Taking a break every 15 or 20 minutes to allow your muscles to rest and recuperate.

In addition, using a mouse mat, a rectangular smooth mat, means you can move the mouse – and with it, the cursor on your screen – with greater ease and precision. The top surface of a mouse mat is smooth so that the mouse glides effortlessly over it, while the underside is coarse to prevent it sliding across the physical desktop as you move the mouse over it.

Avoid eyesight damage

Extended periods of staring at a PC screen can lead to fatigue and ultimately to eyestrain. Here's a few tips to minimize this hazard:

■ Avoid locking your eyes into a fixed screen stare.

■ Look away frequently and focus your eyes on objects on the other side of the room, or out of the window.

■ Ensure your work area is adequately lit. The surrounding lighting should roughly equal that of your computer screen.

■ Position your computer screen so that any windows that allow in natural daylight are to the side of you – and not behind or in front of you. If you can see a window's reflection when you look at your screen, use a window blind or shade to reduce its brightness.

Another precaution is to attach an anti-glare filter in front of your computer screen. Made from a transparent material with an anti-reflective coating, these filters can reduce glare (reflected light from windows, light bulbs or other sources) by 95–99%.

Avoid posture problems

Ergonomics is the science of designing and arranging objects, systems and environments so that they are comfortable, safe and efficient for people to use. Here are some important ergonomic principles for computer users:

- Arrange the hardware elements of your PC in such a way as to provide the easiest and most physically comfortable access. Your desk should support your screen at the correct eye level.

- Use a chair that is comfortable and adjustable, and that provides adequate lumbar (lower back) support.

- Ensure that your desk and chair are at a suitable height, and that your keyboard is at a comfortable angle.

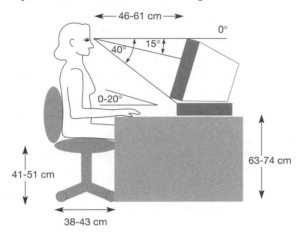

Prevent accidents with electricity and cables

A typical computer system includes a number of different devices: some require cable connections to an electricity socket; all are connected with wires that carry signals to and from the system unit.

- **Electricity supply cables**: The following devices are usually plugged into the mains electricity socket: the system unit, loudspeakers, printers and scanners. On some models the screen takes its electricity supply from the system unit; in others it plugs directly into the mains.

- **Inter-device signal cables**: Your screen, keyboard, mouse, printer and scanner also have cables connecting them to the system box. In addition, the modem is connected to the telephone socket.

That's a lot of cables and wires. Ensure that:

- The mains electricity sockets you use are capable of handling the load safely. Don't plug all the devices into a single adaptor or you risk overloading the circuit.

- Ensure that the cables connecting the components are kept tidy, secure and out of the way, so that there is no danger of tripping over them.

Look after your environment

Ever notice that car drivers say they are stuck in traffic, but never that they are traffic? Information technology impacts on the environment in a number of ways, some good and some bad. Minimizing the negative impacts is our responsibility; it is not just up to hardware manufacturers, software developers and government agencies. Here are some of the ways that you can play your part.

Actions	Comment
Reducing power consumption	Use the Power Options on your PC to eliminate any unnecessary power consumption.
	Turn off your PC and peripherals when they are not in use.
	Only buy a PC that is *ENERGY STAR*® compliant. ENERGY STAR is a US-developed but internationally recognized energy efficiency standard.
Recycle printer toner cartridges	Printer toner cartridges can be refilled and thereby recycled many times over.
Save and recycle paper	Buy only recycled paper, and look for ways to reduce the volume of paper that you use.
	If your printer has a duplex option (can print on both sides of the page), then set that as your default.
	Recycle unwanted printouts.

Conclusion

Eyestrain, repetitive strain injury, electrical overload and improper placement of cables are the main hazards associated with computer usage. All can be avoided by taking sensible precautions. You can reduce the environmental impact of computer usage by choosing energy-efficient monitors, saving and recycling paper, and recycling printer ink cartridges.

Congratulations! You have now completed Module 1 of the ECDL, Basic Concepts of Information Technology. To remind yourself of the key points in this module, cut out the quick reference guide, called **IT essentials**, and keep it beside your computer.

2

Using a computer and managing files

Prepare to take your first practical steps in computing. In this module you will learn the correct ways of starting and shutting down a computer, discover the meaning of the various little pictures on the Windows screen, and find out how to start and close Microsoft® Word, Excel and other software applications that you will meet in later ECDL modules.

Have you ever wondered what information was stored on your computer? After completing this module you will be able to answer such questions as: what drives are installed on a computer? What are the names of its folders and files? What is a processor chip and how much memory does it have? You will even discover how to find a particular file without knowing its name.

Having mastered the basics of Microsoft® Windows, you will be ready to create folders and files of your own, and to rename, move and copy, and delete and undelete them. One important thing to remember: computer files are delicate. It's a very good idea to save your work regularly and to make backup copies of files every so often – just in case something bad happens to the originals. It's always the files you like and need most that seem to disappear the quickest. Better to learn this from this module than from real life.

2.1

First steps in Windows

Learning goals   At the end of this lesson you should be able to:

- power up and power down a computer;
- use the **Start** menu to open Word, Excel and other applications;
- switch between open applications;
- click, double-click, right-click and drag with the mouse;
- use the control buttons at the top right of a window;
- move, resize and scroll windows;
- restart a computer when problems occur.

New terms   At the end of this lesson you should be able to explain the following terms:

Powering up/Booting	The technical terms for starting a computer and displaying the Windows desktop on the screen. You don't 'switch on' a computer; you 'power it up' or 'boot' a computer.
Taskbar	A horizontal bar across the bottom of the Windows desktop that displays the **Start** button, plus the names of any open applications. Click an application's name to display it in the foreground.
Cursor	A symbol, usually an arrow, that you move around the computer screen by moving the mouse across your (physical) desktop.
Menu	A list of items displayed on the computer screen that allows you to work with applications and files, and get more information. Some menus offer sub-menus of further options.
Multi-tasking	The ability of Windows to open several applications and files at one time.
Dragging	Moving a selected item across the screen by clicking on it with the left mouse button, and holding down the button as you move the mouse.
Double-clicking	Pressing the left mouse button twice in quick succession.

Starting, up, shutting down

Are you ready to take your first practical steps in computing? In this lesson you will learn the correct ways of starting and shutting down a computer.

Never just switch off your computer – you risk damaging your computer's hard disk drive and losing information saved on it. Always follow the correct steps to shut down your computer safely.

The Windows desktop

When you start your computer, your screen displays the desktop: little pictures called icons set against a coloured background.

Working with the mouse

You can use the mouse to interact with the desktop and the icons. As you move the mouse around your (physical) desktop, the mouse cursor moves around the Windows desktop. In this way you can perform actions such as selecting, repositioning and resizing items.

Windows within Windows

Windows, the operating system, takes its name from windows – rectangular areas that appear on the desktop when you start applications such as Microsoft Word.

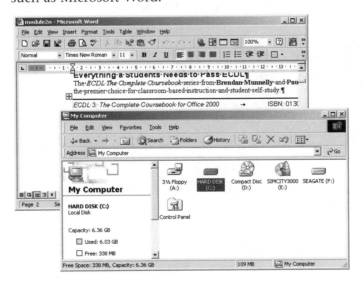

These windows also appear when you open a folder – an icon that represents a number of items grouped together.

Different windows generally share the same features and you can work with them in similar ways.

Start your computer

Follow these steps to start (*power up, boot*) your computer:

1 Check that your computer is plugged into the electricity socket.

2 Press the button to switch on your computer.

Typical locations of computer and screen on/off

On some computers, a single button switches on both the computer and the computer's screen.

Other computers have two buttons: one for the computer itself and a second for the screen.

Your computer will make some humming noises and some messages will flicker on your screen. Don't worry: this is just your computer warming up and checking that everything is in working order.

View your computer's desktop

Your computer displays the Windows desktop – a coloured background with little pictures called icons.

Along the bottom of your screen you will see a grey bar. At its left is a button named **Start**. At its right is a clock.

 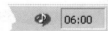

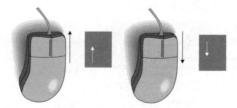

This is called the *Taskbar*.

Move the mouse

Place your hand over the mouse and move it around your (physical) desktop. As you move the mouse, the mouse pointer or *cursor* moves around the Windows desktop, allowing you to point to the item you want to work with.

View your Start menu

Let's see what choices are available on your Start menu.

1 Move your cursor to the bottom left of your screen so that it is over the **Start** button.

2 Press down the left mouse button for about a second, and then release it. This action is called clicking.

When you click the **Start** button it displays a list or *menu* of items. Some items have a small arrow to their right. This means that they contain another menu (or sub-menu) of further items.

Items listed on a menu are called options.

View the sub-menus of your Start menu

Move your mouse up and down over the items in the **Start** menu. As you do you can see sub-menus appear to the right. Some sub-menus have further sub-menus. Don't click on any options just yet.

Click on any part of your computer's desktop to close the **Start** menu and any sub-menus.

Launch Microsoft Word

Let's discover how you start (launch) applications such as Microsoft Word and Excel.

1   Click the **Start** button.

2   Move your cursor over the option named **Programs**. Another menu appears to its right.

3   On this sub-menu, move your cursor over the **Microsoft Word** option, and click on it.

Well done. You have launched the word-processing application.

Launch Microsoft Excel and Notepad

Why stop at one application? Windows enables you to *multi-task* – to open several at one time.

1   Click the **Start** button.

2   Hold your cursor over the **Programs** option to display its sub-menu.

3   Click the **Microsoft Excel** option.

You have now launched a spreadsheets application. Let's launch a third.

4   Click the **Start** button.

5   Click **Start | Programs**.

(This is a shorthand way of saying: 'Click the **Start** button and then click the **Programs** option.')

6   Hold your cursor over the **Accessories** option to display a further sub-menu.

7   Click **Start | Programs | Accessories | Notepad**.

(This is a shorthand way of saying: 'Click the **Start** button, and select the **Programs** option. Next, on the **Programs** menu, click the **Accessories** option. Finally, on the **Accessories** menu, click the **Notepad** option.')

Congratulations! You now have three applications open on your Windows desktop.

Switch between open applications

Only one application can be in the foreground; the others wait behind it in the background. Use the Taskbar to tell Windows which application you want to bring to the foreground.

1 Look at your Taskbar. Notice how it displays the names of all your open applications.

2 Click the Word icon on the Taskbar to bring Word to the foreground.

3 Click the Excel icon on the Taskbar to bring Excel to the foreground.

Use the four control buttons

Windows, the operating system, takes its name from windows – rectangular areas on the desktop such as those created when you launched Microsoft Word, Excel and Notepad. At the top left of every window you will see three control buttons that enable you to manipulate that window. There are four buttons in total, but only three are displayed at any one time.

Control button	Name	Description
✕	**Close**	Closes the window.
🗗 or 🗖	**Restore or Maximize**	Reduces the window size or makes it fill the entire desktop.
＿	**Minimize**	Shrinks a window so that it appears only on the Taskbar.

Let's practise using the control buttons, beginning with the **Close** button.

1 Is Notepad in the foreground? If not, click its icon on the Taskbar.

2 Move your cursor to the top-right of the Notepad window, and click the **Close** button to close (quit or exit) the Notepad application.

Close button

Next, let's try the **Restore** and **Maximize** buttons.

1 Is Excel in the foreground? If not, click its name on the Taskbar.

2 Move your cursor to the top-right of the Excel screen, and click the **Restore** button.

Restore button

This reduces the size of the Excel screen; it no longer fills your entire Windows desktop.

3 Using the Taskbar, switch to Word.

4 Click on Word's **Restore** button.

You should see both applications on your screen, with Word overlapping Excel.

To bring Excel to the foreground, click on any part of its window.

You do not need to click its name on the Taskbar. The Excel window now overlaps the Word window.

To return the Word window to the foreground, click on any part of it.

When you click on a **Restore** button to reduce the size of a window, the **Restore** button disappears and is replaced by the **Maximize** button. Clicking this button reverses the effect of **Restore**: it increases the size of the window so that it again fills the Windows desktop. Try it and see.

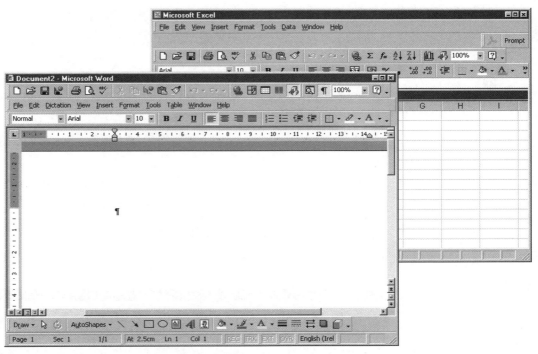

Maximize button

Minimize button

One control button remains: the **Minimize** button. Let's try that.

1 Is Word in the foreground? If not, click on any part of its window.

2 Click on Word's **Minimize** button so that Word appears only as an icon on the Taskbar.

3 Click on any part of the Excel window to select it, and then click its **Minimize** button.

Both applications now appear only in the Taskbar.

To display Word and Excel again, click on their icons on the Taskbar.

Reposition a window with the title bar

You can move a window to a different position on your desktop by using a window's title bar – the identifying bar that runs across the top of the window.

1 Is Excel in the foreground? If not, click on any part of its window.

2 Click on Excel's title bar – but do not release the mouse button.

3 With your finger still on the mouse button, move the mouse to reposition the window.

4 When you have positioned the window where you want it, release the mouse button.

This sequence of click–move–release actions is called *dragging*.

5 Using its **Close** button, close Word.

6 Only Excel is now open on your desktop. Using its **Close** button, close that application too.

Open a desktop window

My Computer

A window created by launching an application such as Word or Excel is called an application window. A second type of window is known as a desktop window. Let's open one.

1 On your Windows desktop locate the icon named My Computer.

2 Hold your cursor over the My Computer icon, and click it once.

Your single click highlights (selects) the icon – but does not perform any action on it.

3 Now, click anywhere on the desktop to deselect the My Computer icon.

4 Once again, hold your cursor over the My Computer icon.

5 Now, click once and then, very quickly, click a second time on My Computer.

This two-click action (called *double-clicking*) opens the My Computer icon so that you can see its contents in a desktop window.

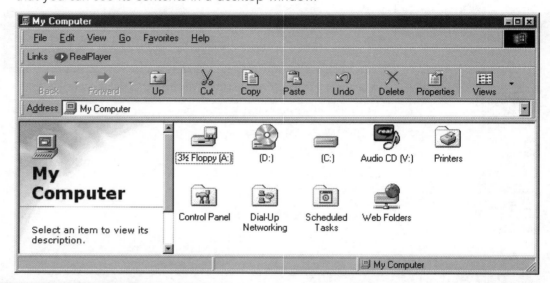

Change the shape and size of a window

You can change the shape and size of a window by dragging any of its four sides.

Changing the width

■ **Width**: To change the width of a window, click on its left or right edge. The cursor changes to a double-headed arrow. Then drag with the mouse. As you do, its edges change to dashed lines.

■ **Height**: To make a window taller or shorter, click on its top or bottom edge. Again, the cursor changes to a double-headed arrow. Drag the edge with the mouse.

Changing width and height

■ **Width and height**: To change both, click the bottom-right corner of the window. The cursor changes to a double-headed, diagonal arrow. Drag the corner with the mouse.

Practise your window resizing skills with the My Computer folder window.

Scroll a window

Sometimes a window may not be large enough to display all its contents. In such cases, scroll-bars appear on the right and/or along the bottom of the window.

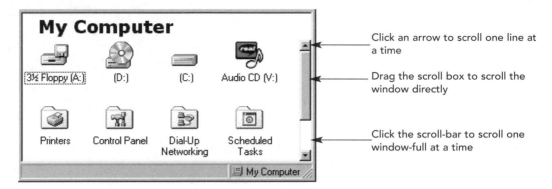

Click an arrow to scroll one line at a time

Drag the scroll box to scroll the window directly

Click the scroll-bar to scroll one window-full at a time

The position of the scroll box in relation to the scroll-bar indicates which area of the window you are viewing. When the scroll box is in the middle of the scroll bar, for example, the window is positioned halfway through its contents. The size of the scroll box tells you how much of the window's contents are visible. If the scroll box is half the length of the scroll-bar, you can see half the window's contents.

Practise your window scrolling skills by reducing the My Computer window to about half its normal size, and then scrolling the window.

Right-click to display pop-up menus

In addition to clicking (to select), dragging (to move) and double-clicking (to perform an action), Windows offers a fourth kind of mouse movement: right-clicking. To right-click something is to click on it once with the right mouse button.

Right-clicking on anything – whether an icon or even the desktop itself – displays a pop-up menu (sometimes called a shortcut menu). The menu options shown depend on the item you right-click. One option that a right-click always displays is called **Properties**.

Practise right-clicking on icons and on the desktop background. In each case:

1   Click the **Properties** option at the bottom of the pop-up menu.

2   When finished, click the **Close** button at the top right of the item displayed.

Shut down your computer

To shut down your computer safely, follow these steps.

1 Click the **Start** button.

2 Click the **Shut Down** option.

Windows displays a rectangular box (dialog box) that prompts you for further choices.

3 Click the **Shut down** option.

4 Click **OK**.

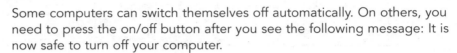

Some computers can switch themselves off automatically. On others, you need to press the on/off button after you see the following message: It is now safe to turn off your computer.

Now, power up your computer again – but wait at least twenty seconds. Otherwise, you may damage your computer's hard disk drive.

Restart your computer

The **Restart the Computer** option has the same effect as powering down the computer and powering it up again very quickly – but without the risk of damage to the computer hardware.

1 Click **Start | Shut Down**.

2 Select the **Restart** option, and click **OK**.

When an application 'hangs' or 'freezes'

An application may occasionally hang or freeze. This means that it does not respond to the pressing of any keys or any clicking with the mouse. Respond as follows:

1 Press the following three keys simultaneously: **CTRL**, **ALT** and **DELETE**.

You are then shown a window similar to the following, which lists all the applications currently open on your computer. The frozen application is indicated by the message Not Responding.

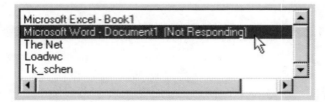

2 Click the frozen application to select it.

3 Click on the **End Task** button.

Windows closes the application, and the Close Program window. You can then reopen the application in the usual way.

Tip: Most computer users do this by holding down the **CTRL** and **ALT** keys with the fingers of their left hand, and then pressing the **DELETE** key with a finger of their right.

When Windows 'hangs' or 'freezes'

Occasionally, Windows itself may fail to respond to any user action, with the result that the entire computer hangs. What do you do?

■ Press **CTRL+ALT+ DELETE** twice in quick succession.

This has the effect of powering down the computer and powering it up again very quickly – but without the risk of damage to the computer hardware.

If you power down your computer in any way other than using **Start | Shut Down**, Windows will typically suggest that you run a program called ScanDisk when you next power up the computer. This checks your hard disk drive(s) for errors. Windows restarts when ScanDisk finishes.

Get to know dialog boxes

The **Close Program** window described previously is an example of a dialog box. You will meet many such dialog boxes when you use Word and other applications, so it's a good idea to become familiar with them.

Dialog boxes typically contain some or all of the following elements:

■ **Command button**: A button that performs or cancels an action. **OK** and **Cancel** are the two most common buttons. Here are some more.

■ **Pull-down list box**: A list of options that you can select from. Click in the list to view all the options available. The example below is from the **Print** dialog box. It shows the printer options available to you. You click an option to select it.

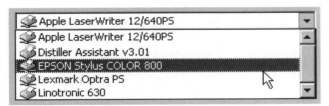

■ **Option buttons**: A group of round buttons indicating alternative choices. The example below is also from the **Print** dialog box. Option buttons indicate exclusive choices: if you click one to select it, all others are automatically deselected.

■ **Checkboxes**: A set of square boxes you can select or deselect to turn options on or off. Unlike option buttons, you can select more than one checkbox at a time.

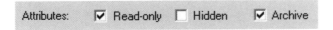

Most dialog boxes offer preselected (default) settings. Unless you choose otherwise, the default settings decide which options and actions are performed. When you choose **Start | Shut Down**, for example, the default option is **Shut Down**.

If you are happy with a dialog box's default options and values, simply press the **ENTER** key. Pressing **ENTER** with any open dialog box has the same effect as clicking the **OK** command button.

Some dialog boxes contain too many elements to fit in a single area. You will recognize such dialog boxes because they have small headings called tabs along the top.

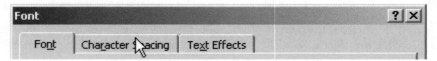

Click a tab to display the details on it.

Quit Windows

You can shut down Windows and power down your computer. You have now completed Lesson 2.1 of the ECDL Using a Computer and Managing Files Module.

2.2

Two words: 'personal' and 'computer'

Learning goals

At the end of this lesson you should be able to:

- view your computer's specifications;
- customize your wallpaper, scheme and screen resolution;
- select a screen saver;
- change your computer's date/time settings;
- adjust your computer's sound volume;
- change your computer's regional settings;
- use Windows online help.

New term

At the end of this lesson you should be able to explain the following term:

Screen Saver

A program that takes over the computer's display screen if there are no keystrokes or mouse movements for a specified period of time. Screen savers either blank out the screen entirely or display a series of continually moving images.

Personalizing your desktop

You can personalize the appearance of your Windows desktop to suit your working needs or personal taste using two main features:

- **Wallpaper:** This is the name given to an image such as a repeated pattern, a scanned photograph or a picture downloaded from the Internet that you can insert as the background of your Windows desktop.

- **Scheme:** This is a combination of colours, fonts and spacing that controls the appearance of such items as title bars, scroll-bars and icons.

Screen savers

If a specified amount of time goes by without any keys being pressed or the mouse moved, a program called a *screen saver* can blank out your screen or show a series of continually moving images. Windows offers a variety of built-in screen savers, and you can obtain others from the Internet and other sources.

Screen resolution

Your screen is composed of tiny squares called pixels, and your screen resolution is the number of pixels displayed.

At lower resolution settings (such as 640 × 480) everything on your screen appears bigger and blockier. At higher resolution settings (such as 1024 × 768) everything appears smaller and more defined.

Date/time, volume and regional settings

A small battery inside your computer ensures that Windows remembers the date and time settings, even when your computer is turned off. You can update your date and/or time settings as needed. You can also adjust the sound volume of attached loudspeakers or headphones.

A feature called Windows Regional Settings allows you to set a default currency symbol shown in your applications, and the conventions Windows uses when displaying times, dates and numbers.

Online help

Windows offers a searchable online help system. The 'help' means that the information is there to assist you in understanding and using the operating system. And the 'online' means that the material is presented on the computer screen rather than as a traditional printed manual.

View your computer's specifications

System

What are your computer's specifications? Find out by following these steps.

1 Choose **Start | Settings | Control Panel** to display the Control Panel desktop folder.

2 Double-click the System icon.

3 On the **General** tab of the **System Properties** dialog box you can see various details regarding your PC, including the operating system type, processor type, and amount of RAM.

4 When finished, click the **Cancel** button to close the dialog box.

Change your wallpaper

My Computer

Would you like to change your Windows desktop background? Here's how.

1 Right-click on the desktop, and choose **Properties** from the pop-up menu.

2 Is the **Background** tab of the dialog box selected? If not, click it.

3 You are shown a list of wallpaper options. Click one to select it.

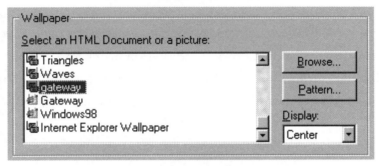

4 Click in the **Display** pull-down list to view your options.

Choose your
wallpaper options

Select **Center** to position the image in the middle of your desktop, **Tile** to repeat the image horizontally and vertically until it fills the entire desktop, or **Stretch** to distort the image to cover the entire desktop.

5 When finished, click **OK** to close the dialog box and apply the new wallpaper settings.

Practise changing your wallpaper a number of times.

Change your scheme

This is the combination of colours, fonts and spacing that controls the appearance of such items as title bars, scroll-bars and icons. Follow this procedure to view or adjust your scheme.

1 Right-click on the desktop, and choose **Properties** from the pop-up menu.

2 On the **Appearance** tab of the dialog box, click the **Scheme** pull-down list to view your options.

3 Click an option on the list to select it.

4 When finished, click **OK** to close the dialog box and apply the new scheme.

You can change your wallpaper and scheme as often as you wish. The relevant dialog boxes offer a preview area where you can view the effect of any changes before you apply them. Don't be afraid to experiment with different settings. You can always change them back again afterwards.

Change your screen resolution

The most commonly used screen resolution settings are 640 × 480 and 1024 × 768. You can change your screen resolution as often as you wish.

1 Right-click on the desktop, and choose **Properties** from the pop-up menu.

2 Click the **Settings** tab of the dialog box displayed.

3 Drag the Desktop area slider left to decrease the resolution or right to increase it.

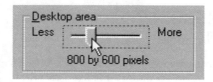

You can see the effect of a new screen resolution in the preview area.

4 When finished, click **OK** to save your new settings and close the dialog box.

Change the number of colours displayed

You can set the maximum number of colours that can be displayed on your PC's monitor. The options available are determined by your combination of monitor and display adapter. The *High Color* option can display over 65,000 colours. Either of the *True Color* options increases the upper limit to over 16 million colours. The more colours displayed, the greater the demand on your PC's processor. Follow these steps:

1 Right-click on the Windows desktop, and choose **Properties** from the pop-up menu.

2 On the dialog box displayed, click the **Settings** tab.

3 Click in the *Colors* drop-down list box to display a list of options, and then click the one you require.

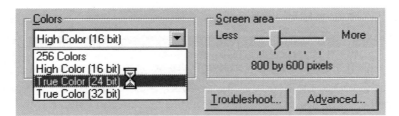

4 When finished, click **OK** to save your new settings and close the dialog box.

Set the screen saver

Screen Savers were originally developed to prevent damage to monitors that could arise if one fixed image was displayed continuously over a long period – such as a weekend, for example. Today's monitors are less likely to suffer from the problem that *screen savers* were designed to prevent, and they are now mostly an adornment. Follow this procedure to apply a new screen saver, or change the settings of your current one.

1 Right-click on the Windows desktop, and choose **Properties** from the pop-up menu.

2 On the dialog box displayed, click the **Screen Saver** tab.

3 Click in the **Screen Saver** pull-down list box to display a list of options, and click the one you require from the list.

4 In the **Wait** box, type the number of minutes of inactivity before which the screen saver will activate.

5 When finished, click **OK**.

To clear the screen saver after it has started, move your mouse or press any key. You can amend your screen saver and its settings as often as you wish.

Set the time and date

Is your computer set to the correct date and time? If not, the files you create and edit, and the e-mails you send, will show misleading dates or times. Here's how to set the date and time.

1 Click **Start | Settings | Control Panel**.

Date/Time

2 On the desktop folder displayed, double-click the Date/Time icon.

3 At the top of the dialog box displayed, click the **Time Zone** tab.

4 If the current zone is incorrect, click in the list of time zones, and then click your correct one.

5 At the top of the dialog box displayed, click the **Date & Time** tab. You can now change the month, the day of the month, the year, and the time.

6 When finished, click **Apply** and then **OK**.

Change your regional settings

Regional Settings

Different regions and countries can use different currency symbols, and different ways of formatting times, dates and numbers. Here's how to change your computer's regional settings.

1 Choose **Start | Settings | Control Panel**, and click the Regional Settings icon.

2 On the **Regional Settings** tab, select the relevant region from the pull-down list.

3 To override the default conventions for your selected region, use the options on the **Number**, **Currency**, **Time** and **Date** tabs. It's unlikely that you will ever need to do this.

4 To specify the keyboard language, click the **Input Locales** tab. If the country you require is not listed, click the **Add** button, select an Input locale and Keyboard layout, and click **OK**.

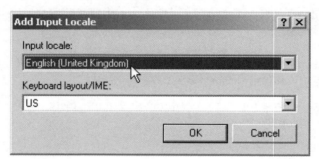

5 In the upper area of the **Input Locales** tab, click to select your required Input language.

6 When finished, click **OK** to save your new settings and to close the dialog box.

Get online help from the Start menu

Choose **Start I Help** to display the **Help & Support** dialog box. Along the top you will see the following options:

Home: Click here and you will see a list of topic areas on the left. Click on any of these to see a list of related sub-topics. Click on one of these to see the text of that topic on the right of the screen.

Index: Click here and you will see an index of help topics on the left. You can either scroll through the list to the topic of interest or enter the term which you are interested in in the box at the top left. The related help text is then shown on the right of the screen.

Tours & Tutorials: Click here and you will see on the left a list of 'how to' subjects that are dealt with in some detail. Click on the one you are interested in and the related text is shown on the right.

In each case, two buttons are shown at the top of the help text: one to print the topic you have displayed, and one to hide the topic list on the left (or to reveal it if you have hidden it).

Take a few minutes to familiarize yourself with the Windows online help system.

Get online help from a dialog box

You can also access online help directly from a dialog box, as the following example demonstrates.

1 Choose **Start I Settings I Control Panel**.

2 Double-click the **System** icon to display the **System Properties** dialog box.

3 On the **Device Manager** tab, click the option View devices by type.

4 Press the **F1** key. Windows displays online help text telling you the purpose of the selected item.

5 Click anywhere on the **System Properties** dialog box to remove the online help text.

Practise this with other dialog boxes in Windows.

Quit Windows

You can shut down Windows and power down your computer. You have now completed Lesson 2.2 of the ECDL Using a Computer and Managing Files Module.

2.3

Drives, folders and files

Learning goals

At the end of this lesson you should be able to:

- distinguish between files, folders and drives;
- use My Computer to view drives, folders and files;
- change the order in which folders and files are displayed in My Computer;
- view information about your computer's operating system, processor type, and amount of RAM;
- explain file name extensions and recognize the most common types;
- search for folders and files;
- create shortcuts to files, folders and applications.

New terms

At the end of this lesson you should be able to explain the following terms:

Drive	A physical storage device for holding files and folders. Typically, A: is the floppy diskette drive, C: the hard disk, and D: is the CD-ROM drive.
File	The computer's basic unit of information storage. Everything on a computer is stored in a file of one type or another.
Folder	A container for files or other folders. Files grouped into folders are easier to find and work with.
Sub-folder	A folder located within another folder.
My Computer	A desktop folder in which you can view almost everything on your computer, including drive contents.
File Name Extension	A three-letter addition to a file name that indicates the type of information stored in the file. A full-stop (dot) separates the extension from the remainder of the file name.
Windows Find	A search feature that enables you to locate folders or files on any of the following bases: all or part of their name, date of creation or last modification, or their content.

How your computer stores information

If you throw all your belongings in a heap together on the floor, you will have a difficult time finding anything. How much easier to sort your valuables beforehand, dividing them neatly between shelves or drawers? When you need to find something, you know exactly where it is.

As with your belongings, so with information stored on a computer. In this lesson you will learn about files, folder and drives – the three levels at which information is organized on a computer.

About drives

A *drive* is a physical device that stores folders and files. Typical PCs have a hard disk drive that is named the C: drive. Some computers may have two hard disks, typically named the C: drive and D: drive.

The next available letter after the hard disk drive is given to the CD/DVD drive. This can be D: or E:. The floppy diskette drive is named the A: drive.

Where is the B: drive? Early personal computers had just two floppy diskette drives, A: and B:. The advent of hard disks, which were named as C: drives, eliminated the need for a second floppy drive.

If your computer is on a network you may be able to access the hard disk drives of other computers on that network. Similarly, other network users may be able to access your hard disk drive. A hard disk drive on a networked computer that is accessible by others on the same network is known as a *network drive*.

About folders

A computer may contain many thousands of *files*. To make it easier for you (and the computer) to find and keep track of files, you can group files together in *folders*. A folder can also contain one or more *sub-folders*, thereby forming a tree-like hierarchy.

About files

All the information and applications on your computer are stored in individual files. Think of a file as the computer's basic unit of storage. In the example below, the Word Documents folder contains two sub-folders: Letters and Reports, and each folder contains a number of individual files.

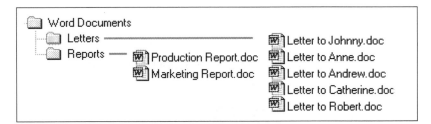

Another advantage of placing files in a folder or sub-folder is that you can work with the files as a group. For example, you can copy or delete all files in a folder in a single operation.

Open My Computer

My Computer

Power up your computer and take a look at your Windows desktop. Can you see a folder named *My Computer*? If not, resize or minimize any open windows until the My Computer icon is visible.

Double-click the My Computer icon on the Windows desktop.

Notice that an icon for the My Computer window is displayed on your Taskbar.

View your drives

In the example below, double-clicking the My Computer icon has revealed four *drives*: a floppy diskette drive (A:), one hard disk drive (C:), a DVD drive (D:), a CD-ROM drive (E:), and a network drive (P:).

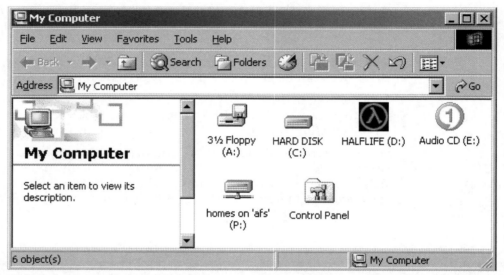

Also displayed by My Computer is an icon for the Control Panel, in which you can change your computer's settings. What drives has My Computer found on your computer?

View your C: drive's properties

Now you know how to discover what drives are installed on your PC – or on any other PC. Let's learn how to view information about a drive.

1 In the My Computer window, right-click the C: drive icon and choose the **Properties** option.

The **General** tab of the dialog box displayed reveals a number of details about your drive:

■ **Disk name**: In the **Label** box you can see your hard disk's name. To change the name, type in another.

■ **Size**: Your can see the size of your hard disk, measured in bytes.

- **Usage**: You can see how much space is occupied on your hard disk, and how much is still free.

■	Used space:	6,447,050,752 bytes	6.00 GB
□	Free space:	382,980,096 bytes	365 MB

2 When finished looking at the drive's details, click **OK**.

As further practice, view the properties of your computer's other drives. To view a floppy diskette or CD/DVD drive, you must have a diskette or CD/DVD in that drive.

Explore folders and files on your C: drive

You can use My Computer to view the folders and files on any drive.

- With the My Computer window open, double-click your C: drive icon.

My Computer opens a second window showing your drive's contents – that is, its folders and files. Leave this second window open.

Change how you view a drive's contents

You can view a drive's folders and files in different ways. Here's how.

1 Click the **View** menu.

2 Choose from the following four main view options.

- **Large icons**: Displays folders and files as shown below.

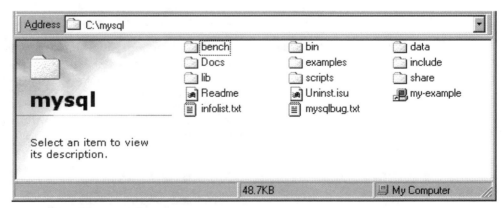

Mp3s   munnelly_com   Music   napv2b6.exe   later1.PDF   rutles.doc

- **Small icons**: Displays folders and files in columns, with folders at the top of each column and files underneath.

Address C:\mysql

mysql

Select an item to view its description.

bench	bin	data
Docs	examples	include
lib	scripts	share
Readme	Uninst.isu	my-example
infolist.txt	mysqlbug.txt	

48.7KB   My Computer

- **List**: Displays folders and files in columns, but lists all your folders before it shows the files.

■ **Details**: Lists folders first and then files in a single column, and displays additional information about each item.

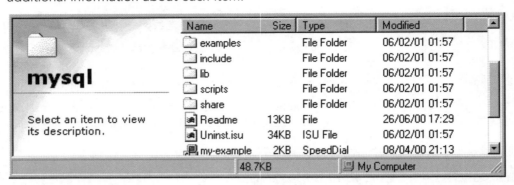

The **View | Details** option is best. It provides the most information about your drive's contents.

Along the bottom of the My Computer window, in the Status bar, you can see the number of items in the window, and the disk space that they occupy. Can't see the Status bar or toolbar? Click the relevant options on the **View** menu to display them.

Sort folders and files

You can vary the order in which My Computer lists folders and files.

1 With your C: drive's contents displayed in My Computer, click on **Name** in the window heading.

Name	Size	Type
zappkif.zip	155KB	WinZip File
ymsgr.exe	1,374KB	Application
ws_ftple.exe	691KB	Application

My Computer sorts the folders and files in reverse alphabetical (Z–A) order. Click again on **Name** to resort them in their original order.

2 Click **Size** in the window heading. My Computer sorts the folders and files in order of decreasing size, with the largest shown first. Click again on **Size** to re-sort them so that the smallest files are listed first.

3 Click on **Modified** in the window heading. My Computer sorts the folders and files so that the most recently created or changed are shown first. Click again on **Modified** to re-sort them so that the oldest are listed first.

You can make any column narrower or wider by clicking on the boundary line in the window heading and holding down the mouse button. The cursor changes to a cross-hair. Next, drag the boundary left or right.

View a folder's properties

To display information about a folder in My Computer, right-click its name. From the pop-up menu displayed, click the **Properties** option.

Type:	File Folder
Location:	C:\
Size:	362MB (379,641,323 bytes), 379,953,152 bytes used
Contains:	176 Files, 41 Folders

Among details shown on the **General** tab of the dialog box displayed are the number of folders and files within the folder.

You can also see the drive on which the folder is located (in this example, C:), and the size of the folder (in this case, 362 megabytes).

View a file's properties

To display information about a file in My Computer, right-click its name. From the pop-up menu displayed, click the **Properties** option.

Among the details displayed on the **General** tab of the dialog box displayed are the file's location, size, and the dates on which it was created and last modified.

View and amend a folder's or file's attributes

Every folder and file has one of the following three so-called attributes.

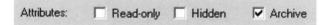

To view or set the attribute values of a file or folder, right-click on the file or folder name in My Computer and choose **Properties** from the pop-up menu. The **General** tab then shows the currently selected attribute and the options available.

■ **Read-only**: A folder or file with this option selected cannot be changed or deleted.

■ **Hidden**: A folder or file with this option selected is invisible. It can be opened and read, but only if you know its name.

■ **Archive**: This option specifies whether the folder or file should be included in an automated backup operation. It is unlikely that you will want to change this from its default value of selected.

If an attribute checkbox displays a grey tick mark, that means that you have selected a folder (or several files), and that some of the files have that option selected but others don't.

Recognize file name extensions and icons

In My Computer you can see that different files are represented by different icons. The icon that Windows uses to represent a file depends on the file's three-letter *file name extension*. The following table lists some common application file name extensions and their icons.

Application file type	Extension	Icon
Microsoft Word document	.doc	
Microsoft Excel spreadsheet	.xls	
Microsoft Access database	.mdb	
Microsoft PowerPoint presentation	.ppt	
Plain text file	.txt	
Online help file	.hlp	
Web page file	.htm (or .html)	
Temporary file	.tmp	
Compressed archive file	.zip	
Image file	.jpg, .gif, .tif, .bmp, .pcx, .psp, .ai	
Music/audio file	.mp3, .wav	
Video/movie file	.avi	

When you name and save a file within an application (for example, a Word document within Microsoft Word), Windows automatically attaches the appropriate three-letter extension to that file. A file name extension is separated from the remainder of the file name by a full stop.

Temporary files are created and used by Windows and some applications to hold information that is required while a particular task is being performed.

A compressed file, as you will learn in Lesson 2.4, is typically created by the WinZip application, and has a file name extension of zip. Image, sound and video files may have different icons on different computers depending on which application is set up to open those files.

View list of recently used files

Follow these steps to view the names of files that were opened most recently on your PC:

1 Choose **Start | Documents**.

2 The files you used most recently are shown in the submenu. You can open a file by clicking its name.

Not every program adds files to the most recently used list. If the file that you are looking for is not listed, you can locate it with **Start | Search | Files or Folders**. See the next topic.

Find folders and files

You can quickly find a folder or file on your computer as follows:

1 Click the **Start** button, and choose the **Search | Files or Folders** option.

2 In the **Search** area on the left of dialog box displayed, click in the **Search for files or folders named:** box and type the name of the file of folder you are looking for.

3 In the **Look in** box, you can specify My Computer (all your drives), a particular drive, or a folder within a drive. The **Browse** option enables you to explore your drives and folders to identify the one you want.

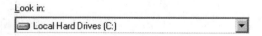

4 Click the **Search Now** button to begin the search operation.

Windows displays the results of the search on the right of the dialog box. You can open any file listed by double-clicking it. To close the **Search Results** dialog box, click the **Close** button in the top-right corner.

Perform a wildcard search

If you cannot remember the full name of the item you want to search for, type a wildcard character in place of the missing letter(s). The asterisk character (*) stands for 'any character or characters or none'; the question mark character (?) stands for 'any single character or none'. For instance, report*.doc finds all files that begin with 'report' and have the .doc extension, such as report3.doc, reportnew.doc and report-a.doc; ???report.doc finds all files that begin with up to three characters followed by 'report' and the .doc extension, such as newreport.doc, oldreport.doc and j-report.doc.

If you search for *.xls, Windows finds all files on your computer that have the Microsoft Excel file name extension. Try it and see!

1 Choose **Start | Search | Files or Folders**.

2 In the **Search for files and folders named:** box, type type *.xls.

3 In the **Look in** box, specify the C: drive.

4 Click **Search Now**.

Perform date- or content-based searches

You can perform more sophisticated searches, based, for example, on date ranges or content.

1 Choose **Start | Search | Files or Folders**, and click the **Date** tab of the dialog box.

2 In **Search Options**, select **Date**.

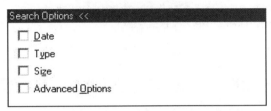

3 You can specify that you want to find files or folders created or modified within the previous number of months or days, or within a certain range of dates.

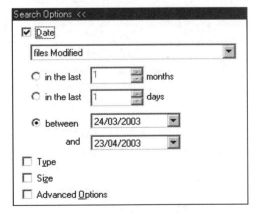

A date search can be combined with a file or folder name specification (for example, you can search for all Word files created yesterday), or you can leave the **Search for files or folders named:** box blank, in which case the search will retrieve all files created or modified in the specified date range.

If you have absolutely no idea of the name of the item that you are looking for, or when it was created or modified, you can search by content. Click in the **Containing text:** box and type one or more words you think are contained within the files you are searching for.

Again, you can use this option on its own or in conjunction with specifications for the file name and dates (for example, you could search for all PowerPoint files created in the last month containing the words 'Sales Forecast').

Create a desktop shortcut icon to an application

You can create an icon on your desktop for any application, and double-click the icon whenever you want to start that application. Such an icon is known as a shortcut icon. Follow these steps to create a shortcut icon for Notepad.

1 Using My Computer, display the Windows folder and locate the Notepad application.

Name	Size	Type	Modified
Notepad.exe	62KB	Application	23/04/99 22:22
notify.dat	1KB	DAT File	17/02/01 17:14
NPSExec.exe	43KB	Application	02/04/99 16:37

Shortcut to Notepad.exe

2 Right-click the Notepad icon, drag it from the My Computer window onto your Windows desktop, and release the right mouse button. If asked, confirm that you want to create a shortcut here.

3 If you don't like your shortcut's default name, right-click it, choose **Rename**, type a new name, and press the **ENTER** key.

You can leave the Notepad icon on your desktop, or drag it to a desktop folder.

Create a desktop shortcut icon to a file

You can create a shortcut icon on your desktop to any file or folder, and double-click the icon whenever you want to open it. Try this simple exercise.

1 Using My Computer, display the Windows folder and locate any text file.

Name	Size	Type ▽	Modified
setuperr	9 KB	Text Document	28/06/2001 19:40
setupapi	3,320 KB	Text Document	01/04/2003 21:03
setupact	103 KB	Text Document	09/02/2002 21:08
SchedLgU	32 KB	Text Document	02/04/2003 19:47

Desktop shortcut

2 Right-click the text file, drag it from the My Computer window onto your Windows desktop, and release the right mouse button. If asked, confirm that you want to create a shortcut here.

3 If you don't like your shortcut's default name, right-click it, choose **Rename**, type a new name, and press the **ENTER** key.

Create a desktop folder with shortcut icons

You can make your Windows desktop look tidier by creating desktop folders and placing icons in them. You create a desktop folder as follows:

- Right-click on the desktop to display a pop-up menu.

- Choose **New | Folder**. Windows creates a desktop folder with the default name New Folder.

- Type your folder name, and press **ENTER**.

Next, double-click the folder to open it, and drag icons into it, either from the desktop or from other desktop folders.

Let's create a desktop folder named Office 2000, and create desktop shortcuts for four Office applications within it.

1 Right-click on your desktop. On the pop-up menu displayed, choose **New | Folder**.

2 Windows creates a folder with the default name New Folder. Type the following folder name, and press **ENTER**: Office 2000

3 Double-click your new folder to open it. You are now ready to create desktop shortcuts and place them within the folder.

4 Let's start with a shortcut to Microsoft Word. Choose **Start | Search | For Files or Folders**.

5 In the **Search for files and folders named:** dialog box, type winword.exe and click **Search Now**.

6 When Winword.exe is found, right-click its icon, and drag it from the **Search Results** dialog box into your Office 2000 desktop folder.

7 Repeat steps 5 and 6 for the following other Office 2000 application files: Excel.exe, Powerpnt.exe and Msaccess.exe.

When finished, you may wish to rename the shortcut icons as shown.

Word 2000   Excel 2000   PowerPoint   Access 2000
                         2000

You can now close the new Office 2000 desktop folder.

Quit Windows

You can shut down Windows and power down your computer. You have now completed Lesson 2.3 of the ECDL Using a Computer and Managing Files Module.

24

Using Windows Explorer

Learning goals   At the end of this lesson you should be able to:

- start Windows Explorer;
- create, name and rename folders in Windows Explorer;
- create, save, name and rename files in Windows Explorer;
- delete and restore folders and files;
- create, name and save a file using an application program;
- copy, cut and paste folders and files;
- capture a screen image;
- create an archive by compressing the files in a folder;
- decompress an archive;
- install and uninstall a software application;
- scan your computer for viruses;
- set up background scanning.

New terms   At the end of this lesson you should be able to explain the following terms:

Windows Explorer	A Windows application for viewing the hierarchy of folders and files, and for performing such actions as renaming, moving and deleting.
Clipboard	A temporary storage area to which you can copy or cut folders or files. You can paste from the clipboard to any location within the same or a different drive.
Recycle Bin	A storage area where Windows holds deleted files. You can retrieve items that you deleted in error, or empty the Bin to free more disk space.
Virus	A program that is loaded on to a computer without the user's knowledge and that damages software or data files in some way. Most viruses have the ability to replicate themselves.

In previous lessons you explored the folders and files on your PC. Now you will learn how to perform actions on folders and files: how to create, name and rename, move and copy, and delete and undelete them. Instead of My Computer you will use the more powerful feature named *Windows Explorer*.

The panes of Windows Explorer

Windows Explorer displays two sub-windows or panes. Use the left pane to select a particular drive or folder. Use the right pane to view folders and files in the drive or folder selected in the left pane.

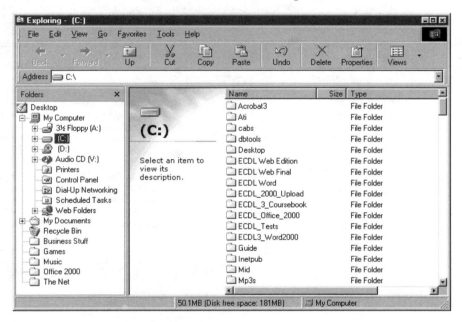

Working with folders and files

Windows Explorer enables you to create a folder, and to rename, delete and restore (undelete) folders and files. Files are created by applications. For example, you can create a letter in Microsoft Word, and a plain-text file in Notepad.

Unless you save a new file, it exists only in the computer's memory. The first time that you save a file, Windows asks you to give that file a name, and to specify the drive and folder in which you want your file stored.

The Windows clipboard

The *clipboard* is a temporary storage area to which you can copy or cut folders or files. You can paste from the clipboard to any location within the same or a different drive.

To copy a folder or file means to make a copy of it, and to place that copy in a new location. When you cut a folder or file, you remove it from its current location. You can copy, cut and paste selected folders and files in two ways: by clicking the buttons at the top of the Windows Explorer window, or by using the commands on the **Edit** menu.

Unlike My Computer, Windows Explorer does not have an icon on the desktop. You can start Windows Explorer in either of two ways:

■ Right-click on the **Start** button, and click the **Explore** option from the pop-up menu.

■ Choose **Start | Programs | Accessories | Windows Explorer**.

Windows Explorer differs from My Computer in that its window is divided into left and right sub-windows (panes).

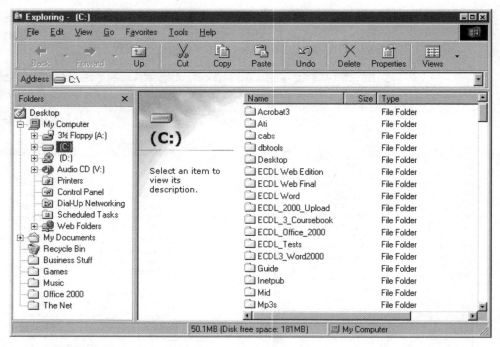

■ In the left pane you can see a hierarchical diagram of your computer's storage space:

– **Top level**: The Windows desktop.

– **Second level**: System folders such as My Computer and Recycle Bin, and any user-created desktop folders.

– **Third level**: Disk drives, Control Panel and Printers.

Click on any drive in the left pane to display, in the right pane, the folders and files stored on that drive. You cannot view individual files in the left pane.

■ You use the right pane to view the folders and files in the drive or folder selected in the left pane. It looks and works in a similar way to My Computer. Double-clicking any folder in the right pane will display any sub-folders and files contained within that folder.

Follow these steps to practise your Windows Explorer skills.

1 In the left pane, click on the C: drive icon.

2 In the right pane, scroll down until you see the Windows folder. Double-click on it.

You can now see the folders and files stored within it. Folders are listed first. Scroll down through the Windows folder to see what files are within it.

Change how you view a drive's contents

As with My Computer, Windows Explorer offers a number of options that let you control how you view your drives, folders and files. Choose **View | Details** – it's the option that provides the most information in the smallest screen space.

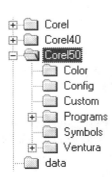

Along the bottom of the Windows Explorer window, in the Status bar, you can see the number of items in the currently open folder (the one whose contents are shown in the right pane), the disk space occupied by the folder's contents, and the remaining free space on the drive.

Can't see the Status bar or Toolbar? Click the relevant options on the **View** menu to display them.

Expand and collapse folder views

A folder with a plus (+) sign has folders inside it, and perhaps files too.

- To open such a folder, click on the folder name or the + sign. This is known as expanding your view of the folder so that you can see its contents.

A minus (-) sign in front of a folder indicates that the folder is already open (expanded) – its sub-folders and files are currently visible.

- To close your view of an open folder, so that its contents are no longer visible, click the folder name or the - sign. This is known as collapsing your view of the folder.

A folder without a plus (+) or a minus (-) sign in front of it is either empty or has only files inside it.

Create a new folder

You can create new folders to hold files and other folders. Let's create two new folders as practice.

1   In the left pane of the Windows Explorer window, click on the C: drive.

2   Choose **File | New | Folder**.

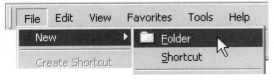

3   Window displays a new folder at the bottom of the list in the right pane. It gives it the default name of 'New Folder'.

4   Type a name for your new folder. If your initials are KB, for example, call it KB Folder 1.

5   Repeat steps 1, 2 and 3. Name your second folder (say) KB Folder 2.

You will use these two new folders throughout the remainder of this lesson.

Create a sub-folder

A sub-folder is simply a folder inside another folder. Let's practise creating one.

1 In the right pane of the Windows Explorer window, double-click on the first folder that you created previously – it was named KB Folder 1 or similar.

2 Choose **File | New | Folder.** Windows displays a new sub-folder.

3 Type a name for your new folder. If your initials are KB, for example, call it KB Subfolder 1.

The first of your two practice folders now contains a sub-folder.

Change a folder's name

You can change a folder's name at any stage. Here's how.

1 Right-click on the first of your new practice folders to display a pop-up menu. It was named KB Folder 1 or similar.

2 Choose **Rename**.

3 Type a new folder name. For example, KB Folder 1 New Name.

Well done! You have given your folder a new name.

About the Recycle Bin

Windows stores files that you delete in an area it calls the *Recycle Bin*. Can you see its icon on your Windows desktop? If not, resize or minimize some open windows until you can.

   You can tell from the Recycle Bin's appearance whether or not it contains any deleted files.

   You can empty your Recycle Bin by choosing **File | Empty Recycle Bin**. Emptying your Bin increases the free space available on your C: drive.

Recycle Bin   Recycle Bin

Delete a folder

Suppose that you don't need a folder any more? Here is how to delete an unwanted folder.

1 In the left pane of the Windows Explorer window, click on the first practice folder that you created. It's called KB Folder 1 New Name or similar.

2 In the left pane of the Windows Explorer window, right-click on the sub-folder. It's named KB Subfolder 1 or similar. From the pop-up menu, select **Delete**.

Alternatively, click once on the sub-folder to select it, and click the **Delete** button on the Windows Explorer toolbar.

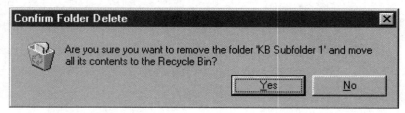

3 Click **Yes** to confirm that you want to remove the folder.

The folder is deleted, as are any sub-folders and files it may have contained.

Restore a folder's files

Where did your deleted folder go? If it contained no files or folders, Windows has deleted it permanently. If it did contain files or folders, Windows moves the files to the Recycle Bin. Recovering deleted items from the Recycle Bin is known as restoring.

1   In the left pane of the Windows Explorer window, scroll down until you can see the Recycle Bin, and click on it.

Windows Explorer now displays the contents of the Recycle Bin in the right pane.

2   Click the deleted folder, named **KB Subfolder 1** or similar, to select it, and choose **File | Restore**.

Create a new file

Files are created by applications. For example, you can create a letter in Microsoft Word and a spreadsheet in Microsoft Excel. The simplest type of file that you can create on a computer is a plain-text file. A file of this kind contains just words, numbers and punctuation marks – no fancy formatting or graphics of any kind. The Windows application for creating plain text files is called Notepad.

1   Choose **Start | Programs | Accessories | Notepad**.

A blank Notepad window appears on your screen, ready to accept text.

2   Type the following words: Just testing

You have now created a file and entered content in that file. But your file is not saved on your hard disk. It exists only in the computer's memory. If the computer were to switch off for any reason, your file would be lost. Leave the new, unsaved file open on your desktop.

Name and save a file

The first time that you save a file, Windows asks you to give that file a name. Follow the steps below.

1   Choose **File | Save** to view the **Save As** dialog box. By displaying this dialog box, Windows is asking:

– What drive do you want to save your folder in?

– What folder (or sub-folder) do you want to save your file in?

– What name do you want to give your new file?

2   Click in the **Save in** pull-down list.

3   Scroll up until you see the C: drive icon. Click on it.

Windows now displays a list of folders on your C: drive.

4   Locate the first of your two practice folders. It's named **KB Folder 1 New Name** or similar. Double-click it.

You have now told Windows the drive and folder where you want to save your file.

All that remains is for you to give your new file a name.

5 Click in the **File name** box, delete any text there, and type a name for your new file. If your initials are KB, for example, name it KB New File.

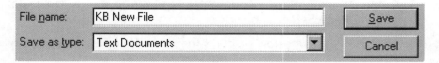

When finished, click **Save**.

Windows automatically adds the three-letter file name extension of .txt to all plain-text files created with the Notepad application.

Well done! You have learnt how to name and save a file.

6 Move the mouse to the top-right of the Notepad window, and click on the **Close** box to close it.

Change a file's name

You can use the following procedure to change a file's name.

1 Using Windows Explorer, open the folder containing your saved Notepad file.

2 Right-click on the file to display a pop-up menu.

3 Choose **Rename**.

4 Type a new file name. For example, KB Renamed File. Do not change or delete the file name extension (.txt).

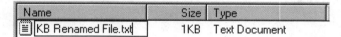

You have given your file a new name. Another skill mastered!

Do not change a file's extension name when renaming a file. If you do, Windows may attempt to open the file with an incorrect application, or fail to open the file at all.

Delete a file

When you have been working on your computer for a while, you may find that its hard disk is taken up by files and folders you no longer use or need.

You can delete these files, but be careful not to delete any files that your computer needs to run programs! If in doubt, don't delete! Here's how to delete an unwanted file.

1 Using Windows Explorer, display and right-click on your practice Notepad file.

Delete button

2 From the pop-up menu, select the **Delete** command.

3 Click **Yes** to confirm that you want to remove the file to the Recycle Bin.

Alternatively, click once on the file in Windows Explorer, and click the **Delete** button on the Windows toolbar.

Restore a file

Let's bring back your deleted Notepad file.

1 In the left pane of the Windows Explorer window, scroll until you can see the Recycle Bin, and click on it.

Windows Explorer now displays the contents of the Recycle Bin in the right pane.

2 Click the Notepad file to select it, and then choose **File | Restore**.

About the Windows clipboard

Suppose you want to place a folder or file in a different location on your computer. Or reproduce a folder or file so that two copies of it appear in different locations. Can you do it? Yes. This is a two-step process:

1 Copy/Cut: You select and then copy the folder or file to the clipboard, a temporary storage area. The selected folder or file remains in its original location. Alternatively, you select and then cut the folder or file to the clipboard. The selected folder or file is no longer in its original location.

2 Paste: You paste the folder or file from the clipboard into a different part of your computer – into a different folder, or even a different drive.

Three points you should remember about the Windows clipboard:

- It's temporary. Turn off your computer and the clipboard contents are deleted.
- It can hold only a single, copied item at a time. If you copy or cut a second item, the second overwrites the first.
- Items stay in the clipboard after you paste from it, so you can paste the same folder or file into as many locations as you need.

Copy a folder

Copy button

Cut button

Paste button

To copy a folder means to make a copy of it, and to place that copy in a new location. Let's try it.

1 In the left pane of Windows Explorer, click your first practice folder to select it.

It's named KB Folder 1 New Name or similar.

2 Choose **Edit | Copy**, click the **Copy** button on the Windows Explorer toolbar, or press **CTRL+c**.

3 Scroll down the left pane until you can see the Windows folder. Click it to display its contents in the right pane.

4 Choose **Edit | Paste**, click the **Paste** button on the toolbar, or press **CTRL+v**.

This places a copy of your folder within the Windows folder.

Cut and paste (move) a folder

To cut a folder means to remove it from its original location. Having cut it, you can then paste it in a new location.

1 In the right pane, display the folder that you copied to the Windows folder in the previous example. It's named KB Folder 1 New Name or similar. Click it to select it.

2 Choose **Edit | Cut**, click the **Cut** button on the toolbar, or press **CTRL+v**.

3 Scroll back up the right pane to locate the folder named System.

4 Double-click the System folder to open it.

5 Choose **Edit | Paste**, click the **Paste** button on the toolbar, or press **CTRL+v**.

This places your folder within the System sub-folder of the Windows folder.

Copy a file

You can copy, cut, and paste files in the same way as you can folders.

1 In the left pane, display the folder the containing your saved Notepad file. The folder is called KB Folder 1 New Name or similar.

2 In the right pane, click the file KB Renamed File.txt (or similar) to select it.

3 Choose **Edit | Copy** or click the **Copy** button on the toolbar.

4 In the left pane, scroll down to locate the Windows folder, and click it to select it.

5 Choose **Edit | Paste** or click the **Paste** button on the toolbar.

You have now placed a copy of your file within the Windows folder.

Cut and paste (move) a file

Cutting a file removes it from its original location, and places it in the clipboard. Pasting a file copies it from the clipboard to a new location.

1 In the right pane, display the Notepad file that you copied to the Windows folder. It's named KB Renamed File or similar. Click it to select the file.

2 Choose **Edit | Cut** or click the **Cut** button on the toolbar.

3 Scroll back up the right pane to locate the folder named System.

4 Double-click the System folder to open it.

5 Choose **Edit | Paste** or click the **Paste** button on the toolbar.

You have now moved the file to the System sub-folder of the Windows folder.

Working with multiple files

Selecting adjacent files

Windows Explorer provides an easy method of copying or moving several files in a single operation. This method works only when:

- The files you want to copy or move are in the same folder.
- The place you want to copy or move them to is also a single folder.

When you list the files to copy or move in Windows Explorer, two situations are possible:

- The files are adjacent. They are positioned immediately below or above one another.
- The files are non-adjacent. They are not positioned immediately below or above one another.

If the files are adjacent, follow these steps:

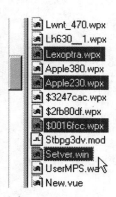

Selecting non-adjacent files

1 Click on the first file.

2 Press and hold down the **SHIFT** key.

3 Click on the last file.

All the files – the first, last and in-between – are now selected, and you can copy or cut them in a single operation.

If the files are non-adjacent, follow these steps:

1 Click on the first file.

2 Press and hold down the **CTRL** key.

3 Click the relevant files, one after the other, to select them.

Again, all the files are now selected, and you can copy or cut them in a single operation.

When selecting several files, you can scroll down or up as you make your selection. This method works for folders as well as files. Another operation that you can perform on selected folders or files is deletion. Simply select the adjacent or non-adjacent files or folders, and click the **Delete** button on the Windows toolbar.

Capture a screen image

PRINT
SCREEN key

Windows allows you to take a snapshot of what's on your computer screen. You have two options:

■ Press the **PRINT SCREEN** key to take a snap of the entire screen.

■ Press **ALT+ PRINT SCREEN** to take a snap of the currently active window or dialog box.

Each option copies an image to the Windows clipboard. You can then paste the image from the clipboard to an application such as Microsoft Word. Try this simple exercise to take a snap of the Windows Calculator.

1 Click **Start | Programs | Accessories | Calculator**.

2 With the calculator displayed as the currently active window, hold down the **ALT** key and press the **PRINT SCREEN** key. This copies an image of the Windows Calculator to the clipboard.

3 Click the **Close** button at the top right of the Calculator window to close it.

4 Click **Start | Programs | Accessories | Paint**.

5 In the Paint application, choose **Edit | Paste** to paste the image from the clipboard.

The upper part of the Paint window should look as shown.

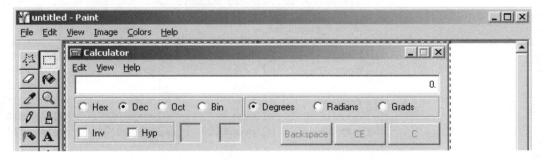

You can close the Paint application without saving the file.

About file compression

Compression – also known as zipping – means 'squeezing' computer files so that they occupy less space. The most widely used file compression application is WinZip. A compressed file is known  as an archive and, when created with the WinZip application, has a file name extension of zip. File compression is a three-step process:

■ Launch WinZip, and create and name a new, empty archive file.
■ You select one or more files for inclusion in your archive. (For ECDL, you need only know how to compress all the files in a particular folder.)
■ You save the archive file that now contains the selected files.

At a later stage you can then decompress or unzip the archive, and open and work with the original file or files.

Compress the files in a folder

Follow these steps to compress all the files in a folder.

1 Choose **Start | WinZip**.

2 Click the **New** button on the WinZip toolbar to display the **New Archive** dialog box.

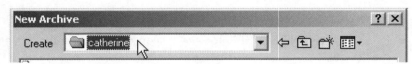

New button

3 At the top of the dialog box, use the **Create** pull-down list to specify the drive and folder on your computer where you want to store your archive file.

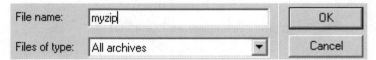

At the bottom of the dialog box, enter a name for the file, and click the **OK** button.

| File name: | myzip | OK |
| Files of type: | All archives | Cancel |

Well done. You have created a new, empty archive file. You next step is to add files to it.

4 WinZip displays the **Add** dialog box. At the top of the dialog box, use the **Add** pull-down list to select the drive and folder that contains the file or files that you want to include in your archive.

In the example below a folder named mod3_images has been selected.

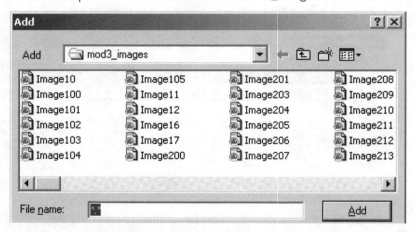

5 Click the **Add with Wildcards** button to include all the files in the selected folder in the archive, and to save the archive after the files have been added. Your WinZip window should now look something like that shown opposite.

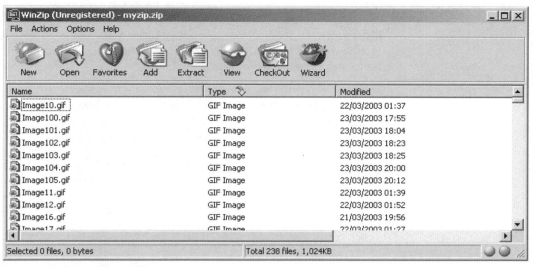

6 You can click the **Close** button at the top right of the WinZip window to close the archive file.

If you view your archive file in My Computer or Windows Explorer it should look as shown below.

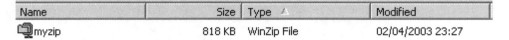

Decompress an archive

The opposite of file compression (or zipping) is decompression (or unzipping). Follow these steps to decompress an archive:

1 In My Computer or Windows Explorer, right-click the archive file.

2 From the pop-up menu displayed, click the **Extract to** command. Windows launches the WinZip application.

3 In the background WinZip displays a list of the files in the archive. In the foreground you can see the **Extract** dialog box. In the Folders/drives area, select the drive and folder into which you want to decompress the contents of the archive.

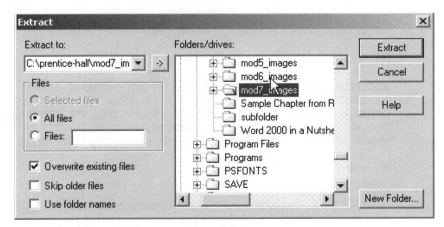

4 Click the **Extract** button. WinZip decompresses the archive into the selected folder. This may take a few seconds. Extracting files from an archive does not affect the archive file.

5 You can click the **Close** button at the top right of the WinZip window to close the archive file.

Most software applications consist of more than just a single file that ends in .exe. In fact, they contain dozens – even hundreds – of different files that may be located in various folders on your PC.

To help you install them correctly on your computer, applications usually come as a single setup file that contains all the necessary component files. To install the application, you simply launch the setup file, and it does all the work for you. All setup files work in a largely similar way.

Let's try a simple example. EditPlus is a text editing application used mainly by web designers. A free trial version can be downloaded from the company's website at www.editplus.com. The setup file is named epp210C.exe. In this exercise it is assumed that you have this setup file on your computer.

1 In My Computer or Windows Explorer, locate the epp210C.exe setup file, and double-click it.

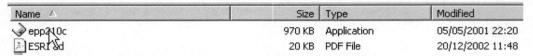

Name △	Size	Type	Modified
epp210c	970 KB	Application	05/05/2001 22:20
ESRI3d	20 KB	PDF File	20/12/2002 11:48

2 EditPlus shows the following dialog box. Click **Setup** to continue.

3 As is usual with application setup files, you are shown a licence agreement, and prompted to accept or decline. Read the licence agreement, and if you accept it, click **Yes**.

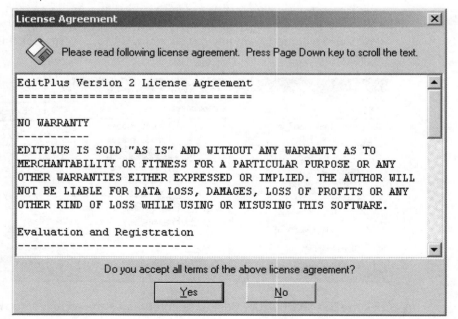

4 Again as is usual, you are shown the application's default installation folder (directory), and prompted to accept this location or specify another one. Click **Start Copy** to begin the installation.

5 You are now shown a progress screen, telling you how the installation is proceeding. For larger applications this may takes several minutes.

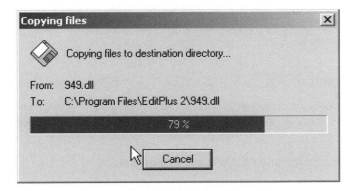

6 Next, EditPlus prompts you to specify how you want the application to appear on the Windows interface. Deselect all options except the **Create shortcut at Desktop** one, and click **OK**.

7 Finally, you are informed that the installation is complete. Click **OK**.

EditPlus 2
icon

Take a look at your desktop. Can you see the EditPlus 2 icon? Next, click **Start | Programs** and locate the EditPlus 2 option with its sub-menu.

You can see that, in addition to the application itself, the EditPlus sub-menu contains three other items: an online manual, a Readme file (containing technical details), and an Uninstall file.

One difference between the install procedure for free trial applications and for full commercial versions is that the second type will usually ask you for a product serial number before the install takes place.

Uninstall a software application

Most applications come with an uninstall option that works in a similar way to a setup file, only in reverse. To uninstall Edit Plus 2, for example, follow these few steps:

1 Click **Start | Programs | EditPlus 2 | Uninstall**.

2 When shown the dialog box below, click **Yes**.

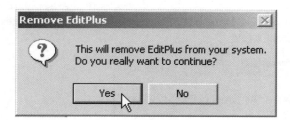

3 Follow the onscreen instructions to remove the application from your computer.

About viruses

Computer *viruses* are programs that attack your files, and are designed to transfer easily and stealthily from one computer to another. Viruses are spread through files downloaded from the Internet, through e-mail attachments and through the exchange of infected floppy disks.

Reputable anti-virus software on your computer can automatically scan your disks (hard drive and floppy disk), and detect and remove any viruses found. In some cases it is possible to disinfect files that have been infected. Anti-virus software usually consists of a number of components:

- **Periodic complete check-up**: It is good housekeeping to perform regular anti-virus checks on your PC.
- **E-mail scanning**: Anti-virus software can be set up to check incoming e-mails and attachments.
- **Background scanning**: This can protect your computer from infected floppy diskettes and other virus threats in the course of your normal working day.

Anti-virus software must be kept up to date – new viruses are being concocted all the time, and the software used to detect and remove them needs to be the very latest.

Scan your computer for viruses

VirusScan is an example of an application that is designed to prevent and cure virus infection. Follow these steps to use VirusScan to check your computer for infection.

1 Choose **Start | Programs | Network Associates | VirusScan** and click the **Where & What** tab.

2 Specify the drive you want to scan – in this example, drive C:.

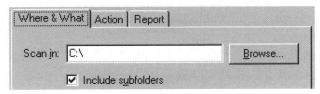

3 To perform the most complete scan, include the following options:

- **Include sub-folders**: Select this to include every folder on drive C: in the scan.

- **All files**: Select this to include all files (not just program files).

- **Compressed files**: Select this to include the contents of compressed files.

4 Click the **Scan Now** button to begin the scanning.

Set up background scanning

VShield icon

You can configure VirusScan so that it runs continually in the background, checking any file you use, open or download. This utility is called VShield. If VShield is running, you see its icon in the Taskbar.

Follow these steps to set up background scanning with VShield.

1 Choose **Start | Programs | Network Associates | VirusScan Console**.

2 In the VirusScan Console window, click **VShield** to select it.

3 Choose **Task | Properties**, and click the **System Scan** tab.

4 Click the **Properties** button to display the **System Scan Status** dialog box.

5 Select the **Enable System Scan** option, and any other options you want. Click **OK** and then **Close**.

Protect against e-mail-borne viruses

1 Choose **Start | Programs | Network Associates | VirusScan Console**.

2 In the VirusScan Console window, click **VShield** to select it.

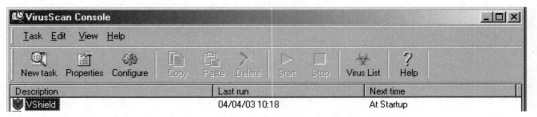

3 Choose **Task | Properties**, and click the **System Scan** tab.

4 Click the **Properties** button to display the **System Scan Status** dialog box.

5 Click **Enable scanning of e-mail attachments** and any other options you want. Click **OK** and then **Close**.

Quit Windows

You can shut down Windows and power down your computer. You have now completed Lesson 2.4 of the ECDL Using a Computer and Managing Files Module.

2.5

Diskettes and printing

Learning goals	At the end of this lesson you should be able to:

- format a diskette;
- copy a file to a diskette;
- save a file to a diskette;
- use various print features and options;
- use an application's menu bars, toolbars and keyboard shortcuts.

New terms	At the end of this lesson you should be able to explain the following terms:

Print Queue	A list of files (print jobs) that are waiting to be printed. The printer pulls the files off the queue one at a time.
Pull-down Menu	A list of options that appears when you click on a menu name. The menu name is generally on a menu bar along the top of the window, and the menu appears below that bar, as if you pulled it down.
Toolbar	A collection of buttons that you can click to perform frequently used actions, such as creating, opening or saving files, and for clipboard operations.

Working with diskettes

You can copy files and folders from your hard disk to a floppy diskette to:

- make a copy of your work that you can give to a colleague or friend.

- have a backup copy of your work in case your computer is damaged and the files on it are 'lost'.

The more regularly you make backups, the more up-to-date your files will be if your computer fails.

Formatting diskettes

You can only copy files to a diskette that is formatted. Most new diskettes come already formatted. When Windows formats a floppy diskette, it:

- sets up a 'table of contents' on the diskette that it later uses to locate files stored on the disk;

- checks for any damaged areas, and, when it finds them, marks those areas as off-limits for file storage.

Formatting a disk overwrites any table of contents there may have been previously on the disk, so making it impossible for Windows to find files that were saved on the diskette before it was formatted. For that reason, don't even think about formatting your computer's hard disk.

The print queue

What happens to a file after you choose to print it? The answer is that it goes to a temporary storage area called a *print queue*.

The print queue can store a number of files, which the printer then collects in turn as it becomes ready to print them. The time it takes to print a file depends on the number and size of the other print jobs in the print queue.

You can view your print queue to see what print jobs are waiting in it, delete print jobs from the queue, and reorder the sequence in which print jobs are listed.

Menu bars, toolbars and keyboard shortcuts

Most applications offer three ways that you perform actions: menu commands, toolbar buttons, and keyboard shortcuts. A menu bar is displayed as a line of words just under the title bar. Each word represents a *pull-down menu* of commands

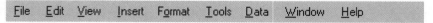

A *toolbar* is a collection of buttons that you can click to perform frequently used actions. Most menu commands have a toolbar button equivalent.

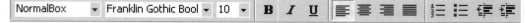

A third option is to press the **CTRL** key in combination with a particular letter key. Examples of such keyboard shortcuts include **CTRL+c** to copy to the clipboard and **CTRL+v** to paste from it.

Format a floppy diskette

Follow these steps to format a floppy diskette:

1 Insert the floppy diskette you want to format into the diskette drive.

2 Choose **Start | Programs | Accessories | Windows Explorer**.

3 Right-click the A: drive icon in the left pane and choose **Format** from the pop-up menu displayed.

4 Select the following two options in the dialog box displayed, and click **Start**.

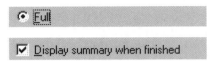

5 When Windows has formatted the disk, click **OK** to display the **Format Results** dialog box.

6 Click **Close** to close the dialog box.

Copy a file to a diskette

You can copy a file to a diskette using the copy and paste options available with Windows Explorer.

1 Insert a formatted diskette in the A: drive of your computer.

2 Start Windows Explorer. In the right pane, display the file that you want to copy – for example, the Mouse.txt file from the Windows folder.

License.txt	32KB	Text Document	23/04/99 22:22
Modemdet.txt	1KB	Text Document	11/12/99 14:39
Mouse.txt	6KB	Text Document	23/04/99 22:22
Msdosdrv.txt	45KB	Text Document	23/04/99 22:22
Ndislog.txt	0KB	Text Document	27/04/01 00:25

3 Click the file to select it, and choose **Edit | Copy** or click the **Copy** button on the toolbar.

4 In the left pane, click on the A: drive icon.

If there are currently any files on the diskette, Windows Explorer lists them in its right pane.

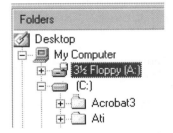

5 Choose **Edit | Paste** or click the **Paste** button to copy the file to the diskette.

Save a file to a diskette

A second way to copy a file to a diskette is to use the **File | Save As** command of the application in which you created and worked with the file. If you currently have the application open on your screen, this is faster than using Windows Explorer.

1 Click **Start | Programs | Accessories | Notepad**.

2 Choose **File | Open** and locate the file you created in Lesson 2.4, named KB Renamed File or similar. When you find it, click it to select it, and click the **Open** button.

3 Choose **File | Save As**, locate the A: drive, and click **Save** to save the file.

A copy of the Notepad file is now stored on the diskette. You can close the Notepad application.

Format a Zip disk

Zip disks from Iomega can store much more data than floppy diskettes. Zip disk types are available with capacities of 100, 250 and 750 MB. Zip disks are available preformatted, but you can format Zip disks to erase all of the files on the disk quickly, or to attempt to repair a disk that has developed bad sectors. Here is the procedure:

1 Insert your Zip disk (label side up and the edge with the metal guard first) in the drive.

2 In My Computer or Windows Explorer, right-click the Zip disk icon.

3 From the pop-up menu displayed, choose **Format** and then select one of the following two options:

- **Short format**: Select this to quickly erase all data on a disk.

- **Long format**: Select this option if you are formatting a disk where you have forgotten the password, or if you need to repair a disk that has developed read/write errors due to bad sectors.

4 Click **Start** to begin formatting the Zip disk.

Print a file

Print button

You can print the contents of files so you can see your work on paper.

1 Open the file, for example, a Word document.

2 Click the **Print** button on the toolbar or choose **File | Print**.

3 Click **OK** in the **Print** dialog box.

If your printer is connected and set up correctly, your file should print.

Preview a file

Print preview button

Most applications offer the ability to preview a file on your screen before you print it.

- To preview your file, click the **Print Preview** button on the toolbar or choose **File | Print**. Click **Close** to return to your file.

View the print queue

What jobs are currently in the *print queue*? Here's how to find out.

1 Click **Start | Settings | Printers**.

2 Double-click the icon for the printer you want to check.

Windows displays a list of all the print jobs in the queue.

Pause or resume a print job in the queue

You can pause and then resume a print job. Here's how:

1 Choose **Start | Settings | Printers**.

2 Double-click the icon for the printer you want to look at. Windows displays a list of all the print jobs in the queue.

3 Right-click the required document, and choose the **Pause** or **Resume** option from the pop-up menu displayed.

Once a file has begun printing you cannot pause it. You may or may not be able to cancel it, depending on how far the printing has progressed.

Cancel a print job in the queue

There are many reasons why you may decide to cancel a print job – you may discover that the job is not printing correctly, you may realize that you already have a copy of the printout, or you may simply change your mind about printing the file. Follow these steps to cancel a job.

1 Choose **Start | Settings | Printers**.

2 Double-click the icon for the printer you are printing to. Windows displays a list of all the print jobs in the queue.

3 Select the file you want to cancel printing by clicking it.

4 Choose **Document | Cancel Printing**.

Change the order of jobs in the print queue

You can change the current sequence of jobs in the print queue. Here's how.

1 Choose **Start | Settings | Printers**.

2 Double-click the icon for the printer you want to look at. Windows displays a list of all the print jobs in the queue.

3 Select the file you want to move by clicking it, and drag it to the required place in the queue.

You can't move a file that is already in the process of printing.

Delete all jobs from the print queue

Follow these steps to remove all pending print jobs from the print queue.

1 Choose **Start | Settings | Printers**.

2 Double-click the icon for the printer you are printing to. Windows displays a list of all the print jobs in the queue.

3 Choose **Printer | Purge Jobs**.

Change the default printer

If your PC is attached to a network, you may have a number of printers available to you. It's a good idea to set the printer you use most often as the default printer. When you choose the **File | Print** command in Microsoft Word or other applications, your file outputs to the default printer unless you specify otherwise.

Follow this procedure to set a printer as the default printer:

■ Choose **Start | Settings | Printers**.

■ Right-click on the icon of the printer you want to set as the default.

■ Select the **Set As Default** command from the pop-up menu.

If there is a check mark beside this command, the printer is already selected as the default printer.

Using the Print dialog box

When you choose the **File | Print** command within an application, you are shown a dialog box that typically offers the following options:

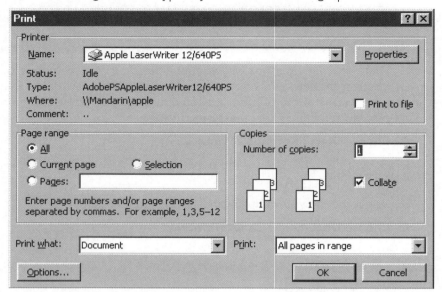

■ **(Printer) Name**: To choose a different printer, click in the **Name** pull-down list box, and then click the printer you require.

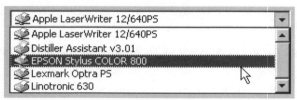

■ **Page range**: You can choose to print all pages, the currently displayed page only or a range of pages.

To print a group of continuous pages, enter the first and last page number of the group, separated by a dash. For example, 2-6 or 12-13.

To print a non-continuous group of pages, enter their individual page numbers, separated by commas. For example, 3,5,9 or 12,17,34. You can combine continuous with non-continuous page selections.

■ **Copies**: You can specify how many copies of the file you want to print. For multiple copies, select the **Collate** checkbox to print each copy of the entire document separately.

■ **Properties button**: Clicking the **Properties** button in the **Print** dialog box displays some further print choices that will vary with the type of printer selected – colour or black-and-white, inkjet or laser.

All printers offer choices about paper size (A4 is standard) and orientation (Portrait means 'standing up', Landscape means 'on its side').

When you have selected your options, you can click **OK** to print your file.

Install a new printer

Follow these steps to install a new printer on your PC:

Add Printer

1 Connect the printer to the appropriate port on your computer.

2 Windows 2000 may automatically install the printer for you. If not, choose **Start | Settings | Printers**, double-click the **Add Printer** icon to start the *Add Printer* Wizard, and then click **Next**.

3 When prompted by the Wizard, select the **Local Printer** option, and ensure that the **Automatically Detect My Printer** check box is deselected. Click **Next**.

If the printer is directly attached to your computer, click Local printer. If it is attached to another computer, or directly to the network, click Network printer.

◉ Local printer
　　☑ Automatically detect and install my Plug and Play printer
○ Network printer

4 Follow the on-screen instructions for selecting the port, the printer manufacturer and model, and then type a name for your printer.

Explore application menu bars

In the final part of this lesson, you will discover the three ways that you can perform actions in a Windows application: menu commands, toolbar buttons, and keyboard shortcuts. Let's start with menu commands.

1 Start the Microsoft Word application.

2 Take a look at the line of words that runs just under the title bar. Each of these words represents a *pull-down menu*.

File　Edit　View　Insert　Format　Tools　Data　Window　Help

3 Click the **File** menu name to display the commands (actions) available on this menu.

You tell Word that you want to perform a particular action by clicking the action's name on the pull-down menu.

4 Click **File | Exit** command to close Word.

Whenever you see an arrow to the right of a menu option, selecting that option displays a further sub-menu of choices.

All Windows applications share a number of common menus. Understand their general purpose and you will be able to use most applications. The common menus are:

- **File**: Use the commands on this menu to create a new (blank) file, open an existing file, save the current file, save the current file with a new name (Save as), print the current file, and quit the application.

- **Edit**: Use the commands on this menu to copy and move selected files, or items (such as text or graphics) within files.

- **View**: Use the commands on this menu to display your file in different ways, including a zoomed-in (up close) view or zoomed out (bird's eye) view.

- **Help**: Use the commands on this menu to display online help information about the application you are using.

Explore application toolbars

A second way of performing an action is to click a button on a *toolbar*. Instead of choosing **File | Save** to save a file, for example, you could click the **Save** button on the toolbar. Not every menu command has a toolbar button equivalent, but the most commonly used commands do.

Here are the toolbar buttons that you will find on almost every Windows application:

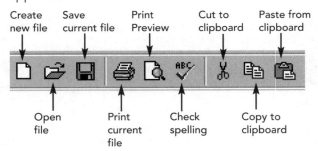

Explore keyboard shortcuts

A third way of performing actions in Windows is to use keyboard shortcuts. You may find using these faster than either menu commands or toolbar buttons, as you need not take either hand away from the keyboard.

An example of a keyboard shortcut is **CTRL+c**, which means 'Hold down the control key and press the letter c key'. This has the same effect as choosing **Edit | Copy** or clicking the **Copy** button on the toolbar.

Here are the most commonly used shortcut keys:

Keyboard shortcut	Action performed	Menu command
CTRL+o	Opens an existing file	**File	Open**
CTRL+n	Opens a new file	**File	New**
CTRL+s	Saves the current file	**File	Save**
CTRL+c	Copies to the clipboard	**Edit	Copy**
CTRL+x	Cuts to the clipboard	**Edit	Cut**
CTRL+v	Pastes from the clipboard	**Edit	Paste**
CTRL+z	Undoes the last action	**Edit	Undo**
CTRL+y	Repeats the last action	**Edit	Redo**

Quit Windows

You can shut down Windows and power down your computer. Congratulations! You have now completed Module 2 of the ECDL, Using a Computer and Managing Files. To remind yourself of the main features of Microsoft® Windows, cut out the quick reference guide, called **Windows essentials**, at the back of the book and keep it beside your computer.

3

Word processing

Back in the days when people thought they could predict the future, someone came up with the phrase 'paperless office'. As computers found their way into more and more workplaces, the theory was that paper-based communication would disappear. Forever. But alongside affordable computers came affordable printers. Result: computerization has led to more rather than less paper usage. The office supplies people have never been busier.

In this module you will learn how to add further to the world's output of computer-generated paperwork. There is a lot more to word processing than just typing and editing words, but these are the two foundation skills to which you are introduced at the beginning of this module. You will also learn how to access and search through Microsoft® Word's online help, which is a great place to find answers and advice on using any of the application's features.

You will then move on to more advanced tasks: changing the appearance of text, changing the position of text on the page, locating and replacing a particular word or phrase, inserting line and page breaks, importing and manipulating pictures, placing page numbers and other details in the page header or footer.

Also covered in this module are the secrets for generating personalized form letters that contain individual names and addresses (as in 'Dear Ms Murray') but have the same basic text (as in 'Allow us to introduce our Spring Promotion...'). A more commonly used term might be junk mail. How is it done? Read this module to find out.

3.1

Your first steps in Word

Learning goals	At the end of this lesson you should be able to:

- start and quit Word;
- enter and edit text;
- recognize Word's non-printing characters;
- use the **SHIFT**, **BACKSPACE**, **DELETE**, **ARROW** and **TAB** keys;
- use Word's Insert Date feature;
- save, name, open, create and close Word documents;
- undo, redo and repeat actions;
- use online help to learn more about Word.

New terms	At the end of this lesson you should be able to explain the following terms:

Word Document	A Microsoft Word file containing text and sometimes graphics too. For example, a letter or a report.
Paragraph Mark	A symbol shown on the screen (but not printed) to indicate the end of a paragraph (¶). Word displays another one each time you press the **ENTER** key.
Text wrap	Word's automatic moving of the cursor to the beginning of a new line when the text reaches the end of the previous one.
Non-printing Characters	Symbols that Word displays on the screen to help you type and edit your document, but that are not printed.

About Word documents

A *Word document* is a file containing text (and sometimes pictures too). Word's *non-printing characters*, such as a single dot to represent a space, do not appear on printouts. They are displayed on the screen only as a guide to typing and editing.

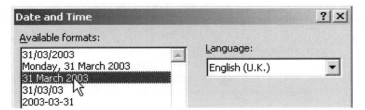

Test cursor and paragraph mark

Every new Word document contains a text cursor and a *paragraph mark* (¶). Whenever you type text, Word places the text at the text cursor's location. Whenever you press the ENTER key to type a new paragraph of text or insert a blank line, Word inserts another paragraph mark at that point. Word's Undo feature enables you to reverse your most recent typing or editing actions if they have produced unwanted results.

Keys you need to know

You can remove text with the following two keys:

- BACKSPACE: Removes text to the left of the text cursor.

- DELETE: Removes text to the right of the text cursor.

Press the SHIFT key in combination with a letter, number or symbol key to type an upper-case (capital) character or symbol.

Press the TAB key repeatedly to move text to the right. When typing a letter, for example, use TAB to position the address and related details at the top right of the letter.

Date and time insertion

As its name suggests, Word's **Insert | Date and Time** command inserts the current date and/or time in a document.

You can choose from a wide range of date formats.

Online help

Word offers a searchable online help system that you can access in two ways: from the **Help** menu, and from the question-mark button at the top-right of individual dialog boxes. Online help is a great place to find answers and advice on using any of Word's features.

Launch Microsoft Word

Word 2000

Double-click the Microsoft Word icon or choose **Start | Programs | Microsoft Word**.

Word starts and displays a window containing a new, empty document ready for you to type into.

> Every·man·a·king,·but·no·man·wears·a·crown.¶

You can type text in your new document, or open an existing document and work with that.

About the text cursor and paragraph mark

Near the top left corner of a new document you can see two items, side by side:

- **Text cursor (|)**: A blinking vertical line that says: 'You are here'. Whenever you type text, Word places the text at the location of the text cursor.
- **Paragraph mark (¶)**: Every new Word document contains at least one of these. Whenever you press the ENTER key to begin a new paragraph, Word inserts another one at that point.

Hide and display the paragraph marks and other non-printing characters

Show/Hide Paragraph Mark button

Can't see the paragraph mark in your document? Click the **Show/Hide Paragraph Mark** button on the Standard toolbar near the top right of your Word window. Except for the wavy underlines, all non-printing characters are displayed or hidden by pressing this button.

Non-Printing·Characters·Displayed¶
What·is·not·nailed·down·is·mine.·↵
What·I·can·prise·loose·is·not·nialed↵
down.¶

Non-Printing·Characters·Hidden
What is not nailed down is mine.
What I can prise loose is not nialed
down.

About non-printing characters

The paragraph mark is an example of a *non-printing character*: it appears on the screen only and not on printouts. Others include a small dot (indicating a blank space), and wavy underlines (possible spelling or grammar errors).

You may find these characters distracting, even annoying, and be tempted to hide them. Don't. Non-printing characters are there to help and guide you as you work with your documents.

Type new text

To type new text, just click with the mouse to position the cursor, and type. Try this:

1 Type the following number: 7

2 Press the SPACEBAR.

7·dwarfs¶ **3** Type the following six letters: dwarfs

That's it. Congratulations! You have typed your first text in Word.

Edit previously typed text

⁊dwarfs¶
⬇
|dwarfs¶
⬇
seven|dwarfs¶

Often you will want to change or remove text that you have typed. This is called editing.

1 Using the mouse, click to the right of the 7.

2 Press the **BACKSPACE** key. (You will find it directly above the **ENTER** key.)

3 Type the following word: seven

Use the SHIFT key

1 Click to the left of the letter s in seven.

2 Press the **DELETE** key to delete the letter s.

3 Hold down the **SHIFT** key and type the letter s. Word displays an upper-case S.

4 Move the cursor to the right of the letter d in dwarfs.

5 Press the **BACKSPACE** key to delete the letter d.

6 Hold down the **SHIFT** key and type the letter d. Word displays an upper-case D.

|seven·dwarfs¶ ➜ |even·dwarfs¶ ➜ S|even·dwarfs¶ ➜ Seven·d|warfs¶ ➜ Seven|warfs¶ ➜ Seven·D|warfs¶

Press ENTER to type new paragraph marks

When you want to begin a new paragraph, press the **ENTER** key. You will see the *paragraph mark* (¶) on screen indicating that the **ENTER** key has been pressed. Try this simple exercise:

1 Type the following four names, pressing **ENTER** after the first three only:

John	John¶
Paul	Paul¶
George	George¶
Ringo	Ringo

Remove a paragraph mark

Any paragraph mark that you insert by pressing **ENTER** you can also remove. Here's how:

1 Click at the left of the paragraph mark.

2 Press the **DELETE** key.

When you remove the paragraph mark, any text that follows the deleted paragraph mark is joined to the previous paragraph. In the example on the right 'Ringo' moves up to join 'George' when 'Ringo' no longer appears on a separate paragraph.

John¶   John¶
Paul¶   Paul¶
George¶ → GeorgeRingo
Ringo

Watch that text wrap

When the text that you type reaches the right side of the page, Word automatically moves further text onto the next line. You do not need to press the **ENTER** key to make this happen: the text is said to *wrap* to the next line. In the example below you can see that the text wraps to a second line without a paragraph mark.

Hospitals·will·normally·meet·your·wishes·in·this·regard,·except·where·it·would·be·considered·that· this·would·cause·serious·harm·to·your·physical·or·mental·health.¶

Insert and remove manual line breaks

Sometimes you will want your text to break to a new line before the text reaches the edge of the page.

To insert a line break directly, hold down the **SHIFT** key and press **ENTER**.

There·was·a·young·girl·from·Glouchester↵
Whose·parents·thought·they·had·lost·her↵
Till·at·last·safe·and·sound↵
In·a·fridge·she·was·found↵
But·the·problem·was·how·to·defrost·her.¶

In the example on the right, the first four lines end with a line break, and the fifth with a paragraph mark.

To remove a so-called manual line break, click at the left of the line break and press the **DELETE** key.

Move the cursor with the ARROW keys

Rather than use the mouse to move the cursor around your document, you can press any of the four **ARROW** keys, located to the right of the **ENTER** key. You may find this method faster than moving and clicking the mouse, because you need not take either hand away from the keyboard.

Type a horizontal line

Word offers a quick way to create a horizontal line, such as the line that appears under a hand-written signature near the bottom of a letter.

Hyphen key

1 Click in your document where you want the horizontal line to appear and press **ENTER** to create a blank paragraph.

2 Hold down the **SHIFT** key and press the **hyphen** key (-) about 20 times. (The **hyphen** key is the second key to the left of the **BACKSPACE** key.)

3 Release the **SHIFT** key.

Move text to the right with the TAB key

Tab key

When addressing a letter, you will usually want your address to begin near the top right of the page. You can push text to the right with the **TAB** key. Follow this simple example to discover how.

1 Type the following four address lines in a Word document:

> XYZ·Training·Centre,¶
> Unit·56A,¶
> Newpark·Office·Centre,¶
> Anytown¶

2 Click at the beginning of the first line, just to the left of the 'X'.

> |XYZ·Training·Centre,¶

3 Press the **TAB** key six or seven times.

4 Repeat step 3 for the remaining three address lines. Your document should look as follows.

> XYZ·Training·Centre,¶
> Unit·56A,¶
> Newpark·Office·Centre,¶
> |Anytown·¶

You will learn more about tabs in Lesson 3.7.

About tabs and non-printing characters

When you press the **TAB** key repeatedly to push a paragraph of text to the right, Word does not display any non-printing characters. If you press **TAB** to move an empty paragraph, however, Word does display non-printing arrow characters of the type shown below.

Insert the current date/time

Letters typically contain the current date. You can tell Word to insert the current date (as recorded on your computer) for you. Here's how:

1 Click in your document where you want the date and/or time to appear. In the sample letter below, the cursor is located in a blank paragraph after the sender's address.

2 Choose **Insert I Date and Time** to display a dialog box that shows a variety of formats.

3 Select the date and/or time format you want, and click **OK**.

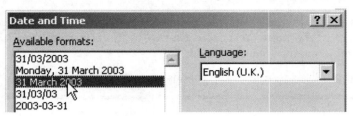

Word inserts the date in your document, and closes the dialog box.

Undo and redo actions

Enter the wrong text? Press a wrong key? Don't panic. Word allows you to undo your most recent text entry or editing action if it has produced unwanted results.

Undo button

- To undo an action, click the **Undo** button on the Standard toolbar or choose **Edit | Undo**.

- To reverse the effect of the **Undo** button, click **Redo**.

- Click **Undo** (or **Redo**) repeatedly to undo (or redo) your last series of actions.

Redo button

- To view a list of recent actions that you can undo or redo, click the arrow to the right of either button.

Practise using the undo and redo options by typing and deleting text in a document, and then reversing your deletions.

Repeat actions

To repeat your most recent previous action, choose **Edit | Repeat** or press **CTRL+y**.

If Word cannot repeat your last action, it changes the **Repeat** command to **Can't Repeat**.

Work with Insert and Overtype modes

By default, Word operates in so-called *Insert* mode. When you click in the middle of previously typed text, and then type some new text, Word 'pushes' the existing text forward to make room for the new characters that you type.

If you prefer, you can tell Word to work in *Overtype* mode, in which Word will replace any previously typed text with new characters that you type.

The Status Bar at the bottom of the Word document window tells you which mode you are in. If the letters OVR are dimmed ('greyed out'), you are in Insert mode. If they are shown in bold, you are in Overtype mode.

- To switch from one editing mode to the other, double-click the letters OVR on the Status Bar.

You can also switch between editing modes by pressing the **INSERT** key in the group of special keys to the right of the main typing keys on your keyboard. Most Word users rely on Insert mode and rarely use Overtype mode.

Save and name a document

Save button

Follow these steps to save a new document, and to give it a name:

1 Click the **Save** button on the Standard toolbar or choose **File | Save**.

2 In the **Save** dialog box, enter the document's file name and click **Save**.

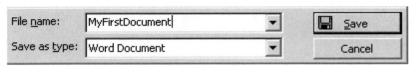

Word assumes that the file type is Word document. You need not type the file name extension of .doc. Word adds it automatically.

Save a document with a different name to a diskette

It's a good idea to save copies of your documents to a diskette or other backup medium.

1 Insert a diskette in your computer's diskette drive.

2 Choose **File | Save As** and locate your A: drive.

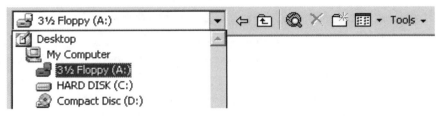

Word suggests the current file name for you to accept or amend.

3 Type a different name in the **File Name** box, and click **Save**.

4 When finished, use **File | Save As** again to resave the document to its original location on your hard disk, and with its original name. (You will be asked if you want to replace the original file: click **OK**.)

If you do not resave your document to its original location, saving the file in future (by clicking the **Save** button on the Standard toolbar or choosing **File | Save**) will save the document to the diskette and not to your computer's disk drive.

Close a document

- Choose **File | Close** or click the **Close** button at the top-right of the document window.

    If you have made changes to your document since you last saved it, you are prompted to save or discard them.

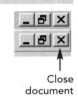

Close document

Create a new document

- Choose **File | New** or click the **New** button on the Standard toolbar. A new blank document is opened on screen for you.

Open an existing document

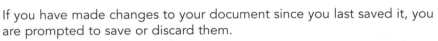

Open button

1 Click the **Open** button on the Standard toolbar or choose **File | Open**.

2 Select the file you want from the **Open** dialog box, and click **Open**.

Switch between open documents

If you have more than one document open, you can switch between them by clicking their names on the Windows taskbar.

Alternatively, click Word's **Window** menu, and then click the document's name from the list of documents at the bottom of the menu.

Display all commands on menus

By default, when you first choose a menu, Word displays only some of its commands. To see them all, you must click the double-arrow at the bottom of each menu. To view a complete list every time, follow these steps.

1 Choose **Tools | Customize** and click the **Options** tab.

2 Deselect the checkbox below, and click **Close**.

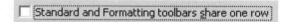

Display the Standard and Formatting toolbars on separate rows

By default Word displays the Standard and Formatting toolbars on a single row across the top of the screen. To display them as two, individual toolbars, follow these steps.

1 Choose **Tools | Customize** and click the **Options** tab.

2 Deselect the checkbox below, and click **Close**.

☐ Standard and Formatting toolbars share one row

Word toolbars

Only two of Word's toolbars are relevant to this ECDL module. The Standard toolbar includes buttons for managing files – that is, documents – and for inserting tables.

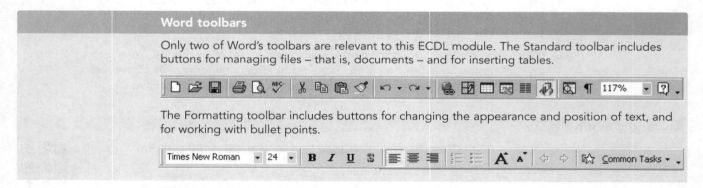

The Formatting toolbar includes buttons for changing the appearance and position of text, and for working with bullet points.

Hide and display toolbars

1 Choose **View | Toolbars**.

2 Select or deselect the various toolbar options from the pull-down menu displayed.

The check marks indicate which toolbars are already selected for display on screen.

Remove and redisplay toolbar buttons

Follow these steps to remove one or more buttons from a toolbar.

1 Display the toolbar that you want to change.

2 Hold down the **ALT** key, and drag the button off the toolbar.

Word removes the selected button. Want to bring it back again? Here's how.

3 Display the toolbar. Click the **More Buttons** button (at the very right of the toolbar) and then the **Add or Remove Buttons** button.

4 Click the button you want to display again.

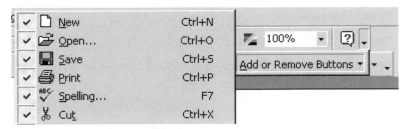

Buttons with a check mark beside their names are displayed on the toolbar.

5 Click anywhere outside the menu to close it. Word redisplays the button on the toolbar.

Get online help from the Help menu

1 Choose **Help | Microsoft Word Help**, or click the **Help** button on the Standard toolbar, or press **F1**.

Help button

2 Word displays the Help window with the following three tabs:

■ **Contents**: Here you will find descriptions of Word's main features. Where you see a heading with a book symbol, double-click it to view the related sub-headings. Double-click on a question-mark symbol to read the online help text.

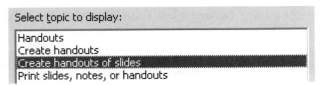

■ **Answer Wizard**: Type your question in the box at the top-left of the dialog box, and click **Search**. Word displays a list of suggested help topics in the lower-left. Click a topic to display the associated text in the right pane.

> Select topic to display:
>
> Handouts
> Create handouts
> Create handouts of slides
> Print slides, notes, or handouts

■ **Index**: Type the word or phrase and click **Search**. Word displays all matches from the online help in the lower left of the dialog box. Click on a topic to display the associated text.

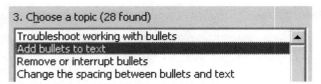

3. Choose a topic (28 found)

Troubleshoot working with bullets
Add bullets to text
Remove or interrupt bullets
Change the spacing between bullets and text

You will see the following buttons, left to right, at the top of the online help window:

- **Hide/Show**: Hides or displays the left pane of the dialog box.
- **Back/Forward**: Moves you backwards and forwards through previously visited help topics.
- **Print**: Prints the currently displayed help topic.
- **Options**: Offers a number of display choices.

Take a few minutes to look through Word's online help system.

Get online help from a dialog box

1   Choose **View | Print** to display the **Print** dialog box.

2   Click on the question-mark symbol near the top-right of the dialog box. Word displays a question mark to the right of the cursor.

3   Move the mouse down and left, and click anywhere in the **Name** box.

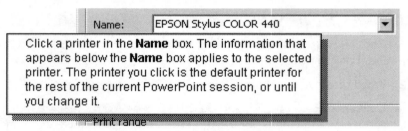

Name: EPSON Stylus COLOR 440

Click a printer in the **Name** box. The information that appears below the **Name** box applies to the selected printer. The printer you click is the default printer for the rest of the current PowerPoint session, or until you change it.

Print range

Word displays online help text that tells you about the selected option. Click **Cancel** to close the dialog box. Practise this with other dialog boxes in Word.

Quit Word

To quit Microsoft Word, choose **File | Exit** or click the **Close** button at the top right of the Word window. You are prompted to save any open documents containing unsaved work.

You have now completed Lesson 3.1 of the ECDL Word Processing Module.

3.2

Working with text and the clipboard

Learning goals At the end of this lesson you should be able to:

- select and deselect text in a document;
- format text (bold, italic and underline);
- apply fonts and font sizes, and super- and subscripts;
- use Word's change text case feature;
- insert symbols and special characters;
- apply built-in paragraph and character styles;
- use Word's Format Painter feature to copy formatting;
- copy, cut and paste text within and between documents;
- print all or part of a Word document;
- use Word's Zoom feature to enlarge and reduce the document display;
- use Word's different page views.

New terms At the end of this lesson you should be able to explain the following terms:

Selecting Text	Highlighting a piece of text in order to perform an action on it such as formatting or alignment.
Font	A typeface: a particular style of text. The two main font families are serif and sans serif.
Superscript	Text that is raised above other text on the same line and is reduced in font size. Commonly used in maths texts for indices.
Subscript	Text that is lowered beneath other text on the same line and is reduced in font size. Commonly used in chemistry texts for formulas.
Clipboard	A temporary storage area to which you can copy and from which you can paste text (or graphics). You can paste to any location within the same or a different document.
Print Layout View	A view of a Word document that displays it exactly as it will appear when you print it.
Normal View	A view of a Word document that displays only the text.
Outline View	A view of a Word document that displays it's structure, with text indented progressively to reflect its level of importance.

Text selection

Typically it is only some text in a document that you want to work with, and not the entire document. You tell Word which part of the document you want to format by first *selecting* that text. When you select text, Word displays that text in reverse (white text on black background).

Typically·it·is·only·some·text·in·a·document·that·you·want·to·format,·and·not·the· entire·document·.You·tell·Word·which·part·of·the·document·you·want·to·format·by·

About text formatting

Text formatting
buttons

The most common formatting effects are **bold** (heavy black text, often used for headings), *italic* (slanted text, often used for emphasis) and <u>underline</u> (a line under the text, often used beneath signatures on letters). You will find the relevant text formatting buttons on the Formatting toolbar.

Fonts and other text effects

A *font* or typeface is a particular style of text. You can change the font, size and colour of selected text, apply *superscript* and *subscript* text effects, and insert special characters and symbols such as á and ©.

Choosing a font from the **Font** pull-down list

Working with the clipboard

Suppose you want to use the same text more than once in a document. Do you need to retype it each time that you need it? No. With Word, you can type the text just once, and then insert it as many times as you need. This is a two-step process:

- **Copy:** You select and then copy the text to the *clipboard*, a temporary holding area.

- **Paste:** You insert or paste the text from the clipboard into a different part of the same document, or even a different document.

Similarly, you can cut (remove) the text from it's original location and paste it to a new location in the same or a different document.

Select text in a document

Follow these steps to *select text* in a Word document.

■ Click to position the cursor at the beginning of the text that you want to select.

> Typically·it·is·only·|some·text·in·a·document·that·you·want·to·format,·and·not·the·
> entire·document.·You·tell·Word·which·part·of·the·document·you·want·to·format·by·

■ To select text on a single line, drag the mouse to the right until you have selected the characters or words.

> Typically·it·is·only·**some**·text·in·a·document·that·you·want·to·format,·and·not·the·
> entire·document.·You·tell·Word·which·part·of·the·document·you·want·to·format·by·

■ To select a text on multiple lines, drag the mouse to the right and down the page.

> **Typically·it·is·only·some·text·in·a·document·that·you·want·to·format,·and·not·the·
> entire·document.**·You·tell·Word·which·part·of·the·document·you·want·to·format·by·

Word offers a number of convenient shortcuts for selecting text:

■ To select a single word, double-click anywhere in the word.

■ To select a sentence, treble-click anywhere in the sentence.

■ To select an entire document, choose **Edit | Select All**. Alternatively, hold down the **CTRL** key and click anywhere in the empty area (margin) at the left of the text.

> **Typically·it·is·only·some·text·in·a·document·that·you·want·to·format,·and·not·the·
> entire·document.·You·tell·Word·which·part·of·the·document·you·want·to·format·by·
> first·*selecting*·that·text.·When·you·select·text,·Word·displays·that·text·in·reverse·
> (white·text·on·black·background),·rather·like·the·negative·of·a·photograph.¶**

Deselect text in a document

You can deselect text that is currently selected by clicking anywhere outside the selected area.

Apply bold format

Follow these steps to apply the bold format to text in a document.

Bold button

1 Select the text by dragging or other means.

2 Click the **Bold** button on the Formatting toolbar or press CTRL+b.

3 Deselect the bold text by clicking anywhere else in the document.

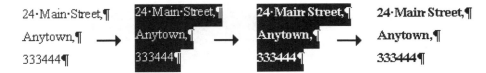

Apply italic format

Italic button

Follow these steps to apply the italic format to text in a document.

1 Select the text by dragging or other means.

2 Click the **Italic** button on the Formatting toolbar or press **CTRL+i**.

3 Deselect the italic text by clicking anywhere else in the document.

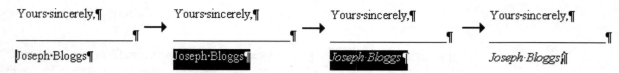

You can apply both bold and italic format to the same text.

Apply underline format

Underline button

Follow these steps to underline text in a document.

1 Select the text by dragging or other means.

2 Click the **Underline** button on the Formatting toolbar or press **CTRL+u**.

3 Deselect the underlined text by clicking anywhere else in the document.

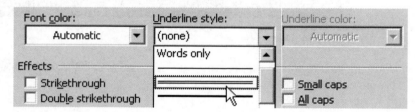

For a wider range of underline options that you can apply to selected text:

1 Choose **Format | Font**, and click the **Font** tab.

2 Click in the **Underline style** pull-down list, and then click an underline option to select it.

3 Click **OK** to apply the underline format and close the dialog box.

4 Deselect the underlined text by clicking anywhere else in the document.

Discover the fonts on your computer

A *font* or typeface is a particular style of text. To see what fonts are installed on your computer, click the arrow at the right of the pull-down **Font** box on the Formatting toolbar.

There are two main kinds (families) of fonts: serif (those with tails or squiggles at their edges) and sans serif. Sans serif just means without serifs.

Word's default font is a serif font called Times New Roman. Other popular serif fonts include Garamond and Century Schoolbook. Word's default sans serif font is Arial. Other common sans serif fonts include Verdana and Trebuchet.

This text is written in a serif font named Times New Roman.

This text is written in a serif font named Garamond.

This text is written in a serif font named Century Schoolbook.

This text is written in a sans serif font named Arial.

This text is written in a sans serif font named Verdana.

This text is written in a sans serif font named Trebuchet.

Change text font

To change the font of selected text in a document:

1 Click the arrow at the right of the **Font** pull-down list on the Formatting toolbar to display the fonts installed on your computer.

2 Click your required font from the list to apply the font to your selected text.

Set font size

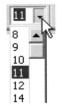

Font Size
pull-down list

Font size is measured in a non-metric unit called the point. About 72 points equals one inch. To change the font size of selected text:

1 Click the arrow at the right of the **Font Size** pull-down list box on the Formatting toolbar.

2 Click your required font size from the list to apply it to your selected text.

For the body text of letters or longer business documents such as reports, 10, 11 or 12 points is a good choice. For headings, use larger font sizes in the range 14 to 28 points.

Headers, footers, endnotes, footnotes and captions are often in 8 or 9 point font size.

Change font colour

Do you have a colour printer? Then you may want to select a text colour other than Automatic. Even without a colour printer, you may want to print your headings in grey.

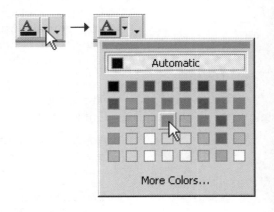

What colour is Automatic? It's black, unless the background is black or another dark colour, in which case Automatic switches to white. To change the colour of selected text:

1. Click the arrow at the right of the **Font Color** button on the Formatting toolbar. Word displays a range of colour choices. If you don't see a colour that you want, click the **More Colors** button to view further choices.

2. Select your required colour from the options displayed to apply it to your selected text.

Apply superscript and subscript text format

The *superscript* text effect raises the selected text above the other text on the same line, and reduces its font size. It is used most commonly for mathematical symbols. For example: 2^2, x^8, 10^3.

The opposite of superscript is *subscript*. For example: H_2SO_4. To apply superscript or subscript:

1. Select the text.

   Q4. ·· Find·the·square·root·of·16x2. ¶

2. Choose **Format | Font**, and click the **Font** tab.

3. In the **Effects** area, select the **Superscript** or **Subscript** checkbox.

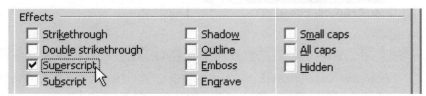

4. Click **OK** to apply the text effect and close the dialog box.

   Q4. ·· Find·the·square·root·of·16x². ¶

5. Deselect the text by clicking anywhere else in the document.

Change text case

You can change the case of selected text with the **Format | Change Case** command.

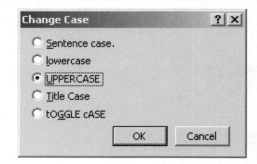

The options are **lowercase**, **UPPERCASE**, **Title Case** (initial capital for every word), **Sentence case** (initial capital for the first letter of the first word in the selected text), and **tOGGLE cASE** (changes the current case of all letters).

Insert symbols and special characters

Word allows you to insert symbols and special characters in your documents:

■ **Symbols**: Among the symbols are foreign language letters with accents (such as á, é, ä and ë) and fractions (such as ¼ and ½).

■ **Special Characters**: These include the copyright (©), registered (®) and trademark (™) symbols, plus typographic characters such as the en dash (a short dash the width of the letter 'n'), the em dash (a longer dash the width of the letter 'm'), and various types of opening and closing quotes.

To insert a symbol or special character in a document:

1 Click in your document at the location where you want to insert the symbol.

Water·boils·at·100 C.¶

2 Choose **Insert | Symbol**, and, as required, click the **Symbols** or **Special Characters** tab.

3 Click the symbol or character you want to insert and click the **Insert** button.

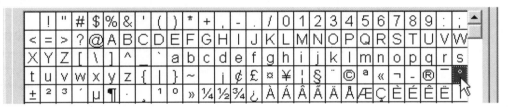

4 Word inserts the selected symbol or character in your document.

Water·boils·at·100°C.¶

5 Word leaves the dialog box open on your screen. Click **Close** to close it.

Discover the styles available to your document

Style pull-down list

A style is a collection of formatting and positioning attributes that you can apply to text in a single operation. To see what styles are available to your currently open document, click the arrow at the right of the **Style** pull-down list on the Formatting toolbar.

Word contains about 100 built-in, ready-to-use styles. The ones that you are likely to use most often are listed below, together with their default values.

Built-in Style Name	Font	Style	Font Size (points)	Additional Spacing (points)
Heading 1	Arial	Bold	16	12 before, 3 after
Heading 2	Arial	Bold, italic	14	12 before, 3 after
Heading 3	Arial	Bold	13	12 before, 3 after
Normal	Times New Roman	Normal	12	None

Although somewhat plain, Word's built-in styles are adequate for many documents. Word's styles are of two types:

- **Paragraph Styles:** You can apply these only to entire paragraphs – and not to selected text within a paragraph.

- **Character Styles:** You can apply these to an entire paragraph or to selected text within a paragraph.

Take a look at the styles in the **Style** pull-down list. Notice that only paragraph styles have the paragraph mark (¶) symbol beside their style name.

Apply a paragraph style

Follow these steps to apply a paragraph style to a paragraph:

- To apply a style to a single paragraph, click anywhere in the paragraph to position the cursor in it, and then click a paragraph style from the **Style** pull-down list on the Formatting toolbar.

- To apply a style to multiple paragraphs, select the paragraphs, and then click a paragraph style from the **Style** pull-down list on the Formatting toolbar.

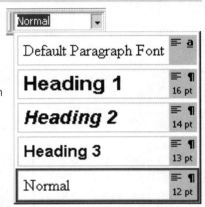

Apply a character style

Follow these steps to apply a character style to text.

1   Select the text, whether a single character, a word, a line or one or more paragraphs.

2   Click a character style from the **Style** pull-down list on the Formatting toolbar.

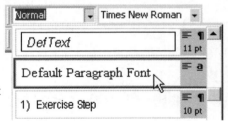

Use Format Painter

Word's Format Painter provides a quick, convenient way to copy formatting and styles from one piece of text to another. Follow these steps:

- Click anywhere in the text that contains the formatting you want to copy.

- Click the **Format Painter** button on the Standard toolbar.

- Drag across the text to which you want to apply the formatting.

- Release the mouse button for Word to apply the formatting.

Format
Painter
button

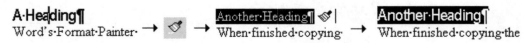

To copy formatting to several locations, begin by double-clicking the **Format Painter** button. When finished copying the formatting, click the **Format Painter** button again or press the **ESC** key.

Copy and paste text within a document

Follow these steps to copy and paste text within the same Word document.

1 Select the text you want to copy and paste, whether a character, word or paragraph.

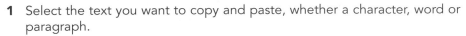

2 Click the **Copy** button on the Standard toolbar, choose **Edit | Copy**, or press **CTRL+c** to copy the text to the clipboard.

Copy button

3 Position the cursor at the location where you want to paste the text.

4 Click the **Paste** button on the Standard toolbar, or choose **Edit | Paste**, or press **CTRL+v**.

Paste button

Our·staff·will·introduce·themselves·to·you·and·explain·how·they·can·help.·All·staff·will·wear·a·name·badge·to·enable·you·to·identify·them.·Our·staff·will·introduce·themselves·to·you·and·explain·how·they·can·help.¶

Word pastes the text from the clipboard to the cursor location.

Copy and paste text between documents

Follow these steps to copy and paste text between documents.

1 Select the text you want to copy and paste, whether a character, word or paragraph.

Copy button

2 Click the **Copy** button on the Standard toolbar, or choose **Edit | Copy** or press **CTRL+c**.

3 Switch to the document into which you want to paste the copied text.

4 Position the cursor at the location in the second document where you want to paste the text.

Paste button

5 Click the **Paste** button on the Standard toolbar, or choose **Edit | Paste**, or press **CTRL+v**.

Cut and paste text

Sometimes, you may want to remove text from one part of a document and place it in a different part. Rather than deleting the text and then retyping it elsewhere, Word allows you to move the text by cutting it from its current location and pasting it to the new location.

Cut button

Cut-and-paste differs from copy-and-paste in that Word removes the cut text, whereas copied text remains in its original location.

You can cut selected text by clicking the **Cut** button on the Standard toolbar, or by choosing **Edit | Cut** or by pressing **CTRL+x**.

Copy, cut and paste by right-clicking

In addition to clicking a button on the Formatting toolbar, choosing a command on the Edit menu or pressing a keyboard shortcut, there is a fourth method exists for performing a copy, cut or paste operation: right-clicking.

When you right-click on selected text, Word displays a pop-up menu offering the **Cut**, **Copy** and **Paste** commands.

When you want to paste text from the clipboard, right-click at the location and choose the **Paste** command from the pop-up menu displayed.

Preview a document

Print Preview
button

Word offers a wide range of printing options, including the ability to preview a document on your screen before you print it.

■ To preview a document, click the **Print Preview** button on the Standard toolbar or choose **File | Print Preview**. Click **Close** to return to your document.

Print a document

When you choose **File | Print**, you have the following options regarding which parts of your document you may print:

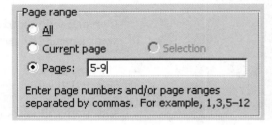

■ **All**: The current document.

■ **Current Page**: The page in which the text cursor is currently located.

■ **Pages**: To print one or a range of pages from the current document, enter the page number(s) here. To print a group of contiguous pages, enter the first and last page number of the group, separated by a dash. For example, 2–6 or 12–13.

To print a non-contiguous group of pages, enter their individual page numbers, separated by commas. For example, 3,5,9 or 12,17,34. You can combine contiguous with non-contiguous page selections.

■ **Selection**: Prints only the currently selected text of the current document.

Other options on the **Print** dialog box allow you to specify how many copies you want to print, and whether you want the pages collated or not.

Change the magnification view

You can change the screen magnification in either of the following two ways.

Zoom box

1 Click in the **Zoom** box on the Standard toolbar.

2 Enter a number between 10 and 400, and press **ENTER**.
(You need not type the percent (%) symbol.)

Alternatively:

1 Choose **View | Zoom**.

2 Select a magnification option from the **Zoom** dialog box.

You can choose a preset option (25–200%), or select **Custom** and enter a number from 10 to 400. To return to normal view, select a magnification of 100%

The Zoom feature affects only the way that Word displays a document on-screen – and not how a document is printed.

Other document views

Word offers four document views, that is, ways of displaying an open document:

- **Print Layout view**: This is Word's default view for all new documents. While this view is necessary when working with images and graphics, *Print Layout view* may slow down such tasks as typing, editing and scrolling. To switch to Print Layout view, choose **View | Print Layout**.

- **Normal view**: It is the fastest view for typing, editing and scrolling. It shows only the text in the document. Any graphics or images in the document are not displayed in this view. To switch to *Normal view*, choose **View | Normal**. If you are working with a long document that contains a small number of graphics, you may want to switch to Normal view.

- **Outline view**: Using styles to format your Word documents offers another advantage: it allows you to display documents in a way that reflects their structure. Such a structured view of a document is called an *Outline view*. An Outline view of a document that is formatted using styles would typically look as follows:

> ⊕ **This·is·Heading·One·Style¶**
> ▫ This·is·body·text·(in·Normal)¶
> ⊕ **This·is·a·Heading·Two·Style¶**
> ▫ This·is·body·text·(in·Normal)¶
> ⊕ **This·is·Heading·One·Style¶**
> ▫ This·is·body·text·(in·Normal)¶

In the above example, three styles are applied: Heading 1, Heading 2 and Normal (the default, used for body text). Notice that Word progressively indents styled text according to its level of importance in the document. To switch to Outline view, choose **Views | Outline**.

- **Web Layout view**: This view displays a document as it would appear in Internet Explorer or other web browser. You may want to use this view when creating a web page in Word. To switch to Web Layout view, choose **View | Web View**.

Quit Word

You can close any open documents and quit Microsoft Word. You have now completed Lesson 3.2 of the ECDL Word Processing Module.

3.3

Working with paragraphs

Learning goals

At the end of this lesson you should be able to:

- align paragraphs: left, right, centred and justified;
- apply left and right indents;
- apply a first line indent to a paragraph;
- apply a hanging indent to a paragraph;
- change the spacing between lines;
- change the spacing between paragraphs;
- apply and format a bulleted or numbered list;
- insert and remove manual page breaks.

New terms

At the end of this lesson you should be able to explain the following terms:

Alignment	The horizontal positioning of lines in a paragraph. They can share a common centre-point, begin at the same point on the left, end at the same point on the right, or begin and end at the same points.
Indent	The positioning of a paragraph of text a specified distance in from the left and/or right margin.
Bulleted and Numbered Lists	A list of short items that are bulleted (preceded by a dot or other symbol) or numbered (preceded by a sequentially increasing number).
Hanging Indent	The positioning of the first line of the paragraph closer to the left margin than the remaining lines of the same paragraph.
Inter-line Spacing	The vertical space between lines within a paragraph of text. Word's default is single line spacing.
Inter-paragraph Spacing	The spacing between successive paragraphs of text.
First Line Indent	The positioning of the first line of a paragraph a greater distance in from the left margin than the remaining lines of the same paragraph.

In this lesson you will work with actions in Word that apply only to entire paragraphs, and not to selected text within a paragraph.

Alignment: left, right, centred and justified

Alignment is a way of positioning text in a paragraph so that it lines up beside the left margin, beside the right margin, beside both left and right margins (justification) or an equal distance from both left and right margins (centring).

You have the right to request the hospital to make details of your relevant medical records available to you.	You have the right to request the hospital to make details of your relevant medical records available to you.	You have the right to request the hospital to make details of your relevant medical records available to you.	You have the right to request the hospital to make details of your relevant medical records available to you.

Buttons for the alignment options are provided on the Formatting toolbar.

Indents: in from the margin

Indenting is a way of moving text a specified distance in from the left or right margin of the page – or from both.

suppliers,·and·save·time·and·money.¶

Another·successful·year·has·seen·revenues·rise·by·35%·and·profits·by·47.5%.·Our·company·is·well·placed·to·face·the·challenges·of·the·future.¶

Refine·your·procurement·strategy·by·choosing·from·a·global·network·of·suppliers.¶

Bulleted and numbered lists

Use lists to communicate short statements or instructions. *Bulleted lists*, in which each item is preceded by a symbol such as a square or diamond, are suitable when the reading order is not critical.

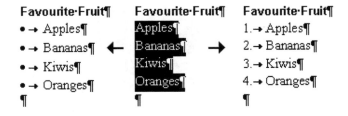

Numbered lists, in which each item is preceded by a sequentially increasing number or letter, are used for instructions and directions, where the order of reading is important.

Align a paragraph

To align a paragraph means to line it up in a particular horizontal (left-right) way. Below are Word's four *alignment* options with examples of each.

Button	Alignment	Description
≣	Left	The default and easiest to read. Commonly used for letters and business documents.
		My·problem·is·that·I·have·been·persecuted·by·an·integer.·For·seven· years·this·number·has·followed·me·around,·has·intruded·in·my·most· private·data,·and·has·assaulted·me·from·the·pages·of·our·most·public· journals.·This·number·assumes·a·variety·of·disguises,·being·sometimes·
≣	Centre	Places text between the left and right margins. Commonly used for headings.
		The·Magical·Number·Seven¶ My·problem·is·that·I·have·been·persecuted·by·an·integer.·For·seven· years·this·number·has·followed·me·around,·has·intruded·in·my·most·
≣	Right	Aligns against the right of the page. Commonly used for decorative effect.
		artscentre¶ Welcome·to·our·official·web·site.·The·largest·arts·and·entertainment· complex·in·the·UK·outside·London,·we're·based·at·the·University·of
≣	Justified	Both left and right aligned at the same time! Commonly used for narrow columns of text in newspapers and magazines.
		Smallsville· United· have· launched· an· official· complaint· against· referee· Ed· Blissem· after· he· / Smallsville· revealed· they· have· been· inundated· with· com¬ plaints· from· supporters·

- To align a single paragraph, click anywhere in the paragraph to position the cursor in it, and click any of the four alignment buttons on the Formatting toolbar.

- To align multiple paragraphs, select the paragraphs, and then click any of the four alignment buttons on the Formatting toolbar.

Apply left and right indents

You can push (*indent*) a paragraph a specified distance in from the left margin, right margin, or both. To indent a selected paragraph:

1 Choose **Format | Paragraph**, and click the **Indents and Spacing tab**.

2 In the **Left** and/or **Right** Indentation boxes, enter or select your required values.

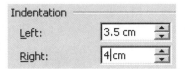

3 Click **OK** to apply the indent and close the dialog box.

In long documents, you may sometimes see indenting used as a way of attracting attention to a particular part of the text. Below is an example that combines a left and right indent with italics.

suppliers,·and·save·time·and·money.¶

> *Another·successful·year·has·seen·revenues·*
> *rise·by·35%·and·profits·by·47.5%.·Our·*
> *company·is·well·placed·to·face·the·*
> *challenges·of·the·future.*¶

Refine·your·procurement·strategy·by·choosing·from·a·global·network·of·suppliers.¶

Apply a hanging indent

A *hanging indent* is where all the lines of a paragraph are indented – except the first one. Hanging indents are sometimes used for lists such as bibliographies. Below is an example.

The·Memoirs·of·James·II·Translated·by·A.·Lytton·Sells·from·the·Bouillon·
Manuscript.·Edited·and·collated·with·the·Clarke·Edition.·With·an·
introduction·by·Sir·Arthur·Bryant.¶

To apply a hanging indent to a selected paragraph:

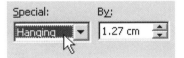

1 Choose **Format | Paragraph**, and click the **Indents and Spacing** tab.

2 In the **Special** pull-down list, select the **Hanging** option, and select or type a value in the **By** box.

3 When finished, click **OK** to apply the hanging indent and close the dialog box.

Set inter-line spacing

Line spacing pull-down list

Inter-line spacing is the vertical space between lines within a paragraph of text. By default, Word applies single inter-line spacing. Below you can see the same text with different inter-line spacing values.

Confidentiality¶
You·have·the·right·to·total·confidentiality·

You·have·the·right·to·request·the·hospital·
available·to·you.·Hospitals·will·normally·
be·considered·that·this·would·cause·seriou
circumstances,·the·information·may·be·co
your·family·doctor.¶

Confidentiality¶

You·have·the·right·to·total·confidentiality·

You·have·the·right·to·request·the·hospital·

available·to·you.·Hospitals·will·normally·

be·considered·that·this·would·cause·seriou

To increase or decrease the inter-line spacing of a selected paragraph:

1 Choose **Format | Paragraph**, and click the **Indents and Spacing** tab.

2 In the **Line spacing** pull-down list, select your required value.

3 When finished, click **OK** to apply the inter-line spacing and close the dialog box.

Set inter-paragraph spacing

Pressing the **ENTER** key to add a blank line between paragraphs of text is a crude – if effective – way of controlling the *inter-paragraph* spacing (*spacing* between paragraphs) in your document.

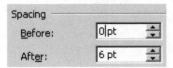

For longer documents, you may instead wish to use the **Format | Paragraph** command, and enter an inter-paragraph space value in the **Spacing Before** and/or **Spacing After** boxes.

■ For body text, enter a value of about 6 points in the **Spacing After** box to separate the next paragraph from the current one.

■ For headings, enter a value of about 12 points in the **Spacing Before** box to place an extra area of blank space above the headings, helping them to stand out from the rest of the text.

Privacy¶
You·have·the·right·to·have·your·privacy·respected,·especially·when·the·nature·of·your·clinical·condition·is·being·discussed·with·you·or·your·relatives·by·hospital·staff.¶

Confidentiality¶
You·have·the·right·to·total·confidentiality·in·respect·of·your·medical·records.¶

You·have·the·right·to·request·the·hospital·to·make·details·of·your·relevant·medical·records·available·to·you.¶

Hospitals·will·normally·meet·your·wishes·in·this·regard,·except·where·it·would·be·considered·that·this·would·cause·serious·harm·to·your·physical·or·mental·health.¶

In·such·circumstances,·the·information·may·be·communicated·through·a·health·professional,·normally·your·family·doctor.¶

Apply a first line indent

Word also lets you indent the first line of a paragraph only, so that it starts a greater distance in from the left margin than the other lines of the same paragraph. Do not use a *first line indent* for the first paragraph after a heading.

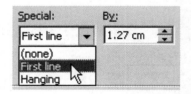

For long documents, you can set inter-paragraph spacing for body text to zero, and use first line indenting as a way of indicating where each new paragraph begins.

Confidentiality¶
You·have·the·right·to·total·confidentiality·in·respect·of·your·medical·records.¶
    You·have·the·right·to·request·the·hospital·to·make·details·of·your·relevant·medical·records·available·to·you.·¶
    Hospitals·will·normally·meet·your·wishes·in·this·regard,·except·where·it·would·be·considered·that·this·would·cause·serious·harm·to·your·physical·or·mental·health.¶
    In·such·circumstances,·the·information·may·be·communicated·through·a·health·professional,·normally·your·family·doctor.¶

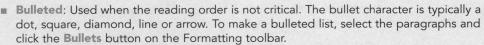

About bulleted and numbered lists

Lists are good ways to format a series of short statements or instructions. Lists are of two types:

- **Bulleted**: Used when the reading order is not critical. The bullet character is typically a dot, square, diamond, line or arrow. To make a bulleted list, select the paragraphs and click the **Bullets** button on the Formatting toolbar.
- **Numbered**: Used when the order of reading is important, for example, in directions and instructions. Each item is assigned a sequentially increasing number or letter. To make a numbered list, select the paragraphs and click the **Numbering** button on the Formatting toolbar.

You can also make lists by choosing **Format | Bullets and Numbering**. Word offers you a wide range of options, such as the style of bullet or number character, and the distance between the bullet or number character and the bulleted or numbered text.

Apply a bulleted or numbered list

Follow these steps to format a number of paragraphs as a list.

Numbering and Bullets buttons

1 Select the paragraphs to which you want to apply the list format.

2 Click either the **Bullets** or **Numbering** button on the Formatting toolbar.

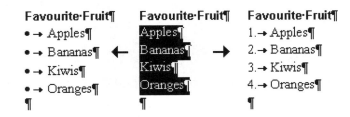

Word applies the bulleted or numbered list format as appropriate.

Remove a bulleted or numbered list format

Follow these steps to remove the bulleted or numbered list format from one or more paragraphs:

- To remove the list format from a single paragraph in a list, click anywhere in the paragraph, and then click either the **Bullets** or **Numbering** button on the Formatting toolbar.

Favourite·Fruit¶	Favourite·Fruit¶	Favourite·Fruit¶	Favourite·Fruit¶
•→ Apples¶	•→ Apples¶	1.→ Apples¶	1.→ Apples¶
•→ Bananas¶ →	Bananas¶	2.→ Bananas¶ →	Bananas¶
•→ Kiwis¶	•→ Kiwis¶	3.→ Kiwis¶	3.→ Kiwis¶
•→ Oranges¶	•→ Oranges¶	4.→ Oranges¶	4.→ Oranges¶
¶	¶	¶	¶

- To remove the list format from multiple or all paragraphs in a list, select the paragraphs, and then click either the **Bullets** or **Numbering** button on the Formatting toolbar.

Change the bullet style in a list

Follow these steps to change the symbol used in a bulleted list:

1 Select all the paragraphs in the bulleted list. (Notice that you cannot select the bullet symbols. Why? Because they are not entered text – they are generated automatically by Word.)

2 Choose **Format I Bullets and Numbering**, click the **Bulleted** tab, and click the **Customize** button.

3 At the top of the **Customize Bulleted List** dialog box you can see a range of suggested bullet symbols. Click one of these to select it.

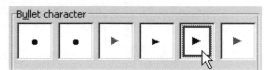

Alternatively, click the **Bullet** button to display a much wider range of symbol choices. Click any of these, and then click **OK** to return to the **Customize Bulleted List** dialog box.

4 Click **OK** to apply the new bullet symbol and close the **Customize Bulleted List** dialog box.

Change the number style in a list

Follow these steps to change the style of numbering used in a numbered list:

1 Select all the paragraphs in the numbered list. (Notice that you cannot select the numbers. Why? Because they are not entered text – they are generated automatically by Word.)

2 Choose **Format I Bullets and Numbering**, click the **Numbered** tab, and click the **Customize** button.

Number style pull-down list

3 Click in the **Number Style** pull-down list, and then click a style option to select it. Word offers a range of choices that includes sequential series of numbers and letters.

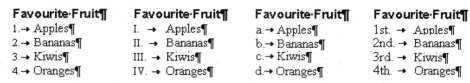

4 Further options are available if you click the **Font** button. In the **Font** dialog box displayed you can change the font, style, size and colour of the numbering symbol.

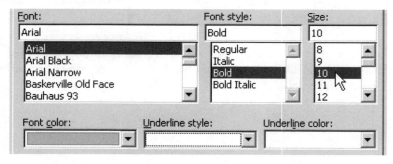

When finished, click **OK** to close the **Font** dialog box.

Insert and remove manual page breaks

When a page of a Word document fills with text (or graphics), Word automatically creates a new page to hold further content. You can insert a page break directly at any point in a document by pressing **CTRL+ENTER**. Alternatively, choose the **Insert | Breaks** command, select the **Page break** option, and click **OK**. Below is an example of Word's so-called manual page break.

¶

··Page Break··

To remove such a break, simply click on it and press the **DELETE** key.

Quit Word

You can close any open documents and quit Microsoft Word. You have now completed Lesson 3.3 of the ECDL Word Processing Module.

3.4

Borders, fills, graphics and charts

Learning goals At the end of this lesson you should be able to:

- apply borders to text and paragraphs;
- add shading to selected text and paragraphs;
- insert a Clip Art image in a document;
- insert an image file in a document;
- resize an inserted image or chart;
- reposition an inserted image or chart;
- delete an inserted image or chart.

New term At the end of this lesson you should be able to explain the following term:

Clip Art Standard or stock images that can be used and reused in a wide range of documents.

Decorative borders

You can draw attention to areas of text in a document with borders (decorative boxes). Word's **Format | Borders and Shading** command offers a range of border options, with Box and Shadow the most common choices. By default, a border covers all four edges, but you can choose to place a border on only one, two or three edges.

Special·Offer¶

Special·Offer¶

Special·Offer¶

Background fills

Coloured backgrounds (what Word calls shading) can brighten your documents. The three main shading options available with the **Format | Borders and Shading** command are fills, patterns and colours.

Special·Offer¶
Announcing·a·new·range·of·gardening·products·at·unbelievably·low·prices.¶

You can apply both a border and shading to the same text or paragraph, and use the border to extend the shaded area around the text or paragraph.

Clip Art images

Word contains 16 categories of so-called *Clip Art* images that you can use and reuse in a wide range of documents. Clip Art is also available on CD-ROMs and on the Internet.

Home & Family   Household   Industry   Lost & Found   Maps

You can insert Clip Art images, and any other image files that you may have, in a Word document. You can also insert charts created in other applications such as Microsoft Excel.

Create your sample document

1 Launch Word. In the new document, type the following text, and format the heading in Arial Narrow, 14 point, bold:

Special·Offer¶
Announcing·a·new·range·of·gardening·products·at·unbelievably·low·prices.¶

2 Save your document with the following file name:

Gardening

You will use this document throughout this lesson.

Apply borders to text and paragraphs

You can draw attention to areas of text in a document with borders (decorative boxes). Word's **Format | Borders and Shading** command offers a range of border options, with **Box** and **Shadow** the most common choices. By default, a border covers all four edges, but you can choose to place a border on only one, two or three edges, if required. Let's try it in your sample Gardening document.

1 Select the text or paragraph around which you want to place a border.

Special·Offer¶
Announcing·a·new·range·of·gardening·products·at·unbelievably·low·prices.¶

Box border option

2 Choose **Format | Borders and Shading** and click the **Borders** tab.

3 At the left of the dialog box click the **Box** border style option.

4 Use the **Style**, **Colour** and **Width** pull-down lists to select your required border options.

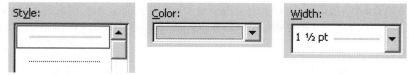

Top edge button

5 Use the **Preview** section on the right of the dialog box to select the edges that you want bordered. Click an edge button once to hide a border, and again to redisplay it. Below are some of the effects that you can achieve.

Special·Offer¶

Special·Offer¶

Special·Offer¶

Apply to pull-down list

6 Pay attention to the **Apply to** pull-down list at the bottom right of the dialog box. Your choice affects how Word draws the border. See the two examples below.

Special·Offer::·Border·Applied·to·Text¶

Special·Offer::·Border·Applied·to·Paragraph¶

If you select the **Paragraph** option in the **Apply to** pull-down list, you can click the **Options** button and set the spacing between the text and the border that surrounds it.

7 Experiment with the various border settings. When finished, click **OK** to apply your chosen border settings and close the dialog box.

Add shading to selected text and paragraphs

Coloured backgrounds (what Word calls shading) can brighten your documents. The three main shading options available with the **Format | Borders and Shading** command are as follows:

- **Fill**: This is the text background colour. If placing a grey shade behind black text, use 25% or less of grey. Otherwise, the text will be difficult to read.

- **Style**: This allows you to apply tints (percentages of a colour) or patterns of a second colour (selected in the **Color** box) on top of the selected Fill colour. Usually you will not want to apply a second colour, and will leave the **Style** box at its default value of **Clear**.

- **Colour**: If you have selected a pattern in the **Style** box, select the colour of the lines and dots in the pattern here. Otherwise, you can ignore this box.

Let's try a shading exercise with your sample Gardening document.

1 In your sample Gardening document, copy the heading and text, and paste it twice beneath the existing text.

2 Remove any borders that may be applied to your copied text. It should look as shown.

Special·Offer¶
Announcing·a·new·range·of·gardening·products·at·unbelievably·low·prices.¶
¶
Special·Offer¶
Announcing·a·new·range·of·gardening·products·at·unbelievably·low·prices.¶

3 Select the first of the two headings, choose **Format | Borders and Shading** and click the **Shading** tab.

4 Click the **Gray-10%** option, ensure that the **Apply to** pull-down list shows the **Paragraph** option, and click **OK**.

5 Repeat steps 3 and 4 for the second of the two headings, select the **Text** option in the **Apply to** pull-down list, and click **OK.**

6 Notice the difference between applying shading to text and to a paragraph.

Special·Offer¶
Announcing·a·new·range·of·gardening·products·at·unbelievably·low·prices.¶
¶
Special·Offer¶
Announcing·a·new·range·of·gardening·products·at·unbelievably·low·prices.¶

For darker shaded backgrounds, you will want to change the text colour to white or another lighter colour. Here is a sample effect.

Special·Offer¶
Announcing·a·new·range·of·gardening·products·at·unbelievably·low·prices.¶

7 Experiment with the various shading settings. When finished, click **OK** to apply your chosen shading settings and close the dialog box.

You can apply both a border and shading to the same text or paragraph, and use the border to extend the shaded area around the text or paragraph. In the example below, background shading is combined with a 3 point-wide border.

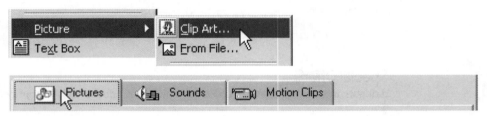

Special·Offer¶

Announcing·a·new·range·of·gardening·products·at·unbelievably·low·prices.¶

Insert a Clip Art image in a document

Word contains 16 categories of so-called *Clip Art* images that you can use and reuse in a wide range of documents. Clip Art is also available on CD-ROMs and on the Internet. Follow these steps to insert a Clip Art image into a document:

1 Position the cursor where you want the Clip Art image to appear in your document.

2 Choose the **Insert I Picture I Clip Art** command, and click the **Pictures** tab.

3 Click a Clip Art category to display the images contained within the category.

Home & Family   Household   Industry   Lost & Found   Maps

4 When you see the individual image that you want to insert, right-click it and choose the **Insert** command from the pop-up menu displayed.

5 The Clip Art image is inserted in your document.

6 Word leaves the **Insert ClipArt** dialog box open on your screen. Click the **Close** button at the top right of the **Insert ClipArt** dialog box to close it.

As practice, insert a Clip Art image from the Plants category at the top of your sample Gardening document.

Insert an image file in a document

You can insert an image file in a Word document as follows:

1   Position the cursor where you want the image to appear in your document.

2   Choose **Insert | Picture | From File**.

3   In the **Insert Picture** dialog box, locate the relevant graphic – it may be on your hard disk, on a diskette in the A: drive, or on a CD-ROM.

4   Click **OK** to insert the image in your document and close the dialog box.

Insert image files with copy and paste

Another way to insert an image file in a Word document is to use copy (or cut) and paste. This method is possible only if you can open the file containing the relevant graphic. To do so, you need to have installed on your computer a software application that can read that graphic format.

For example, to copy into Word a graphic created in Adobe Photoshop, you need Adobe Photoshop installed and open on your computer. Or, failing that, another graphics program capable of opening Adobe Photoshop (.psd) files.

When you have the graphic open in your graphics program, select it (or part of it, as you require), and choose **Edit | Copy** to copy it to the clipboard. Then, switch to Word, position the cursor where you want the graphic to appear in your document, and choose **Edit | Paste**.

Create an Excel chart for inserting into Word

Follow these steps to create in the Microsoft® Excel application a chart that you will paste into Word.

1   Choose **Start | Programs | Microsoft Excel** to open a new Excel worksheet on your screen. You can see lots of the little boxes called cells, arranged in rows and columns. You can enter a number or text in any cell by first clicking on it, and then typing.

2   Enter text and numbers anywhere in the Excel worksheet as shown below.

Jan	1200
Feb	1300
Mar	890
April	1432

Chart Wizard button

3   Drag across the eight cells to select them, click the **Chart Wizard** button on Excel's Standard toolbar, and, in the dialog box displayed, click the **Finish** button.

Chart legend

4 At the right of the chart you can see the chart legend.

Click the legend to select it, and press the **DELETE** key to remove it.

Excel expands the width of the chart columns to fill the area left by the deleted legend.

Your chart should look as shown to the right.

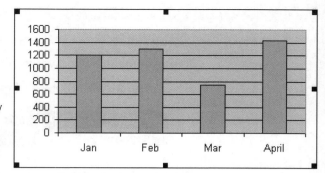

5 With the chart selected, choose **Edit | Copy** to copy it to the clipboard.

You may now close the Excel worksheet file without saving it, and quit Microsoft Excel. But the copied chart must remain in the clipboard.

Insert an Excel chart in a Word document

Follow these steps to insert an Excel chart, created in the previous topic, into a Word document.

1 Position the cursor in the Word document where you want the Excel chart to appear. (For the purposes of this example, create a new, empty document, and click at the paragraph mark at its beginning.)

2 Choose **Edit | Paste**.

This pastes the Excel chart data from the clipboard to the Word document.

Resize an inserted image or chart

You can change the shape or size of an image or chart as follows.

1 Click anywhere inside the image or chart to select it.

2 Click on any of its eight sizing handles.

3 Hold down the mouse button and drag to change its shape.
As you drag the image or chart, Word changes its border to a dashed line.

Use the corner handles to increase or reduce the size of the image or chart while maintaining it's proportions. Use the handles in the middle of the sides to distort it by resizing it in one dimension only.

Reposition an inserted image or chart

To reposition an image or chart on the same page, a different page or document, follow these steps:

1 Click anywhere inside the image or chart to select it.

Copy button

2 Click the **Cut** button on the Standard toolbar, or choose **Edit | Cut** or press CTRL+v.

3 Position the cursor at the location where you want to paste the image or chart.

If necessary, switch to the document into which you want to paste the image or chart. When you have more than one Word document open at a time, you can switch between them by choosing the document's name in the **Window** menu.

Paste button

4 Click the **Paste** button on the Standard toolbar, or choose **Edit | Paste**, or press CTRL+v.

Word pastes the image or chart from the clipboard to the cursor location.

Delete an inserted image or chart

To remove an image or chart, click it to select it and press the **DELETE** key.

Quit Word

You can close any open documents and quit Microsoft Word. You have now completed Lesson 3.4 of the ECDL Word Processing Module.

3.5

Page setup, headers and footers

Learning goals At the end of this lesson you should be able to:

- set page size;
- set page orientation;
- set page margins;
- specify left/right or common headers and footers;
- create and format headers and footers;
- insert automatic page numbers in a header or footer;
- insert a document's creation or modification date in a header or footer;
- insert a document's file name and location in a header or footer.

New terms At the end of this lesson you should be able to explain the following terms:

A4 The standard page size for letters and most other business documents throughout Europe.

Margin The distance of the text and graphics from the edge of the printed page. Word lets you specify separate top, bottom, left and right margins.

Headers and Footers Standard text and graphics that are printed in the top and bottom margins of every page of a document.

You have learnt how to control where text appears on the printed page, using text alignment, indenting, inter-line spacing and inter-paragraph spacing. But what about the page on which the text appears? What options does Word offer you?

You can use the **Margins** and **Paper Size** tabs of the dialog box displayed by the **File | Page Setup** command to view and set your options.

The standard page size is *A4* (21 cm wide and 29.7 cm high), and pages can be oriented in Portrait ('standing up') or Landscape ('on its side').

A *margin* is the distance of the text (and graphics) from a particular edge of the page. Word's default margin values – top and bottom, 1 inch (2.54 cm), left and right, 1.25 inches (3.17 cm) – are acceptable for most letters and business documents.

Headers and footers

Headers and footers are small text items that reoccur on every (or every second) page. Word places headers and footers in the top and bottom page margins, set with the **File | Page Setup** command.

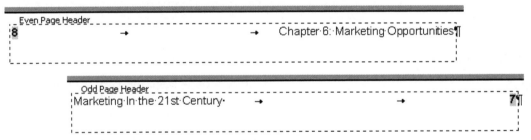

Headers and footers typically contain such details as the document title and an automatically generated page number.

Set page size

You can specify the size of the page on which Word positions the content (text, images and graphics) that you create and edit.

1 Choose **File | Page Setup**, and click the **Paper Size** tab.

2 Select an option from the **Paper size** pull-down list.

It is unlikely that you will want to change from the default of A4. This is the European standard paper size (21 cm wide and 29.7 cm high).

A4 is used for almost all letters and other business documents.

3 When finished, click **OK** to apply your page size settings and close the dialog box.

Set page orientation

Orientation is the direction in which the page is printed. To set page orientation:

1 Choose **File | Page Setup**, and click the **Paper Size** tab.

2 Select an option from the **Orientation** area.

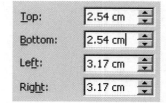

Your options are Portrait ('standing up') and Landscape ('on its side').

Letters and most other business documents are printed in portrait.

3 When finished, click **OK** to apply your orientation setting and close the dialog box.

Set page margins

A *margin* is the distance of a page's printed content (text and graphics) from the edge of the paper. You can set each of the page's four margins (top, bottom, left and right) independently as follows:

1 Choose **File | Page Setup**, and click the **Margins** tab.

2 Amend the **Top**, **Bottom**, **Left** and **Right** margin values, as required.

Word's default margin values – top and bottom, 2.54 cm (1 inch), left and right, 3.17 cm (1.25 inches) – are acceptable for most letters and business documents.

3 Ensure that the **Apply to** pull-down list is set to Whole document.

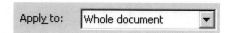

4 When finished, click **OK** to apply your margin settings and close the dialog box.

Specify left/right or common headers and footers

Before inserting headers and footers in a document, first specify the type that you want.

1 Choose **File | Page Setup**, and click the **Layout** tab.

2 Deselect the **Different odd and even** checkbox if you want the same headers and the same footers to appear on both odd-numbered (right) pages and even-numbered (left) pages.

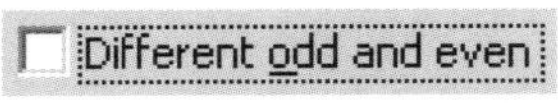

☐ Different odd and even

In the example below, you can see that left and right page footers both contain a page number that is aligned horizontally in the page centre.

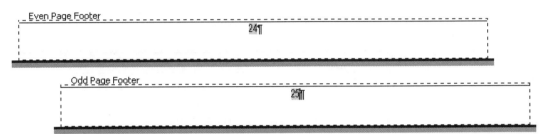

Select the **Different odd and even** checkbox if you want different headers and different footers to appear on odd-numbered (right) pages and even-numbered (left) pages.

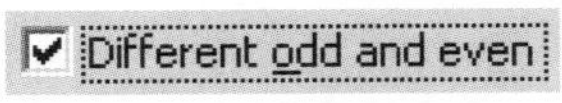

☑ Different odd and even

In the example below, you can see that the even (left) page header contains a page number and a chapter title, while the odd (right) page header contains a document title and a page number.

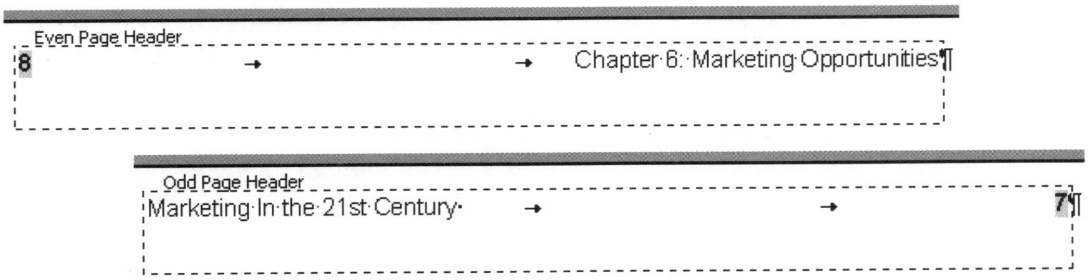

<!-- Even Page Header: 8 → → Chapter 6: Marketing Opportunities¶ -->
<!-- Odd Page Header: Marketing In the 21st Century · → → 7¶ -->

3 When finished, click **OK** to apply your header and footer settings and close the **Page Setup** dialog box.

Specify different headers/footers on first pages

By convention, the first or title page of a document should not contain a header or footer.

1 Choose **File | Page Setup**, and click the **Layout** tab.

2 Select the **Different first page** checkbox if you want the first page of your document to have a different header or footer from the remainder of your document – or no header or footer.

3 When finished, click **OK** to apply your header and footer settings and close the **Page Setup** dialog box.

Display the header and footer area

To enter, edit or format header and footer text, you must first display the header and footer areas.

1 Choose **View | Header and Footer**.

This command displays the header or footer area (surrounded by a dashed border), and the document text in grey (which you cannot edit when working with headers and footers).

You can also see a Header and Footer toolbar that gives you quick access to the commonly used actions.

2 You can click the following navigation buttons on the Header and Footer toolbar to display different header and footer areas of your document.

 Click the **Switch between Header and Footer** button to view the footer area when in the header area, and vice versa. The two areas are similar in appearance and operation.

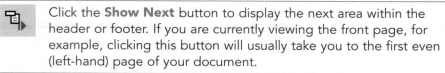 Click the **Show Next** button to display the next area within the header or footer. If you are currently viewing the front page, for example, clicking this button will usually take you to the first even (left-hand) page of your document.

 Click the **Show Previous** button to display the previous area within the header or footer.

3 When finished viewing the header and footer areas, click the **Close** button at the right of the Header and Footer toolbar.

Type header and footer text

Before inserting a header or footer, ensure that you have selected the correct checkboxes on the **Layout** tab of the dialog box displayed by the **File | Page Setup** command. Now follow these steps:

1   Choose **View | Header and Footer** to display the header and footer area.

2   If necessary, click the navigation buttons on the Header and Footer toolbar to move to the area where you want to type text.

3   Word positions the paragraph mark at the left of the header or footer area, ready for you to type text.

Word provides two preset tab stops to make it easy for you to centre-align or right-align headers or footers. Press **TAB** once to centre a header or footer, and press **TAB** twice to line it up against the right margin.

> *Odd Page Header*
> ECDL·Training·Notes →   Final·Draft   →   3¶

4   When finished typing or editing your header and footer text, click the **Close** button at the right of the Header and Footer toolbar.

Format header and footer text

Any formatting that you can apply to text in your document, such as bold, italics, alignment, borders and shading, you can also apply to text in the headers and footers.

1   Choose **View | Header and Footer** to display the header and footer area.

2   If necessary, click the navigation buttons on the Header and Footer toolbar to move to the area where you want to type text.

3   Select the text that you want to format.

4   To apply font formatting, choose **Format | Font**, click the **Font** tab, select your required options, and click **OK**.

Typically, the header and footer text is 2 or 3 points smaller than the body text. At that size, sans serif fonts such as Arial are easier to read than serif ones.

5   To apply borders, choose **Format | Borders and Shading**, and click the **Borders** tab.

A common option for headers and footers is a paragraph-wide top or bottom border.

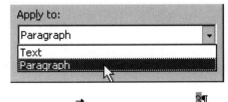

ECDL·Training·Notes →   Final·Draft   →   3¶

→   Not·for·Distribution¶

When finished with the **Borders and Shading** dialog box, click **OK**.

6   When finished typing or editing your header and footer text, click the **Close** button on the Header and Footer toolbar.

Insert automatic page numbers in headers and footers

You can insert an automatic page number in the header or footer – that is, a page number that is updated automatically when you add or remove pages in the document. The same formatting options are available for the page number as for header and footer text.

1   Choose **View | Header and Footer**.

2   If necessary, click the navigation buttons on the Header and Footer toolbar to move to the area where you want to insert page numbers.

Insert Page Number button

3   Click the **Insert Page Number** button on the Header and Footer toolbar. Word inserts the page number and displays it against a grey background.

4   If necessary, repeat steps 2 and 3 to insert page numbers on other pages.

Place page numbers at the outside margin (left for left-hand side pages, right for right-hand pages) or at the centre of the header or footer area.

5   When finished typing or editing your header and footer text, click the **Close** button on the Header and Footer toolbar.

Set automatic page numbers options

Follow these steps to view and apply your options for automatic page numbers in header and footers:

1   Choose **View | Header and Footer**.

2   If necessary, click the navigation buttons on the Header and Footer toolbar to move to the area with the page numbers you want to format.

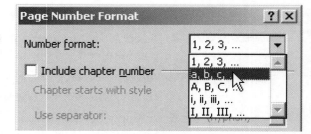

Format Page Number button

3   Click at the page number that you want to format, and then click the **Format Page Number** button on the Header and Footer toolbar.

4   You can number the pages using numbers, letters, or Roman numerals. And you can also start at a number other than 1.

5   When finished formatting your page numbers, click **OK** in the **Page Number Format** dialog box, and then click the **Close** button on the Header and Footer toolbar.

Insert the document creation date in a header/footer

To insert the date on which a document was created in a header or footer, follow these steps:

1 Choose **View | Header and Footer**.

2 If necessary, click the navigation buttons on the Header and Footer toolbar to move to the area where you want to insert the document's date.

3 Position the cursor where you want to insert the date.

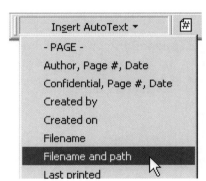

Insert Date button

4 To insert the current date, click the **Insert Date** button; to insert the date on which the document was created, click the **Insert AutoText** button at the left of the Header and Footer toolbar.

5 From the pull-down menu displayed, click the **Created on** option.

6 When finished, click the **Close** button on the Header and Footer toolbar.

Insert the document's file name and location in a header/footer

To insert the name and location of your document file in a header or footer, follow these steps:

1 Choose **View | Header and Footer**.

2 If necessary, click the navigation buttons on the Header and Footer toolbar to move to the area where you want to insert the file location details.

3 Position the cursor where you want to insert the current file location.

4 Click the **Insert AutoText** button at the left of the Header and Footer toolbar.

5 From the pull-down menu displayed, click the **Filename and path** option.

Word inserts the relevant details.

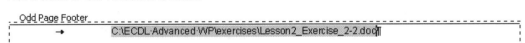

6 When finished, click the **Close** button on the Header and Footer toolbar.

Quit Word

You can close any open documents and quit Microsoft Word. You have now completed Lesson 3.5 of the ECDL Word Processing Module.

3.6

Working with content

Learning goals   At the end of this lesson you should be able to:

- find and replace text, text with formatting, and special characters;
- use Word's spelling and grammar checkers;
- hyphenate justified text;
- apply automatic hyphenation options.

New term   At the end of this lesson you should be able to explain the following term:

Hyphenation   The process of splitting a long word across two successive lines to avoid unsightly amounts of white space. Used mostly in narrow, justified columns of text.

Finding text in your documents

Use Word's **Edit | Find** command to locate a particular piece of text. You can refine your search by telling Word to find only text with specific formatting. You can also search a document for special characters such as paragraph marks and tabs.

Finding and replacing text

Anything that you can locate with the **Edit | Find** command, you can replace with **Edit | Find and Replace** – including text formatting, text positioning, tabs and special characters.

For example, you may want to find and replace all occurrences of a word or phrase in a document with a different word or phrase. You might have misspelled a word consistently throughout a document, or maybe you want to substitute 'person' for 'man' or 'woman'.

You can perform a replace operation in two ways: you can replace the relevant text one occurrence at a time, or you can replace all occurrences in a single operation. Use the second option only if you are certain that you want to replace every instance of the text you are searching for!

Checking your spelling and grammar

How's your spelling and grammar? Word can check your typing and suggest corrections to errors in two ways: as you type and edit your document (the automatic option) or whenever you choose the **Tools | Spelling and Grammar** command (the on-request option).

A word of caution: if the word that you have typed is correctly spelt but inappropriate – for example, 'their' instead of 'there'– your spelling checker will not detect it as an error. Therefore, you should always read over the final version of the document to ensure that it doesn't contain any errors.

About hyphenation

You can use Word's *hyphenation* feature to remove unsightly amounts of white space by splitting long words across successive lines. Hyphenation is applied mostly to the kind of narrow columns of justified text found in newspapers and magazines.

> Word spreads out the text in order to align it with both margins simultaneously. This is particularly true when the text contains a lot of long words.

> Word spreads out the text in order to align it with both margins simultaneously. This is particularly true when the text contains a lot of long words.

Find text: basic options

Need to locate a particular word or phrase in a long document quickly? Word's **Edit | Find** command can take you straight to the text that you are looking for. Follow these steps:

1 Choose **Edit | Find**, and click the **Find** tab.

2 In the **Find what** box, type (or paste in from the clipboard) the text you want to find.

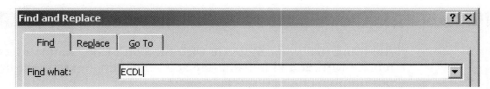

3 Click the **Find Next** button. Word takes you to the first occurrence of the relevant text in your document. The dialog box stays open on your screen.

> When·finished,·you·can·close·Internet·Explorer·by·clicking·the·
> Close·button·or·choosing·**File | Close**.·You·have·now·completed·
> this·Section·7.1·of·the·ECDL·Information·and·Communication·
> Module.¶

4 Click **Find Next** to continue searching for further occurrences, or click **Cancel** to close the dialog box and end your search.

By default, Word searches the whole document. To limit the text that Word searches through, first select only that part of the document. When Word has finished searching the selected text, it asks whether you want to search the remainder of the document or not.

Find text: search options

By default, Word's **Edit | Find** command finds parts of words as well as whole words. When you search for 'the', Word also finds 'then'. You can tell Word to find whole words only by clicking the **More** button in the **Find and Replace** dialog box, and then selecting the **Find whole words only** checkbox.

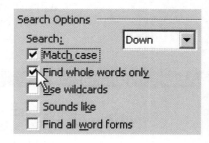

Another option is to select the **Match case** checkbox. So, for example, a search for 'The' does not find 'the' or 'THE'.

To find paragraph marks, tabs or other special or non-printing characters, click the **Special** button and then click on the relevant character.

Find text: format options

You can tell Word to find only text that is in a certain format. Click the **Format** button in the **Find and Replace** dialog box, and then select the formatting option that you require.

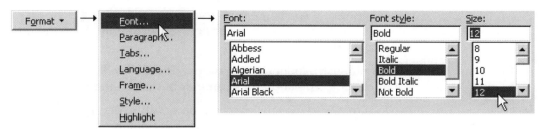

In the example above, the **Find** operation will only find text that is Arial, Bold, 12 point.

Find and replace text

Anything that you can locate with the **Edit | Find** command, you can replace with **Edit | Replace** – including text formatting, text positioning, tabs and special characters. To replace text:

1   Choose **Edit | Replace**, and click the **Replace** tab.

2   Enter the text you want to replace in the **Find what** box.

3   Enter the text you want to substitute for the replaced text in the **Replace with** box.

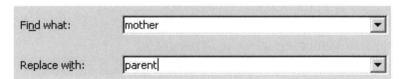

4   If you click the **Replace** button, Word replaces your text one occurrence at a time. At each occurrence, you are asked whether you want to make the replacement or not. This is the 'safe' option.

If you click the **Replace All** button, Word replaces all occurrences in a single operation. Use this option only if you are certain that you want to replace every instance of the text you are searching for!

Set your spellcheck options

they·beleive

Wavy red underline
denotes a possible
spelling error

How's your spelling? Word can check your spelling and suggest corrections to errors in two ways:

- **Automatically**: As you type and edit text. Wavy red underlines indicate words with possible spelling errors. To correct the spelling, right-click an underlined word, and then choose the option you want from the pop-up menu displayed.

- **On request**: Whenever you choose **Tools | Spelling and Grammar**, press **F7** or click the **Spelling and Grammar** button on the Standard toolbar.

Spelling and
Grammar
button

To turn automatic spellchecking on or off, select or deselect the **Check spelling as you type** checkbox on the **Spelling & Grammar** tab of the dialog box displayed by the **Tools | Options** command.

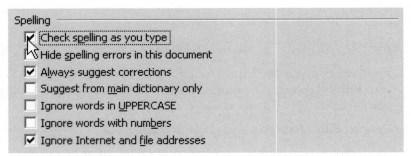

Correct misspelled words

When automatic spellchecking is switched on, a wavy red line under words indicates possible spelling errors. To correct an error:

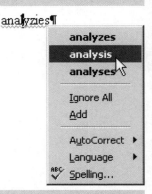

1 Right-click the word with a wavy underline.

2 Select from the list of alternative correct spellings displayed on the pop-up menu.

Selecting the last menu option, **Spelling**, displays Word's **Spelling and Grammar** dialog box.

Perform a spellcheck

When you run a spellcheck on a document with the **Tools | Spelling and Grammar** command, Word identifies suspect text, and, in the **Spelling and Grammar** dialog box, shows suggested alternatives.

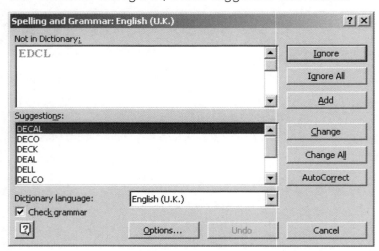

Your options include the following:

- **Ignore**: Leave this occurrence of the word unchanged.

- **Ignore All**: Leave this and all other occurrences of the word in the document unchanged.

- **Add**: Add the word to the spelling dictionary, so that Word will recognize it during future spellchecks of any document. Use this option for the names of people or places, or abbreviations or acronyms that you type regularly.

- **Change**: Correct this occurrence of the word, but prompt again on further occurrences.

- **Change All**: Correct this occurrence of the word – and all other occurrences, without further prompting.

In addition to misspelled words, the spelling checker also identifies repeated words.

The·last·train·to·to·Clarksville.¶

When Word's spelling checker finds no further errors, it displays a box telling you that the spellcheck is complete.

Spellchecking: a word of caution

If the word that you have typed is correctly spelt but inappropriate – for example, 'their' instead of 'there' – your spelling checker will not detect it as an error. Therefore, you should always read over the final version of the document to ensure that it doesn't contain any errors.

Set your dictionary language

Before spellchecking your documents, you might want to choose **Tools | Language | Set Language** to verify that your current spelling dictionary language is the correct one.

If the currently selected language is incorrect (perhaps US English instead of UK English), select your required language from the list displayed, and choose **Default**.

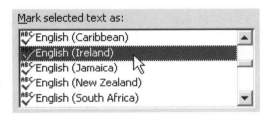

Set your grammar checking options

Word can check your grammar and suggest corrections to errors in two ways:

- **Automatically**: As you type and edit text. Wavy green underlines indicate words with possible grammar errors. To correct the error, right-click the underlined text, and then choose the option you want from the pop-up menu displayed.

- **On request**: Whenever you choose **Tools | Spelling**, press **F7** or click the **Spelling and Grammar** button on the Standard toolbar.

Spelling and Grammar button

To turn automatic grammar checking on or off, select or deselect the **Check grammar as you type** or the **Check grammar with spelling** checkbox on the **Spelling & Grammar** tab of the dialog box displayed by the **Tools | Options** command.

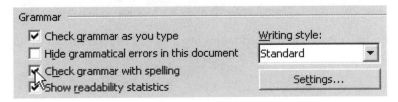

You use Word's grammar-checking and correction features in the same way as its spelling checker.

About hyphenation of justified text

The narrow columns found in newspapers and magazines are typically justified. Such columns can contain a lot of white space (that is, blank space), because Word spreads out the text in order to align it with both margins simultaneously. This is particularly true when the text contains a lot of long words.

Hyphenation is the process of breaking up long words and splitting them across two lines. This can give justified text a more professional appearance, as the example on the right shows.

> Word spreads out the text in order to align it with both margins simultaneously. This is particularly true when the text contains a lot of long words.

> Word spreads out the text in order to align it with both margins simultaneously. This is particularly true when the text contains a lot of long words.

Word applies two rules when hyphenating text: certain words are never hyphenated, and words that are hyphenated are split only in certain places.

Word allows you to hyphenate unjustified text, but it is unlikely that you would ever want to do so.

Set automatic hyphenation

You can hyphenate text in two ways: automatically or manually. For ECDL you need only know how to switch the automatic option on and off.

1 Choose **Tools | Language | Hyphenation**.

2 Select or deselect the **Automatically hyphenate document** checkbox, as required.

If you select automatic hyphenation, Word offers you a number of options that let you control how it applies hyphenation to your document.

☐ Hyphenate words in CAPS

Deselect this checkbox if you don't want Word to hyphenate words written entirely in capital letters. Typically, only headings and acronyms are in capitals. Typically, you will not want Word to hyphenate those.

Hyphenation zone: 0.63 cm

Enter the amount of space that you want Word to leave between the end of the last word in a line and the right margin. This setting applies only to unjustified text, which you are unlikely to want to hyphenate anyway. Make the zone wider to reduce the number of hyphens, or narrower to reduce the raggedness of the right margin.

Limit consecutive hyphens to: 2

Select the number of consecutive lines of text that can end with a hyphen. Too many such consecutive lines can look unsightly. A number of 2 is probably the best option.

3 When finished, click **OK** to apply your automatic hyphenation settings and close the dialog box.

Quit Word

You can close any open documents and exit Microsoft Word. You have now completed Lesson 3.6 of the ECDL Word Processing Module.

3.7

Tables and tabs

Learning goals   At the end of this lesson you should be able to:

- create tables in a document;
- insert and edit text and numbers in a table;
- select table cells, rows, columns and an entire table;
- insert and delete table rows and columns;
- modify column width and row height;
- add borders and shading to all or part of a table;
- use tabs to position text.

New terms   At the end of this lesson you should be able to explain the following terms:

Table	An array of cells arranged in rows and columns that can hold text and graphics.
Tabs	Predefined horizontal locations between the left and right page margins that determine where typed text is positioned. Using tabs on successive lines gives the effect of side-by-side columns of text.

About tables and tabs

On most Word documents, you want text to flow left to right across the width of the page. Sometimes, however, you may want to create narrow, side-by-side columns of text, numbers and graphics.

In this lesson you will learn about Word's two options for creating such side-by-side columns: tables and tabs.

Tables in Word

A *table* consists of rectangular cells, arranged in rows and columns. Inside cells, text wraps just as it does on a page. As you type text into a cell, the cell expands vertically to hold each new line. You can format text and numbers in a table just as you can in a paragraph, and apply decorative borders and shading to all or part of a table.

Sales·Region¤	Number·of·Units·Sold¤
Europe¤	1234﹡
Latin·America¤	5678﹡
China¤	4321﹡

¶

As required, you can insert and delete rows and columns in a table. Word's AutoFormat option provides a quick way to improve the appearance of any table.

Tabs in Word

Tabs are predefined horizontal locations that, when used on successive lines, give the appearance of columns. The effect of using tabs is similar to using tables: text appears in side-by-side columns rather than running continuously from the left to the right margin on the page.

Cajun·Heat·Fries·　→　　→　£1.45→　　→　Primo·Mozzarella·Poppers　→　→ £3.25¶
Onion·Rings →　　→　　→　£1.65→　→　Breaded·Zucchini·Sticks　→　→ £2.75¶

If you want to position small amounts of text such as the address lines at the top of a letter, tabs are quicker to use than tables.

Create a new table: toolbar button

You can create a *table* in two ways. Follow these steps to create a new table in a document using the toolbar button.

1 Click at the location in your document where you want the table to appear.

2 Click the **Insert Table** button on the Standard toolbar.

3 Drag over the cells to tell Word the number of rows and columns that you want, and then click.

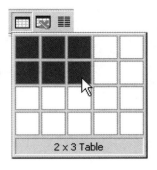

2 x 3 Table

Word inserts the new, empty table in your document, and positions the cursor in the first cell of the table.

Create a new table: menu command

Follow these steps to create a new table in a document using the menu command.

1 Click at the location in your document where you want the table to appear.

2 Choose **Table | Insert | Table**.

3 In the **Insert Table** dialog box, type or select your required number of columns and rows.

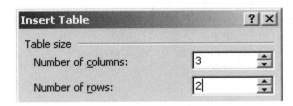

4 In the **AutoFit behavior** area, accept the default **Fixed column width** option of **Auto**. This creates columns of equal size across the width of your page.

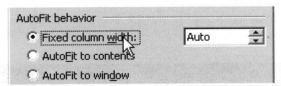

5 Click **OK** to close the dialog box.

Word inserts the new, empty table in your document. The cursor is located in the first cell of the table.

Insert and edit text and numbers in a table

After creating a new table in a document, you will want to insert text in its cells. The following simple exercise shows you how.

1 Create a new table with 2 columns and 4 rows.

2 If the cursor is not in the top left cell, click in the cell and type: Sales Region

3 Press the **TAB** key. In a table, pressing **TAB** does not insert a tab stop. Instead, it moves the cursor to the next cell.

SHIFT+TAB moves the cursor back to the previous cell. You can also use the **ARROW** keys or the mouse to move the cursor between different cells. (To insert a tab in a table, press **CTRL+TAB**.)

With the cursor in the top-right cell, type the text: Number of Units Sold

4 Continue moving the cursor and typing text until your table looks as shown.

Sales·Region¤	Number·of·Units·Sold¤
Europe¤	1234¤
Latin·America¤	5678¤
China¤	4321¤

Congratulations. You have created your first table in Word. You will use this simple table in further exercises in this lesson.

Select table cells

You can format and align table text in the same way as text outside a table. Here are the rules on selecting table text:

■ To select text in a cell, drag the mouse across the text.

■ To select a single cell, use the mouse to position the cursor over the left edge of the cell, wait for the cursor to change to a thick arrow, and then click to select the cell.

■ To select a horizontal row, position the cursor just outside the left edge of the row, wait for the cursor to change to a thick arrow, and then click to select the row.

Europe¤	1234¤
Latin·America¤	5678¤

Alternatively, click in any cell of the row and choose **Table | Select | Row**.

- To select a vertical column, position the cursor at the top edge of the column, wait for the cursor to change to a thick, downward arrow, and then click to select the column.

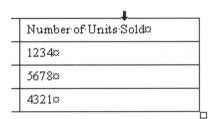 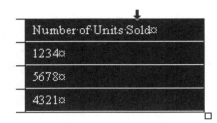

Alternatively, click in any cell of the column and choose **Table | Select | Column**.

- To select the entire table, position the cursor anywhere over the table. Notice that Word displays the table's move handle at the top-left of the table.

Click on the move handle to select the entire table.

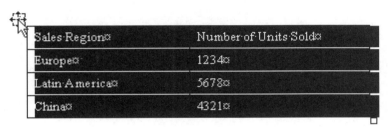

Alternatively, you can select a table by clicking in any of its cells and choosing **Table | Select | Table**.

When you have selected a cell, row column or entire table, you can then apply formatting to it.

Insert or delete table rows or columns

Here are the rules for making changes to a table:

- To add a new row, select the row beneath or above the position where you want to insert the new row, and choose **Table | Insert | Rows Above** (or **Rows Below**).

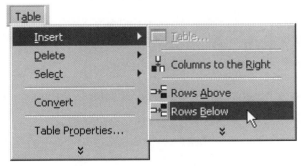

- To add a new column, select the column to the left of where you want to insert the new column, and choose **Table | Insert | Columns to the Right**.

- To delete a row or column, select it, and choose **Table | Delete | Rows** or **Table | Delete | Columns**.

Modify column width

Cursor shape when changing column width

You can change the width of a table column at any stage as follows:

1 Hold the mouse cursor over the left or right vertical edge of any cell in the column. Notice that the cursor changes shape.

2 Drag with the mouse until the column is the width that you require.

As you make a column wider or narrower, Word adjusts the width of the other columns so that the overall table width stays the same. If you hold down the **SHIFT** key while dragging a column edge, Word changes the width of the whole table accordingly.

To set a column's width precisely:

1 Click in any cell in the column, choose **Table | Table Properties**, and click the **Column** tab.

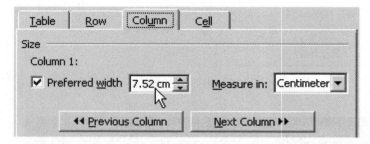

2 Select the **Preferred width** checkbox, type or select your required column width, and click **OK**.

Modify row height

Currsor shape when changing row height

You can change the height of a table row at any stage as follows:

1 Hold the mouse cursor over the top or bottom horizontal edge of any cell in the row. Notice that the cursor changes shape.

2 Drag with the mouse until the row is the height that you require.

To set a row's height precisely:

1 Click in any cell in the row, choose **Table | Table Properties**, and click the **Row** tab.

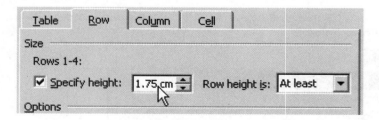

Select the **Specify height** checkbox, type or select your required row height, and click **OK**.

Add borders to a table

You can apply borders to all or part of a table to make its contents easier to read, or simply more attractive to look at. Select the cells, rows or columns, choose **Format | Borders and Shading**, and select your required options. Try this simple exercise with your sample table.

1   Select your entire table.

2   Choose **Format | Font**, and set the text to Arial, Regular, 10 point.

3   Choose **Format | Paragraph**, and set the **Spacing Before** and **Spacing After** to 2 points.

4   Select the top row of your table, and click the **Bold** button on the Formatting toolbar.

5   Click in the cell that contains the word Europe, and then drag down over the three cells beneath it. Click the **Italic** button on the Formatting toolbar.

Click anywhere outside your table to deselect it. Your sample table should look as shown.

Sales·Region¤	**Number·of·Units·Sold¤**
Europe¤	1234※
Latin·America¤	5678※
China¤	4321※

6   Select the entire table again, choose **Format | Borders and Shading**, and click the **Borders** tab.

7   In the **Preview** area at the right of the dialog box, click in turn on each of the three vertical border edges: left, centre and right. This removes the vertical borders. (Clicking on them again would bring them back.)

8   Click **OK** to apply your border settings, and close your dialog box. Click anywhere outside your table to deselect it. Your sample table should look as shown.

Sales·Region¤	**Number·of·Units·Sold¤**
Europe¤	1234※
Latin·America¤	5678※
China¤	4321※

When you turn off table borders, Word displays non-printing gridlines – thin grey lines that make it easier to see where the rows and columns are in the table. You can turn gridlines off and on with the **Table | Hide/Show Gridlines** command. This command applies to your entire document, and not just a particular table.

9   Let's try one more border option. Select the top row of your table, choose **Format | Borders and Shading**, and click the **Borders** tab.

10 Click in the **Width** pull-down list, and click to select a border width of 1½ point.

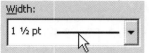

Next, in the **Preview** area at the right of the dialog box, click the top border.

11 Click **OK** to apply your border settings, and close your dialog box.

12 Click anywhere outside your table to deselect it. Your sample table should look as shown.

Sales·Region¤	Number·of·Units·Sold¤
Europe¤	1234¤
Latin·America¤	5678¤
China¤	4321¤

Add shading to a table

As with borders, you can apply shading to all or part of a table. Select the cells, rows or columns, choose **Format | Borders and Shading**, and select your required options. Try this simple exercise with your sample table.

1 Select the top row of your table, choose **Format | Borders and Shading**, and click the **Borders** tab.

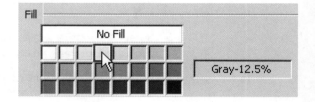

2 Click in the box for Gray 12.5%.

3 Click **OK** to apply your shading setting, and close your dialog box.

4 Click anywhere outside your table to deselect it. Your sample table should look as shown.

Sales·Region¤	Number·of·Units·Sold¤
Europe¤	1234¤
Latin·America¤	5678¤
China¤	4321¤

Use the table AutoFormat option

Word's AutoFormat option offers a range of predefined formats for your table, including borders and shading. To apply AutoFormat:

1 Select your table and choose **Table | Table AutoFormat**. The **Table AutoFormat** dialog box offers a preview area where you can view the formatting effects on your table.

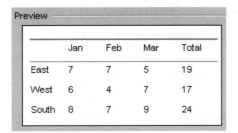

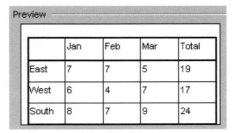

2 Select your preferred AutoFormat, and click **OK**.

Practise by selecting your table and applying a series of AutoFormats.

Insert tab stops

TAB key

Pressing the **TAB** key has the effect of moving text or a paragraph mark a specified distance to the right. These distances are called *tab* stops. Try it and see.

1 Create a new empty, Word document.

2 Click at the paragraph mark, and press the **TAB** key six or seven times. Your screen should look as shown.

Word automatically positions tab stops at intervals of 1.27 cm (0.5 inch) from left to right. Each time that you press **TAB**, Word moves the cursor 1.27 cm to the right.

Position text with left-aligned tabs

By default, tabs are left-aligned. That is, a tab stop of 5.08 cm means that the relevant text or number is positioned so that it begins 5.08 cm in from the left margin.

Try the following simple exercise to create text with left-aligned tabs.

1 Open a new document and type the following text:

   Cajun·Heat·Fries·£1.45·Primo·Mozzarella·Poppers·£3.25¶

   Onion·Rings·£1.65·Breaded·Zucchini·Sticks·£2.75¶

2 Are Word's tabs measured in centimetres or inches? Find out by choosing **Format | Tabs** to display the **Tabs** dialog box.

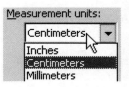

   If inches, click **OK** to close the dialog box. Next, choose **Tools | Options**, click the **General** tab, select Centimeters, and click **OK**.

3 On the first line of your document, position the cursor at the end of the word Fries, and press **DELETE** to remove the space between Fries and £1.45. Press **TAB** repeatedly to move £1.45 rightwards to the 5.08 cm default tab stop.

4 Repeat this action for the second line. Your text should look as below.

   Cajun·Heat·Fries   →   →   £1.45·Primo·Mozzarella·Poppers·£3.25¶

   Onion·Rings →   →   →   £1.65·Breaded·Zucchini·Sticks·£2.75¶

5 On the first line, position the cursor after £1.45, and press **DELETE** to remove the space before Primo. Press **TAB** twice to move Primo Mozzarella Poppers rightwards to the 7.62 cm default tab stop.

6 Repeat this action for the second line. Your text should look as below.

   Cajun·Heat·Fries·   →   →   £1.45→   →   Primo·Mozzarella·Poppers   →   → £3.25¶

   Onion·Rings →   →   →   £1.65→   →   Breaded·Zucchini·Sticks   →   → £2.75¶

   Well done. You have used Word's tabs to create a restaurant menu.

Use multiple tab alignment options

In addition to left-aligned tabs, Word offers three other tab alignment options:

- **Centred:** The tabbed text or number is positioned so that its centre is (say) 5.08 cm from the left margin.

- **Right-aligned:** The tabbed text or number is positioned so that it ends (say) 5.08 cm from the left margin.

- **Decimal:** If the tabbed item is a number that contains a decimal point, the number is positioned so that the decimal point is (say) 5.08 cm from the left margin. If the tabbed item is a number that does not contain a decimal point, or is text, a decimal tab stop has the same effect as a right-aligned tab.

Any tab stop position that you insert in a paragraph of a document applies only to that paragraph. This means that different paragraphs of the same document may contain tabs of different types, and at different positions. Try this simple exercise to practise your tab alignment skills.

1 Create a new document, and type the text and numbers as shown. Make the text 'Unit Cost' bold.

> **Unit·Cost¶**
> .853·¶
> 621¶
> 45¶
> 26.82¶

2 In turn, select each of the five lines (but not the paragraph mark), and copy and paste it three times to its right. Your document should now look as shown below.

> **Unit·CostUnit·CostUnit·CostUnit·Cost¶**
> .853.853.853.853¶
> 621621621621¶
> 45454545¶
> 26.8226.8226.8226.82¶

3 Insert four tab stops on each line as shown below. (The tab positions are Word's default ones.)

> **Unit·Cost → Unit·Cost → Unit·Cost → Unit·Cost¶**
> .853 → .853 → .853 → .853¶
> 621 → 621 → 621 → 621¶
> 45 → 45 → 45 → 45¶
> 26.82 → 26.82 → 26.82 → 26.82¶

4 Select the five lines of text, choose **Format | Tab**, and click **Clear All** to remove all the default tabs.

5 Set the following tab positions and alignments:

Tab stop position	Alignment
2 cm	Left
6 cm	Centre
10 cm	Right
13 cm	Decimal

In each case, type the tab position, select the alignment, and click **Set**.

6 When finished, click **OK**. Your document should now look as shown.

> → **Unit·Cost** → **Unit·Cost** → **Unit·Cost** → **Unit·Cost¶**
> → .853 → .853 → .853 → .853¶
> → 621 → 621 → 621 → 621¶
> → 45 → 45 → 45 → 45¶
> → 26.82 → 26.82 → 26.82 → 26.82

Use tabs with the ruler

You can display and amend Word's default tab stops by choosing **View | Ruler**. The ruler appears along the top of the document window. You can see the default tab stops, indicated by thin vertical lines, at evenly spaced positions along the base of the ruler.

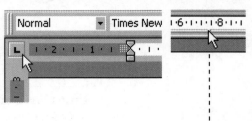

You can change the position of a tab stop by dragging it left or rightwards to a new location on the ruler. The space between all default tab stops changes proportionately. As you drag a tab stop, Word displays a vertical, dashed line stretching down from the tab ruler to the document itself.

The four tab alignment options

At the left of the ruler you can see the **Tab Alignment** button. As you successively click this button, it cycles through the four possible tab alignment options: left-aligned (default), centre-aligned, right-aligned, and decimal point-aligned.

- To add a new tab stop, click the tab button to display the type of tab you want, and then click the ruler where you want to place the tab.

- To remove a tab stop, click on it and drag it to the right off the ruler.

Quit Word

You can close any open documents and exit Microsoft Word. You have now completed Lesson 3.7 of the ECDL Word Processing Module.

3.8

Mail merge

Learning goals

At the end of this lesson you should be able to:

- create the two components of a merged letter: the form letter and the data source;
- select the appropriate merge fields and insert them in a form letter;
- merge a form letter with a data source to produce a mail merge;
- use mail merge to create address labels.

New terms

At the end of this lesson you should be able to explain the following terms:

Form Letter
A Word document containing information (text, spaces, punctuation and graphics) that remains the same in each copy of the merged letter.

Data Source
A file containing information (such as names and addresses) that will be different in each merged copy of the final letter.

Merge Field
An instruction to Word to insert a particular type of information, such as job title or a line of an address, in a specified location on the form letter.

About mail merge

Mail merge is the process of combining a *form letter* (which holds the unchanging letter text) and a *data source* (which holds the names, addresses and other details that are different in every merged letter).

The data source can be created in Word, or in a spreadsheet (such as Excel) or database (such as Access). Whichever the file type, the data source contents must be arranged in a table. Along the top row must be the titles identifying the information categories in the columns underneath, such as Title or Last Name. *Merge fields* in the form letter indicate which details are taken from the data source, and where they are positioned on the final, merged letter.

Main steps in a mail merge

Open your form letter and choose **Tools | Mail Merge**. In the **Mail Merge Helper** dialog box, section 1, click **Create**, then **Form Letters** and then **Active Window**. In the **Mail Merge Helper** dialog box, section 2, click **Get Data**, then **Open Data Source**, select your data source document, and click **Open**. Click **Edit Main Document** to begin inserting merge fields. The Merge toolbar is displayed.

Click in your form letter where you want the first merge field to appear. Click the **Insert Merge Field** button to insert your first merge field. Continue until all your merge fields are inserted.

View
Merged
Data button

When finished, inspect your merged letters by clicking the **View Merged Data** button, and the associated **Forward** and **Backward** buttons.

Click the **Mail Merge** button to display the **Merge** dialog box. Select **Merge to Printer**, then **Merge** and then **OK** to output copies of your merged letters.

Mailing labels

To create mailing labels, create a new Word document and choose **Tools | Mail Merge**. In the **Mail Merge Helper** dialog box, section 1, click **Create**, select the **Mailing Labels** option, and then click **Active Window**. In Section 2 of the **Mail Merge Helper** dialog box, click **Get Data**, then **Open Data Source**, and select your data source.

Click **Set Up Main Document**, select the printer and the labels you want to use, and click **OK**. In the **Create Labels** dialog box, insert the merge fields for the address information. In the **Mail Merge Helper** dialog box, click **Merge**. Inspect your mailing labels by clicking the **View Merged Data** button, and the associated **Forward** and **Backward** buttons. In the **Merge to** box, click **Printer** to merge to the selected printer.

You can think of a mail merge as a five-step process. Steps one and two are about preparing the ingredients: the form letter and the data source.

In step three, you make the connection between the two by inserting the merge fields in your form letter – one merge field for every item of information that you want to merge to the form letter from the data source.

Step four is optional, but recommended. Before you produce your merged letters, take a preview of the first one or two to check that the merge has worked successfully.

Finally in step five, you print your merged letters.

1 Prepare Your Form Letter

This is simply a Word document. Using the **Tools | Mail Merge** command, you can do one of the following:

- Select a letter you have already typed as the form letter, and delete any details that relate to a specific recipient.

- Create a new letter especially for the merge operation.

2 Prepare Your Data Source

Again, using the **Tools | Mail Merge** command, you can do one of the following:

- Create a new Word file and enter the names, addresses and other details of the people you plan to send the merged letter to.

- Select a file created in another software application such as Microsoft Access or Excel.

3 Insert Merge Fields in Your Form Letter

When you open your *form letter* on screen, Word displays a special Mail Merge toolbar. One of its buttons is called **Insert Merge Field**. This is the one you use to select and then position the merge fields in your form letter.

«FirstName»

A merge field

The merge fields are special instructions that you insert in your form letter. They tell Word which details you want to merge from your data source, and where Word is to position them in your merged letter.

4 Preview Your Merged Letters

View
Merged Data
button

Before you produce your (perhaps hundreds or thousands!) of merged letters, click on the Toolbar's **View Merged Data** button to preview the first few merged letters.

5 Print Your Merged Letters

If you are happy with the preview, click on the **Mail Merge** button to perform the complete merge operation. Select the **Merge to Printer** option to output copies of your merged letters.

Word gives you the option of saving all the merged letters in a single file. You don't need to do this, because you can quickly recreate them at any stage by rerunning the merge operation.

Use an existing document as a form letter

You can use an existing Word document as the basis of a form letter. The sample letter below contains the name and address of a particular person.

```
To: →  Dr·Mary·Mulligan,¶
    →     Unit·46,·New·Business·Park,¶
    →     Anytown,¶
    →     FGB·123.¶
    →    →    →    →    →    →    →    →    →    →    17.10.03¶
¶
Dear·Dr·Mulligan,¶
```

By removing these specific details, you can then use the letter's content as a general-purpose form letter.

```
To: →  ,¶
    →     ,¶
    →     ,¶
    →     ,¶
    →    →    →    →    →    →    →    →    →    →    17.10.03¶
¶
Dear·,¶
```

Let's follow the steps of using an existing document as the basis of a form letter.

1   Open your document and delete any details that relate to a specific recipient.

2   Choose **Tools | Mail Merge** to display the **Mail Merge Helper** dialog box.

3   In the Main document area, click the **Create** button. From the pull-down list of options click the **Form Letters** option.

4   On the next dialog box displayed, click the **Active Window** button.

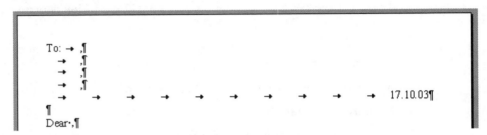

5   Using the **Mail Merge Helper** dialog box, you can now select or create a data source for your letter.

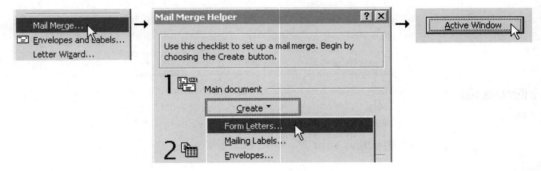

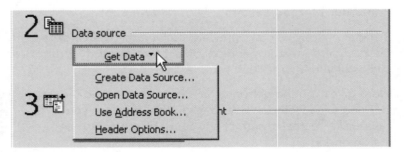

6   Alternatively, click the **Close** button to close the **Mail Merge Helper** dialog box.

Create a new form letter

Follow the steps below to create a new, blank form letter:

1 Choose **Tools | Mail Merge** to display the **Mail Merge Helper** dialog box.

2 In the **Main Document** area, click the **Create** button. From the pull-down list of options click **Form Letters**.

3 On the next dialog box displayed, click the **New Main Document** button.

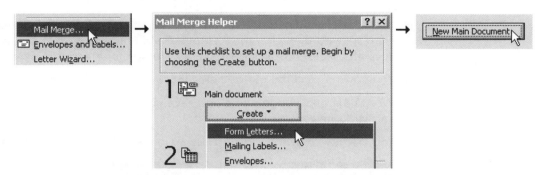

Word displays a new version of the **Mail Merge Helper** dialog box. In the **Main Document** area you can see an **Edit** button to the right of the **Create** button.

4 Click the **Edit** button, and then click the button showing the document name (such as Document3) beneath it.

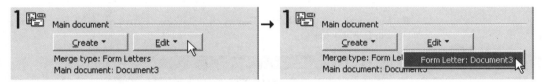

Word opens a new form letter document on your screen for you to enter the text.

5 Save and name your new, empty form letter document. You later select or create a data source for your form letter.

Create a data source

You create a *data source* to hold the names, addresses and other information that will vary on each copy of a final, merged letter. Follow this simple exercise:

1 If your form letter is not already open, open it now.

2 If the **Mail Merge Helper** dialog box is not already displayed, choose **Tools | Mail Merge** to display it.

3 In the **Data source** area, click the **Get Data** button to display a pull-down list of options, and, from the list, click the **Create Data Source** option.

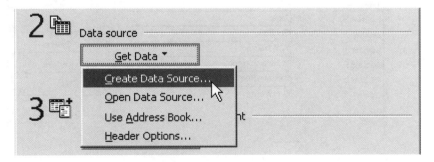

Word now displays the **Create Data Source** dialog box.

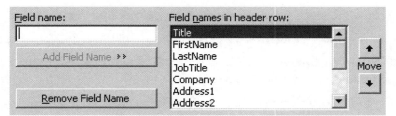

4 In the case of each of the following merge fields, click the field name in the list displayed then click the **Remove Field Name** button to delete them: JobTitle, State, PostalCode, Country, HomePhone and WorkPhone.

5 You now have all the merge fields that you need. Click **OK**.

6 Word next asks you to name and save your data source file. Type a file name and click **Save**.

7 You are now shown the dialog box below. Click **Edit Data Source**.

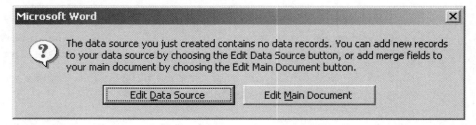

8 Word displays a **Data Form** dialog box. Enter the information as shown and click **Add New**.

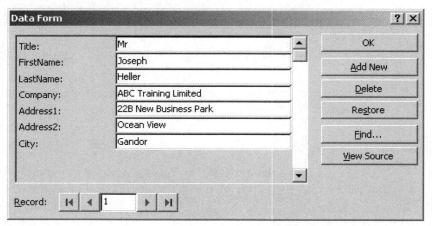

9 Enter a second set of details in the **Data Form** dialog box as shown below. Click **Add New** and then click **OK**.

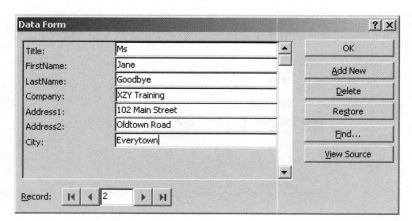

10 When finished, click **OK** to close the dialog box.

You have now created a data source with two records. But you can easily imagine a data source with hundreds or thousands of records, each record holding the name, address and other information regarding a particular person or organization.

View a Word data source

You can open, view and edit your data source file just as you can any other Word document. If you open the data source you created in the previous exercise it should look as shown below.

Title¤	FirstName¤	LastName¤	Company¤	Address1¤	Address2¤	City¤
Mr¤	Joseph¤	Heller¤	ABC· Training· Limited¤	22B·New· Business· Park¤	Ocean· View¤	Gandor¤
Ms¤	Jane¤	Goodbye¤	XZY· Training¤	102·Main· Street¤	Oldtown· Road¤	Everytown¤

¶

You can see a header row containing the merge field names such as FirstName and LastName. And under the header row are the records themselves, each in a row of its own.

Work with a non-Word data source

Does your data source have to be a Word document? No. You can also use files created in a database such as Access or, as shown below, a spreadsheet such as Excel.

	A	B	C	D	E	F	G
1	Title	First Name	Last Name	Company	Address1	Address2	City
2	Mr	Joseph	Heller	ABC Training Limited	22B New Business Park	Ocean View	Gandor
3	Ms	Jane	Goodbye	XZY Training	102 Main Street	Oldtown Road	Everytown

The only requirement is that the information is arranged in the same type of table format: a single, top row of merge field titles, followed by other rows holding individual records.

Insert merge field codes in a form letter

Follow these steps to insert *merge field* codes in a form letter.

1 If your form letter document is not already open, open it now. Along the top of the document window you should see the Mail Merge toolbar.

2 For each merge field:

- Position the cursor at the location in your document where you want to insert the merge field code.

- Click the **Insert Merge Field** button on the Mail Merge toolbar to display a list of the fields in the associated data source.

- Click the relevant field name from the pull-down list.

Continue until you have inserted all the merge field codes.

A sample form letter with inserted merge field codes is shown below

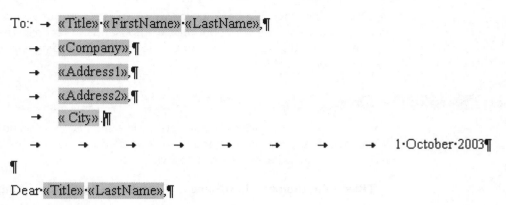

To:· → «Title»·«FirstName»·«LastName»,¶
  →   «Company»,¶
  →   «Address1»,¶
  →   «Address2»,¶
  →   «City».¶

  →   →   →   →   →   →   →   1·October·2003¶
¶
Dear·«Title»·«LastName»,¶

Do not forget to type spaces between merge fields just as you would
between ordinary text. Also, type commas or full stops at the end of lines.

3 Save and name your form letter when finished.

Now everything is in place for the mail merge operation.

Preview a mail merge

Before performing a mail merge, it's a good idea to preview the first one or
two merged letters.

**View Merged
Data button**

1 If your form letter is not already open, open it now .

2 Click the **View Merged Data** button on the Mail Merge toolbar. Word
displays the first merged letter. It might look as shown below.

To: → Dr·Mary·Mulligan,¶
  →   Clamour·Chemicals,¶
  →   Unit·46,¶
  →   New·Business·Park.¶

  →   →   →   →   →   →   →   1·October·2003¶
¶
Dear·Dr·Mulligan,¶

¶

You can preview the second and further merged letters by
clicking the **Forward** and **Backward** buttons on the Mail
Merge toolbar.

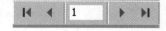

You are now ready to perform the mail merge.

Perform a mail merge

The simplest mail merge produces a number of one-page letters. Typically, you will want these letters output to a printer. You can then put your letters in addressed envelopes and send to them to their recipients. Here are the steps for merging a form letter with its data source, and outputting the merged letters to a connected printer.

1 Open your form letter. Ensure that it is the active window – in other words, that the form letter is in the foreground in front of any other open window.

2 Click the **Start Mail Merge** button on the Mail Merge toolbar.

Word now displays the **Merge** dialog box.

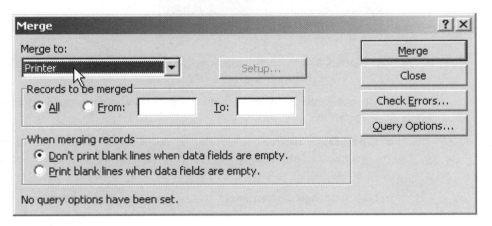

3 In the **Merge to** pull-down list, select the **Printer** option. Ensure the other dialog box options are as shown, and click **Merge**.

4 Word now displays the **Printer** dialog box. Click **OK**. Your form letter and the records from the data source are now merged to your printer.

Congratulations! You have performed a mail merge in Word.

Perform a mail merge to a document

You may not always want to print the results of a mail merge immediately to a printer. Instead, you may want to store your merged letters in a Word document.

To output your merged letters to a Word document, select the **New document** option in the **Merge to** pull-down list displayed in the **Merge** dialog box.

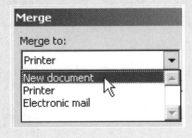

For example, if your form letters are just a single page each, and your data source contains 50 records, then the Word document will consist of 50 pages, each separated by a section break that acts like a page break.

¶ ⋯⋯⋯⋯⋯⋯⋯⋯⋯⋯⋯⋯⋯⋯⋯⋯⋯Section Break (Next Page)⋯⋯⋯⋯⋯⋯⋯⋯⋯⋯⋯⋯⋯

You can save and name your document, perhaps copy it to a different computer, and then output the merged letters to a printer at a later stage.

Merge addresses to labels

You can use Word's mail merge feature to print a list of names and addresses (or any other list of structured information) on adhesive labels. The following exercise shows you how.

1 Open a new Word document.

2 Chose **Tools | Mail Merge**.

3 Click **Create**, select the **Mailing Labels** option, and then click the **Active Window** button.

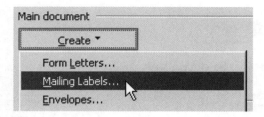

4 Click **Get Data** to select the source of the names and address that you want to use. Word offers three options:

■ **Create Data Source:** Select this to enter the name and address information in Word.

■ **Open Data Source:** Select this to use a list of names and addresses that is contained in an existing Word document (or in a spreadsheet, a database or other list).

■ **Use Address Book:** Select this to use names and addresses from an electronic address book such as that contained in Outlook Express.

For this exercise, choose the **Open Data Source** option, and select the Word document that you created as a data source earlier in this lesson.

5 Click **Set Up Main Document**.

In the **Label Options** dialog box, select the type of printer and the type of labels you want to use, and click **OK**.

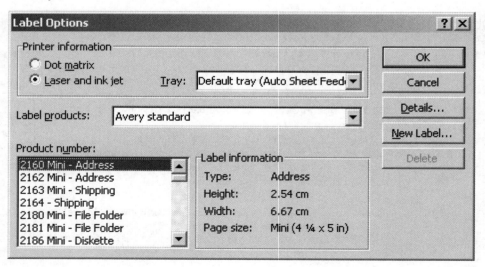

6 In the **Create Labels** dialog box, insert the merge fields for the address information.

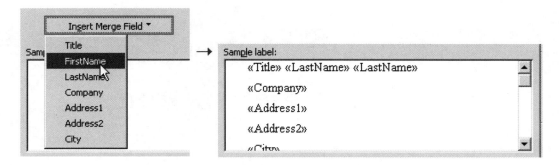

7 In the **Mail Merge Helper** dialog box, click **Merge**.

8 Make sure that your printer is loaded with the correct label stationery. In the **Merge to** box, click **Printer** to merge to the selected printer.

Well done! That completes your mail merge exercises.

Quit Word

You can close any open documents and exit Microsoft Word. You have now completed Lesson 3.8 of the ECDL Word Processing Module.

39

Word file formats

Learning goals	At the end of this lesson you should be able to:
	■ save Word 2000 documents in the following file formats: earlier versions of Word, RTF, WordPerfect, template, text and HTML.
New terms	At the end of this lesson you should be able to explain the following terms:
File Format	A set of rules that translates 1s and 0s into text and graphics on computer screens and printouts, and vice versa.
Word Template	A file that can contain ready-made text, formatting and page settings, and interface controls. Every Word document is based on, and takes its characteristics from, a template of one kind or another.

With Word's **File | Save As** command, you can save your document in a *format* other than Word's own. The options include:

- **Template:** A template file can provide the basis for creating new documents of the same type by holding built-in text, graphics and settings.

- **Earlier Versions of Word:** Saving a Word 2000 file in an earlier file format may result in some adjustment or loss of formatting.

- **HTML (Web page):** You can display and print HTML format files with a web browser application.

- **Rich Text Format (RTF):** This is a format common to all Microsoft Office applications.

- **Text Only:** Each paragraph of the original Word document occupies a single line of the plain-text file, often resulting in very long lines of text.

- **Text Only with Line Breaks:** A paragraph break is inserted everywhere a line ended in the original Word document, so that each line of the Word document becomes a separate paragraph in the plain-text file.

Work with web (HTML) format

Web pages are created using the HTML *file format*. Their file name extension is .htm (or sometimes .html). You can save a Word 2000 file in HTML format in either of two ways:

1 Choose **File | Save As Web Page** for Word to display the **Save** dialog box. In the **Save as type** pull-down list you can see that the option shown below is selected by default.

To change the web page title (the text that appears in the title bar of the web browser), click the **Change Title** button, type the new title in the **Set Page Title** box, and then click **OK**.

2 Click the **Save** button to close the dialog box and save the HTML file. Your original Word document is unaffected.

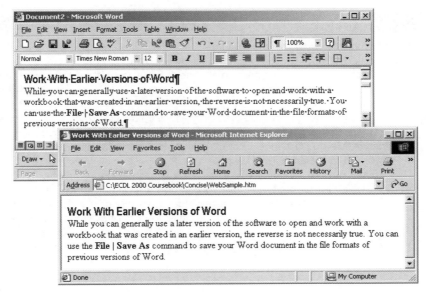

You can display and print HTML files with Internet Explorer or any other web browser application.

Work with earlier versions of Word

While you can generally use a later version of Word to open and work with a document that was created in an earlier version, the reverse is not necessarily true. You can use the **File | Save As** command to save your Word document in the file formats of previous versions of Word. The **Save as type** pull-down list offers two main options:

- Microsoft Word 6.0/95.

- Word 2.x for Windows.

Saving a Word 2000 file in an earlier file format may result in adjustment or loss of formatting.

Work with Rich Text Format (RTF)

This is the common format of all Microsoft Office applications, including Word. A Word 2000 document saved in this file format looks just like one saved in Word 2000's own file format. You can save a Word 2000 file in RTF as follows:

- Choose **File | Save As**, select the file format option shown below, and click **Save**.

The file name extension that is added is .rtf.

Work with non-Word formats

You can use the **File | Save As** command to convert your Word documents into other, non-Word 2000 file formats, so that they can be opened and read by people who work with applications such as WordPerfect.

Of the WordPerfect options in the **Save as type** pull-down list, the most commonly used is WordPerfect 5.x for Windows. Converting a document to WordPerfect may result in adjustment or loss of formatting. The file name extension of WordPerfect for Windows files is also .doc.

About Word templates

Word allows you to save a document as a *template* that you can later use and reuse as a basis for quickly creating other, similar documents. A template can contain built-in text and graphics (such as your company's name and logo), preset formatting (such as font settings) and text positioning (such as alignment and inter-paragraph spacing), and preset page settings (such as margins and page orientation).

For example, you could save everyone in your organization time by creating a memo template that contained preset margins, the company logo, and text for standard headings such as 'Memo', 'To:' and 'From:'. With much of the formatting and typing already done, users simply fill in the additional text.

Every new Word document you create is based on a template. And unless you choose otherwise, the template used is Normal.dot. In addition to this standard, all-purpose template, Word provides templates for specific document types such as letters, memos and reports.

A single template can provide the basis for lots of documents. But each document can be based on only a single template at a time. A template, like a document, is a Word file. Whereas document file names end in .doc, template file names end in .dot.

Save a document as a template

Follow these steps to save a Word document as a template:

1 Choose **File | Save As**.

2 Click the **Save as type** box and select the option below from the list displayed.

3 Typically, Word suggests that you save your templates in the following folder.

C:*os*\Profiles*user_name*\Application Data\Microsoft\Templates

where os is the operating system folder – for example, Windows.

Accept or amend this location and default file name, as required, and click **Save**.

Open a document based on a saved template

The next time you want to create a document, you can start with that saved document template. Word shows a template in the **File | New** dialog box if you have saved your template in the default templates folder. Click the template that you want to base your new document on, and then click **OK**.

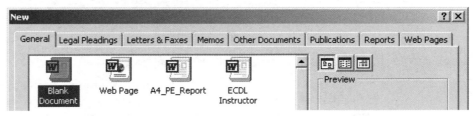

Note that when you click the **New** button on the Standard toolbar, Word automatically bases your new document on the Normal.dot template.

Work with text-only formats

As its name suggests, this format saves only the text of a file: any text formatting or graphics are lost. The file name extension added is .txt. This format is also called plain-text or ASCII format.

Of the various plain-text options offered by the **Save as type** pull-down list in the **File | Save As** dialog box, only two are relevant:

■ **Text Only:** Each paragraph of the original Word document occupies a single line of the plain-text file, often resulting in very long lines of text that you can view only by scrolling horizontally.

■ **Text Only with Line Breaks:** A paragraph break is inserted everywhere a line ended in the original Word document, so that each line of the Word document becomes a separate paragraph in the plain-text file.

Because line width remains the same as in the original Word document, the text is easier to read on screen. However, the text file contains many more paragraph marks than the original Word document file, with the result that editing the plain-text file can be awkward.

Plain-text files can be opened and read by just about all software applications on virtually every type of computer. This format is most commonly used in e-mail messages on the Internet.

Set the default folder for opening and saving documents

Unless you specify otherwise, Word presents the following folder when you click the **Open** or **Save** buttons on the Standard toolbar, or choose their equivalent menu commands:

C:\Documents and Settings\UserName\My Documents

-or-

C:/My Documents

Follow these steps to change the default folder for opening and saving files:

1 Choose **Tools | Options**, and click the **File Locations** tab.

2 Click the **Documents** item in the **File Types** list, and then click the **Modify** button.

3 Navigate to the folder that you want to use as the new default, and click **OK**.

You can change the default folder as often as you wish.

Set the user name for Word documents

Word can insert the user's name in document elements such as comments and headers and footers. Word takes the user name from the **User Information** tab of the dialog box accessed with the **Tools | Options** command. This information is entered and recorded during Word installation, but it may be amended at any stage.

Follow these steps to change the current user name that is stored in Word:

1 Choose **Tools | Options**, and click the **User Information** tab.

2 Edit the details in the **Name** and **Initials** boxes.

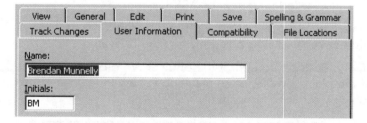

3 When finished, click **OK** to close the dialog box and save your changes.

When working on another person's PC, you can use **Tools | Options** to change the user information details, and then change them back again when you have completed your tasks.

Quit Word

You can close any open Word documents, and quit Word. Congratulations! You have now completed Module 3 of the ECDL, Word Processing. To remind yourself of the main features of Word, cut out the quick reference guide, called **word processing essentials**, at the back of the book and keep it beside your computer.

4

Spreadsheets

Evidence was once discovered of an ancient, primitive tribe that used just three numbers: one, two and many – a simple life with few or no possessions requires little knowledge of arithmetic. As society has moved on, the number of things to count has increased, out of which there grew a need for better ways to count them.

A spreadsheet program, such as Microsoft® Excel, is a modern solution to the need to manipulate numbers – quickly, easily and accurately. You can use Excel to add, subtract, multiply and divide numbers, sort numbers in increasing or decreasing order, find the average of a group of numbers, and identify the largest and smallest numbers in a group. You can also present your numbers in charts or graphs.

Excel shares with other Microsoft® Office programs a number of common features: you can reproduce (copy) or move (cut) text and numbers within and between files, find-and-replace items, perform spell-checks, insert images, apply font formatting, and set print options. You can also save Excel files in non-Excel formats such as text-only and HTML (web format).

Think of this module as your chance to count rather than be counted.

4.1

Your first steps in Excel

Learning goals	At the end of this lesson you should be able to:

- start and quit Excel;
- enter numbers and text in worksheet cells;
- edit and delete the contents of a cell;
- save, name, rename, open, create and close Excel workbooks;
- switch between, rename, create and remove worksheets;
- control the display of toolbars and toolbar buttons;
- change magnification views;
- undo, redo and repeat actions;
- use Excel's online help.

New terms	At the end of this lesson you should be able to explain the following terms:
Worksheet	A page that is made up of little boxes (cells) arranged in rows and columns. Relationships can be created between the cells so that changing the contents of one cell affects the contents of the related cells.
Workbook	A file containing worksheets.
Cells	The little boxes that make up a worksheet.
Row	A horizontal line of cells that stretches left-to-right across the worksheet.
Column	A vertical line of cells from the top of the worksheet to the bottom.
Active Cell	The cell in which the cursor is currently located.
Cell Reference	The location or 'address' of a cell on a worksheet.
Name Box	The rectangular area above the top-left corner of a worksheet in which Excel displays the cell reference of the active cell.
Label	A piece of text in a worksheet cell that provides information about the number in an accompanying cell, usually either below it or to its right.

This ECDL Module is about *spreadsheets*. But Excel uses two other words – *worksheet* and *workbook*. When you launch Excel, it opens a new workbook file that contains three blank, ready-to-use worksheets. In Excel, a worksheet is a spreadsheet. A worksheet is much larger than your screen. You can see only a very small part of it at one time.

Think of worksheets as pages in a book, and the workbook as the book containing those pages.

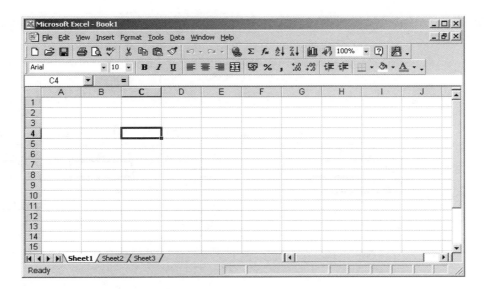

Near the bottom of the Excel window you can see the worksheet names – Sheet1, Sheet2 and Sheet3. Excel displays Sheet1 by default.

Worksheet cells

Cells, the little boxes that make up a worksheet, are arranged in (horizontal) *rows* and (vertical) *columns*. Only one cell can be the *active cell* at any one time.

Each cell in a worksheet has a unique address known as its *cell reference*. A cell reference is made up of two parts:

- column letter (A, B, C, ...) and

- row number (1, 2, 3, ...).

When you open a new workbook in Excel, the active cell is the one on Sheet1 with the cell reference A1. Remember: column letter first, row number second. For example, B6, C8 and J12.

Launch Microsoft Excel

Microsoft Excel

- Double-click the Microsoft® Excel icon.

Alternatively:

- Choose **Start | Programs | Microsoft Excel**.

Excel displays a new *workbook* with three *worksheets*. It names the workbook Book1.

Create a new workbook

New button

1 Click the **New** button on the Standard toolbar.

Alternatively:

2 Choose **File | New**, click the Workbook icon on the **General** tab of the New dialog box, and click **OK**.

By default Excel names additional workbooks Book2, Book3 and so on.

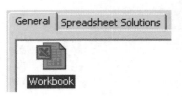

Select a cell in a worksheet

A worksheet contains over 16 million cells, but you can enter something in only one cell at a time. Excel surrounds the active cell with a thicker border. You can select a cell in two ways.

■ Click the cell with the mouse. For example, click cell A2, then B1, and finally A3.

The *Name Box* at the top left of the worksheet shows the cell reference of the active cell.

Alternatively:

■ Press the **ARROW** keys. Press these keys a few times and notice the effect.

Enter text and/or numbers in a cell

To enter something in a cell, click it, type your entry, and press the **ENTER** key. Let's practise.

1 Click cell B2. Type the following word and press **ENTER**: Add

2 Click cell B3. Type the following number and press **ENTER**: 1274

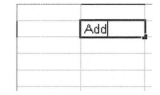  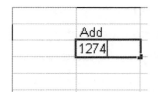 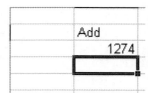

Text that describes a number on a worksheet is known as a *label*.

Why does Excel right-align numbers but left-align text?

Notice that Excel aligns numbers against the right border of a cell. When you write a list of numbers on paper to add them, you line up the numbers from the right. Excel right-aligns numbers for the same reason. While Excel right-aligns numbers, it left-aligns text.

Edit the content of a cell

To change whatever is in a cell, first double-click the cell. The following provides an example.

1 Double-click cell B3. Excel displays a blinking cursor in the cell. (The location of the cursor within the cell depends on which part of the cell you double-clicked on.)

2 Using the **ARROW** keys, move the blinking cursor to the left of the 4.

3 Press the **DELETE** key once, removing the 4.

4 Type 5 and press **ENTER**. This moves the cursor from B3 down to B4.

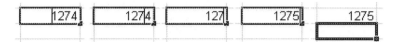

Excel has replaced 1274 with 1275.

Delete the content of a cell

1 Click cell B2.

2 Press **BACKSPACE** or **DELETE**.

This deletes only the cell content – it does not remove the cell itself from the worksheet!

Undo and redo actions

Undo button

1 Click cell B2.

2 Click the **Undo** button on the Standard toolbar or choose **Edit | Undo**. Excel restores the word Add to cell B2.

3 Click the **Redo** button on the Standard toolbar or choose **Edit | Redo**. Excel again removes the word Add from cell B2.

Redo button

4 Click the **Undo** button one more time to redisplay the word Add.

Using **Undo** (or **Redo**) repeatedly undoes (or redoes) your last series of actions. To view a list of recent actions that you can undo or redo, click the arrow at the right of the buttons.

Repeat actions

1 Click the heading of row 2. This has the effect of selecting the entire row.

Click here ⟶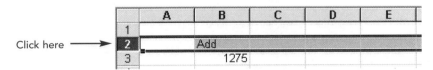

2 Choose **Insert | Rows** to insert a new row immediately above the selected one.

3 Choose **Edit | Repeat** (or press **CTRL+y**). Excel inserts another row, repeating your last action.

4 Repeat the row insertion a few more times. When finished, click the **Undo** button repeatedly to remove the inserted rows.

If Excel cannot repeat your last action, it changes the **Repeat** command to **Can't Repeat**.

Save and name a new workbook

In Excel, as in other applications, always save your work as you go along.

Save button

1 Click the **Save** button on the Standard toolbar or choose **File | Save** to display the **Save** dialog box.

2 Excel names the first workbook file Book1, and assumes that its file type is Microsoft Excel Workbook.

You can accept or amend the suggested file name.

3 Save your workbook with the following file name and click the **Save** button:

FirstSteps

You need not type the file name extension of xls. Excel adds this automatically.

Save a workbook with a different name to a diskette

It's a good idea to save a copy of your workbook to a diskette or other backup medium.

1 Insert a diskette in your computer's diskette drive.

2 Choose **File | Save As** and locate your A: drive.

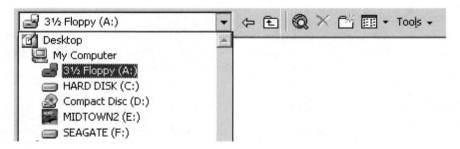

3 Excel suggests the current file name for you to accept or amend. Type a different name in the **File Name** box.

4 Click the **Save** button to save the file and close the dialog box.

5 When finished, use **File | Save As** again to resave the workbook to its original location on your hard disk, and with its original name. (You will be asked if you want to replace the original file: click **OK**.)

If you do not resave your workbook to its original location, saving the file in future (by clicking the **Save** button on the Standard toolbar or choosing **File | Save**) will save the workbook to the diskette and not to your computer's disk drive.

Switch between and rename worksheets in a workbook

An Excel workbook contains three worksheets.

- To display a different worksheet, click its tab near the bottom of the workbook window. For example, to display Sheet3, click the tab with that name.

- To rename a worksheet, right-click its tab, choose **Rename** from the pop-up menu displayed, and type the new name.

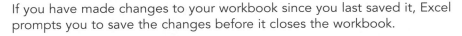

Add and delete worksheets

- To add a new worksheet, right-click one of the existing tabs, and choose **Insert** from the pop-up menu.

- To remove a worksheet, right-click its tab, and choose **Delete** from the pop-up menu.

Switch between open workbooks

- If you have more than one workbook open, you can switch between them by clicking the workbooks' names on the Windows Taskbar.

| Start | section4-3 | Book4 | Book5 | Book6 | | 21:21 |

- Alternatively, click the Excel **Window** menu, and then click the workbook name from the list at the bottom of the menu.

Close a workbook

Close workbook

- Choose **File | Close** or click the **Close Workbook** button at the top-right of the workbook window.

  If you have made changes to your workbook since you last saved it, Excel prompts you to save the changes before it closes the workbook.

Open an existing workbook

Open button

1 Click the **Open** button on the Standard toolbar or choose **File | Open**.

2 Select the file you want from the **Open** dialog box.

3 Click the **Open** button.

Display the Standard and Formatting toolbars on separate rows

By default Excel displays the Standard and Formatting toolbars on a single row across the top of the screen. To display them as two, individual toolbars, follow these steps.

1 Choose **Tools | Customize** and click the **Options** tab.

2 Deselect the checkbox below, and choose **Close**.

☐ Standard and Formatting toolbars share one row

Display all commands on menus

By default, when you first choose a menu, Excel displays only some of its commands. To see them all, you must click the double-arrow at the bottom of the menu. To view a complete list every time, follow these steps.

1 Choose **Tools | Customize** and click the **Options** tab.

2 Deselect the checkbox below, and choose **Close**.

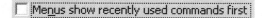

Excel toolbars

Only two of Excel's toolbars are relevant to this ECDL Module. The Standard toolbar includes buttons for managing files and working with numbers in cells.

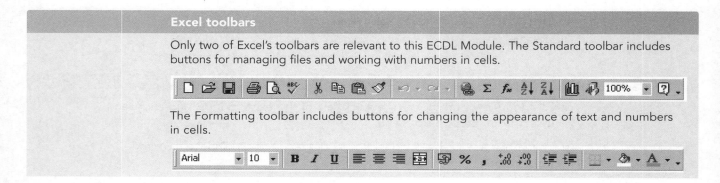

The Formatting toolbar includes buttons for changing the appearance of text and numbers in cells.

Hide and display toolbars

1 Choose **View | Toolbars**.

2 Select or deselect the various toolbar options from the pull-down menu displayed.

The check marks indicate which toolbars are already selected for display on screen.

Remove and redisplay toolbar buttons

Follow these steps to remove one or more buttons from a toolbar.

1 Display the toolbar that you want to change.

2 Hold down the **ALT** key, and drag the button off the toolbar.

Excel removes the selected button. Want to bring it back again? Here's how.

1 Display the toolbar. Click the **More Buttons** button (at the very right of the toolbar) and then the **Add or Remove Buttons** option.

2 Click the button you want to display again.

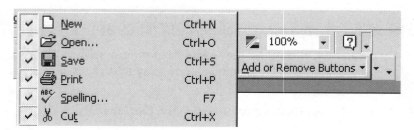

Buttons with a check mark beside their names are displayed on the toolbar.

3 Click anywhere outside the menu to close it. Excel redisplays the toolbar button.

Change the magnification view

Zoom box

You can change the screen magnification in the following two ways.

1 Click in the Zoom box on the Standard toolbar.

2 Enter a number between 10 and 400, and press **ENTER**.

(You need not type the percent (%) symbol.)

Alternatively:

1 Choose **View | Zoom**.

2 Select a magnification option from the **Zoom** dialog box.

You can choose a preset option (25–200%), or select **Custom** and enter a number from 10 to 400. The **Fit Selection** option magnifies or reduces the selected cell or cells so that they occupy the full screen.

To return to normal view, select a magnification of 100%

Display different areas of a worksheet

To view areas of your worksheet, drag the horizontal or vertical scroll-bars at the right and bottom of the Excel window.

Alternatively, press the **PAGE UP**, **PAGE DOWN** or **ARROW** keys.

Get online help from the Help menu

Microsoft Excel Help button

1 Choose **Help | Microsoft Excel Help**, or click the **Microsoft Excel Help** button on the Standard toolbar, or press **F1**.

2 Word displays the **Help** window with the following three tabs:

Contents: Here you will find descriptions of Excel's main features. Where you see a heading with a book symbol, double-click it to view the related sub-headings. Double-click on a question mark symbol to read the online help text.

⊞ 📕 Editing Worksheet Data
⊟ 📖 Formatting Worksheets
　　　❓ About worksheet formatting

Answer Wizard: Type your question in the box at the top-left of the dialog box, and click **Search**. Excel displays a list of suggested help topics in the lower-left. Click a topic to display the associated text in the right pane.

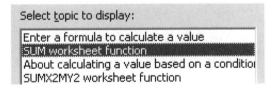

Index: Type the word or phrase and click **Search**. Excel displays all matches from the online help in the lower-left of the dialog box. Click on a topic to display the associated text.

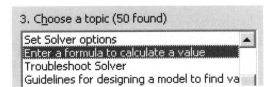

You will see the following buttons, left to right, at the top of the online help window:

Hide/Show: Hides or displays the left pane of the dialog box.

Microsoft Excel Help

Back/Forward: Moves you backwards and forwards through previously visited help topics.

Print: Prints the currently displayed help topic.

Options: Offers a number of display choices.

Take a few minutes to look through Excel's online help system.

Get online help from a dialog box

1 Choose **View | Zoom** to display the **Zoom** dialog box.

2 Click on the question mark symbol near the top-right of the dialog box. Excel displays a question mark to the right of the cursor.

3 Move the mouse down and left, and click the **Fit Selection** option.

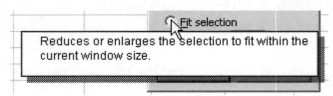

Excel displays online help text that tells you about the selected option. Practise this using other dialog boxes in Excel.

Quit Excel

To leave Excel, choose **File | Exit** or click the **Close** button at the top right of the Excel window. Excel prompts you to save any open files containing unsaved work.

You can close your FirstSteps.xls workbook and quit Excel. You have now completed Lesson 4.1 of the ECDL Spreadsheets Module.

4.2

Calculations with formulas

Learning goals	At the end of this lesson you should be able to:

- use Excel formulas to add, subtract, multiply and divide numbers;
- apply the rules of arithmetic to calculations in Excel;
- insert and format dates in worksheet cells;
- use Excel's AutoFill feature;
- insert symbols and special characters;
- select adjacent and non-adjacent cell ranges.

New terms	At the end of this lesson you should be able to explain the following terms:
Formula	An equation that performs operations such as addition, subtraction, multiplication or division on data that is stored in a worksheet.
Operators	Symbols that specify the type of calculation you want to perform on the arguments of a formula. Excel's four main arithmetic operators are +,-,* and /.
Argument	The inputs to a calculation that generate the result.
AutoFill	An Excel tool for quickly copying or incrementing (increasing in a defined sequence) the entries in a cell or range.
Adjacent Cell Range	A group of cells that are directly beside, above or below one another. Adjacent cells are sometimes called contiguous cells.
Non-Adjacent Cell Range	A group of cells that are not directly beside, above or below, one another. Also called non-contiguous cells.

Calculations in Excel

You can perform calculations on worksheet cells in one of two ways: using *formulas* or using functions. Functions are covered in Lesson 4.3.

Formulas and operators

You begin a *formula* by pressing the EQUALS (=) key to the left of the BACKSPACE key.

Formulas contain one or more *operators*. These indicate the type of arithmetic operation that you want the formula to perform: addition (+), subtraction (-), multiplication (*) or division (/).

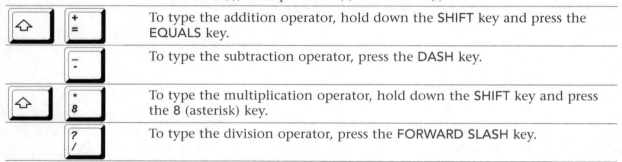

To type the addition operator, hold down the SHIFT key and press the EQUALS key.

To type the subtraction operator, press the DASH key.

To type the multiplication operator, hold down the SHIFT key and press the 8 (asterisk) key.

To type the division operator, press the FORWARD SLASH key.

Formulas and arguments

The components or *arguments* of a formula can be cell references, numbers, or both. A sample formula would be:

=A12+B12+3

Excel follows the rules of arithmetic in calculating formulas: division is done first, followed by multiplication, then addition and finally subtraction.

You can use parentheses (brackets) to force Excel to calculate your formula in a particular order. For example:

=C5*(A4+A7)-(C4/C7)

AutoFill: letting Excel do the work

This convenient Excel feature removes the need to type text and/or numbers that contain a predictable pattern.

Create and save your formulas workbook

Save button

1 Launch Excel, click the **Save** button on the Standard toolbar or choose **File I Save**.

2 Enter the following file name and click **Save**:

Formulas

Excel adds the file name extension of .xls automatically. You will use this workbook throughout this lesson. Don't forget to save the workbook as you go along!

Add, subtract, multiply and divide numbers

Now it's time to perform some arithmetic in Excel.

1   Enter the text and numbers in the cells as shown below.

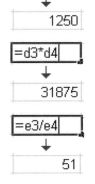

	A	B	C	D	E	F
1						
2		Add	Subtract	Multiply	Divide	
3		1275	1275	1275	1275	
4		52	25	25	25	
5						
6						

2   Click B5, and enter the following formula: =B3+B4 (That is, type =B3+B4 and press **ENTER**.)

3   In cell C5, enter the formula: =C3-C4

4   In cell D5, enter the formula: =D3*D4

5   In cell E5, enter the formula: =E3/E4

After you enter each of the four formulas, Excel displays its result as shown on the left.

Edit a formula

You can edit previously typed formulas just as you can edit text or numbers.

1   Enter the text shown below in cell G8, and the numbers in B9, C9, D9, E9 and F9.

8						Total
9		1234	4532	5693	3512	239

2   In cell G9, enter the formula: =B9+C9+D9+E9+F9

Excel displays the result of adding the specified cells (15210) in G9.

3   Double-click G9. Using either the **BACKSPACE** or **DELETE** keys, delete from the formula the argument F9 and the plus operator (+) in front of it, and press **ENTER**.

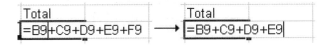

Excel now displays in G9 the result of adding B9, C9, D9 and E9 only.

You will usually see cell references written with the column letters in upper-case letters (for example, A1, B10 and W90) rather than in lower-case ones (for example, a1, b10 and w90). This is true for Excel's online help – and this book.

Column letters: upper- or lower-case?

You will usually see cell references written with the column letters in upper-case letters (for example, A1, B10 and W90) rather than in lower-case ones (for example, a1, b10 and w90).

You can type a cell reference into Excel using an upper- or lower-case column letter, however. Excel accepts either. You may find it easier to enter column letters in lower-case, because you need to type only the letter key, and not the letter key in combination with the **SHIFT** key.

Use constants in formulas

Excel formulas can contain numbers as arguments instead of (or as well as) cell references. Excel calls these numbers constants.

1 Enter the following formula in cell G2 and press **ENTER**: =26*109

2 Enter the following formula in cell G2 and press **ENTER**: =E3/5

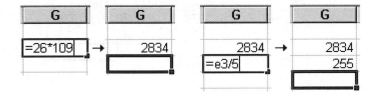

Combine multiple operators in a single formula

Let's perform a more complex task: calculating the total cost of each of four products, and then determining the profit on each product.

1 Enter the text and numbers in the cells shown below.

	A	B	C	D	E	F	G	H
12		Name	Fixed	Variable	Total Cost	Discount	Price	Profit
13		Product 1	12	2		2	21	
14		Product 2	34	6		8	56	
15		Product 3	56	28		12	112	
16		Product 4	127	92		19	290	

2 In cells E13, E14, E15 and E16, enter the formulas shown below to calculate the total cost of each product. The total cost of each product is the sum of its fixed costs (in the C column) and its variable costs (in the D column).

3 In cells H13, H14, H15 and H16, enter the formulas shown below to calculate the profit on each product. The profit is the price (in the G column) minus the sum of the total cost and the discount.

Total Cost		Total Cost
=C13+D13	→	14
=C14+D14	→	40
=C15+D15		84
=C16+D16		219

Profit		Profit
=G13-(E13+F13)	→	5
=G14-(E14+F14)	→	8
=G15-(E15+F15)		16
=G16-(E16+F16)		52

Arithmetic: the order of precedence

Excel follows the rules of arithmetic in calculating formulas that combine different operations. The following formula gives a result of 11 because Excel first multiplies 2 by 3 (resulting in 6) and then adds 5:

=5+2*3

You can use parentheses (brackets) to force Excel to calculate your formula in a particular order. For example, the following formula gives a result of 21 because Excel first adds 5 and 2 (because they are within parentheses) and then multiplies that result by 3 to give 21:

=(5+2)*3

Ensure that you follow every opening bracket with a matching closing bracket. Here's a way to help you remember the order of precedence among arithmetical operators:
Oh **D**ear! **M**y **A**unt **S**ally!

Perform a fixed factor calculation

Your company sells a range of five products, priced at £10, £15, £20, £25 and £30, to the USA and Japan. At given sterling-to-dollar and sterling-to-yen exchange rates, your task is to create a currency conversion table that shows the prices of your products in sterling, dollars and yen.

This is an example where you need to apply the same number – a so-called fixed factor – several times to different numbers. In this case the fixed factor is a currency exchange rate; in others, it could be an employee tax rate or sales commission rate. It's best to place a fixed factor in a cell of its own, and enter its cell reference as needed in formulas.

1 Enter the text labels and numbers as shown below.

	A	B	C	D
18				
19		GBP/USD	1.62	
20		GBP/JPY	195.82	
21				
22		Sterling	Dollars	Yen
23		10		
24		15		
25		20		
26		25		
27		30		

2 In cells C23 to C27, enter formulas to calculate the price of each product in dollars, obtained by multiplying its price in sterling by the dollar exchange rate (the fixed factor) in cell C19.

3 In cells D23 to D27, enter formulas to calculate the price of each product in yen, obtained by multiplying its price in sterling by the yen exchange rate (another fixed factor) in cell C20.

Dollars
=B23*C19
=B24*C19
=B25*C19
=B26*C19
=B27*C19

⟶

Dollars
16.2
24.3
32.4
40.5
48.6

Yen
=B23*C20
=B24*C20
=B25*C20
=B26*C20
=B27*C20

⟶

Yen
1958.2
2937.3
3916.4
4895.5
5874.6

When you press **ENTER** after typing each formula, Excel displays the calculated result.

Recalculate a fixed factor calculation

The power and convenience of a spreadsheet is not so much the ability to calculate as the ability to recalculate. Excel recalculates an arithmetic operation whenever numbers in the operation change.

1 Double-click cell C19, change the dollar exchange rate to 1.72, and press **ENTER**.

2 Double-click cell D19, change the yen exchange rate to 195.62, and press **ENTER**.

Excel recalculates the converted amounts as shown on the right.

Dollars	Yen
17.2	1956.2
25.8	2934.3
34.4	3912.4
43	4890.5
51.6	5868.6

Insert a date in a cell

To enter a date in a cell, type a forward slash (/) or a dash (–) to separate the parts of a date. Here are two examples:

1 In B30 type the following and press **ENTER**: 17/10/03

Notice how Excel converts your entered two-digit year (03) to a four-digit year (2003). If you type in just the day and the month, Excel assumes the current year.

2 In B31 type the following and press **ENTER**: 26-Nov-01

Change date display format

Want to change the way that Excel displays an entered date? Follow these steps:

1 Click the cell containing the date.

2 Choose **Format | Cells**, and select the **Number** tab.

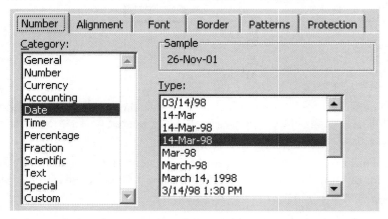

3 Select Date in the **Category** list, select a display format in the **Type** list, and click **OK**.

AutoFill numbers and text

Excel's *AutoFill* feature can reproduce a cell's content in other cells. Here's how.

1 In cell B34 enter the word Text, and in cell C34 the number 6534.

2 Click cell B34 and position the cursor over the fill handle – the black square at the bottom-right of the selected cell.

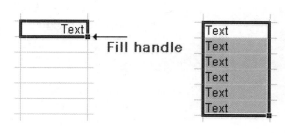

3 Drag the fill handle down to cell B39.

4 Repeat steps 2 and 3 for cell C34.

Excel copies the text and number into the cells that you dragged over.

AutoFill a number series

AutoFill can recognize that two selected cells contain numbers in an increasing series, and can increment the numbers in the cells that you drag across.

1   Enter 12 in cell D34, and enter 13 and in D35.

2   Click on cell D34 and drag down to select D35 also.

3   Click the fill handle at the lower-right of cell D35, and drag down to cell D39.

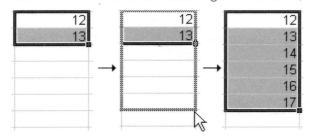

AutoFill a date

AutoFill can recognize a date and can increment the date in the cells that you drag across.

1   Enter the following date in cell E34: 26/11/03

2   Click the fill handle at the lower-right of cell E34, and drag down to cell E39.

| 26/11/2003 |
| 27/11/2003 |
| 28/11/2003 |
| 29/11/2003 |
| 30/11/2003 |
| 01/12/2003 |

Insert symbols in cells

You can paste symbols from Word into Excel, which has no command for entering them directly.

1   In cell G34 enter the following: 100C.

2   Start Microsoft® Word. It should open with a new, blank document ready for you to use.

3   Choose **Insert | Symbol**, select the **Symbols** tab, and double-click the degree character (°) in the dialog box. Click **Close** to close the dialog box.

4   Select the degree character (°) in the Word document, and press **CTRL+c**. You can now close the Word document and Word itself. You need not save the Word document.

`100°C`

5   Switch to Excel, double-click cell G34 to make it editable, position the cursor between the 100 and the C, and press **CTRL+v**. Cell G34 should now look as shown to the left.

Select an adjacent cell range

An *adjacent cell range* is a group of cells that are directly beside, above or below one another.

■   To select an adjacent cell range, click the top-left cell, and then drag with the mouse.

Add	Subtract	Multiply	Divide
1275	1275	1275	1275
52	25	25	25
1327	1250	31875	51

Excel displays the selected cells with a coloured background. Although several cells are selected, only one cell is the active cell. It's shown as black text against a white background.

- To cancel a selection, click anywhere outside the selected cell or range.

Select a non-adjacent cell range

A *non-adjacent cell range* can consist of individual cells dotted around the worksheet or a number of smaller, sub-groups of adjacent cells.

- To select a non-adjacent cell range, select the first cell (or first sub-group of adjacent cells), hold down the **CTRL** key, and then select further cells (or adjacent ranges).

Add	Subtract	Multiply	Divide
1275	1275	1275	1275
52	25	25	25
1327	1250	31875	51

Identifying cell ranges

You identify an *adjacent cell range* by the cell reference of the top-left cell, a colon (:) and the cell reference of the bottom-right cell. For example, the adjacent cell range A1:B2 includes the following four cells: A1, A2, B1 and B2. Adjacent cell ranges may include cells in one column only (such as B2:B5) or in one row only (such as D9:F9).

You identify a *non-adjacent cell range* by inserting commas between the individual cells (for example, A2, B3, C4) or between the smaller sub-groups of adjacent cells (for example, A2:A6, H4:H8).

Select rows or columns

- To select several adjacent rows (or columns), click the heading of the top row (or left column), and hold down the mouse button as you drag down (or right).

- To select several non-adjacent rows (or columns), click the heading of the first, hold down the **CTRL** key, and the click on the other row (or column) headings.

- To select an entire worksheet, click on the top-left of the worksheet, where the row heading meets the column heading.

Quit Excel

You can close your Formulas.xls workbook and quit Excel. You have now completed Lesson 4.2 of the ECDL Spreadsheets Module.

4.3

Calculations with functions

Learning goals   At the end of this lesson you should be able to:

- use the following Excel functions: SUM, AVERAGE, MIN, MAX, COUNT and IF;
- use the **AutoSum** button;
- enter text across multiple columns;
- recognize and correct Excel error messages.

New term   At the end of this lesson you should be able to explain the following term:

Function   A predefined formula built in to Excel and used for a specific purpose.

About functions

In Lesson 4.2 you used formulas to add, subtract, multiply and divide numbers. Excel offers a second way to perform calculations: *functions*.

As with formulas, functions always begin with an equals (=) symbol. And as with row and column letters, you can type function names in upper- or lower-case letters. In the same way that Excel accepts A4 or a4, it accepts SUM or sum, AVERAGE or average. The components of a function, like those of a formula, are called arguments.

The SUM function

With the SUM function, you need enter only two arguments when totalling a vertical or horizontal list of cells: the first and last cell references. An example of a SUM function would be:

=SUM(A2:A6)

AutoSum button

AutoSum button

A fast way to total a vertical or horizontal list of cells is to select them and click the **AutoSum** button. Excel tries to 'guess' which cells you want to add. If Excel has guessed correctly, just press **ENTER** to confirm the suggested arguments. If not, edit the arguments of the SUM function.

The AVERAGE function

As its name suggests, this function calculates the average of a vertical or horizontal list of numbers. For example:

=AVERAGE(D5:F5)

The MAX, MIN and COUNT functions

Excel's MAX and MIN functions find the largest and smallest numbers respectively in a range of cells. You can use the COUNT function to find the number of cells in a cell range that contain numbers or calculations that display numbers as their result.

The decision-making IF function

IF is a so-called conditional function: it tests how two other cells (or constants) relate to one another, and gives a different result depending on the result of the test. Depending on whether the value under test is equals (=), less than (<), greater than (>), greater than or equal to (>=) or less than or equal to (<=) a specified value, the IF function will perform one of two different calculations, or display one of two different texts.

Create and save your functions workbook

Save button

1 Launch Excel, click the **Save** button on the Standard toolbar or choose **File | Save**.

2 Enter the following file name and click **Save**:

Functions

Excel adds the file name extension of .xls automatically. You will use this workbook throughout this lesson. Don't forget to save the workbook as you go along!

Total numbers with the SUM function

1 Enter the numbers and text shown below.

2 Type the following function in B6 and press **ENTER**: =SUM(B3:B5)

	A	B
3	Conway	2356
4	Murphy	4921
5	Smith	2903
6	Totals	=sum(b3:b5)
7		

→

	A	B
3	Conway	2356
4	Murphy	4921
5	Smith	2903
6	Totals	10180
7		

Well done! You have used Excel's SUM function to add numbers.

Total a vertical list of numbers with the AutoSum button

Because SUM is such a commonly used function, Microsoft put a button for it on the Standard toolbar. It looks like a sideways letter 'M' and is called the **AutoSum** button.

1 Click cell B6, press the **BACKSPACE** or **DELETE** button, and then press **ENTER**.

This removes the SUM function.

Σ

AutoSum button

2 Click cell B6 again to select it, and then click the **AutoSum** button on the Standard toolbar.

Excel 'guesses' which cells you want to add. It assumes (correctly) that the cells begin at B3 and end at B5. Click the AutoSum button again to confirm that B3, B4 and B5 are the cells for adding.

	A	B
3	Conway	2356
4	Murphy	4921
5	Smith	2903
6	Totals	=SUM(B3:B5)

3 Enter more text and numbers as shown below.

	A	B	C	D	E
1					
2		January	February	March	Totals
3	Conway	2356	3261	4560	
4	Murphy	4921	4055	3542	
5	Smith	2903	3308	3622	
6	Totals	10180			

4 To total the C column, click cell C6, and click the **AutoSum** button twice.

5 Total the D column by clicking cell D6, and clicking the **AutoSum** button twice. Your totals should look as shown below.

		B	C	D
6		10180	10624	11724

Total a horizontal list of numbers with the AutoSum button

AutoSum can total numbers horizontally as well as vertically.

1 Calculate the total of the top (Conway) row by clicking cell E3 and clicking the **AutoSum** button.

3	Conway	2356	3261	4560	=SUM(B3:D3)

Excel 'guesses' that the cells you want to add are B3, C3 and D3. Click the **AutoSum** button a second time to confirm the operation.

3	Conway	2356	3261	4560	10177

2 Repeat this action for the second (Murphy) row by clicking cell E4, and then clicking the **AutoSum** button twice to add its three numbers.

4	Murphy	4921	4055	3542	12518

3 Click cell E5, and then click the **AutoSum** button. This time Excel incorrectly assumes that you want to add the two cells above E5, E3 and E4.

4 Double-click cell E5 to make the cell editable. Press **DELETE** or **BACKSPACE**. This does not remove the SUM function from E5. It just removes the two arguments of the function, the cell references, E3:E4.

5 Type B5:D5 within the parentheses (brackets) of the SUM function, and click the **AutoSum** button to confirm your entry.

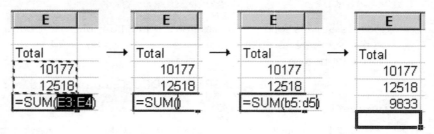

Find averages with the AVERAGE function

This Excel function – you guessed it – finds the average of a group of numbers. As with the SUM function, the AVERAGE function begins with the = sign. Then follows the function name, and finally the arguments within parentheses.

1 In cell A8 enter the following text: Average

2 In cell B8 enter the following formula:

=AVERAGE(B3:B5)

3 Repeat step 2 for columns C and D. Row 8 should now look as shown.

8	Average	3393.333	3541.333	3908	

Recalculate function results

Excel automatically recalculates functions whenever the numbers used in the functions change.

1   Double-click cell B5, and change its value to 2902.

2   Double-click cell C3, and change its value to 3260.

See how Excel's SUM and AVERAGE functions now display new, updated results.

	A	B	C	D	E
1					
2		January	February	March	Totals
3	Conway	2356	3260	4560	10176
4	Murphy	4921	4055	3542	12518
5	Smith	2902	3308	3622	9832
6	Totals	10179	10623	11724	
7					
8	Average	3393	3541	3908	

Discover the biggest and smallest with the MIN and MAX functions

The MAX and MIN functions find the largest and smallest numbers respectively in a range of cells.

1   Enter the text Max and Min in cells A9 and A10.

2   In cell B9 enter the following function: =MAX(B3:D5)

The cell range B3:D5 includes all the cells in the rectangular area that has B3 at its top left and D5 at its bottom right.

3   In cell B10, enter the following function: =MIN(B3:D5)

Your MAX and MIN function results should look as shown below.

9	Max	4921
10	Min	2356

SUM, MAX, and MIN ignore empty and non-numeric cells

These three are tolerant functions. If any cell contains text instead of a number, or is empty, the functions do not display an error message. They just ignore the non-numeric cells or empty cells.

Count numbers with the COUNT function

Excel's COUNT function finds the number of cells in a cell range that contain numbers or calculations that display numbers as their result.

1   Enter the text Count in cell A11.

2   In cell B11 enter the following function: =COUNT(A2:E6)

The cell range A2:E6 includes all the cells in the rectangular area that has A2 at its top left and E6 at its bottom right. The cells in this cell range include text, numbers and calculations.

As you can see, Excel correctly finds that of 25 cells in the cell range A2:E6, only 15 contain numbers and calculated results.

11	Count	15

Calculate sales commission with the IF function

Your company awards 12% commission to sales representatives who sell up to £19,999 worth of products. Those who sell £20,000 or more receive a 15% commission. You can use Excel's conditional IF function to determine which one of the two commission rates to apply.

1 Enter the text and numbers shown below. 12% and 15% are entered as 0.12 and 0.15.

	A	B	C
14	Comm1	0.12	
15	Comm2	0.15	
16			
17		Sales	Amount
18	Smith	12345	
19	Jones	19421	
20	Brown	25891	

2 In cell C18 enter the following function: =IF(B18<19999, B18*B14, B18*B15)

If the sales amount is less than 19999, Excel will multiply the amount by the lower rate (0.12). Otherwise, Excel will multiply the sales amount by the higher rate (0.15)

3 In cell C19 enter the following function: =IF(B19<19999, B19*B14, B19*B15)

4 In cell C20 enter the following function: =IF(B20<19999, B20*B14, B20*B15)

Amount		Amount
=IF(B18<19999, B18*B14, B18*B15)	→	1481.4
=IF(B19<19999, B19*B14, B19*B15)		2330.52
=IF(B20<19999, B20*B14, B20*B15)		3883.65

Display conditional text with the IF function

You can use the IF function to display one of two different texts depending on the value in a cell.

1 Enter the text and numbers shown on the right.

2 In cell G18 enter the following function:

=IF(E18<=F18, "OK", "Over")

3 In cell G19 enter the following function:

=IF(E19<=F19, "OK", "Over")

	E	F
17	Actual	Budget
18	34897	35000
19	45821	45000
20	63298	65000

4 In cell G20 enter the following function: =IF(E20<=F20, "OK", "Over")

Notice that the text for display is enclosed within quotes.

Format of the conditional IF function

Excel's IF function has the following format:
    IF(value under test, result if value passes test, result if value fails test)
The value under test contains one of the following comparison operators: = (equal to), > (greater than), >= (greater than or equal to), < (less than) or <= (less than or equal to).
    If the value passes the test, Excel performs the calculation or displays the text in the second part of the function. If the value fails the test, Excel performs the calculation or displays the text in the third part of the function. Always enclose any text that you want the IF function to display within quotes (" ").

Enter text across multiple columns

You can enter multi-column text (text that is longer than the width of a single cell) provided the other, over-typed cells are blank.

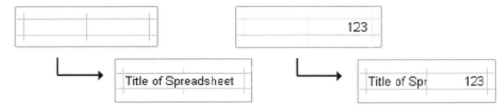

1 In cell F15 enter the following: Text Here

2 In cell E15 enter the following: Budget Variance Calculation

E	F	G
Budget Va	Text Here	

Notice that the text in E15 does not display across multiple columns.

3 Click cell F15, press **BACKSPACE** or **DELETE**, and press **ENTER** to remove the words Text Here.

E	F	G
Budget Variance Calculation		

Notice that the text in E15 now displays across multiple columns.

Excel's error messages

If a formula or function cannot properly calculate a result, Excel displays an error message in the calculated cell indicating the type of error that has taken place.

The most common error messages indicate that you have used a cell containing text in a calculation (#VALUE!), or a cell that has been deleted (#REF!). Another message indicates that you have tried to divide by zero or by an empty cell (#DIV./0!).

The ##### message indicates that a cell contains a number or a calculation result that is too wide for the cell to display. This is not really an error: Excel has the correct information; it just can't display it.

Display the #VALUE! error message

In this and the next four examples you will deliberately generate error messages to understand better how they can be avoided and, if not avoided, corrected.

1 Enter the text and numbers shown below.

	A	B	C	D	E
23		Error Messages			
24		Profit	6341	348	1235678
25		4532	0	24	

2 In cell B26 enter the following formula: =B24/B25

Excel displays the #VALUE! error message because you have used a text cell (B25) in a calculation.

Display the #DIV./0! error message

1 In cell C26 enter the following formula: =C24/C25

Excel displays the #DIV./0 error message because you tried to divide by zero (C25).

2 Delete the zero from cell C25.

The error message remains. Excel regards an empty cell and a cell containing zero in the same way.

Display the #REF! error message

1 In cell D26 enter the following formula: =D24/D25

Excel responds by displaying the calculated result (14.5) in cell D26.

2 Click D25 to select it, and choose **Edit | Delete**.

3 In the Delete dialog box displayed, select the **Shift Cells Up** option, and click **OK**.

The cell that was previously cell D26 now moves up one row to fill the space that was occupied by the deleted D25 cell.

Excel displays the #REF! error message because the calculation includes a deleted cell.

Display the ##### error message

1 Hold the mouse pointer over the right border of the E column heading

2 Drag the border a little to the left, reducing the column width.

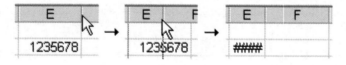

Excel displays the ##### error message in column E because it is now too narrow for its content.

Quit Excel

You can close your Functions.xls workbook and quit Excel. You have now completed Lesson 4.3 of the ECDL Spreadsheets Module.

Number styles and cell formatting

Learning goals	At the end of this lesson you should be able to:

- choose the appropriate number format for the type of numbers that you want to enter and store in your worksheet;
- enter numbers as text;
- change font, font style (bold and italic) and font size;
- apply borders and fills (coloured backgrounds to cells);
- hide and unhide rows and columns;
- freeze row and column titles;
- wrap text over multiple lines in a cell.

New term	At the end of this lesson you should be able to explain the following term:

Number Style	The way in which Excel displays a number on screen and on printouts. Number format affects only the appearance and not the value of numbers.

Excel recognises many types of numbers, and calls each a *number style*. Do not confuse this with stylistic formatting such as bold and italic. Number style affects only the way that a number looks on screen and on printouts – and not its value.

The table below summarizes Excel's four main number styles.

Style	Button	Examples	Description
General		12.34 3.4575 45	This default style does not display trailing zeros (a zero entered as the last digit after a decimal point). Nor does it insert commas to separate thousands.
Percent	%	1234% 346% 4500%	Multiplies numbers by 100, and places the percent sign (%) after each one. Useful for displaying decimal fractions (such as 0.0525) as percentages (such as 5.25%).
Comma	,	12.34 3.46 45.00	Automatically inserts a comma to separate thousands, and displays all numbers to two places of decimals.
Currency		£ 12.34 £ 3.46 £ 45.00	Automatically inserts your national currency symbol, and follows your currency's convention for decimal places.

The best way to apply a non-default number format is to select the empty cell or range, apply the relevant format, and then enter the numbers.

Custom number formats and options

For numbers that require several places of decimals, apply the customizable format called Number format.

Text as numbers

You can set numbers as text. This can be useful when the numbers are identifiers (part numbers, phone numbers and so on) rather than amounts.

Fonts, borders and background colours

You can use buttons on Excel's Formatting toolbar to change the font, font size, font colour, borders or background colours of a selected cell or cell range.

Create and save your numbers-formatting workbook

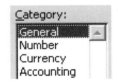

Save button

1 Launch Excel, click the **Save** button on the Standard toolbar or choose **File | Save**.

2 Enter the following file name and click **Save**:

Numbers-Formatting

Excel adds the file name extension of .xls automatically. You will use this workbook throughout this lesson. Don't forget to save the workbook as you go along!

Enter the text and numbers shown below.

	A	B	C	D	E
2		January	February	March	Totals
3	Conway	2356	3260	4560	10176
4	Murphy	4921	4055	3542	12518
5	Smith	2902	3308	3622	9832
6	Totals	10179	10623	11724	

Apply the Comma number format

Comma Style button

1 Click the heading of column B to select the entire January column.

2 Click the **Comma Style** button on the Standard toolbar.

Excel inserts commas and two places of decimals for all numbers in the column. Text entries are unaffected.

You may need to widen column B for its cell contents to display correctly.

B
January
2356
4921

→

B
January
2,356.00
4,921.00

Change back the default General Number format

1 Click the heading of column B to select the entire January column.

2 Choose **Format | Cells**, and click the **Number** tab.

3 In the category list, click General, and click **OK**.

The numbers in column B revert to the default General style.

Category:
General
Number
Currency
Accounting

Apply the Currency number format

1 Click on the top-left of your worksheet, where the row headings meet the column headings.

Click here ———→

2 Click the **Currency Style** button on the Standard toolbar.

Excel inserts the currency symbol (£), the thousands separator (,) and two places of decimals (including, where necessary, trailing zeros).

	A	B	C	D	E
2		January	February	March	Totals
3	Conway	£ 2,356.00	£ 3,260.00	£ 4,560.00	£ 10,176.00
4	Murphy	£ 4,921.00	£ 4,055.00	£ 3,542.00	£ 12,518.00
5	Smith	£ 2,902.00	£ 3,308.00	£ 3,622.00	£ 9,832.00
6	Totals	£ 10,179.00	£ 10,623.00	£11,724.00	

Click any cell in the worksheet to deselect the entire worksheet. You may need to widen some of the columns for their cell contents to display correctly.

Calculate the percentage contribution

A common spreadsheet task is to find the percentage contribution of one person or organizational unit to an overall amount. In this example you will calculate the total contribution of three individuals, and then find the percentage contributed by each one.

1   Click cell E6, and click the **AutoSum** button twice to calculate the total of the row totals. E6 should now display £32,526.

2   Click cell G2, and enter the percentage symbol (%). You'll find it above the number 4 on the keyboard.

Percent button

3   Click the heading of column G, and click the **Percent** button on the Formatting toolbar.

4   In cell G3, enter the formula =E3/$E$6 to calculate the proportion of the overall total contributed by Conway.

(You will learn more about the $A$1 format for absolute cell references in Lesson 4.5.)

=E3/$E$6		31%
=E4/$E$6	→	38%
=E5/$E$6		30%

5   Click G3, click the fill handle at the lower-right of the cell, and drag down to G5.

The G column now shows the percentage contribution of each of the three individuals.

Apply the number format called ... Number format

Numbers such as the results of laboratory experiments may require several places of decimals. The format to apply in such situations is the customizable Number format.

- Select the cell or range, choose **Format I Cells** and click the **Number** tab.

- In the **Category** list, select Number, and select (say) 4 places of decimals.

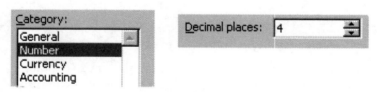

Where an entered number has more than four decimal places, Excel rounds up or down to four. Where the number has less, Excel adds trailing zeros.

- Also available on the **Number** tab of the **Format I Cells** dialog box is the option to specify the thousands separator (,).

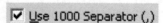

Increase and decease the number of decimal places

Increase Decimal button

The **Increase Decimal** and **Decrease Decimal** buttons on Excel's Formatting toolbar offer quick ways of changing the number of decimal places displayed in a selected cell or range. Each time you click a button, Excel increases or decreases by one the number of decimal places displayed.

Decrease Decimal button

The buttons work with numbers in the General, Currency and Number formats.

Enter a number as text

You can also format numbers as text. This can be useful when the numbers are identifiers (part numbers, phone numbers and so on) rather than amounts. You do this in two ways:

- Click in the cell, type the single quote symbol ('), and then enter your number.

- Select the blank cell or cell range and choose **Format | Cells**. On the **Number** tab, select Text from the **Category** list. Now, enter your number or numbers.

You cannot apply the Text format to already-entered numbers.

Applying non-default number formats

You can change the number format by selecting the cell or cell range containing already entered numbers, and then clicking the **Percent**, **Comma** or **Currency** toolbar buttons.

When changing cells to a non-default number format, it is generally better to do so before you enter your numbers. Numbers that are entered as text will be left- rather than right-aligned.

Regional Settings

Regional Settings

Options you select in the **Regional Settings** tab of the Windows Control Panel affect both the currency and the date conventions applied by Excel to your cell entries:

- **Changing Currency**: To use a different currency in your workbooks, choose **Start | Settings | Control Panel**, and double-click on the **Regional Settings** icon. On the **Regional Settings** tab, select the required country. On the **Currency** tab, accept or amend the currency conventions such as symbol, number of decimal places, and digit grouping symbol.

- **Changing Date**: To use the date conventions of another country in your workbooks, select the required country on the **Regional Settings** tab, and, on the **Date** tab, accept or amend the calendar conventions.

Change font, font style, font size and font colour

1 Click the heading of row 1 to select the entire row.

2 Choose **Insert | Rows**, and then **Edit | Repeat Insert Rows** to insert a second row.

3 In C2, enter the following text:

First Quarter Sales Figures for 2003

4 With C2 selected, click the **Font** pull-down list box, and select Arial Narrow. Next, click the **Font Size** pull-down box, and select 14 point.

Bold, Italic and Underline buttons

Font Color button

5 With C2 still selected, click the **Bold** and then the **Italic** buttons on the Formatting toolbar.

6 With C2 still selected, click the pull-down arrow at the right of the **Font Color** button on the Formatting toolbar, and click the Dark Blue option.

7 Select cells A5:A8, and click the **Italic** button on the Formatting toolbar.

8 Select the cell range B4:H4.

9 Click the **Bold** button on the Formatting toolbar. Click anywhere else on the worksheet to deselect the cells. They should look as shown.

January	February	March	Totals		$

Underline cell content

To underline the content of one or more cells, select the cell(s) and click the **Underline** button on the Formatting toolbar. To apply one of a range of alternative underline styles, such as double underline, select the cell and choose **Format | Cell**. Then, in the Underline drop-down list, select the style of underline you require and click **OK**.

Change horizontal alignment

Alignment buttons

1 Select the cell range B4:H4.

2 Click the **Centre-align** button on the Formatting toolbar.

January	February	March	Totals		$

Change borders

Bottom border button

All Borders button

1 Select cells A7:E7, click the pull-down arrow at the right of the **Borders** button on the Formatting toolbar, and click the **Bottom Border** option.

2 Select cells G5:G7, click the pull-down arrow at the right of **Borders** button on the Formatting toolbar, and click the **All Borders** option.

Change background colours

Fill Color button

1 Select cell range A4:G4, click the pull-down arrow at the right of the **Fill Color** button on the Formatting toolbar, and click the Gold option.

2 Select cell range A5:F8, click the pull-down arrow at the right of the **Fill Color** button on the Formatting toolbar, and click the Light Yellow option.

3 Select the cell range G5:G8, click the arrow on the right of the **Fill Color** button, and click the Light Turquoise option.

Your worksheet should look as shown below (use your imagination to see all the colours!).

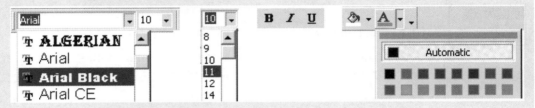

	A	B	C	D	E	F	G
2			First Quarter Sales Figures 2003				
3							
4		January	February	March	Totals		$
5	Conway	£ 2,356.00	£ 3,260.00	£ 4,560.00	£ 10,176.00		31%
6	Murphy	£ 4,921.00	£ 4,055.00	£ 3,542.00	£ 12,518.00		38%
7	Smith	£ 2,902.00	£ 3,308.00	£ 3,622.00	£ 9,832.00		30%
8	Totals	£ 10,179.00	£ 10,623.00	£ 11,724.00	£ 32,526.00		

Working with fonts

By default Excel shows worksheet cells in Arial, 10pt, Normal. The text colour is black. To change them, select the cell or cells, and use the list boxes or buttons on the Formatting toolbar.

Working with background colours and borders

By default Excel shows worksheet cells with a white background. To change the background colour of a selected cell or cells, use the **Fill Color** button on the Formatting toolbar.

By default cells have no borders. Do not confuse cell borders with gridlines. Gridlines are covered under printing in Lesson 4.6. The **Borders** button on the Formatting toolbar offers a range of options.

Some commonly used border types are shown below. The Thick Bottom Border is a common choice for totals.

Bottom Border	Thick Bottom Border	Top and Double Bottom Border	Top and Double Thick Border	Outside Borders
12345	454	553	54353	4534

Change column width and row height

To change the width of a column, move the mouse to the column heading, and then drag the right border of the column heading until the column is the width you want.

To change row height, move the mouse to the row heading, and then drag the bottom border of the row heading until the row is the height you want.

1 Click the right border in the new column F heading, and drag it to the left, making the column narrower.

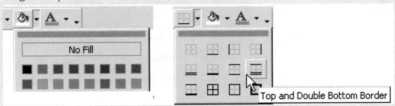

	A	B	C	D	E	F
2			First Quarter Sales Figures 2003			

2 In the row heading area, click the border between rows 2 and 3, and drag down about 1 cm with the mouse.

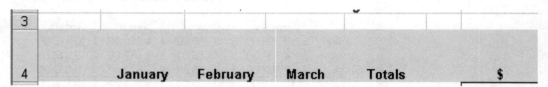

Align cells vertically

The three alignment buttons (left, centre and right) on the Formatting toolbar enable you to position cell contents horizontally (left-to-right). You can use the **Alignment** tab in the dialog box displayed by the **Format | Cells** command to align cell contents vertically (top-to-bottom).

1 Select row 4 by clicking the row heading.

2 Choose **Format | Cells**, select the **Alignment** tab, select the Center option from the Vertical list, and click **OK**.

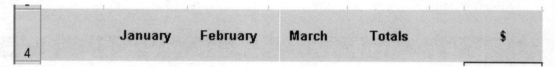

Excel now aligns the cells' content vertically so that it is centred between the top and bottom of the cells' boundaries.

Change cell orientation

Excel offers the ability to rotate or 'orient' cell contents to a specified angle.

1 Select row 4, and choose **Format | Cells**.

2 Click the **Alignment** tab, type 90 in the **Degrees** box, and click **OK**.

Entering a positive number in the **Degrees** box rotates the cell content in the anticlockwise direction. A negative number of degrees rotates the cell content in the clockwise direction. You may need to increase the row's height to hold the reoriented text.

Hide and unhide rows and columns

You can hide rows and columns of information that you don't want to print or display.

- To hide a row or column, select it by clicking its heading and choosing **Format | Row** or **Column | Hide**.

- To unhide a row, select the rows above and below the hidden row, and choose **Format | Row | Unhide**.

- To unhide a column, select the columns at the left and right of the hidden column, and then **Format | Column | Unhide**.

Freeze row and column titles

When working in a long worksheet, it's easy to forget which information is held in each column once you have scrolled down past your text headings.

To set a particular row so that it is always displayed:

1   Click the heading of the row directly beneath the one you want to be always displayed.

2   Choose **Window | Freeze Panes**.

Your selected row remains visible ('frozen' in place) as you scroll down through the remainder of your worksheet.

■ To unfreeze a row, choose **Window | Unfreeze Panes**.

Wrap content in a cell

To display multiple lines of text within a cell:

■ Select the cells you want to format.

■ Choose **Format | Cells**, and click the **Alignment** tab.

■ Under **Text control**, select the Wrap text checkbox.

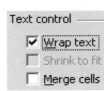

To start a new line of text at a specific point, click where you want to break the line, hold down the **ALT** key and hit **ENTER**.

Quit Excel

You can close your Numbers-Formatting.xls workbook and quit Excel. You have now completed Lesson 4.4 of the ECDL Spreadsheets Module.

45

Copying, inserting and sorting

Learning goals

At the end of this lesson you should be able to:

- copy, cut and paste the contents of cells between cells, worksheets and workbooks;
- use relative and absolute cell references;
- sort cells according to one or two criteria;
- insert and delete cells and cell ranges;
- insert and delete rows and columns.

New terms

At the end of this lesson you should be able to explain the following terms:

Marquee	A flashing rectangle that Excel uses to surround a cell, or cell range, that you have copied to the Clipboard.
Absolute Cell Reference	A reference to a cell or cell range in the format $A$1, A$1 or A$1. Excel does not adjust an absolute cell reference when you copy or move a calculation containing such a reference.
Relative Cell Reference	A reference to a cell or cell range in the format A1. Excel changes a relative cell reference when you copy or move a formula or function containing such a reference to a new location.
Sorting	Rearranging columns of cells based on the values in the cells. Sorting does not change the content of cells, only their location.
Sort Order	A particular way of ordering cells based on value. A sort order can be alphabetic or numeric, and can be in ascending (0 to 9, A to Z) or descending (9 to 0, Z to A) order.

Copy, cut and paste

Copy button

You can reproduce (copy) or move (cut) a selected cell or cell range within the same worksheet, between different worksheets in the same workbook, or between different workbooks.

A variety of methods are available, including drag-and-drop, commands on the pop-up menu activated by right-clicking, Edit menu commands, and buttons on the Standard toolbar.

Cut button

When you copy (or cut) a cell or cell range by any means other than drag-and-drop, Excel surrounds the selected cells with a flashing rectangle called a *marquee*. If you remove a marquee by pressing the ESC key, Excel removes the contents of the selected cell or cell range from the Clipboard.

Paste button

Cell references: relative and absolute

Errors can arise when pasting a calculation cell that contains a cell reference that must always refer ('point to') the same cell in the worksheet. To prevent Excel from adjusting cell references in a paste operation, specify the pasted cell address as an *absolute cell reference* in the format $A$1. Entering a reference such as $B$9 in a calculation says to Excel 'always use cell B9'.

Cell references in the form A1 are called *relative cell references*.

Inserting and deleting rows and cells

Sometimes you need to insert a row or column to hold new data within a range of cells that already contain text and numbers. To insert a new row or column, select the row or column heading immediately below or to the right of where you want to insert, and choose Insert | Rows or Insert | Columns.

To delete a row or column, select the row or column heading and choose Edit | Delete.

Sorting: reordering rows by content

Sort Ascending button

The order in which you originally typed entries in a worksheet may not be the order in which, later on, you would prefer to display or print that information.

By selecting the cell range and choosing the Sort Ascending (A-Z) or Sort Descending (Z-A) button on the Standard toolbar, you can rearrange the cells so that Excel displays them in order of increasing or decreasing value.

Sort Descending button

You can sort a cell range based on the values in more than a single column. This is called a multiple sort. *Sorting* does not change the content of cells, only their location.

Create and save the copy-insert-sort workbook

1 Launch Excel, click the **Save** button on the Standard toolbar or choose **File | Save**.

2 Enter the following file name and click **Save**:

Copy-Insert-Sort

Save button

Excel adds the file name extension of .xls automatically. You will use this workbook throughout this lesson. Don't forget to save the workbook as you go along!

Copy and paste a cell with drag-and-drop

1 Click cell B2 and enter in it the following number: 1234

2 Click cell B2 to select it. See how the cursor is shaped like a plus sign (+).

3 Move the cursor to any edge of the selected cell and hold down the **CTRL** key.

Excel changes the cursor from a plus sign to an arrow with a smaller plus sign.

4 Holding down the **CTRL** key, drag to the destination cell – for example, F2.

5 Release the mouse button first, and then the **CTRL** key.

(If you release **CTRL** first, Excel cuts rather than copies the cell contents.)

	A	B	C	D	E	F
1						
2		1234				1234

If there is already something in cell F2, Excel overwrites it with the pasted number.

Copy and paste a cell by right-clicking

1 Click cell B4 and enter in it the following number: 1234

2 Right-click cell B4 with the mouse and choose **Copy** from the pop-up menu. Excel places the contents of B4 in the Clipboard.

3 Right-click cell F4 with the mouse, and choose **Paste** from the pop-up menu. Excel pastes the content of the Clipboard in F4.

If there is already something in cell F4, Excel overwrites it with the pasted number.

You can use drag-and-drop and right-click methods with cell ranges as well as single cells.

About the Clipboard

When you copy (or cut) and paste by any means other than drag-and-drop, the copied (or cut) cells are held in the Clipboard. This can hold up to twelve items at a time. When you copy second and further items, Excel displays the Clipboard toolbar. (If it doesn't appear, choose **View | Toolbars | Clipboard** to display it.) If you attempt to copy a thirteenth item, Excel asks you if you want to overwrite the oldest of the twelve items.

To paste the most recently copied item, right-click and choose **Paste** from the pop-up menu, click the **Paste** button on the Standard toolbar, choose **Edit | Paste** or press **CTRL+v**. To paste a different item, click its icon on the Clipboard toolbar.

Copy and paste adjacent and non-adjacent cell ranges

1 In cell B6 enter the number: 1234. Click B6 again, and drag its fill handle to F6.

2 Select the cell range B6:F6 by clicking in B6 and dragging to F6.

6	1234	1234	1234	1234	1234
7					

3 Press **CTRL+c** to copy the cell range B6:F6 to the Clipboard.

4 Click cell B8, and press **CTRL+v** to paste from the Clipboard. Excel copies the cells to the new cell range B8:F8 as shown below.

6	1234	1234	1234	1234	1234
7					
8	1234	1234	1234	1234	1234

5 With cell range B6:F6 still in the Clipboard, select the cell range B10:F13.

6 Press **CTRL+v** to paste to the cells. All four rows of the destination cell range now contain the pasted cells.

7 With cell range B6:F6 still in the Clipboard, select the non-adjacent cell range B15:F15, B17:F17, B19:F19.

8 Press **CTRL+v**. The three non-adjacent rows of the destination cell range now contain the pasted cells. The lower part of your worksheet should look as shown.

	A	B	C	D	E	F
9						
10		1234	1234	1234	1234	1234
11		1234	1234	1234	1234	1234
12		1234	1234	1234	1234	1234
13		1234	1234	1234	1234	1234
14						
15		1234	1234	1234	1234	1234
16						
17		1234	1234	1234	1234	1234
18						
19		1234	1234	1234	1234	1234

Copy and paste rows and columns

1 Click cell B21, and enter the following number: 5678

2 Copy B21 to the Clipboard, select cell range C21:F21, and paste.

3 At the left of the worksheet, click the heading of row 21. This selects the entire row. Press **CTRL+c**.

21	5678	5678	5678	5678	5678

4 Click the heading of row 22 to select the entire row.

21	5678	5678	5678	5678	5678
22					

5 Press **CTRL+v**. Excel copies the contents of row 21 to row 22.

6 Click the F column heading to select the entire column, and press **CTRL+c**.

7 Click the H column heading, and press **CTRL+v**. Excel copies the contents of column F to column H.

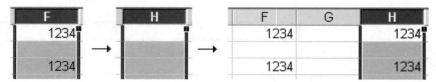

To copy or cut multiple rows or multiple columns, first drag across multiple row or column headings to select them.

Copy and paste between worksheets and workbooks

1 At the bottom of your worksheet click the Sheet2 tab to display the second worksheet.

File open button

2 Click the **File Open** button on the Standard toolbar or choose **File | Open**. Open the file named Functions that you created in Lesson 4.3.

3 Select the cell range A2:E6, and press **CTRL+c**. You can close the Functions workbook.

4 On Sheet2 of this lesson's workbook, click cell A2, and press **CTRL+v**. Click anywhere on the worksheet to deselect the pasted cell range. It should look as shown below.

	A	B	C	D	E
1					
2		January	February	March	Totals
3	Conway	2356	3260	4560	10176
4	Murphy	4921	4055	3542	12518
5	Smith	2902	3308	3622	9832
6	Totals	10179	10623	11724	

You will work with these cells in Sheet2 in the remainder of this lesson.

Cut and paste cell contents

Copy button

Cut and paste differs from copy and paste in that cutting removes the content of the original cells, whereas the contents of copied cells remain in their original location. Cutting does not remove the cells. It just removes their contents, leaving behind empty cells.

- To cut and paste using drag-and-drop, do not hold down the **CTRL** key while dragging the cell contents to their new location.

Cut button

- To cut and paste using the pop-up menu, choose **Cut** rather than **Copy**.

- The keyboard shortcut for cutting a cell or cell range is **CTRL+x**.

- **Cut**, **Copy** and **Paste** commands are also available on Excel's **Edit** menu.

Paste button

Yet another method is to use the relevant buttons on the Standard toolbar.

Copy and paste a calculation: relative cell references

The effect of copying (or cutting) a calculation that contains cell references depends on whether the cell references are written in relative (A1) or absolute ($A$1) form. As you will discover, Excel automatically adjusts relative cell references when you copy them.

1   Delete the calculations from cells C6 and D6, and cells E4 and E5.

2   Cell B6 contains the function =SUM(B3:B5). Click B6 and press **CTRL+c** to copy the calculation to the Clipboard.

3   Select cells C6 and D6, and press **CTRL+v** to paste to them from the Clipboard.

6		=SUM(B3:B5)	=SUM(C3:C5)	=SUM(D3:D5)

As you can see by clicking on C6 and D6 and displaying the functions that they contain, Excel has amended the cell references so that they total the two cells above C6 and D6 – not the two cells above B6.

4   Cell E3 contains the function =SUM(B3:D3). Click E3 and press **CTRL+c** to copy the calculation to the Clipboard.

5   Select cells E4 and E5, and press **CTRL+v** to paste to them from the Clipboard.

Excel amends the cell references so that E4 and E5 total the two cells to their left – not the two cells to the left of E3.

Convert relative cell references to absolute cell references

=e3/e6

↓

0.312869

=E3/$E$6

Σ

AutoSum
button

To prevent Excel adjusting cell references in a formula or function after copying or cutting, change them from relative cell references (the default format) to absolute cell references.

■   Double-click the cell containing the cell reference, and preface the column letter and row number with a dollar sign ($).

The following provides an example.

1   In cell G2, enter the percent symbol (%).

2   Click cell E6, click the **AutoSum** button twice on the Standard toolbar. E6 now contains the total of the three rows (32526).

3   In cell G3 enter the following formula: = E3/E6

4   This shows the proportion of the total contributed by the top (Conway) row.

5   Double-click G3 and change the cell reference of the cell that contains the total amount to $E$6. Press **ENTER** when finished.

You have converted the relative cell reference E6 to the absolute cell reference $E$6.

Copy and paste a calculation: absolute cell references

1   Select G3, and copy it to the Clipboard.

2   Select cells G4 and G5, and paste to them.

As you can see, Excel adjusts the cell reference E3 to E4 and E5, but the absolute cell reference $E$6 remains unaltered.

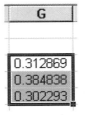

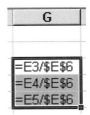

AutoFill a calculation: absolute cell references

1 Select cells G4 and G5, and delete their contents.

2 Click cell G3, click the fill handle at the bottom-right of the cell, and drag down to cell G5.

As with copy-and-paste, AutoFill adjusts the cell reference E3 to E4 and E5, but the absolute cell reference $E$6 remains unaltered.

Copy and paste fixed factor calculations: absolute cell references

1 Enter the text and numbers shown below.

	A	B	C
9		GBP/USD	1.72
10			
11		Sterling	Dollars
12		10	
13		15	
14		20	
15		25	
16		30	

2 In cell C12 enter the formula: =B12*$C$9.

3 Click C12, click the fill handle at the lower-right of the cell, and drag down to C16.

Excel changes the relative cell reference B12 to B13, B14, B15 and B16 in the different rows. The absolute cell reference of the exchange rate, $C$9, remains unaltered.

Cell references: relative and absolute

In the first lesson of this Module you learnt that each worksheet cell has a unique reference, written in the form A1. In fact, Excel supports two cell reference types: relative (the A1 type) and absolute (the $A$1 type).

Why is one type of cell reference not enough? The answer lies in the way that Excel copies and pastes calculations that contain cell references.

Excel changes a relative cell reference when you copy or move a calculation (formula or function) containing such a reference to a new location.

Excel does not adjust an absolute cell reference when you copy or move a calculation containing such a reference. Accordingly, you should use absolute cell references when entering fixed factor type calculations.

You can make part of a cell reference absolute and part relative. For example, G$13 or $D17.

Insert rows and columns

1 Click the heading of row 5 to select the entire row.

2 Choose **Insert | Rows**. Excel inserts a new row of blank cells beneath your selected row.

4	Murphy	4921	4055	3542	12518	0.384861
5						

3 Click the heading of column E to select the entire column. Then choose **Insert | Columns**. Excel inserts a new column of blank cells to the left of your selected column.

	A	B	C	D	E	F	G	H
1								
2		January	February	March		Totals		%

4 Enter the text and numbers in your new column and row as shown below. Notice that Excel recalculates the column and row totals automatically as you insert the new numbers.

1								
2		January	February	March	April	Totals		%
3	Conway	2356	3260	4560	4872	15048		0.340106
4	Murphy	4921	4055	3542	3498	16016		0.361984
5	Jones	6381	2591	1472	5823			
6	Smith	2902	3308	3622	3349	13181		0.297909
7	Totals	16560	13214	13196		44245		

5 Click cell E7, and click **AutoSum** twice to total the four cells above it (17542). In cell F5, use the =SUM(B5:E5) function to total the new, inserted Jones row (16267).

6 Click cell H4, and drag its fill handle down to H5 to find Jones' contribution to the total.

7 Let's improve the worksheet appearance. Click the column H reading, and click the **Percent style** button on the Formatting toolbar. Click the row 2 heading, and click the **Bold** and **Centre-align** buttons on the Formatting toolbar. Click the A column heading, and click the **Italics** button on the Formatting toolbar. Sheet2 should look as shown.

1								
2		**January**	**February**	**March**	**April**	**Totals**		**%**
3	*Conway*	2356	3260	4560	4872	15048		25%
4	*Murphy*	4921	4055	3542	3498	16016		26%
5	*Jones*	6381	2591	1472	5823	16267		27%
6	*Smith*	2902	3308	3622	3349	13181		22%
7	*Totals*	16560	13214	13196	17542	60512		

Remove rows and columns

- To delete a row, select the row heading and choose **Edit | Delete**. The row beneath moves up to fill the space previously occupied by the deleted row.

- To delete a column, select its heading and choose **Edit | Delete**. The column to the right moves left and fills the space previously occupied by the deleted column.

Insert and delete cells

- To insert individual cells on a worksheet, first select a cell immediately below or to the right of where you want to insert the new cell, and then choose **Insert | Cells**.

- To delete a cell, select it and choose **Edit | Delete**.

  Be careful about inserting or deleting a cell or cell range, because Excel adjusts the position of the surrounding cells accordingly. Excel prompts you, when inserting, to choose whether the surrounding cells should move right or down, and, when deleting, whether they should move left or up.

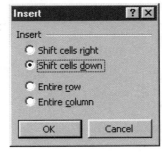

Perform a simple alphabetical sort

Sort Ascending
button

Sort Descending
button

1 In cells B20, C20 and D20 enter the words Original, Ascend and Descend.

2 In B21: B25 enter the country names Japan, Ireland, Brazil, Australia and Belgium.

3 Select B21:B25, and copy the cell contents to C21:D25.

4 Select C21:C25, and click the **Sort Ascending** (A–Z) button on the Standard toolbar.

5 Select D21:D25, and click the **Sort Descending** (Z–A) button on the Standard toolbar. Your worksheet should look as shown.

Original	Ascend	Descend
Japan	Japan	Japan
Ireland	Ireland	Ireland
Brazil	Brazil	Brazil
Australia	Australia	Australia
Belgium	Belgium	Belgium

→

Original	Ascend	Descend
Japan	Australia	Japan
Ireland	Belgium	Ireland
Brazil	Brazil	Brazil
Australia	Ireland	Belgium
Belgium	Japan	Australia

Perform a simple numerical sort

1 In cells F20, G20 and H20 enter the words Original, Ascend and Descend.

2 In F21: F25 enter the numbers 5324, 4661, 1278, 6589 and 3197.

3 Select F21:F25, and copy the cell contents to G21:H25.

4 Select G21:G25, and click the **Sort Ascending** (A–Z) button on the Standard toolbar.

5 Select H21:H25, and click the **Sort Descending** (Z–A) button on the Standard toolbar. Your worksheet should look as shown.

Original	Ascend	Descend
5324	5324	5324
4661	4661	4661
1278	1278	1278
6589	6589	6589
3197	3197	3197

→

Original	Ascend	Descend
5324	1278	6589
4661	3197	5324
1278	4661	4661
6589	5324	3197
3197	6589	1278

Perform a multiple criteria sort

In the following example you will sort rows by first name within surname.

1 Enter the text and numbers in cell range B28:D31 as shown below left.

2 Select cell range B28:D31 and choose **Data I Sort** to display the **Sort** dialog box.

3 By default, Excel shows the first column in the selected range (in this case, the B column of surnames) in the **Sort by** box. In the **Then by** list box, select Column C.

4 Select the *sort order* of Ascending for both columns B and C, and click **OK**.

Where the surnames in the B column are the same (Dunne), you can see that the first names in the C column are sorted in ascending order.

Callan	John	234
Dunne	Sheila	4567
Dunne	Joyce	23
Dunne	Alan	6543

→

Callan	John	234
Dunne	Alan	6543
Dunne	Joyce	23
Dunne	Sheila	4567

Quit Excel

You can close your Copy-Insert-Sort.xls workbook and quit Excel. You have now completed Lesson 4.5 of the ECDL Spreadsheets Module.

4.6

Proofing, printing and file format

Learning goals At the end of this lesson you should be able to:

- find and replace worksheet content;
- spell-check a worksheet;
- insert and format headers and footers;
- use Excel's print options;
- save Excel 2000 files in the following file formats: Excel 2000 template, earlier versions of Excel, non-Excel spreadsheet, database, text-only and HTML (web format);
- insert images, graphs and text into an Excel worksheet.

New terms At the end of this lesson you should be able to explain the following terms:

File Format	A set of rules that translates 1s and 0s into text and graphics on computer screens and printouts, and vice versa.
Tab-delimited text file	A text file format in which data items are separated horizontally by tabs and vertically by paragraph breaks.
Comma Separated Values (CSV) Text File	A text file format in which data items are separated horizontally by commas and vertically by paragraph breaks.

Finding and replacing cell content

You use the **Edit | Find** command to search a worksheet or selected range of cells for label text, numbers that were entered directly, numbers resulting from calculations, and calculation components (function names, cell references, arithmetic operators and constants).

With the **Edit | Replace** command you can replace any item (say, F36) with a specified alternative (say, F38).

Headers and footers

These are small text items that occur on every printed page, and typically contain such details as the workbook name, author name and date. They can also contain the automatically generated page number. You insert them with the **Header/Footer** tab of the **File | Page Setup** command.

Printing options

Excel's print options include a print preview feature and the ability to print selected cells only. By default, Excel does not include cell boundary lines or row and column headings on printouts. You can change either or both of these settings on the **Sheet** tab of the **File | Page Setup** dialog box.

Other file formats

Excel 2000 has a **File | Save As** feature that allows you save your workbooks in a format other than its own. The options include:

- **Earlier versions of Excel**: While you can generally use a later version of the software to open and work with a workbook that was created in an earlier version, the reverse is not necessarily true.

- **HTML (web page)**: The worksheet cells are converted to table cells in the HTML file. You can display and print HTML format files with a web browser application.

- **Rich Text Format (RTF)**: To reuse a workbook in another application, the best option is to save the presentation in Rich Text Format (RTF). This is a format common to all Microsoft Office applications.

Importing images, graphs and text

You can paste images, graphs and text into Excel from other applications.

To import text containing numbers which you want Excel to 'interpret' by arranging them correctly across rows and down columns, use the Text Wizard feature within the **File | Open** command. Select the **Delimited** option for a file in which a specific character (such as a comma or a tab) consistently indicates column endings, or the **Fixed Width** option for a file in which blank spaces cause the data to line up vertically.

Open the copy-insert-sort workbook

File Open button

1 Launch Excel, click the **Open** button on the Standard toolbar or choose **File | Open**.

2 Select the following file from Lesson 4.5 and click **Open**:

  Copy-Insert-Sort

You will use Sheet1 of this workbook throughout this lesson.

Finding cell content

You can search a worksheet for label text, numbers that were entered directly, numbers resulting from calculations, and calculation components (function names, cell references, arithmetic operators and constants). Let's try it:

1 Click in any cell, and choose **Edit | Find**.

2 Type the following in the **Find What** box and click **Find Next**: Smith.

Excel should highlight the cell A6.

Excel's Find feature offers the following options:

- **Search**: Select the direction you want to search in: down through columns, or rightwards across rows.

- **Look in**: The type of cells you want to search through: Formulas, Values or Comments.

- **Match case**: Searches only for characters that match the case of the entered search text. For example, a search for 'smith' does not find 'Smith'.

- **Find entire cells only**: Searches only for complete matches. For example, a search for 'Sm' does not find 'Smith', and 330 does not find 3308.

  You can cancel an **Edit | Find** operation in progress by pressing the **ESC** key. To search only part of your worksheet, first select the relevant cell range.

Replacing cell content

Anything that you can search for in a worksheet with **Edit | Find**, you can replace with a specified alternative.

1 Click in any cell, and choose **Edit | Replace**.

2 Type the text below in the **Find what** and **Replace with** boxes, and click **Replace**.

> Find what:
> Smith
>
> Replace with:
> Higgins

To perform a find-and-replace on only part of a worksheet, first select the relevant cell range. You can replace all occurrences of the found characters by clicking **Replace All**. You can delete from the selected cells the characters in the **Find what** box by leaving the **Replace with** box blank.

Spell-checking

Excel can check the spelling of text in all or part of a worksheet. To check your spelling, follow this procedure:

- Select the range of cells whose spelling you want to check. To check the whole worksheet, click any cell.

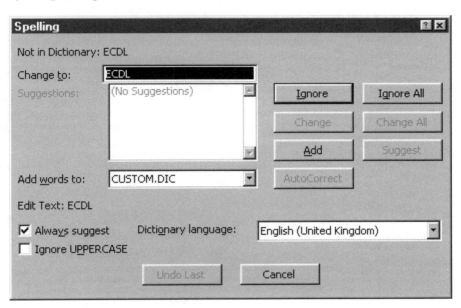

- Click the **Spelling** button on Excel's Standard toolbar.

Spelling button

When Excel meets a word that it does not recognize from its spelling dictionary (the same dictionary used by Microsoft Word), it displays the **Spelling** dialog box.

The following are your main options:

- **Ignore**: Leave this occurrence of the word unchanged.

- **Ignore All**: Leave this and all other occurrences of the word in the selected cells unchanged.

- **Change**: Correct this occurrence of the word, but prompt again on further occurrences.

- **Change All**: Correct this occurrence of the word – and all other occurrences without further prompting.

- **Add**: Add the word to the custom (your personal) dictionary. Use this option for the names of people or places, or abbreviations or acronyms, that you type regularly. Excel will recognize such added words during future spell-checks of any worksheet.

Set up print options

To view Excel's various printing options, choose **File | Page Setup** and inspect the following tabs of the dialog box: **Page**, **Margins**, **Header/Footer**, and **Sheet**.

- **Paper Size**: Located on the **Page** tab of the **File | Page Setup** dialog box, this option allows you to select the size of the paper you want to print on. The default is A4 (21 cm wide and 29.7 cm high).

- **Orientation**: Also on the **Page** tab, this is the direction in which the page is printed. Your options are Portrait ('standing up') and Landscape ('on its side').

- **Scaling**: Two scaling options on the **Page** tab enable you to reduce or enlarge the worksheet printout:

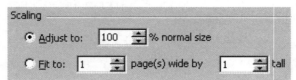

- **Adjust to**: On the **Page** tab you can enter a number in the range 10–400% of normal size. (You need not type the % symbol.)

- **Fit to**: This **Page** tab option reduces the worksheet (or selected cells) so that it fits on the specified number of pages. You can specify the number of pages vertically (tall), horizontally (wide), or both.

- **Margins**: You set the distances that the printed worksheet or selected cells are positioned in from the four edges of the printed page on the **Margins** tab. It is unlikely that you will need to change Excel's default margin values – top and bottom, 2.5 cm, left and right, 1.9 cm.

The **Margins** tab allows you to centre your worksheet or selected cells horizontally (positioned evenly between the left and right margins of the printed page), vertically (between the top and bottom margins), or both.

You can also specify separate margins for headers and footers, which are covered in the next topic.

- **Gridlines**: By default, Excel does not include cell boundary lines on printouts. You can change this setting by clicking the Gridlines checkbox on the **Sheet** tab.

Below is an example of a worksheet printout without and with gridlines selected.

	Jan	Feb	Mar
	323	566	429
	367	992	381
	445	394	1880
	1135	1952	2690

	Jan	Feb	Mar
	323	566	429
	367	992	381
	445	394	1880
	1135	1952	2690

About headers and footers

Headers and footers can be made to appear at the top and bottom of every page of a printed worksheet. They typically contain details such as file name, author name, date, and page number. You need only enter header and/or footer text once, and Excel repeats the text on every page. Here are a few facts about headers and footers in Excel:

- You insert them with the **Header/Footer** tab of the **File I Page Setup** command.
- The **Header/Footer** tab offers a pull-down list of suggested header and footer texts, from which you can choose the one that best suits your needs.
- You can edit and/or format your chosen header or footer text by clicking the **Custom header** or **Custom footer** button on the **Header/Footer** tab, and then selecting the required options.
- The **Custom** buttons enable you to format the header or footer text, and insert any or all of the following items: page number, total number of pages, date, time, Excel file name and worksheet name.
- When setting header and footer margins on the **Margins** tab of the **File I Page Setup** dialog box, ensure that the values are less than the top and bottom page margins – otherwise, the header and footer text may overlap the cells on the printout.

Insert a header and footer

Let's insert a header and footer in your Copy-Insert-Sort worksheet.

1 Click in any worksheet cell, choose **File | Page Setup**, and click the **Header/Footer** tab.

2 On the **Header** pull-down list, select the Excel workbook file name (Copy-Insert-Sort).

3 On the **Footer** pull-down list, select Page 1 of ?.

4 Click the **Custom Header** button, drag across the file name in the Center section to select it, and click the **Text Formatting** button.

5 Make the file name bold, and click **OK**.

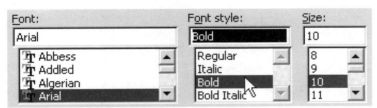

6 In the Left section, type My First Worksheet. In the Right section, type ECDL Module 4.

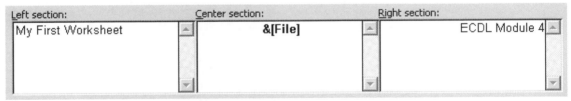

Date button

Time button

7 Click **OK** to return to the **Header/Footer** tab of the **Page Setup** dialog box.

8 Click the **Custom Footer** button, click in the Left section, and then click the **Date** button.

9 Click in the Right section, and then click the **Time** button.

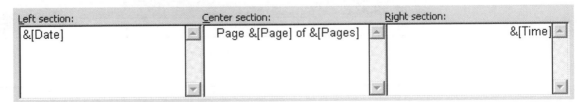

10 Click **OK** to return to the **Header/Footer** tab of the **Page Setup** dialog box. Click **OK** again to close the dialog box.

Well done. You have inserted a header and footer in your workbook. You cannot see headers and footers on screen; they appear on printouts only.

Preview your worksheet

Print Preview button

Excel offers a wide range of printing options, including the ability to preview a worksheet on your screen before you print it.

- To preview your worksheet, click the **Print Preview** button on the Standard toolbar or choose **File | Print Preview**. Click **Close** to return to your worksheet.

Print row titles on every page

For multi-page printouts you may find helpful to show the same cell titles on a single row across the top of every page. Follow these steps to discover how:

1   Click the **Sheet 2** tab at the bottom of your Copy-Insert-Sort worksheet.

2   Insert the following labels and numbers in the cells shown.

	A	B	C	D
1				
2		Jan	Feb	Mar
3		12	34	45
4		13	35	46

3   Select the cells B3:B214, and choose **Edit | Fill | Series**. In the dialog box displayed, select the options shown below, and click **OK**.

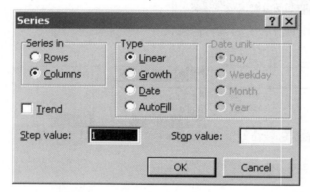

Repeat this action for cell ranges C3:C214 and D3:D214. You have now several pages of numbers to practice with.

4   Choose **File | Page Setup** and click the **Sheets** tab. Click the coloured box at the right of the *Rows to repeat at top* box.

Excel responds by displaying the **Page Setup – Rows to repeat at top** dialog box. You can reposition this dialog box on your screen if required.

5   On the worksheet, click any cell in the row that you want to use as the title row for every printed page. In this example, click anywhere in row 2.

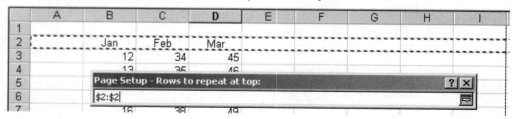

Excel displays a flashing marquee around your selected row.

6 On the *Standard* toolbar click the **Print Preview** button to inspect your work. As you can see from the partial screen below, the various pages all contains the same row of titles along their top top.

	A	B	C	D
1				
2		Jan	Feb	Mar
3		12	34	45

	A	B	C	D
2		Jan	Feb	Mar
54		63	85	96
55		64	86	97

Print your worksheet

When you choose **File | Print**, you have the following options regarding which parts of your workbook you may print:

- **All**: The current worksheet.

- **Pages**: To print one or a range of pages from the current worksheet, enter the page number(s) here.

- **Selection**: Prints only the currently selected cells on the current worksheet.

- **Entire Workbook**: All worksheets that contain data in the workbook.

Other options on the **Print** dialog box allow you to specify how many copies you want to print, and whether you want the pages collated or not. Let's try it.

1 Click in any worksheet cell.

2 Choose **File | Print**, accept the default options, and click **OK**.

About Excel templates

Excel allows you to save a workbook as a template which you can later use and reuse as a basis for quickly creating other, similar workbooks.

For example, you could create a workbook for use as an expense form, enter and format relevant text labels, place borders around certain cells, and enter the function =SUM(C2:C22) in cell C23 so that any numbers typed in the range C2:C22 are totalled and displayed in C23.

By saving such a workbook as a template, you speed up the process of creating further expense forms because the text, formatting and addition calculation need not be re-entered.

Save a workbook as a template

Follow these steps to save a workbook as a template:

1 Choose **File | Save As**.

2 Click the **Save as type** box and select Template from the list displayed.

3 Typically, Excel suggests that you save your templates in the following folder:

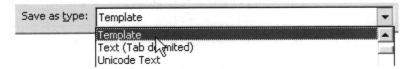

C:\os\Profiles\user_name\Application Data\Microsoft\Templates

where os is the operating system folder – for example, Windows. Accept or amend this location and default file name, as required, and click **Save**.

Open a workbook based on a saved template

The next time you want to create a workbook, you can start with that saved workbook template. Excel lists a template in the **File | New** dialog box if you have saved your workbook template file in the default templates folder.

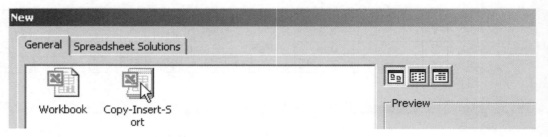

Work with earlier versions of Excel

While you can generally use a later version of the software to open and work with a workbook that was created in an earlier version, the reverse is not necessarily true. You can use the **File | Save As** command to save your Excel 2000 workbook in the file formats of previous versions of Excel. You have two main options:

■ Microsoft Excel 5.0/95 Workbook.

■ Any Earlier Excel Format.

Work with non-Excel formats

Other file formats in which you can save your Excel workbooks include Lotus 1-2-3 or Quattro Pro (two other spreadsheet applications) and dBASE (a database application).

Work with text-only formats

Excel's text-only options save just the currently displayed worksheet. To convert other worksheets of a workbook, switch to each sheet and save it separately. Two of the more commonly used plain-text options are:

■ **Text (tab-delimited):** In this format, cell entries in the same row but in different columns are separated from each other by tabs. Different rows are separated by paragraph breaks. The file name extension added is .txt. As you can see in the example below, text in the tab-delimited format does not necessarily line up vertically in neat columns.

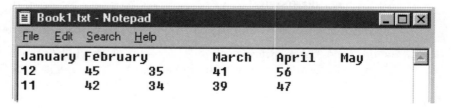

- **CSV (comma-delimited)**: Similar to tab-delimited, but with a comma rather than a tab separating cells on the same row.

The file name extension added is .csv, meaning comma separated values.

Text-only formats save only the text of a file. The word 'text' in this context includes numbers as well as alphabetic characters. All formatting is lost. This format is also called plain-text or ASCII format.

Work with HTML (web) format

You can save an Excel 2000 file in HTML format in either of two ways: choose **File | Save As web Page** or choose **File | Save As**, and select the **web Page** option. The worksheet cells are converted to table cells in the HTML file.

You can display and print HTML format files with a web browser application.

Import an image or graph

To insert an image in a worksheet, click a cell, choose **Insert | Picture**, and then select the relevant option. The range of options available to you depends on whether you have installed the Microsoft Office Clip Art Gallery and whether a scanner is attached to your computer.

- To reposition an inserted image, click on it to select it, and then drag the image to a different part of your worksheet.

- To resize an inserted image, click on it to select it, then click any sizing handle and drag the image to a different shape.

If you drag on a corner handle, the image expands and contracts proportionately to its current size; if you drag on an edge handle, the image expands or contracts in that direction only.

To insert a graph created in PowerPoint or another application, select it, copy it to the Clipboard, click in a worksheet cell, and paste it.

Import text with the Text Wizard

To insert a small amount of text in a single worksheet cell, copy the text to the Clipboard, click in a worksheet cell, and then paste it.

To import text containing numbers which you want Excel to interpret by arranging them correctly across rows and down columns, choose the **File | Open** command and select the text file to launch Excel's Text Wizard. Let's try it.

1 Using Notepad or another text editor, create a new file. Type the following five words, pressing the **TAB** key after each word except the last (do not type spaces between the words):

January February March April May

2 Press **ENTER** to move the cursor to a new line.

3 Type the following five numbers, pressing the **TAB** key after each one except the last (do not type spaces between the numbers):

12 45 35 41 56

4 Press **ENTER** to move the cursor to a new line.

5 Type the following five numbers, pressing the **TAB** key after each one except the last (again, do not type spaces between the numbers):

11 42 34 39 47

Your file should look as shown below. (The columns may not always line up vertically.)

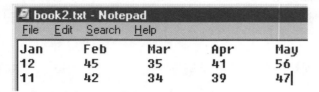

6 Save, name and close your text file. In Excel, choose **File | Open**, and select your text file.

7 Excel displays the first of three **Text Import Wizard** dialog boxes. Ensure that the field values in the top part of the dialog box are as shown.

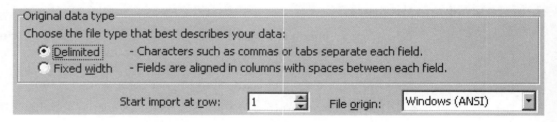

Click **Next**.

8 Excel displays the second **Text Import Wizard** dialog box. Ensure that the field values in the top part of the dialog box are as shown.

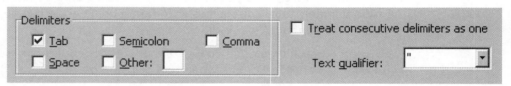

Click **Next**.

9 Excel displays the third **Text Import Wizard** dialog box. Ensure that the field values look as shown.

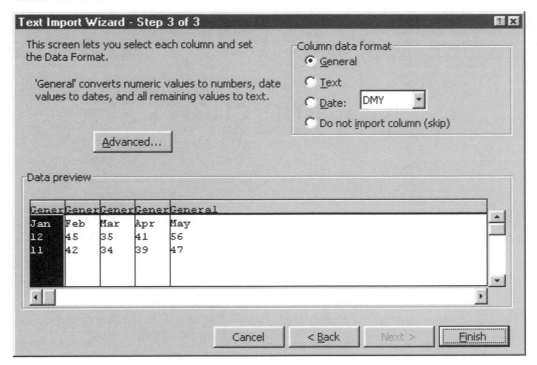

Click **Finish**.

10 Excel closes the Text Import Wizard and displays a worksheet that should look similar to that shown. The workbook file name will be the same as that of the text file.

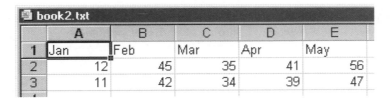

11 You can save and close your workbook, and close Excel.

Quit Excel

You can close your Copy-Insert-Sort.xls workbook and quit Excel. You have now completed Lesson 4.6 of the ECDL Spreadsheets Module.

4.7

Column charts

Learning goals

At the end of this lesson you should be able to:

- use Excel's Chart Wizard to create *column charts*;
- format chart text and change chart colours;
- change the scale of chart axes;
- add and edit chart titles and data labels;
- move, copy, resize and delete charts;
- print charts.

New terms

At the end of this lesson you should be able to explain the following terms:

Chart	A graphic or diagram based on the numbers, text and calculations that are located in the rows and columns of an Excel worksheet.
Chart Area	The margin area inside the chart boundaries but outside the actual plotted chart. It typically holds labels identifying the chart axes.
Plot Area	The area containing the actual plot. It is bounded by the two chart axes and is enclosed within the chart area.
Column Chart	Excel's default chart type, in which items are shown horizontally and values vertically.

You follow two main steps to create a *chart* in Excel:

Chart Wizard
button

- Select the cells whose contents you want to chart.

- Select and run Excel's Chart Wizard.

The Wizard's default options in its four dialog boxes are acceptable in most cases. When in doubt, click the Next button on the first three dialog boxes, and the Finish button on the fourth.

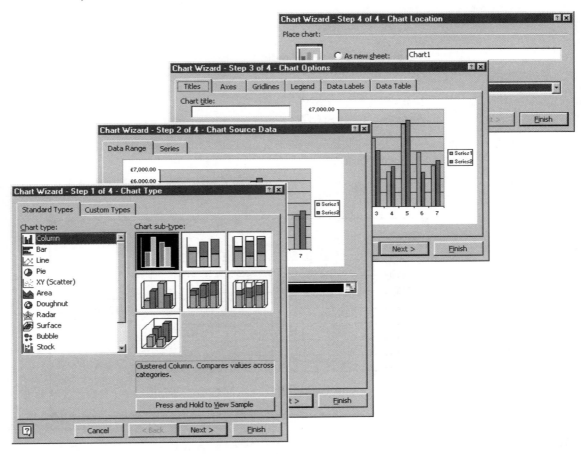

Chart components

A chart has two main regions: the *chart area* and the *plot area*.

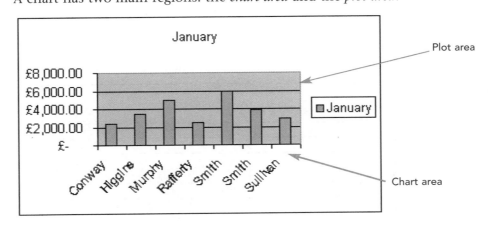

Create and save your Column-Charts workbook

Save button

1 Launch Excel, and choose **File | Save** or click the **Save** button on the Standard toolbar.

2 In the **Save** dialog box, save the new, empty workbook with the following file name and click **Save**:

Column-Charts

Create a column chart

1 In Sheet 1 of the new workbook, enter the text and numbers below in cell range B2:C5.

Jan	1200
Feb	1300
Mar	890
April	1432

Chart Wizard button

2 Select the cell range B2:C5, and click the **Chart Wizard** button on the Standard toolbar.

3 In the dialog box displayed, click **Finish**. Well done. You have created your first Excel chart.

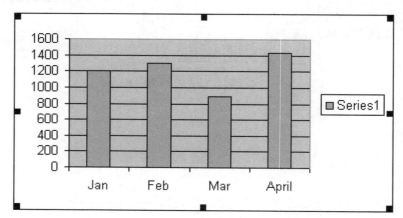

Remove the chart legend

Legend

A chart legend is unnecessary for such a simple chart as the one that you have created.

1 Click the legend in your chart to select it. It's in the chart area to the right of the plot area.

2 Press the **DELETE** key to remove it.

Excel expands the plot area horizontally to fill the chart area.

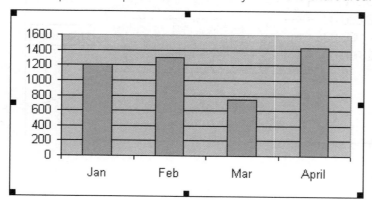

Add a chart title: method 1

A chart should have a title that describes its content. Here's how to insert a title directly in the chart.

1 Right-click on the white chart area, and choose **Chart Options** from the pop-up menu.

2 On the **Titles** tab of the dialog box displayed, type the Chart title of 'Monthly Sales'. Click **OK**.

By default, Excel centres the chart title in the chart area over the plot area.

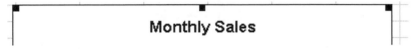

Add a chart title: method 2

A second way to give your chart a title is to type the title text in the worksheet cell directly above the list of numbers on which the chart is based. You then include this text cell in the selected cell range before clicking the **Chart Wizard** button. Follow these steps to discover how.

1 Click the white chart area, and press **DELETE** to remove your chart.

2 In cell C1, enter the following text: Monthly Sales.

3 Select the cell range B1:C5.

	A	B	C	D
1			Monthly Sales	
2		Jan	1200	
3		Feb	1300	
4		Mar	890	
5		April	1432	

4 Click the **Chart Wizard** button, and then click the **Finish** button in the dialog box displayed.

Excel creates a new chart that contains the chart title.

5 The chart legend also contains the chart title text. Click the legend and press the **DELETE** key.

Edit the chart title

1 To edit your chart's title, click it once to select it, and then click it a second time to make it editable. Excel places the text cursor inside the chart title box.

Monthly Sales ⟶ Monthly Sales

The text is now editable. The position of the cursor depends on where you positioned the mouse when you clicked on the chart title the second time.

2 Edit the text of the chart title as shown below.

Monthly Sales 2003

3 When finished, click anywhere else on the chart to deselect the chart title.

Add data labels to your columns

Data labels provide information about the source or size of your chart's columns. The first type are called text labels (or just labels) and the second type are value labels. Let's try each type.

1 Right-click the white chart area, and choose **Chart Options** from the pop-up menu.

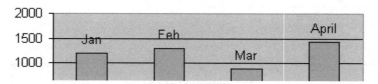

2 On the **Data Labels** tab of the dialog box displayed, select the **Show label** option, and click **OK**.

The tops of your columns now look as shown below.

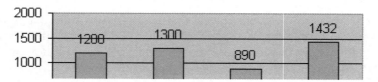

3 Repeat steps 1 and 2, but this time, select the **Show value** option. The tops of your columns now look as shown below.

You can have text or value labels, but not both. Adding data labels to your chart provides more information to the reader, but can make your chart more cluttered.

Format the chart text

You can format the text of the chart title, the data labels, and the axes.

1 To format the chart title, right-click it and choose **Format Chart Title** from the pop-up menu.

2 In the **Font** tab of the dialog box displayed, select a **Font Style** of Bold, a Size of 12, and a **Colour** of Green. Click **OK**.

3 To format the columns' data labels, right-click any label to select all the labels, and choose **Format Data Labels** from the pop-up menu.

4 In the **Font** tab of the dialog box displayed, select a **Font Style** of Italic. Click **OK**.

5 To format the X-(horizontal) axis text, right-click anywhere on the axis, and choose **Format Axis** from the pop-up menu.

6 In the **Font** tab of the dialog box displayed, select a **Font Style** of Bold. Click **OK**.

7 Repeat steps 5 and 6 for the Y-(vertical) axis. Your chart should now look as shown below.

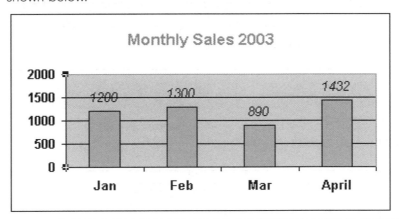

Change the chart colours

Don't like Excel's default chart colours? You can change the colours of the (white) chart area, the (grey) background of the plot area, and the (blue) columns.

1 Right-click the white chart area, and choose **Format Chart Area** from the pop-up menu.

2 On the **Patterns** tab of the dialog box displayed, click the colour Light Yellow in the **Area** section. Click **OK**.

3 Right-click on the grey plot area, and choose **Format Plot Area**.

4 On the **Patterns** tab of the dialog box displayed, click the colour Orange in the **Area** section. Click **OK**.

5 Right-click any column to select all four columns, and choose **Format Data Series**. (The columns represent the data series of the chart.)

6 On the **Patterns** tab of the dialog box displayed, click the colour Red in the **Area** section. Click **OK**. Your chart should now look as shown below (imagination required to see the full range of colours!).

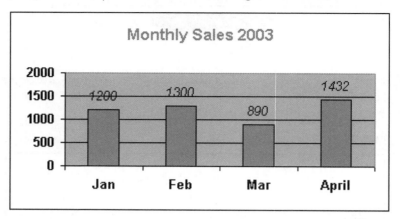

Monthly Sales 2003

Reposition and resize the chart

1 To move the chart to a different location on your worksheet, click the chart area and then drag with the mouse. Try it and see.

2 To make your chart larger or smaller, click the chart area. Next, click any sizing handle and drag the chart to a different shape.

If you drag a corner handle, the chart expands and contracts proportionately to its current size; if you drag on an edge handle, the chart expands or contracts in that direction only. Excel automatically adjusts the font size of text in your chart as you resize.

Practise changing the size of your chart.

Cut, copy or paste the chart

To copy or cut a chart, click the chart area and press **CTRL+c** or **CTRL+x**. You can then paste your chart to a different location on the same worksheet, or to a different worksheet or workbook.

1 Click your chart to select it, and press **CTRL+c** to copy it to the Clipboard.

2 Click cell B26, and press **CTRL+v**. Excel pastes your chart so that its top-left corner is over your selected cell.

3 At the bottom of your worksheet click the tab named Sheet2. Excel displays the second worksheet in your workbook.

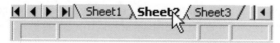

4 Click any cell in Sheet2 and press **CTRL+v** to paste the chart.

5 Choose **Edit | Undo** twice to undo your two paste actions.

Change the values in the chart

If you change the content of worksheet cells on which a chart is based, Excel automatically redraws the chart to reflect the changed value.

1 Double-click cell C4 in your worksheet.

2 Change its value from 890 to 1070.

Notice that Excel redraws the third column of your chart.

Rescale the vertical chart axis

If the chart columns are similar in size, you can focus on the differences between them by changing the minimum and maximum values of the Y-(vertical) axis. In your chart, the smallest column is 1070, and the largest is 1432.

1 Right-click the Y-(vertical axis), and choose **Format Axis** from the pop-up menu.

2 Set the **Minimum** Y value to 1000, and the **Maximum** to 1500. Excel updates the **Major** and **Minor unit** boxes automatically. Click **OK**.

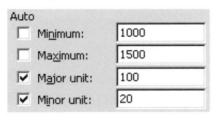

Your chart should now look as shown below.

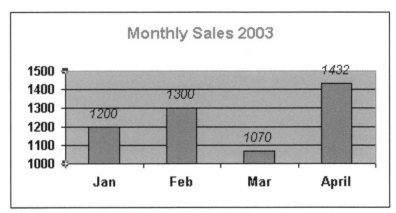

Print the chart

You can control how Excel prints a chart by choosing **File | Page Setup**, selecting your options on the **Chart** tab, and clicking **OK**.

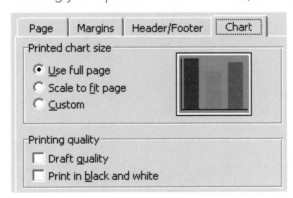

To print only a chart and no other part of a worksheet, click the chart to select it, and choose **File | Print**. In the **Print** dialog box, ensure that the **Selected Chart** option is selected, and click **OK**.

Quit Excel

You can close your Column-Charts.xls workbook and quit Excel. You have now completed Lesson 4.7 of the ECDL Spreadsheets Module.

4.8

Bar, line, pie and comparison charts

Learning goals	At the end of this lesson you should be able to:

- convert a column chart to the following non-default chart types: bar, line and pie;
- add data labels to pie chart slices;
- explode a pie chart slice;
- create a two-data series comparison chart;
- create a three-data series comparison chart.

New terms	At the end of this lesson you should be able to explain the following terms:
Bar Chart	A 'sideways' column chart that shows items vertically and values horizontally.
Pie Chart	These are typically used to illustrate the breakdown of figures in a total. A pie chart is always based on a single data series.
Data Point	An item being measured and its measured value.
Data Series	A group of related data points. For example, your data series may compare different items measured at the same time, or a single item measured at different times.

Excel's default chart type is a column chart. The quickest way to create a *bar*, line or *pie* chart is to first create a default column chart, and then change the chart type.

Most chart types offer sub-types or variations. You can preview how your data will look in a particular chart type by clicking the **Press and Hold to View Sample** button within the **Chart Wizard** dialog box.

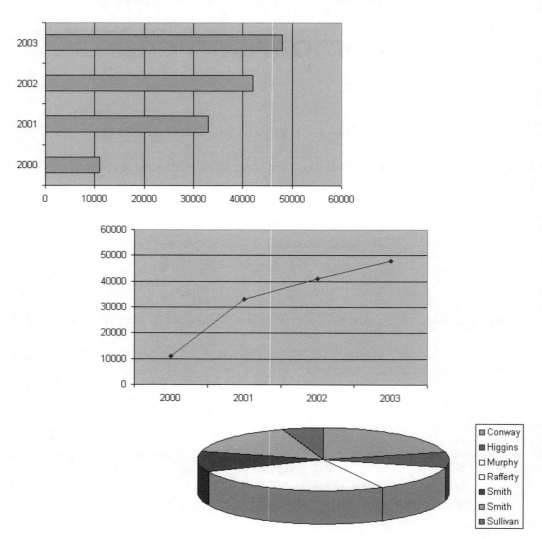

All charting is based on two very basic ideas: the data point and the data series. A *data point* is a single item (such as 1st Qtr Sales) and its numerical value (such as £320,000). A collection of data points is called a *data series*. For instance, a data series may the entire company's sales figures for different months. Or it may compare sales figures for a single month from different departments.

The chart you worked on in the previous lesson was an example of a single data series chart. Charts that contain multiple data series are sometimes called comparison charts.

Create and save your Other-Charts workbook

Save button

1 Launch Excel, and choose **File | Save** or click the **Save** button on the Standard toolbar.

2 In the **Save** dialog box, give the new, empty workbook the following file name and click **Save**:

    OtherCharts

Change from a column to a bar chart

1 Enter the following text and numbers in cell range B1:C5.

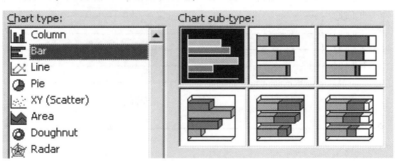

B	C
	Annual Sales
2000	12300
2001	34912
2002	42108
2003	48722

Chart Wizard button

2 Select the cell range B1:C5, click the **Chart Wizard** button on the Standard toolbar, and in the dialog box displayed, click **Finish**.

3 Right-click anywhere on your chart, and choose **Chart Type** from the pop-up menu.

4 In the **Chart type** list, select Bar. In the **Chart sub-type** list, accept the default option of the first sub-type, and click **OK**.

5 Click the chart area, and drag your chart to position it just to the right of cell range B1:C5.

6 Click the chart legend and press the **DELETE** key. You new chart should look as shown below.

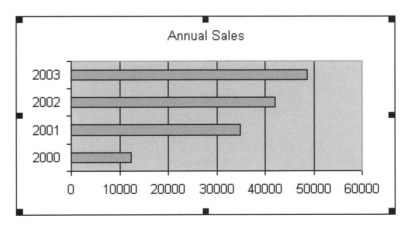

Change from a column to a line chart

1   Click your new bar chart, and press **CTRL+c** to copy it to the Clipboard.

2   Click cell D16, and press **CTRL+c** to paste the bar chart.

3   Right-click anywhere on your chart, and choose **Chart type** from the pop-up menu.

4   Select the options shown, and click **OK**.

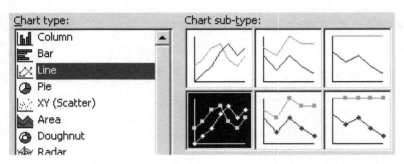

5   Click the chart area, and drag your chart to position it just beneath your bar chart.

6   Click the chart legend, and press the **DELETE** key. You new chart should look as shown below.

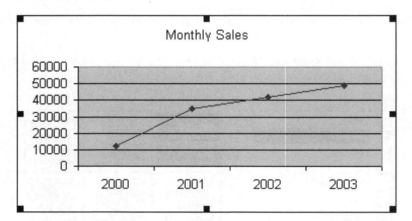

Create a pie chart

1   Enter the text and numbers shown below in cells B29:D35 of your worksheet.

	A	B	C	D
28				
29		Conway	John	2356
30		Higgins	Tracey	3463
31		Murphy	Robert	4921
32		Rafferty	Aidan	2512
33		Smith	Catherine	5951
34		Smith	Zowie	3872
35		Sullivan	Andrew	2903

2   Select the non-adjacent cell range B29:B35, D29:D35, click the **Chart Wizard** button, and in the dialog box displayed, click **Finish**.

3   Right-click anywhere on your chart, and choose **Chart type** from the pop-up menu.

4 In the **Chart type** dialog box, select Pie chart as the **Chart type**, and Pie with a 3D visual effect as the **sub-type**. Click **OK**.

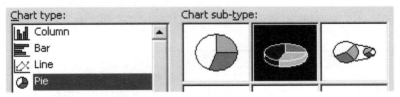

5 Click the chart area, and drag your chart to position it just to the right of cell range B29:D35. Your chart should look as shown below.

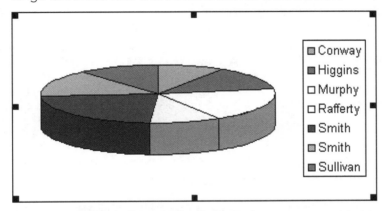

Add data labels to pie chart slices

1 Double-click on the pie chart plot area.

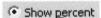

2 On the **Data Labels** tab of the dialog box displayed, select the option **Show Percent**, and click **OK**.

Notice how Excel shrinks the plot area to make room for the percentage data labels.

Explode a pie chart slice

You can emphasize one slice of a pie chart by 'exploding' it – that is, moving the slice away from the remainder of the plot area.

1 Click once in the plot area. This selects all the pie's slices.

2 Click on the slice you want to explode to select that slice only. For example, click the largest slice, the one with the 23% data label.

3 Drag the selected slice down and to the left. Your pie chart should now look as shown.

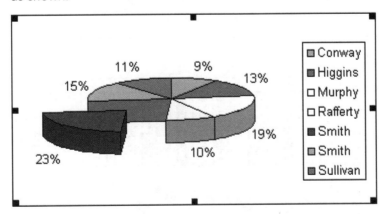

4 Click the chart area of your pie chart, and drag it to the right until its top-left corner is positioned over cell H29.

Create a two-data series comparison chart

1 Enter the additional text and numbers in your worksheet as shown below. You now have data for three data series: one for January, a second for February, and a third for March.

	A	B	C	D	E	F
28				Jan	Feb	March
29		Conway	John	2356	3465	3980
30		Higgins	Tracey	3463	3760	4100
31		Murphy	Robert	4921	5002	5398
32		Rafferty	Aidan	2512	3498	4875
33		Smith	Catherine	5951	6023	6298
34		Smith	Zowie	3872	4002	4321
35		Sullivan	Andrew	2903	3009	3234

2 Select the non-adjacent cell range B28:B35, D28:E35. Your cell range includes the text labels Jan and Feb above the two columns of values.

3 Click the **Chart Wizard** button, and in the dialog box displayed, click **Finish**. Your chart should look as shown below. Excel automatically applies different colours to the columns that represent different data series.

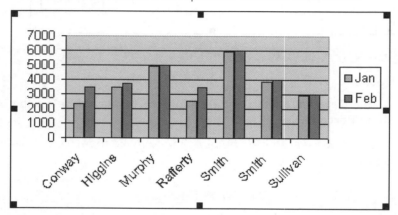

Click the chart area of your comparison chart, and drag it until it is positioned beneath your pie chart.

Create a three-data series comparison chart

1 Select the non-adjacent cell range B28:B35, D28:F35. Your cell range includes the text labels Jan, Feb and March above the three columns of values.

2 Click the **Chart Wizard** button, and in the dialog box displayed, click **Finish**. Your chart should look as shown below.

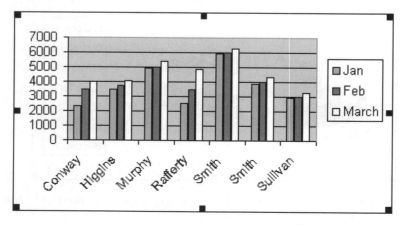

You can close your Other-Charts.xls workbook and quit Excel. Congratulations! You have now completed Module 4 of the ECDL, Spreadsheets. To remind yourself of the main features of Excel, cut out the quick reference guide, called **spreadsheet essentials**, at the back of the book and keep it next to your computer.

Databases

An artist was once asked, if his house was on fire, and he could take only one thing with him, what would that one thing be? His reply was 'I would take the fire, for its passion would inspire me.'

If all the software applications on a computer were similarly threatened, is there a single one that might be more important than others? Yes. Of the many applications that computers can perform, there is one that modern organizations have come to rely on most critically. We are talking about databases.

A database is a collection of information that is related to a particular subject, such as the employees in a firm, the parts in a warehouse, or the collection of music CDs in your home. Databases existed long before computers. Address books, card indexes and telephone directories are all examples of databases. But by storing your facts in a database on a computer, you gain the power to manage and manipulate that information – even very large amounts of information – in a variety of ways.

Microsoft® Access is an application that enables you to create and work with databases. In this module you will discover how to build databases to suit particular needs, view information in a database from different perspectives, sort and select particular pieces you are interested in, and produce printed reports.

5.1

Databases and database objects

Learning goals   At the end of this lesson you should be able to:

- start and quit Access;
- open an Access database;
- view database objects using the tabs of the Database window;
- open, navigate and close a table;
- create a new database;
- save and copy a database with My Computer or Windows Explorer;
- hide and display the main Access toolbar.

New terms   At the end of this lesson you should be able to explain the following terms:

Database Management System (DMBS)	An application such as Microsoft Access that enables you to collect information on a computer, organize it in different ways, sort and select pieces of information of interest to you, and produce reports.
Table	A collection of records that contain the same fields. A database may contain one or more tables.
Record	One complete set of fields relating to the same subject.
Field	A single piece of information about a subject. More precisely, it is the space where that information is held.
Database window	The 'control panel' of Acess. By clicking on its tabs, you can open and work with any of the database objects, including tables, forms, queries and reports.

Databases? What are they?

A database is a collection of information relating to the same topic or subject matter. It is usually organized in such a way that you can easily:

- find the items of information you are interested in, and

- file away the new items that you come across.

A database does not have to be kept on a computer. For example, address books, card indexes and telephone directories are all databases – even though very few people would call them that!

Computer databases

You can manipulate large amounts of information more efficiently with computer-based databases than with paper-based ones. For example, using a paper-based telephone directory, it is relatively easy to find a person's telephone number, but it is very difficult (but not impossible) to find the person's name if you only have their telephone number.

With a computer-based directory, however, you can find that information quickly and easily. You could also find the names of everyone who lives on a particular road, or everyone whose first name was 'Paul'. Or you could print a report showing the five most common surnames.

Microsoft Access is an example of a *database management system* – an application that allows you to work with databases.

Information – and how it's viewed

An Access database holds at least one *table* of information; each table has a number of *records*; and each record has a number of *fields*. A field is a single piece of information about a subject. A record is one complete set of fields relating to the same subject. And a table is a collection of records.

But that is not all. In addition to the information stored in tables, an Access database can also hold different ways of looking at that information. These different views of the information include forms, queries and reports. In common with tables, all these items are called database objects.

Launch Microsoft Access

Microsoft
Access

- Double-click the Microsoft Access icon or choose **Start | Programs | Microsoft Access**.

Access shows a dialog box that offers a number of options, including the following.

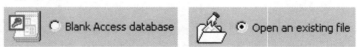

Click **Cancel** to close the dialog box. You can now work with the usual Windows-style toolbar buttons and pull-down menus to create a new database or update an existing one.

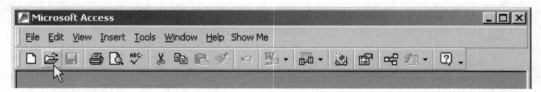

Maximize the Microsoft Access window

Maximize
button

You can open lots of windows from the main Microsoft Access window. For this reason, if the main Access window does not fill your screen when you launch the application, it's a good idea to maximize it by clicking the **Maximize** button near the top right of the window.

Open an Access database

Open
button

1 Click the **Open** button on the Standard toolbar or choose **File | Open**.

2 Select the database file you want from the **Open** dialog box.

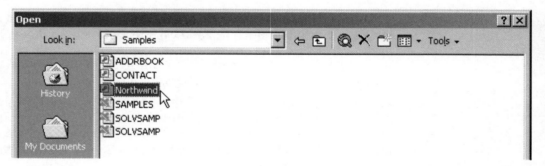

3 Click the **Open** button.

Practise your database-opening skills by locating and opening the sample Northwind database that comes with Microsoft Access. It is usually located in the following folder:

    C:\Program Files\Microsoft Office\Office\Samples\

The file names of Access databases end in .mdb (Microsoft database). This helps you to distinguish Access files from other file types such as Excel spreadsheets (.xls) or Word documents (.doc).

Explore the Database window

It's the first screen that you see when you open an Access database, it's a kind of a 'control centre' – and you really need to get to know your way around it. We are talking about the *Database window*.

Below is the upper part of the Database window that Access displays when you open the sample Northwind database.

The Database window displays a different tab for each type of object associated with the currently open database. For the ECDL, only the first four object types and their tabs are relevant: you don't need to worry about Pages, Macros and Modules.

Click an object type at the left of the Database window to display its tab. Below are the upper parts of four tabs for the sample Northwind database: **Tables**, **Queries**, **Forms** and **Reports**.

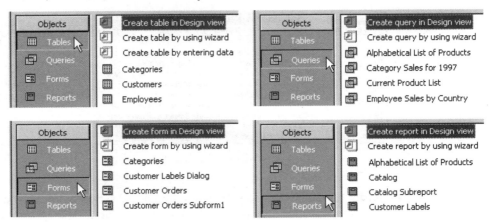

Distinguish between actions and the objects

In a Database window, the tab for each database object type lists two very different types of item:

- **Actions**: The first two or three items listed are always actions. They begin with the word 'Create'. If you double-click an action, Access responds by creating a new object. After you create a new database, only actions are listed on the tabs of the Database window.

- **Objects**: The items listed after the two or three actions are objects – the results of actions. If you double-click one of these, Access responds by opening and displaying the relevant object.

Typically, you will select objects much more frequently than actions. In other words, you will work with already existing objects much more frequently than you will create new ones.

Open a database table

A *table* is the basic, fundamental database object: this is where the data lives. Other types of database objects such as forms, queries and reports are ways of looking at the information that has been entered in a table. A single database can have several tables.

Follow these steps to display a table:

Open button

1 Open the database file that contains the table you want to view. Access displays the Database window for your selected database.

Tables button

2 If the **Tables** tab is not displayed by default, click the **Tables** button at the left of the Database window. Some databases contain several tables. Others contain just one.

Double-click the table to open it

3 Double-click your required table to open it.

When you open a table, Access displays it in a separate window. The Database window remains open in the background.

Explore a database table: records and fields

The screen below shows part of the Employees table from the sample Northwind database. The type of information it contains gives you a good idea of how tables are used.

	Employee ID	Last Name	First Name	Title	Title Of	Birth Date	Hire Date
▶ ⊞	1	Davolio	Nancy	Sales Representative	Ms.	08-Dec-1968	01-May-1992
⊞	2	Fuller	Andrew	Vice President, Sales	Dr.	19-Feb-1952	14-Aug-1992
⊞	3	Leverling	Janet	Sales Representative	Ms.	30-Aug-1963	01-Apr-1992
⊞	4	Peacock	Margaret	Sales Representative	Mrs.	19-Sep-1958	03-May-1993
⊞	5	Buchanan	Steven	Sales Manager	Mr.	04-Mar-1955	17-Oct-1993
⊞	6	Suyama	Michael	Sales Representative	Mr.	02-Jul-1963	17-Oct-1993
⊞	7	King	Robert	Sales Representative	Mr.	29-May-1960	02-Jan-1994
⊞	8	Callahan	Laura	Inside Sales Coordinator	Ms.	09-Jan-1958	05-Mar-1994
⊞	9	Dodsworth	Anne	Sales Representative	Ms.	02-Jul-1969	15-Nov-1994

Record: ◄◄ ◄ 1 ► ►I ►* of 9

Tables arrange information in horizontal rows called *records* and vertical columns called *fields*.

■ **Fields**: Fields are the spaces where individual types of information are held, such as a first name, telephone number or product description.

When a table contains more vertical columns of information than can be shown in the table window, use the horizontal scroll-bar to move right and left. If you can't see the horizontal scroll-bar, click the **Maximize** button at the top right of the table window to display it.

■ **Records**: A record is the set of fields relating to a single record.

When a table contains more records than can be shown in the table window, use the vertical scroll-bar to move up and down the range of records.

Alternatively, click the navigation buttons displayed at the lower left of the table window.

Button	Description
I◄	Places the cursor in the very first record at the top of the table.
◄	Places the cursor in the previous record.
►	Places the cursor in the next record.
►I	Places the cursor in the very last record at the bottom of the table.

10

Entering a record number

You can also enter a record number directly and press **ENTER** to go to that record.

Close a table

To close a table, click the **Close** button at the top right of the table window – not the **Close** button at the top right of the main Access window.

Create a new database

New button

Database
The Database
icon

Follow these steps to create a new database in Access:

1   Click the **New** button on the Access toolbar.

2   In the **General** tab of the **New** dialog box, click the Database icon, and click **OK**.

3   In the **File New Database** dialog box, specify the folder where you want to store your new database file, and enter a database file name.

Access assumes that the file type is Microsoft Access Databases. You need not type the file name extension of .mdb. Access adds it automatically.

4   Click the **Create** button.

Access then displays the Database window, with the **Tables** tab shown by default. Notice that none of the four main tabs – **Tables**, **Queries**, **Forms** and **Reports** – contains any objects.

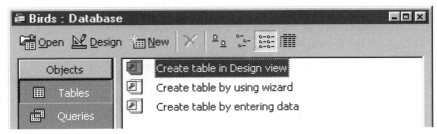

Practise your database-building skills by creating the sample Bookworm database that you will use throughout this module.

■   Click the **New** button on the Access toolbar. In the **New** dialog box, click the **General** tab, click the Database icon, and then click **OK**. Then in the **File New Database** dialog box, specify the folder where you want to store your new database file, type the following database file name, and click the **Create** button:

    Bookworm

That's it. You will add a table to your new Bookworm database in Lesson 5.2.

Save a database

As you work with a table or other object in a database, Access saves the database object as you proceed. So there is no need to save the database file that contains the object.

Copy a database

You cannot copy a database from within Access. Instead, follow these steps to copy a database to another location, such as a diskette or other backup medium.

1 Close the database that you want to copy.

2 Launch Windows Explorer or My Computer, and locate the folder that contains the database file.

3 Select the Microsoft Access database file.

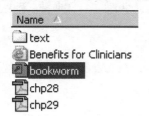 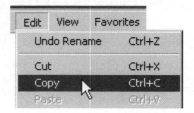

4 Copy the file to the new location.

Delete a database

You cannot delete a database from within Access. Instead, follow these steps:

1 Close the database that you want to delete.

2 Launch Windows Explorer or My Computer, and locate the folder that contains the database file.

3 Select the database file, and delete it, for example by clicking the toolbar **Delete** button.

Delete button

Hide and display Access toolbars

The most frequently used functions are available as buttons on the Access toolbar. Access displays the most suitable buttons for the functions that you are most likely to use at any one time.

If you want to hide the toolbar (and choose all your options from the menus), or if you want to display other toolbars, choose **View | Toolbar** and select the toolbars that you want displayed.

In addition to the main toolbar at the top of the Access window, the Database window itself has its own toolbar. The buttons differ slightly depending on which tab is displayed – **Tables**, **Forms**, **Queries** or **Reports**.

Quit Access

■ To leave Access, choose **File | Exit** or click the **Close** button at the top right of the Access window.

You can close your Bookworm.mdb database and quit Access. You have now completed Lesson 5.1 of the ECDL Databases Module.

5.2

Meet the Table Wizard

Learning goals	At the end of this lesson you should be able to:

- start the Access Table Wizard;
- select a suitable sample table from the list provided by the Table Wizard;
- select from your chosen sample table the fields you want in your table;
- rename fields selected from the Wizard's sample;
- name and save a new table;
- select a primary key to uniquely identify each record in a table.

New terms	At the end of this lesson you should be able to explain the following terms:
Table Wizard	A feature that simplifies the creation of new tables by offering a range of sample tables and a series of easy-to-follow dialog boxes.
Primary key	A field in a table that is used to identify uniquely each record in the table.

Choosing a sample table

Get ready to build your first table in Access! This is not as intimidating a task as it may sound. Access comes with a built-in *Table Wizard* that greatly simplifies the process of creating a new table.

This wizard creates a new table to store data.

The Table Wizard includes dozens of sample tables, so that you can base your new table on an existing one. This is so much easier and faster than creating a new table from scratch.

You simply choose a sample table that most resembles the new table that you want to create, and let the Table Wizard take care of all the behind-the-scenes work for you.

Customizing the sample table

Your chosen sample table may be similar to the new table that you want to create, but it's unlikely to be exactly the same. It would be impossible for anyone – even Microsoft – to anticipate precisely what you want to do with your new table.

Don't worry. The Access Table Wizard allows you to customize your chosen sample table according to your individual requirements.

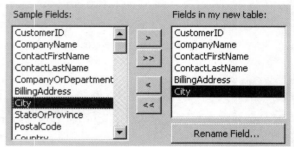

For example, you probably won't want every field from the sample table included in your table, so you can specify which ones you want, and which you don't.

Typically, you will also want to rename at least some of the fields that you have selected from the sample table.

Saving and naming your table

In the same way that you must name and save a database file, you must also name and save an individual table within the database file.

It's essential to select a so-called *primary key* for your new table. The primary key is the field that will identify each record in the table uniquely. Fields selected as the primary key typically have names such as Part Number, Product Code, Employee ID, and so on.

Ready? Let's go and build a table.

Open your Bookworm database

Open button

1 Launch Microsoft Access, click the **Open** button on the Access toolbar or choose **File | Open**.

2 Select the following database file and click **Open**.

Bookworm

This is the database that you created in Lesson 5.1. It is currently empty – that is, it does not contain any database objects: no tables, queries, forms or reports.

In this lesson you will create a table named Books within the Bookworm database.

Explore the Table Wizard

Access contains a Table Wizard that simplifies the process of creating a new table in a database. You start the Table Wizard by double-clicking the option below on the **Tables** tab of the Database window.

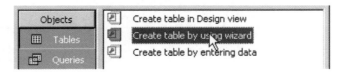

The Wizard presents four dialog boxes. Each is called 'Table Wizard', and contains a number of sub-steps.

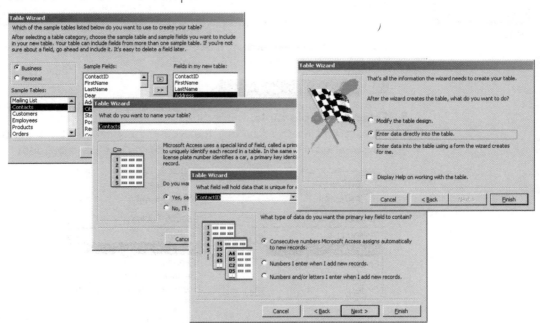

The following table summarizes each of the four **Table Wizard** dialog boxes.

Dialog box	Description
Table Wizard (1)	You select the sample table that most resembles the new one that you want to create. You then select the fields from the sample table that you want to include in your table. Optionally, you can rename one or more of your included fields.
Table Wizard (2)	You enter a table name for your new table, and specify that you want to select the table's primary key. The primary key is the field that identifies each record in the table uniquely.
Table Wizard (3)	You select the primary key, and specify the primary key type: either an automatically assigned number or one that you enter for each record.
Table Wizard (4)	Finally, you tell Access what you want to do with your new table. Typically, you indicate that you want to enter data in your new table.

Use the Table Wizard to create your sample Books table

Practise your table-building skills by creating the sample Books table within your Bookworm database.

Tables button

1 **Open the database:** If the Bookworm database is not already open, open it now. Click the **Tables** button at the right of the Database window.

2 **Start the Table Wizard:** You do this by double-clicking the option below on the Tables tab of the Database window.

3 **Select a sample table:** In this step you 'recycle' an existing sample table that most resembles the new one that you want to create. Click the **Business** or **Personal** options to view the sample tables in each category.

For the new Books table that you want to create, select the **Personal** option, and from the list of tables within that category, select the table named **Books**.

4 **Select your required fields:** You probably don't want every field from the sample table included in your new table. The **Sample Fields** list shows all the fields supplied with the selected sample table. The **Fields in my new table** list shows only the fields that you have decided to include in your new table. Initially, this second list is empty.

You use the following buttons to move fields between the two lists.

Button	Description
>	Moves the selected field from the sample table to your new table.
>>	Moves all fields from the sample table to your new table.
<	Removes the previously selected field from the new table.
<<	Removes all previously selected fields from the new table.

For your Bookworm table, move the following fields from the **Sample Fields** list to the **Fields in my new table** list:

ISBNNumber, Title, Pages, CopyrightYear, PurchasePrice, DatePurchased and Notes.

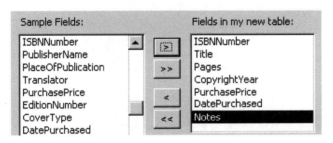

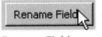
5 **Rename your selected fields:** Typically, you will want to rename at least some of the fields that you have selected from the sample table. To rename a field, click the field to select it in the **Fields in my new table** list, and then click the **Rename Field** button.

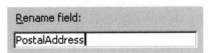

Type the field's new name in the **Rename field** dialog box and click **OK**. Repeat this procedure for as many fields as you want to rename.

For your Books table, rename four of your selected fields as follows.

Old name	New name
ISBNNumber	ISBN
PurchasePrice	Cost
DatePurchased	PurchaseDate
Notes	Comments

When finished, click the **Next** button to display the second of the four **Table Wizard** dialog boxes.

6 **Name your new table:** What name do you want to give your new table? You type it in the box provided at the top of the second dialog box. Type the name shown below.

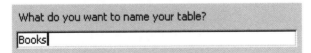

7 **Specify that you want to select your primary key:** Access displays the following question.

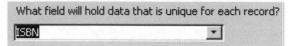

Do you want the wizard to set a primary key for you?

The primary key is the field that identifies each record in the table uniquely. Respond as follows.

    ⊙ No, I'll set the primary key.

Click the **Next** button to display the third of the four **Table Wizard** dialog boxes.

8 **Select your primary key:** At the top left of the new dialog box, confirm that **ISBN** is the field that you want to use as the primary key.

What field will hold data that is unique for each record?

ISBN   ▼

9 **Select your primary key type:** Access prompts you to specify the primary key type. See the box opposite entitled 'About primary keys' for more details about these options.

For your Books table, select the option below.

    ⊙ Numbers and/or letters I enter when I add new records.

Click the **Next** button to display the fourth and final **Table Wizard** dialog box.

10 **Prepare to enter data directly:** In the final dialog box Access prompts you as follows.

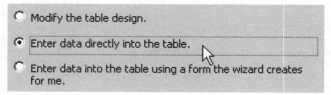

That's all the information the wizard needs to create your table.

After the wizard creates the table, what do you want to do?

Well, a table without data is pretty boring, so you probably want to enter data directly into the table without further delay. So click the second of the three options.

○ Modify the table design.

⊙ Enter data directly into the table.

○ Enter data into the table using a form the wizard creates for me.

Click the **Finish** button to complete the Table Wizard process.

Access now displays your new table in a separate window. Along the top are column headings that show your field names, and underneath is a single, blank row.

ISBN	Title	Pages	Copyright Year	Cost	PurchaseDate	Comments

You will enter data in your new table in Lesson 5.3. For the moment, close your new Books table by clicking the **Close** button at the top right of the table window – not the **Close** button at the top right of the main Access window.

About primary keys

In the telephone directory there are many people listed with the surname Smith; a number of them share the same first name, John. To find the one you want, you need some more information: where do they live? Even that might not be enough – father and son might have the same name and you might have to ask them some further questions to confirm that you are talking to the right one.

In a database table, that obviously is not satisfactory. Access needs to know which John Smith you mean. And you don't want to send a bill, or, worse still, a cheque to the wrong John Smith. So you must give each record an identifier, called a primary key, which is unique to that record – it is not shared with any other. When running the Table Wizard, Access displays the following prompt:

> What type of data do you want the primary key field to contain?

Each of the three possible responses has its particular advantages and disadvantages.

> ⦿ Consecutive numbers Microsoft Access assigns automatically to new records.

This option requires the least user effort, but also offers the least flexibility. Access simply applies the next available number to every new record that you insert in the table. If the previously entered record was 1234, for example, the next one will be record 1235. You don't need to type the 1235, but you cannot change the automatically assigned number either.

> ○ Numbers I enter when I add new records.

> ⦿ Numbers and/or letters I enter when I add new records.

Option two or three is a better choice when the items you want to insert in your table already have product or part numbers that can serve as their primary key. When you insert a new record in the table, you type this number along with the rest of the record's details. Which of these two options you select depends on whether the unique product identifier is a number (such as 1234) or a sequence of numbers and letters (such as 123-ABC/03D).

CopyrightYear or Copyright Year?

You will have noticed that all the field names in your sample Books table consist of a single, continuous string of characters, even when they contain more than one word. Why CopyrightYear and PurchaseDate instead of Copyright Year and Purchase Date?

The answer is that this is a throwback to the times when, due to software limitations, field names in a database table could contain only a single world. Microsoft Access does not impose this restriction. You can, for example, rename the 'Titles' field in your Books table to 'Titles of my Books'. Old database habits die hard, however, and that is why this convention continues to be widely used.

Quit Access

You can close your Bookworm.mdb database and quit Access. You have now completed Lesson 5.2 of the ECDL Databases Module.

5.3

More about tables

Learning goals

At the end of this lesson you should be able to:

- adjust the width of a column in a table;
- enter data in a table;
- edit data previously entered in a table;
- use the Undo option, and recognize its limitations;
- copy, cut and paste records within and between tables;
- delete a record from a table;
- hide and unhide a column in a table;
- freeze and unfreeze a column in a table;
- reorder columns in a table;
- save changes to a table's layout;
- copy a table;
- delete a table;
- use Microsoft Access online help.

New term

At the end of this lesson you should be able to explain the following term:

Table layout changes

Changes to the appearance and/or structure of a table. These will be lost if not saved. Changes to the content of records in a table are saved automatically.

Entering and editing data in a table

One aspect of table creation that no wizard can help you with is data entry: only you can do that. The input and updating of data in a table may be tiresome tasks, but they are essential skills that you need to learn.

When you create a new table, Access displays column headings that show your selected field names above a single, blank row. You can type record details into the blank row. As soon as you enter one record, Access opens up a new line underneath, so that there is always a blank record at the end where you can enter the next one.

	Product ID	Product Name	Product Description	Supplier ID	Units In Stock
▶	1	Widget Big	A Big widget	101	2000
▶	2	Widget Small	A small widget	102	2500
▶	(AutoNumber)				

Products : Table

When you can undo, and when you can't

Undo button

Access behaves differently to other Microsoft Office applications in the way that it saves data. In most applications, you can use the Undo feature to reverse just about every typing action, button click or menu command. Access does have an Undo option, but it's very limited.

When you type something in the field of an Access table, and then press the ENTER or TAB key, or click in another field, there is no going back. Access saves your entry automatically. There is no way to recover the previous field content. The Undo option is available only before you press ENTER or TAB, or click anywhere else.

For this reason, it's a *very* good idea to make regular backup copies of your Access database files and keep them in a safe place.

Columns: hiding, freezing and reordering them

There is nothing so good that it cannot be improved upon. Now that you have built your first table, and entered data in it, you need to learn how to make changes to its appearance.

In this lesson you will discover how to change the width of your table's columns, hide and unhide them, freeze and unfreeze them, and amend the order in which they appear.

Open your Bookworm database

Open button

1 Launch Microsoft Access, click the **Open** button on the Access toolbar or choose **File | Open**.

2 Select the following database file and click **Open**:

Bookworm

This is the database that you created in Lesson 5.1, and contains the table that you built with the Table Wizard in Lesson 5.2.

Adjust column width

When you create a new table, all its columns have the same width. The example below shows the Books table you created in Lesson 5.2.

You may find that some columns are too narrow and others too wide.

Click on the right column boundary to change column width

■ To change the width of a column, click on its right column boundary. Notice that the cursor changes shape to a double-headed arrow. Drag the cursor left or right until the column is the right size.

■ To adjust the width of a column so that it fits the longest entry in that column, double-click its right column boundary in the column header.

Adjust the column widths of your Books table as shown below. Don't worry about the Comments field for the moment.

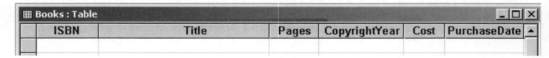

Now that you have adjusted its column widths, you are ready to enter data in your Books table.

Enter data in a table

To enter data in the currently open table, click in a field and type the data. You can move from field to field using the **TAB** key or the **ARROW** keys.

If your primary key is automatically assigned by Access, such as in the example below, the field designated as the primary key contains the word AutoNumber. You cannot enter a new number in this field or change an existing one.

Product ID	Product Name	Product Description	Supplier ID	Units In Stock
1	Widget Big	A Big widget	101	2000
2	Widget Small	A small widget	102	2500
(AutoNumber)				

Products : Table

Enter data in your Books table

Your Books table does not have any data in it. So enter the data shown below. Let's walk through the entry of the first record step by step.

1 Click in the ISBN field, type 597-7, and then click in the Title field to its right.

Notice that as soon as you type the first digit (5) in the ISBN field, Access opens a second, new record beneath it.

2 With the cursor in the Title field, type the following text: The BFG

3 Click in the Pages field, and type the following number: 202

4 Click in the CopyrightYear field, and type the following: 1982

5 Click in the Cost field, and type the following number: 3.99

Notice that Access automatically adds the currency symbol (£).

6 Click in the PurchaseDate field, and type the following date: 01/05/00.

As soon as you type any number in this date field, Access inserts two forward slashes (/) to separate the day from the month, and the month from the year. Access also displays your entered two-digit year (00) as a four-digit year (2000).

When finished, press **ENTER** or click in any field of the next record.

7 Do not enter any text in the Comments fields for the moment.

Well done. You have entered your first record in a table. It should look as shown below.

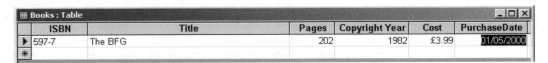

(Note that real ISBN codes have 10 characters. To minimize typing of the sample Books table, only four are used.)

Now enter the following 17 records in your table in addition to the one already present.

ISBN	Title	Pages	CopyrightYear	Cost	PurchaseDate
389-X	Love in the Time of Cholera	370	1985	5.95	24/02/98
670-8	Animal Farm	160	1945	6.99	03/04/99
069-3	Little Women	344	1868	6.99	24/02/98
010-9	Emma	302	1816	4.99	30/11/01
011-7	Jane Eyre	345	1847	4.99	13/09/98
016-8	Great Expectations	412	1861	4.99	13/09/98
066-4	Mansfield Park	287	1814	8.99	03/04/99
414-2	The Name of the Rose	450	1983	5.95	07/07/99
893-1	Chocolat	250	1999	6.99	01/05/00
408-2	The History of the Kelly Gang	432	2000	13.60	23/10/00
439-2	The Return of the Naked Chef	254	2000	24.80	23/10/20
274-5	Harry Potter and the Philosopher's Stone	298	1997	4.99	24/02/98
624-X	Harry Potter and the Goblet of Fire	230	2000	5.95	16/03/03
629-0	Harry Potter and the Prisoner of Azkaban	340	1999	7.50	19/04/01
043-9	Cowboys and Indians	280	1991	8.99	07/07/99
242-4	The Shipping News	289	1993	6.20	03/04/99
624-t	Northanger Abbey	234	1855	5.95	01/03/03
625-X	Sense and Sensibility	334	1876	6.95	01/03/03
712-4	Galileo's Daughter	212	1999	10.40	03/04/99

Try to enter the data exactly as shown. Ignore the Comments column for the moment. Later in this module you will use the data shown here for queries and reports. Your table should now look as shown below.

Close and reopen your Books table: automatic re-sorting by primary key

You can now close the Books table. Reopen it by double-clicking its name in the **Tables** tab of the Database window. Notice anything different?

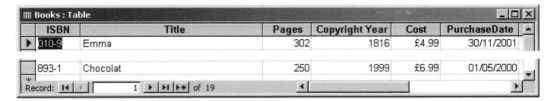

Yes. Access has reordered the records. (The database term for this is 'sorting'.) They are no longer in the order in which you entered them in the table. Access has ordered your records in increasing order of ISBN, the primary key field. The record with the smallest ISBN is first, and the one with the largest is now at the bottom of the table. You will learn more about sorting records in Lesson 5.7.

Edit a field in a table

Enter the wrong data? To change the content of a field, begin by clicking that field:

- If you click anywhere in a field, you can use the **BACKSPACE** or **DELETE** key to remove characters one by one, or you can type new characters.

- If you click the extreme left of the field, the entire field is selected. Anything you type immediately overwrites the whole field. Alternatively, press **DELETE** to remove the contents of the field.

When you have finished editing the content of a field, move to another field, by clicking in it or by pressing the **ENTER** or **TAB** key. Moving to another field confirms and saves your change – there is no way to recover the previous field content.

Undo actions

Undo button

To undo an edit to a field – before you press **ENTER** or **TAB**, or click in another field – click the **Undo** button on the Access toolbar or choose **Edit | Undo**. To view a list of recent actions that you can undo, click the arrow at the right of the **Undo** button.

Save a record

You don't need to save records after you enter or modify them – Access automatically saves a record when you move the cursor to another field. If you do wish to save a record directly, choose **Records | Save Record**.

Sometimes you may want to enter a new record that is very similar to a previously entered record. Instead of typing in the new record's details, you can copy and paste the existing record, and then edit the pasted record's details as necessary. Follow these steps:

Record selector box

1   Right-click the record selector box at the left of the record to select the entire record. An arrow appears in the box, indicating that this is the current record – that is, the record you are currently working on.

2   From the pop-up menu displayed, choose **Copy**.

3   Right-click any other record selector and choose **Paste** from the pop-up menu displayed.

Remember that the primary key must be unique, so if you are pasting into the same table, you will need to update this. If the primary key is an AutoNumber, Access updates it automatically.

Let's try copying a record within your sample Books table.

1   Right-click the record selector box at the left of the last record in the table to select the entire record.

| ▶ | 893-1 | Chocolat | | 250 | 1999 | £6.99 | 01/05/2000 |
| * | | | | | | | |

2   From the pop-up menu displayed, choose **Copy**.

3   Right-click in the next record selector box immediately beneath the record you are copying, and choose **Paste** from the pop-up menu displayed.

4   Access displays the following dialog box.

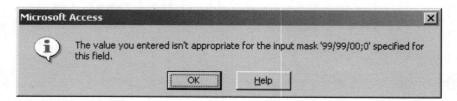

Click **OK** to continue. Access now pastes a copy of the record from the clipboard. The cursor is in the ISBN field.

	893-1	Chocolat	250	1999	£6.99	01/05/2000
⌀	893-1	Chocolat	250	1999	£6.99	01/05/2000
*						

5   Change the ISBN field from 893-1 to 893-2. Remember the primary key must be unique for each record.

You will delete this copied record in the next section.

■   To remove a record from its original location, choose **Cut** rather than **Copy**.

Delete a record

Follow these steps to remove a record from a table:

1 Right-click the record selector to select the entire record.

2 From the pop-up menu displayed, choose **Delete Record**.

You can then confirm that you want to delete the record, or change your mind and leave it alone.

If you delete a record from a table that has an AutoNumber field, Access will not reassign the number of the deleted record to another record.

Let's try deleting a record from your sample Books table.

1 Right-click the record selector for the last record, the record that you copied in the previous section.

2 From the pop-up menu displayed, choose **Delete Record**. Access prompts you as follows.

3 Click **Yes**.

Access deletes the copied record from your Books table.

Hide and unhide a column

You can hide individual columns in a table – if, for example, you are not using all the columns, or if a column contains data that you don't want other people to see. To hide a column:

■ Right-click the column header, and choose **Hide Columns** from the pop-up menu displayed.

The column is not removed from the table. It's still there; it's just not visible.

To unhide one or more previously hidden columns:

1 Choose **Format | Unhide Columns** to display the **Unhide Columns** dialog box. Fields that are currently displayed (unhidden) have check marks in front of them. Hidden fields do not have a check mark.

2 Click to select the column(s) you want to display (unhide).

3 Click the **Close** button.

Practise hiding and unhiding columns in your Books table.

Freeze and unfreeze a column

If you want to ensure a particular column is always visible even when you scroll, freeze it.

■ Right-click the column header, and choose **Freeze Columns** from the pop-up menu displayed.

Access moves the selected column to the left of the table. It remains visible no matter where you scroll.

You cannot unfreeze an individual column. To unfreeze all columns:

■ Choose **Format | Unfreeze All Columns**.

Any column or columns that you previously froze remain at the left of the table. You will need to reorder the column(s) to return them to their original position.

Reorder columns

Follow these steps to change the order in which columns appear in the currently open table:

Hold down the mouse button to move a column

1 Click the header of the column that you want to move. Access selects the entire column.

2 Click it again, but, this time, hold down the mouse button. Notice that a dashed box appears on the tail of the mouse pointer.

3 Drag the column, left or right, to the new location. As you drag with the mouse over each column, Access displays a bold vertical line at the right of that column.

Dragging a column

4 Access is asking you: is this where you want to place the column? If yes, release the mouse button, and the column is relocated.

If not, keep dragging until the bold line appears at your required location, and release the mouse button

Let's practise by moving the Pages column in your Books table.

1 Click the Pages column header, and then click it again.

2 Drag the column to the left until Access displays a bold vertical line just to the right of the ISBN column.

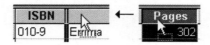

3 Release the mouse button. The Pages column should now be at the new location shown below.

⊞ Books : Table						_ □ ✕
ISBN	**Pages**	**Title**	**Copyright Year**	**Cost**	**PurchaseDate**	▲
▶ 010-9	302	Emma	1816	£4.99	30/11/2001	
011-7	345	Jane Eyre	1847	£4.99	13/09/1998	

Save table layout changes

When you enter and edit data in a table, Access saves your additions and changes automatically. So do you ever need to save a table? Yes, because Access does not automatically save what it calls *layout changes*. These include:

- Changes to the table appearance – for example, if you change a column's width, or hide or freeze it, or amend the order in which columns or records appear. None of these changes affect the data in the table, just the way that the data is displayed.

- Changes to table structure – for example, if you add an extra column.

Save button

To retain layout changes, you need to save them. To do so, click the **Save** button on the Access toolbar or choose **File | Save**.

You are also prompted to save any changes to the layout or design when you close a table.

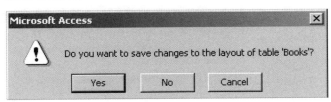

Generally, you will respond to this dialog box by clicking **Yes**.

Copy a table

Follow these steps to copy a table, within the current database or to a different database:

1   In the Database window, right-click the table once to select it.

2   From the pop-up menu displayed, choose **Copy**.

3   To copy the same database, choose **Edit | Paste**.

To copy the table to a different database, close the current database, open the new one, and choose **Edit | Paste** from the new Database window.

4   Access prompts you to name the copy, and you are offered a choice of what you want to copy.

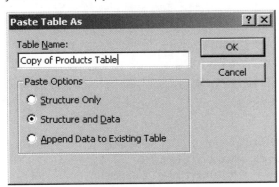

Let's examine what these options mean.

Paste option	Description
Structure Only	Copies the structure of the table only, without any data.
Structure and Data	Copies both the structure of the table and all its data.
Append Data to Existing Table	Access prompts you to enter the name of the table to which you want to append the data. The destination table must have the same structure as the table you are copying from.

Practise your table-copying skills by making a copy of your sample Books table within the Bookworm database. Include both the structure and data in the copy, and name it Books Original.

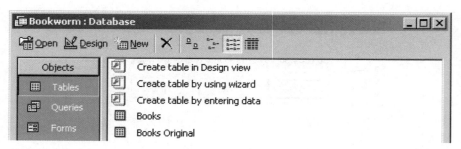

Your copied table should be listed in the **Tables** tab of the Database window.

Delete a table

To remove a table from the currently open database, right-click it in the Database window and choose **Delete** from the pop-up menu. Access prompts you to confirm that you want to delete the table.

Get online help from the Help menu

As with other Microsoft Office applications, Microsoft Access offers an online help system. Follow these steps to display help topics.

Help button

1 Choose **Help | Microsoft Access Help**, click the **Microsoft Access** Help button on the Standard toolbar, or press **F1**.

2 Access displays the Help window with the following three tabs:

- **Contents:** Here you will find descriptions of Access's main features. Where you see a heading with a book symbol, double-click it to view the related sub-headings. Double-click on a question-mark symbol to read the online help text.

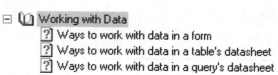

- **Answer Wizard:** Type your question in the box at the top-left of the dialog box, and click **Search**. Access displays a list of suggested help topics in the lower-left. Click a topic to display the associated text in the right pane.

- **Index:** Type the word or phrase and click **Search**. Access displays all matches from the online help in the lower left of the dialog box. Click on it to display the associated text.

You will see the following buttons, from left to right, at the top of the online help window:

Microsoft Access Help

Hide/Show: Hides or displays the left pane of the dialog box.

Back/Forward: Moves you backwards and forwards through previously visited help topics.

Print: Prints the currently displayed help topic.

Options: Offers a number of display choices.

Take a few minutes to look through the Access online help system.

Get online help from a dialog box

You can display online help directly from a dialog box in Access, as the following example shows.

Click the question mark...

...then click the object you want help on

1 Open your sample Books table, and choose **Format | Datasheet**.

2 Click the question-mark symbol near the top right of the dialog box. Access displays a question mark to the right of the cursor.

3 Click the **Flat** option.

Access displays online help text telling you about the purpose of the selected screen element.

> Select a cell effect for the datasheet. The sunken and raised cell effects default to a silver background color.

4 Click anywhere else on the dialog box to remove the online help text, and click **Cancel** to close the dialog box.

Practise this exercise with other dialog boxes in Access.

Quit Access

You can close your Bookworm.mdb database and quit Access. You have now completed Lesson 5.3 of the ECDL Databases Module.

5.4

Design view:
behind the scenes

Learning goals   At the end of this lesson you should be able to:

- switch between Datasheet and Design view;
- know when to use the following data types: Text, Memo, Number, Date/Time, Currency, AutoNumber and Yes/No;
- create a new table in Design view;
- delete a column from a table;
- add a column to a table;
- change the data type of a field;
- add a new field;
- view a table's indexed field(s);
- add and remove indexed fields.

New terms   At the end of this lesson you should be able to explain the following terms:

Design view	A view in which you can display and change the organizational structure of your table.
Data type	This determines the kind of data that can be entered in a field, and how Access treats that data.
Datasheet view	A view of a database table where you can see information presented in rows and columns, with several records visible at the same time.
Indexed field	A field that a table can use to find and sort records. Access automatically makes primary key fields indexed fields. You can index other fields if required.

Ever taken the back off a radio, computer or washing machine, and been confronted with a complex tangle of components and wires? It can be an intimidating experience.

You may feel the same the first time that you display a table in *Design view*. Instead of the familiar rows and columns holding data, you see a split-window: in the upper half is a list of the fields in your table, and in the lower there are further details regarding whichever field is selected in the upper half.

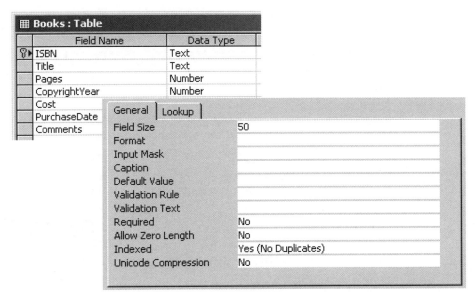

Design view is where you can change the organizational structure of your table. And once you get to know your way around, you will be able to work like a database professional.

Fields – more than one type

As you will learn in this lesson, all fields are not the same. Some hold text, others numbers, dates or financial amounts, and so on. A field's *data type* tells Access how to treat the field, how the data is to be stored, and what kind of data is allowed in it. Knowing which field type to use for particular types of data is an important skill in database design.

Open your Bookworm database

Open button

1 Launch Microsoft Access, click the **Open** button on the Access toolbar or choose **File | Open**.

2 Select the following database file and click **Open**.

    Bookworm

You will use the Bookworm database through this lesson.

Switch between Datasheet and Design view

Until now, when you have opened a table, it looked as shown below. In *Datasheet view*, as it is called, you can see several records arranged in rows and columns.

	ISBN	Pages	Title	Copyright Year	Cost	PurchaseDate
▶	010-9	302	Emma	1816	£4.99	30/11/2001
	011-7	345	Jane Eyre	1847	£4.99	13/09/1998

In fact, this is just one of a number of possible views of a table. Now meet a second view, *Design view*. This view 'takes you behind the scenes' and allows you to change the organizational structure of your table.

Design View button

■ If your table is open in Datasheet view, switch to Design view by clicking the **Design View** button on the Access toolbar, or by choosing **View | Design View**.

Datasheet View button

■ If your table is open in Design view, return to Datasheet view by clicking the **Datasheet View** button on the Access toolbar, or choosing **View | Datasheet View**.

A Design view window is composed of two parts: an upper and a lower.

The upper part lists the fields in the table, and shows the type of data each field is intended to hold. The example below is from your Books table. The key symbol beside the ISBN field indicates that this field is set as the table's primary key.

The lower part of the Design view window shows further details of the field that is selected in the upper part of the window.

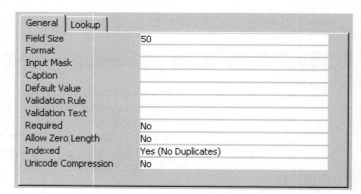

The example above shows details of the ISBN field in the sample Books table.

If your table is not open, you can open it in Design view by clicking it once to select it in the **Tables** tab of the Database window, and clicking the **Design** button on the tab's toolbar.

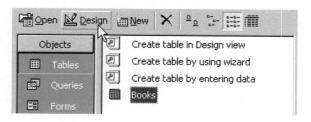

Reorder columns in Design view

In Lesson 5.3 you moved the Pages column from the right of the Title column to its left. Yet, in Design view, you can see that it is still at the location it originally occupied when you created the table. Why? The answer is that modifications to a table's appearance in Datasheet view do not change how the table is presented in Design view. To avoid confusion, let's change the column order in Design view so that it matches the order in Datasheet view.

1 In Design view, click the record selector for the Pages field at the extreme left of the window, and hold down the mouse button.

This selects the entire row. Notice that a hollow rectangle appears at the tail of the cursor.

2 Drag upwards until the Pages row is on top of the Title row.

3 Release the mouse button. The first three rows should now look as shown below.

4 Save your table layout changes by clicking the **Save** button on the Access toolbar or choosing **File | Save**. You can close the table.

Explore field types and properties

In Lesson 5.2, when you were entering records in your sample Books table, you probably noticed that the PurchaseDate field accepted only dates, and that the Pages field accepted only numbers. If you tried entering text into the PurchaseDate field, you would get a message something like that below.

How does it know that the PurchaseDate column should only contain dates and that Pages accepts only numbers? Is Access reading your mind? No, the answer is in the table design. When you set up a table in Access, there are two things you have to give each field:

■ A name, and

■ A data type.

When you used the Table Wizard to set up the Books table, you changed the names of some fields, but you did not change any of the fields' data types. Nor did you need to. The field data types from the sample table provided by Access were suitable for the kind of information that you wanted to enter in those fields.

In Access, all information is not the same. By specifying the data type for a field, you tell Access what kind of information you want to enter and store in the field. The data type controls what kind of information can be entered into the field and how Access treats that information. The following table lists and describes the main data types in Access.

Data type	Used for	Examples
Text	Any kind of alphabetic or numeric data. Typically used where there is a limit on the amount of data. No more than 255 characters may be input. If the data is numeric, it cannot be used in calculations.	Surname, Colour, Post Code, Telephone Number
Memo	Any sort of alphabetic or numeric data. Typically used for free-form input. Up to 64,000 characters may be input. Again, if the data is numeric, it cannot be used in calculations.	Description, Notes
Number	Numeric data that may be used in calculations.	Quantity in Stock, Number Sold
Date/Time	Date or time data.	Date Bought, Best Before Date, Arrival Time, Departure Time
Currency	Money values or other numeric data used in calculations where the number of decimal places does not exceed four.	Price, Current Value
AutoNumber	A number assigned to each new record automatically. Access assigns the numbers in sequence, starting with 1.	User ID, Employee No, Customer Code, Part No
Yes/No	Fields that can have simple yes/no, true/false or on/off values only.	Second Hand Goods?, Buy Again?

When numbers are text, and years are numbers

Text is the default data type for new fields. If a field is to store numbers, it's not always necessary to change its data type from Text. For example, you can store telephone or fax numbers in a text field, because it is unlikely that you will ever want to find the average of a list of phone numbers, or add two phone numbers together and subtract them from a third.

In your sample Books table, the Year field has a data type of Number rather than Date/Time. This is satisfactory, because only a year and not a formatted combination of day/month/year will be entered in this field. And because this field is not text but a number, you can still perform operations on the Year field, such as finding the year you purchased most books.

Use Design view to create a sample Authors table

Now that you have a knowledge of field data types, you can think about building a table directly in Design view, without relying on the Table Wizard to walk you through the table creation process.

You might have noticed that your Books table does not contain a field for author – a rather serious omission! But think about it: if an Author field was in the Books table, you would need to enter the same author's details many times over. To eliminate duplication of this kind, let's create a separate table for authors, and then link it to the Books table. In Lesson 5.6, you will learn how to build links between two tables so that Access can retrieve data from both of them.

The following steps describe the creation of the sample Authors table, but they apply equally to the building of any table in Design view.

1 **Open the database:** If your Bookworm database is not already open, open it now. Click the **Tables** button at the right of the Database window.

2 **Start the table creation process:** You do this by double-clicking the option below on the **Tables** tab of the Database window.

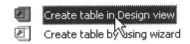

3 **Type the field names:** In the Field Name column, enter the following four field names:

   AuthID, AuthLastName, AuthFirstName and Nationality

After you type Nationality in the fourth **Field Name** box, click its associated **Data Type** box. All four of your new fields now have a default data type of **Text**.

Field Name	Data Type
AuthID	Text
AuthLastName	Text
AuthFirstName	Text
Nationality	Text

4 **Set the field data types:** In the **Data Type** column, click in the top box (the one for AuthID), and select the data type of **AutoNumber**. AutoNumber is an automatically assigned sequence number.

Leave the other three fields with their default data type of **Text**.

5 **Enter field descriptions:** Use the **Description** column to enter a brief description of each field. Your screen should now look as follows.

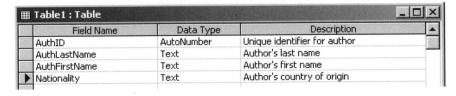

Field Name	Data Type	Description
AuthID	AutoNumber	Unique identifier for author
AuthLastName	Text	Author's last name
AuthFirstName	Text	Author's first name
Nationality	Text	Author's country of origin

6 **Set the primary key:** Now you need to set AuthID as the primary key for the table. Right-click the AuthID field and choose **Primary Key** from the pop-up menu.

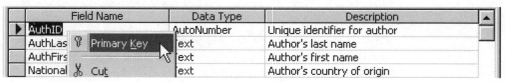

Access displays a key symbol to the left of the AuthID field name.

Save button

7 **Save and name your table:** To save your table, click the **Save** button on the Access toolbar or choose **File | Save**. When prompted, give it the name Authors.

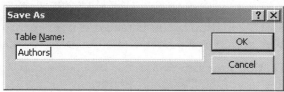

**Datasheet
View** button

8 Switch to Datasheet view. Widen the AuthLastName and AuthFirstName fields a little. You can now begin to enter data in your new table.

9 Type in the details listed below. Because the AuthID field is your chosen primary key, you need not and cannot enter values in it.

AuthID	AuthLastName	AuthFirstName	Nationality
1	Austen	Jane	British
2	Harris	Joanne	British
3	Marquez	Gabriel Garcia	Columbian
4	Rowling	J.K.	British
5	Alcott	Louisa May	American
6	Dahl	Roald	British
7	Bronte	Charlotte	British
8	Dickens	Charles	British
9	Carey	Peter	Australian
10	Oliver	Jamie	British
11	Orwell	George	British
12	Proulx	E. Annie	American
13	Sobel	Dava	British
14	O'Connor	Joseph	Irish
15	Eco	Umberto	Italian

Your Authors table should now look as shown below.

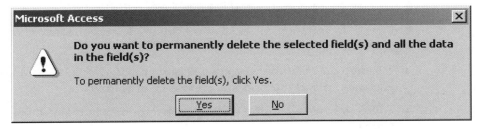

AuthID	AuthLastName	AuthFirstName	Nationality
1	Austen	Jane	British
2	Harris	Joanne	British
3	Marquez	Gabriel Garcia	Columbian
4	Rowling	J.K.	British
5	Alcott	Louisa May	British
6	Dahl	Roald	British
7	Bronte	Charlotte	British
8	Dickens	Charles	British
9	Carey	Peter	Australian
10	Oliver	Jamie	British
11	Orwell	George	British
12	Proulx	E. Annie	American
13	Sobel	Dava	British
14	O'Connor	Joseph	Irish
15	Eco	Umberto	Italian
(AutoNumber)			

You can now close your new table.

Delete a column from a table

Don't want a particular column in a table any more? You can delete it in either view.

- **Datasheet view**: Right-click on column header and choose **Delete Column** from the pop-up menu.

- **Design view**: Click anywhere in the row you want to delete, and choose **Edit | Delete Rows**.

As practice, let's remove the Comments field from the Books table.

1 If your Bookworm database is not already open, open it now. Click the **Tables** button at the right of the Database window, and open the Books table.

2 Right-click on the Comments column header, and choose **Delete Column** from the pop-up menu.

3 Access displays a message similar to the following. Click **Yes**.

Microsoft Access

⚠ **Do you want to permanently delete the selected field(s) and all the data in the field(s)?**

To permanently delete the field(s), click Yes.

[Yes]   [No]

The Comments column is removed. You will recreate this column in the next topic.

Add a new field to a table in Datasheet view

Can you add new fields to your database tables at any time? Yes. However, it is better if you think about the fields you want to add when you are setting up the table, and modify the design as little as possible after that. A danger of adding new fields is that you may have to go back and edit all the records you have already entered. This applies particularly to the following two field types:

■ Numeric fields, where a blank field may be interpreted as 0, and

■ Yes/No fields, where a blank field may be interpreted as No.

Let's recreate the Comments column, which you removed in the previous section, in your Books table.

1 Open your Books table in Datasheet view.

Click anywhere in a column to insert a new one to its left

2 Click anywhere in the column that will be to the right of where you want to place the new column. Let's put it to the left of the Cost column, so click in any field of that column.

3 Choose **Insert | Column**. The new column is inserted with the title Field1.

Field1	Cost
	£4.99

Right-click the column header to rename it

4 Right-click the column header and choose **Rename Column** from the pop-up menu. The column header is now editable.

5 Type the name 'Comments' and press **ENTER**.

6 Drag the new Comments column to the right so that it is positioned to the left of the last column, the PurchaseDate column. Drag the PurchaseDate column to the left of the Comments column. The Comments column is now in its original location.

Save button

7 Click the **Save** button on the Access toolbar or choose **File | Save** to save the changes to the table.

8 Switch to Design view, and drag the Comments field down so that it appears as the bottom field. Close and save your table.

Add a new field to a table in Design view

You have already added a field in Datasheet view. Let's add another field, called Recommended, In Design view.

Design View button

1 Display your Books table in Design view.

2 Where do you want to add a new field: at the end of a record or somewhere in the middle?

■ To add a new field between two existing fields, click in the row above which you want to add the field and choose **Insert | Rows**.

■ To add a new field at the end of the record, click in the next unused **Field Name** box.

3 Enter the name of the new field: Recommended.

Recommended	Text

4 Click in the associated **Data Type** box. Access assigns the default data type of **Text** to your new field.

5 Click the **Save** button on the Access toolbar or choose **File | Save** to save the change to the table.

6 Switch to Datasheet view to see the impact of adding the Recommended field. You may want to widen the column if it is too narrow to display the column name.

Copyright Year	Cost	PurchaseDate	Comments	Recommended
1816	£4.99	30/11/2001		

Change the data type of a field

It's easy to change the data type of a field, but ideally you should get it right before you enter data in the table. If you try to change the data type after a lot of data has been input, you risk confusing Access, and you may lose some of your data.

Let's change the data type of the Recommended field in your Books table from **Text** to **Yes/No**.

1 Display your Books table in Design view.

Click in the **Data Type** box for the Recommended field, and select the **Yes/No** option.

By default, Access uses a checkbox to represent these values: ticked means Yes and unticked means No.

2 Click the **Save** button on the Access toolbar or choose **File | Save** to save the change to the table.

3 Switch to Datasheet view to see the impact on the Recommended field.

Copyright Year	Cost	PurchaseDate	Comments	Recommended
1816	£4.99	30/11/2001		☐

As you can see, the field now contains a checkbox that you can select to indicate a book that you would recommend. Initially, the field is set to No (unticked) for all records.

4 Tick about half of the books listed in the table as recommended. If you have no personal preferences, simply tick every second record.

5 Click the **Save** button on the Access toolbar or choose **File | Save** to save the change to the table.

View a table's indexed fields

Looking up a name in the index at the back of a book is easier than scanning hundreds of pages of text in search of it. Indexes in a database table work in the same way. Table sorting and querying based on indexed fields take less time because Access needs to examine only the indexed fields rather than entire records.

Access automatically makes a table's primary key field an *indexed field*. You can verify that the ISBN field of your Books table is indexed by displaying the table in Design view, clicking the ISBN field in the upper part of the window, and inspecting the field's details in the lower part.

Indexed	Yes (No Duplicates)

Indexes button

Similarly, verify that the AuthID field of your Authors table is indexed by displaying the field's details in Design view.

A quick way to view a table's indexed field or fields is to open the table in Design view, and click the **Indexes** button on the main Access toolbar.

Index non-primary key fields

To index a field means making it an indexed field. You can index fields other than the primary key, and you can decide whether or not you want to allow duplicate values in such fields. Here are the steps:

1 In Design view, click the field in the upper part of the window.

2 In the lower part of the window, click the arrow to the right of the **Indexed** property box to display and select your indexing option: **Yes (Duplicates OK)** or **Yes (No Duplicates)**.

An indexed field need not be unique for each record. If a table of employees, for example, has a primary key field called EmployeeID, Access would automatically index that field and enforce unique field values (**No Duplicates**).

However, you could index another field, such as **Surname**, and allow duplicate field values (**Duplicates OK**).

3 Click the **Save** button on the Access toolbar or choose **File | Save** to save the change to the table.

Remove an index from a field

■ To remove an index from a field that is not the primary key, but not actually remove the field itself, select the field in Design view and set the **Indexed** property to **No**.

Quit Access

You can close your Bookworm.mdb database and quit Access. You have now completed Lesson 5.4 of the ECDL Databases Module.

Protect good tables against bad data

Learning goals

At the end of this lesson you should be able to:

- set a field's default value;
- set a field as required (mandatory) field;
- set specific properties for text, number, currency and date/time fields;
- create validation rules for number, date/time and text fields using comparison operators and literals;
- create validation rules for text fields using the IN operator and literals;
- combine single validation rules using the AND, OR and IN logical operators.

New terms

At the end of this lesson you should be able to explain the following terms:

Default value	In an Access table, a value specified by the table creator when the user does not type information, or select a yes/no checkbox.
Validation rule	This sets limits or conditions on the values that may be entered into a field. When a user enters data into a field, Access checks the data to ensure that it complies with the validation rule.
Field properties	The set of characteristics that you can apply to a field, such as its maximum size or default value. Most field properties depend on the field's data type.
Comparison operator	A symbol indicating an arithmetic relationship between two numbers or dates, such as 'equal to or less than' (=<).
Literal	A literal value, such as a specific number (12), date (26/11/04) or text (Yes).
Logical operator	A symbol indicating how multiple conditions are related in a rule. With the AND operator, all conditions must be met. With OR, only one condition must be met.

Screening for data entry errors

Good database design is about anticipating the type of information that users are likely to enter in each field – and preventing the entry of so-called bad data.

Examples of bad data would be a date entered in a field that is not a date field, and text entered in a field that is intended to hold numbers for use in calculations. Applying the appropriate data type to each field in a table is the most basic way to prevent the input of bad data, but it is not the only one.

Default values and mandatory fields

If you want a field to have a value even when the user does not enter any data in it, you can specify a *default value* for that field. A well-chosen default value can help speed up users' entry of records.

Default Value	12.5

If a particular field is essential for each record, you, the table designer, can insist that it is always completed by making it a required or mandatory field. An example would be a table's primary key field when that field is not automatically generated by Access.

Field data types and properties

Specific field types, such as text, number and date fields, can have properties set for them that determine how they accept and display information.

For text fields, you can limit how many characters can be entered. For number fields, you can specify the type and range of numbers allowed. For currency fields, you can indicate whether or not you want Access to display the currency symbol and thousands separator. Date fields offer a wide range of input and display formats for the database designer to choose from.

Applying validation rules

Another control option available to the designer is the setting of limits or conditions on the actual values that may be entered in fields. Access calls these *validation rules*. For example, you could make it a condition of a number field that only values in the range 0 to 9 can be entered. For a date field, you could restrict valid entries to the current date or a past one.

Validation Rule	>#01/01/2000# AND <#31/12/2010#
Validation Text	Dates must be in range 2000-2110

Validation rules are accompanied by validation text, the words that appear on screen when users attempt to enter invalid data.

Open your Bookworm database

Open button

1 Launch Microsoft Access, click the **Open** button on the Access toolbar or choose **File | Open**.

2 Select the following database file and click **Open**:

Bookworm

You will use the Bookworm database through this lesson.

Set field properties: default values and required fields

Regardless of their data type, all fields have two *properties* that table designers will find useful:

- **Default value:** if you want a field to have a value even when the user does not enter any data in it, specify that value in the **Default Value** property box.

  If you are designing a table to hold records of sales transactions, for example, and the most common tax rate is 12.5%, you may want to specify that as the tax field's default value.

Default Value	12.5

By providing a *default value* for a field, you can speed up users' entry of records. Depending on their data type, fields may contain default text, numbers or dates.

- **Required:** If a field is so important that you want data entered into it whenever a record is inserted or updated, set the value of the **Required** property to **Yes**.

You may want to make the primary key field a required field, for example, if the primary key is not automatically generated by Access but entered manually for each record. In database terms, required fields are sometimes called mandatory fields.

By setting a field as required, you, the designer, are saying to data entry personnel: 'Please enter a value in this field. I *insist*.'

Set field properties: text fields

For fields with a data type of **Text**, you can use the **Size** property to set the maximum number of characters that may be entered in that field. The default is 50 characters.

Set the smallest possible size, because smaller sizes require less memory and the computer can process them faster. Text entries larger than the specified size will be rejected by the field.

Be careful, however, when reducing the size of a field that already contains data. Access will truncate existing field values if their number of characters exceeds your new field size limit.

Set field properties: number fields

For fields with a data type of **Number**, you can use the **Size** property to specify the type and range of numbers that the field will accept.

- **Integers:** Your choices for whole numbers are **Byte**, **Integer** or **Long Integer**.

  Byte stores positive numbers from 0 to 255, **Integer** stores numbers from –32,768 to 32,767, and **Long Integer** stores numbers in the range –2,147,483,648 to 2,147,483,647.

- **Fractions: Single** is adequate for most numbers with fractions. This includes decimal fractions such as 1234.56.

Set field properties: currency fields

For fields with a data type of **Currency**, you can choose from a range of **Format** properties that control what data may be entered, and how entered data is displayed. Your main options are listed in the table below.

Format option	Description	Sample Input
Currency (default)	Access automatically inserts the currency symbol and commas to separate thousands. Choosing this option can save significant effort and time when working with large tables.	£1,234.56
Fixed	Access does not automatically insert the currency symbol and commas to separate thousands.	1234.56
Standard	Access does not automatically insert the currency symbol, but does insert commas to separate thousands.	1,234.56

Access uses the regional settings specified in the Windows Control Panel. The examples used in this book assume that your regional settings are set to English (United Kingdom), so £ is the default currency symbol.

Set field properties: date/time fields

For fields with a data type of **Date/Time**, you can choose from a range of **Format** properties that control what data may be entered, and how entered data is displayed. Your main options are listed in the table below.

Format option	Description	Sample Input
Short Date (default)	Access accepts a date as a group of three, two-digit numbers. The separator character is a forward slash (/). Once entered, years are displayed as four digits.	17/10/04
Medium Date	Access accepts dates as a two-digit day, a three-character month, and a two-digit year. The separator character is a hyphen (-). Once entered, years are displayed as four digits.	17-Oct-03
Long Date	Access accepts dates as a two-digit day, the full month name, and a four-digit year. The separator character is a space.	17 October 2003

As with **Currency** fields, Access uses the regional settings specified in the Windows Control Panel for **Date/Time** formats. The examples used in this book assume that your regional settings are set to English (United Kingdom). The default sequence for dates is therefore: day first, month second, and then year.

Explore validation rules: comparison operators and literals

You can minimize the opportunity for data entry errors by setting limits or conditions on the values that may be entered in the fields. Access calls these validation rules. Typically, you apply validation rules only to fields with a data type of **Number**, **Currency** or **Time/Date**. Validation rules contain the following two elements:

- One or more *comparison operators* (for example, +, >, =).
- One or more *literal* values (for example, 123.5, 23/10/03, 'Yes').

The comparison operators are listed in the table below.

Operator	Description	Example	Comment
=	Equal to	=100	Only a number of 100 is accepted.
<>	Not equal to	<>0	Any number except 0 (zero) is accepted.
<	Less than	<250	Numbers less than 250 are accepted. 250 is not accepted.
<=	Less than or equal to	<=250	Numbers less than 250 are accepted. 250 is also accepted.
>	Greater than	>1234	Numbers greater than 1234 is accepted. 1234 is not accepted.
>=	Greater than or equal to	>=1234	Numbers greater than 1234 are accepted. 1234 is also accepted.

Operators are combined with literal values (such as a particular number or date) to create a validation rule. Literal values are generally referred to as literals.

- To include a number in a validation rule, simply type the number.
- To include a date in a validation rule, enclose it within a pair of hash (#) characters. You will find the **hash** key just to the left of the **ENTER** key.
- To include today's date (as recorded on your computer) in a rule, insert Date().

Hash key

Some examples of validation rules containing numbers and dates are shown in the table below.

Validation rule	Comment
>#17/10/03#	Only dates later 17 October 2002 are accepted, but not that date itself.
<=#26/11/95#	Only dates earlier than 26 November 1995 are accepted, as is the date itself.
<>#09/02/92#	Any date is accepted except 9 February 1992.
=Date()	Only today's date is accepted.
<Date()	Only dates before today's date are accepted. Today's date is not allowed.
>=Date()	Only today's date, or any future date, is accepted.

Validation rules are accompanied by validation text. These are the words that appear on screen whenever a user attempts to enter incorrect data. Validation text should clearly state what values are acceptable and what are not. The right-hand example below is obviously preferable to that on the left.

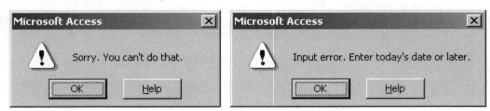

Access enforces validation rules whenever a user tries to insert new data in the table, edit existing data, or paste or otherwise import data from another table.

Create a validation rule for a number field

Let's experiment with validation rules by creating a validation rule for a numeric field (a field with a data type of number).

First, make a copy of your Books table (both its structure and data) in the Bookworm database, and name the table BooksValidation.

1 Open your BooksValidation table in Design view.

2 In the upper part of the window, click the Cost field.

3 In the lower part of the window, type the following validation rule:

>1.99

4 For validation text, enter the following:

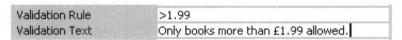

Save button

5 Click the **Save** button on the Access toolbar or choose **File | Save** to save the change to the table. If Access displays the dialog box below, click **No** to continue.

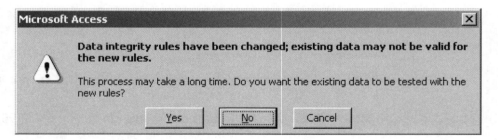

6 Switch to Datasheet view, and try changing the Cost field of the first record (Emma) to £1.00. Access should display the following error message.

7 Click **OK**. Change the **Cost** field back to its original value of £4.99.

Create a validation rule for a date/time field

Follow these steps to impose the restriction on your BooksValidation table that a book's purchase date must be prior to a specified future date.

1 Open your BooksValidation table in Design view.

2 In the upper part of the window, click the PurchaseDate field.

3 In the lower part of the window, type the following validation rule:

   <#01/01/2008#

4 For validation text, enter the following:

| Validation Rule | <#01/01/2008# |
| Validation Text | Dates must be less than year 2008. |

Save button

5 Click the **Save** button on the Access toolbar or choose **File | Save** to save the change to the table.

6 Switch to Datasheet view, and try changing the PurchaseDate field of the first record (Emma) to 24/10/08 (not 24/10/2008). Access should display the following error message.

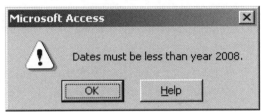

7 Click **OK**. Change the PurchaseDate field back to its original value of 30/11/2001.

Apply validation rules to text fields

Validation rules are less commonly applied to text fields, but it's possible to do so. Note the following important point:

■ To include text in a validation rule, enclose it within a pair of double quotes (" ").

Here are two examples of validation rules applied to text fields.

| <>"Smith" | Any text except Smith is accepted. |
| ="New" | Only the text New is accepted. |

Explore logical operators in validation rules: AND and OR

The terms AND and OR have a special meaning in validation rules. They enable you to group two or more combinations of operators and literals into a single, larger rule. They are known as *logical operators*.

With the AND operator, all conditions in the rule must be met. If not, the entered data is rejected.

■ In a number field, for example, you could apply the rule that entered numbers must be larger than 10 AND smaller than 100.

■ In a date field, for example, you could require that entered dates must be later than 1 January 2003 AND earlier than 31 December 2010.

Here are some examples of the AND operator in use.

Validation rule	Comment
>=10 AND <=100	Only numbers in the range 10 to 100 inclusive are accepted.
>10 AND <100	Only numbers in the range 10 to 100, but not 10 or 100, are accepted.
>=#01/01/03# AND <=#31/12/03#	Only dates in the year 2003 are accepted.
>=Date() AND #<=31/12/06#	Only dates from today's up to the end of 2006 are accepted.
>=#01/01/90# AND =<Date()	Only dates from the beginning of 1990 up to and including today's date are accepted.

With the OR operator, only one condition in the rule need be met for the entered data to be accepted.

In a number field, for example, you could apply the rule that any one of the following three numbers is acceptable: 10, 14 or 16. All other numbers would be rejected as an invalid entries. The following table provides some examples of the OR operator in use.

Validation rule	Comment
="1" OR ="2" OR ="3"	Only the numbers 1, 2 and 3 are accepted
="Small" OR ="Medium" OR ="Large"	Only the words Small, Medium or Large are acceptable.

By convention the AND and OR operators are usually written in upper-case characters. In Access, you can type them in lower-case (and, or) or in capital case (And, Or).

Use the AND operator in a date/time field

Follow these steps to impose the restriction on your BooksValidation table that a book's purchase date must be between two specified dates.

1 Open your BooksValidation table in Design view.

2 In the upper part of the window, click the PurchaseDate field.

3 In the lower part of the window, enter the following validation rule:

>#01/01/2000# AND <#31/12/2010#

4 For validation text, enter the following:

| Validation Rule | >=#01/01/2000# And <=#31/12/2010# |
| Validation Text | Dates must be in range 2000-2010 |

Save button

5 Click the **Save** button on the Access toolbar or choose **File | Save** to save the change to the table. If Access displays the dialog box below, click **No** to continue.

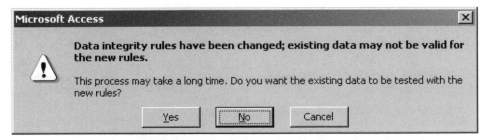

6 Switch to Datasheet view, and try changing the PurchaseDate field of the first record (Emma) to 31/11/20 (not 31/11/2020). Access should display the following error message.

7 Click **OK**. Change the PurchaseDate field back to its original value of 30/11/2001.

Use the IN operator with multiple OR conditions

Usage of the OR operator can become awkward when you want to specify more than two conditions in a validation rule. In the sample rule below, only the name of one of four possible countries is acceptable:

="England" OR "Wales" OR "Scotland" OR "Ireland"

Access offers an alternative to multiple OR combinations in the form of the IN operator. The above validation rule now becomes:

IN("England", "Wales", "Scotland", "Ireland")

Here is an example of the IN operator applied to a number field:

IN(100, 200, 300, 400)

And here is the IN operator applied to a date field:

IN(#01/01/04#, #01/01/05#, #01/01/06#, #01/01/07#, #01/01/07#)

Quit Access

You can close your Bookworm.mdb database and quit Access. You have now completed Lesson 5.5 of the ECDL Databases Module.

5.6

Linking tables in relationships

Learning goals At the end of this lesson you should be able to:

- display the Relationship window in Access;
- create a one-to-one relationship between two tables in a database;
- create a one-to-many relationship between two tables in a database;
- delete a relationship between tables;
- protect relationships with referential integrity.

New terms At the end of this lesson you should be able to explain the following terms:

Table relationship	A link between records in different tables of the same database.
One-to-one relationship	A record in either table has one matching record in the other table. Typically, the two tables have the same primary key.
One-to-many relationship	A record in the first table can have many matching records in the second table. But a record in the second table can have only one matching record in the first table.
Relationship window	A window that displays existing links between tables, and that provides a visual method for working with links.
Relational integrity	A system of rules enforced automatically by Access that prevents the insertion, deletion or changing of data that threatens or breaks a relationship.

Tables can store not just details of people (such as employees or customers) or things (such as test results or products). They can also record events that involve people and transactions that involve things.

When a candidate takes an ECDL test, for example, the test result is stored somewhere in a computer file. But also recorded are the student's name, test date, test location, the identity of the test supervisor, and perhaps some other details too. Similarly, when a product is sold to a customer, the sale transaction details (such as date, price, credit terms, discount, delivery details and so on) can be stored in a sales order entry table.

Entering table data once

If a student retakes an ECDL test a number of times, or when the same product is sold hundreds of times in a day, you can imagine how time-consuming it would be to enter the personal or product details on every occasion.

Good database design, as you learned in the previous lesson, should mean that only the correct information is entered. Intelligent database design means that information should be entered only once.

Linking tables in relationships

The alternative to the repetitive entering of personal or product details is to create separate tables: one table for people or products, and a second table for events or transactions.

You then link the two tables so that it is necessary only to enter a unique personal or product identifier in an event or transaction record, and the database makes the connection to the relevant personal or product record.

When a table contains a link to another table, you can see a plus sign (+) in its leftmost column. Clicking this sign displays the relevant details from the other, linked table.

In old style, so-called flat-file databases, the database file was just a single table of records. In relational databases such as those you can create in Access, however, a single database file can contain lots of different tables that are linked with each other to eliminate duplication of data entry. Moreover, because the information is entered only once and is held in one place, it is easier to update.

Open your Bookworm database

Open button

1 Launch Microsoft Access, click the **Open** button on the Access toolbar or choose **File | Open**.

2 Select the following database file and click **Open**:

Bookworm

You will use this sample database throughout this lesson.

Explore relationship types

For ECDL 4, you need to know about the following two types of *table relationships*.

Relationship type	Description	Example
One-to-one relationship	A record in the first table can have no more than one matching record in the second table. Typically, the two tables have the same primary key.	The storage of sensitive or private information, such as user passwords, salary information, exam grades ordisciplinary records, in a separate table from the one where the main details are held.
	One-to-one relationships are rare in relational databases.	Another reason that a database designer might want to keep information separate is if the content of one table changes more frequently than the data contained in the other, or if the data in different tables need to be updated by different departments.
One-to-many relationship	A record in the first table can have many matching records in the second table, but a record in the second table can have only one matching record in the first table. This is a very common type of relationship.	The first table could list products and the second could list sales transactions. A single product record could link to many sales transaction records in the second table. However, each transaction record can include only a single product.

Access imposes two restrictions on the fields that can be linked in one-to-one and one-to-many relationships:

- Only fields that are either primary keys or have non-duplicated indexes may be linked.

- Only fields of the same data type may be linked: text fields can link to text fields, number fields to other number fields, and so on. In addition, when the linked fields are number fields, they must have the same field size property setting. One exception is the AutoNumber field type. It can link to a field of a different type in another table.

Display tables for linking

Access provides a visual, point-and-click method for creating relationships between tables of the currently open database. The *Relationships window* is where you create, modify and view the links between your tables. To work with links, first display this window, and then display the relevant tables in the window.

1 In the Database window, choose **Tools | Relationships** to view the Relationships window.

Notice that when this window is displayed, Access adds a new menu called **Relationships** to the main menu bar.

The Relationships window is empty the first time that you display it.

Show Table button

2 Your next task is to display the relevant tables. Click the **Show Table** button on the Access toolbar or choose **Relationships | Show Table** to display the **Tables** tab of the **Show Table** dialog box.

3 Hold down the **CTRL** key, click the relevant tables, and click the **Add** button to close the dialog box. The **Show Table** dialog box below is from the sample Northwind database.

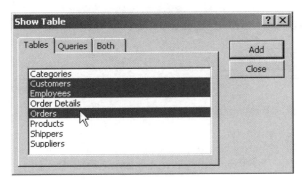

Access now displays your selected tables in the Relationships window.

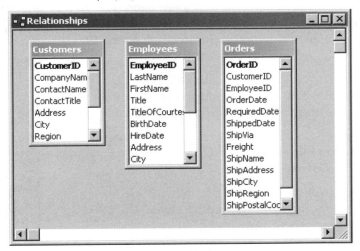

4 You can now use the Relationships window and the commands on the **Relationships** menu to create, modify and delete relationships between the tables.

Create a one-to-one relationship

Show Table button

Follow these steps to create a one-to-one relationship between two tables in the currently open database:

1 Choose **Tools | Relationships** to display the Relationships window. If the two tables are not shown, click the **Show Table** button on the Access toolbar or choose **Relationships | Show Table** to display them.

2 In the first table, click the field that you want to link from, and hold down the mouse button. Notice how the cursor changes shape to a rectangle.

3 Drag the cursor over to the field to which you want to link in the second table. Release the mouse button.

4 Access now displays the **Edit Relationships** dialog box. Select the **Enforce Referential Integrity** option. (Referential integrity is explained below.)

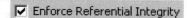

Line shows link between two fields

5 Click the **Create** button to close the dialog box and create the link.

Access now displays a line joining the two fields in the two tables, representing the relationship you have just created.

6 Close the Relationships window and save the layout changes when prompted.

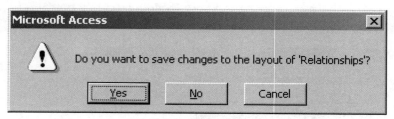

Create a one-to-one relationship between two sample tables

It's time to practise your relationship-building skills. In your Bookworm database, imagine that you want your comments and recommendations to remain private, and don't want them to be part of the Books table itself.

You begin by creating a new table named BookComments to hold the **Comments** and **Recommended** fields from the Books table. Then you will build a one-to-one relationship between the Books table and the new BookComments table.

1 Make a copy of your sample Books table within the Bookworm database. Include both the structure and data in the copy, and name it BooksComments.

2 Your copied BookComments table is now listed in the **Tables** tab of the Database window. Double-click it to open it in Datasheet view.

3 Delete the following columns from the BookComments table: Title, CopyrightYear, PurchaseDate, Cost and Publisher.

Only the following fields should remain: ISBN, Comments and Recommended.

ISBN	Comments	Recommended
010-9		☐
011-7		☑
016-8		☐
043-9		☑
066-4		☐
069-3		☑
242-4		☐
274-5		☑
389-X		☐
408-2		☑
414-2		☐
439-2		☐
597-7		☑
624-t		☐
624-X		☑
625-X		☐
629-0		☑
670-8		☐
712-4		☑
893-1			☐
*		☐

BooksComments : Table

Record: ◄◄ ◄ 20 ► ►► ►* of 20

4 Click the **Save** button on the Access toolbar or choose **File | Save** to save the change to the table.

5 Close your BooksComments table. You cannot create a relationship for a table that is currently open.

(Do not delete the Comments and Recommended columns from the Books table. You will need these columns for exercises in future lessons.)

Now, let's create a one-to-one relationship between the Books and BooksComments tables.

1 In the Database window for your Bookworm database, choose **Tools | Relationships** to display the Relationships window. You should see the three tables you have created in the Relationships window.

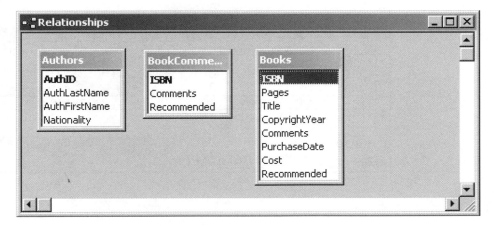

Show Table button

If you don't see all three tables, click the **Show Table** button and add any missing table. You can change the position and size of the individual table windows as required.

2 In the Books table, click the ISBN field and hold down the mouse button. Notice how the mouse pointer changes shape.

3 Drag the cursor over to the ISBN field in the BookComments table and release the mouse button.

4 In the **Edit Relationships** dialog box displayed, select the **Enforce Referential Integrity** option, and click the **Create** button.

Access now displays a line joining the **ISBN** fields in the two tables – this represents the relationship you have just created.

5 Close the Relationships window and save the layout changes when prompted.

Well done. You have successfully created a one-to-one relationship between two tables of a database.

When you open the Books table now, you can see a new column of plus (+) signs at the left of the table. When you click a + sign, Access displays the linked record from the BooksComments table. To close the window showing the linked record, click its minus (-) sign.

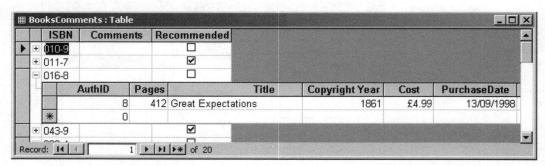

	ISBN	Pages	Title	Copyright Year	Cost	PurchaseDate	
+	010-9	302	Emma	1816	£4.99	30/11/2001	
+	011-7	345	Jane Eyre	1847	£4.99	13/09/1998	
+	016-8	412	Great Expectations	1861	£4.99	13/09/1998	
+	043-9	280	Cowboys and Indians	1991	£8.99	07/07/1999	
+	066-4	287	Mansfield Park	1814	£8.99	03/04/1999	
−	069-3	344	Little Women	1868	£6.99	24/02/1998	

	Comments	Recommended
		☑
*		☐

	ISBN	Pages	Title	Copyright Year	Cost	PurchaseDate	
+	242-4	289	The Shipping News	1993	£6.20	03/04/1999	

Similarly, the BooksComments table contains a column of plus (+) signs to the left of the ISBN column. When you click the + sign beside an ISBN, you see the matching record from the Books table. Click the minus (-) sign to close the record from the second, linked table.

Create a one-to-many relationship

Much more common than one-to-one relationships are one-to-many relationships. This is where a record in the first table can have many matching records in the second table, but a record in the second table can have only one matching record in the first table.

Some of the authors in the Authors table wrote more than one of the books in the Books table (for example, Jane Austen). But no book has more than one author. It is possible, therefore, to create a one-to-many relationship between the Authors table and the Books table.

One (author) ...	... to many (books)
Jane Austen	Pride and Prejudice
	Sense and Sensibility
	Emma

The primary key of the Authors table is AuthID. If an AuthID field is added to the Books table, then books can be linked to their authors, and vice versa.

1 Display the Books table in Design view.

2 Click in the second row, and choose **Insert | Rows**.

3 Enter AuthID as the field name, and select **Number** as the data type.

AuthID	Number

4 Ensure that the **Field Size** property is set to **Long Integer**.

5 Click the **Save** button or choose **File | Save** to save the changes to the Authors table.

6 Switch to Datasheet view to enter the following AuthID details for each of the books.

Book	Author	AuthID
Emma	Austen	1
Jane Eyre	Bronte	7
Great Expectations	Dickens	8
Cowboys and Indians	O'Connor	14
Mansfield Park	Austen	1
Little Women	Alcott	5
The Shipping News	Proulx	12
Harry Potter and the Philosopher's Stone	Rowling	4
Love in the Time of Cholera	Marquez	3
The History of the Kelly Gang	Carey	9
The Name of the Rose	Eco	16
The Return of the Naked Chef	Oliver	10
The BFG	Dahl	6
Northanger Abbey	Bronte	7
Harry Potter and the Goblet of Fire	Rowling	4
Sense and Sensibility	Jane Austen	1
Harry Potter and the Prisoner of Azkaban	Rowling	4
Animal Farm	Orwell	11
Galileo's Daughter	Sobel	13
Chocolat	Harris	2

7 Close the Books table when finished.

You are now ready to create the one-to-many relationship between the Authors and Books tables.

Show Table button

1 In the Database window for your Bookworm database, choose **Tools | Relationships** to display the Relationships window.

If you don't see your Authors and Books tables, click the **Show Table** button and add any missing table.

2 In the Authors table, click the AuthID field, and drag to the AuthID field in the Books table. Notice how the cursor changes to a rectangle. Release the mouse button.

3 Access now displays the **Edit Relationships** dialog box. Select the **Enforce Referential Integrity** option. (Referential Integrity is explained below.)

☑ Enforce Referential Integrity

4 Click the **Create** button to close the dialog box and create the link. The one-to-many symbol (a sideways number 8) represents the one-to-many relationship between the tables.

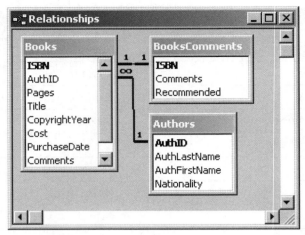

5 Close the Relationships window and save the layout changes when prompted.

When you open the Books table, you can see that it looks the same as it did at the beginning of this exercise. The column of plus (+) signs at the left of the table relates to the BooksComments table, not to the Authors table.

When you open the Authors table, however, you can see that a new column of plus signs has been added. Click any of these to display the linked book in the Books table.

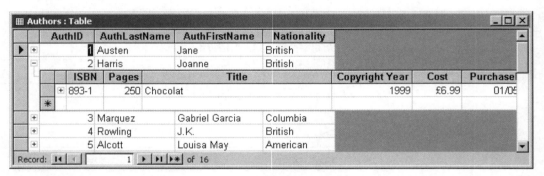

About the primary key and the foreign key

The AuthID field is the primary key for the Authors Table. Within the Books table, however, it is a foreign key – this is the term used to describe a field in one table that refers to the primary key in another table.

Conversely, ISBN is the primary key in the Books table, but it is a foreign key in the BooksComments table.

Delete a relationship

Follow these steps to delete a relationship that you no longer want:

1 In the Database window, choose **Tools | Relationships** to display the Relationships window.

Show Table button

2 If you don't see the relevant tables, click the **Show Table** button and add any missing table.

3 Right-click at or near the centre point of the relationship line, choose **Delete** from the pop-up menu, and click **Yes** to confirm your action when prompted.

You can close the Relationships window when finished.

Protect relationships with relational integrity

When creating a link between two tables, it's normally a good idea to select the **Enforce Referential Integrity** checkbox. Why?

☑ Enforce Referential Integrity

When a table is unlinked to any other, you can work with it without reference to any data that is contained in any other table. But when a table is linked to another, you need to take the details of that relationship into account when working with either table. The restrictions that apply in such situations come under the title of *referential integrity*.

When referential integrity is enforced in tables, Access applies the following restrictions to relationships.

In your sample Books and Authors tables	In general
In the Books table, you cannot enter an AuthID if that AuthID is not present in the Authors table.	You cannot enter a value in a foreign key field if that value doesn't exist in the primary key field of the related table.
In the Authors table, you cannot delete an author if that author's AuthID is referenced in the Books table.	You cannot delete a record from a table if foreign key values in a related table point to that record.
If the AuthID fields of the Authors table were not AutoNumbers but were editable by a user, an AuthID still could not be changed if that value is referenced in the Books table.	You cannot change a primary key value if there are linked values in foreign key fields of a related table.

About the Cascade options

When the **Enforce Referential Integrity** checkbox is selected, two further options become available: **Cascade Update Related Fields** and **Cascade Delete Related Records**. These allow you to perform actions restricted by referential integrity, while ensuring that Access automatically takes action to prevent inconsistencies. Selecting the Cascade options, however, may result in Access automatically deleting or changing many records. As a general rule, these options are better left unselected.

☑ Enforce Referential Integrity
☐ Cascade Update Related Fields
☐ Cascade Delete Related Records

Quit Access

You can close your Bookworm.mdb database and quit Access. You have now completed Lesson 5.6 of the ECDL Databases Module.

5.7

Sorts, filters and queries

Learning goals At the end of this lesson you should be able to:

- sort records in a table based on a single field;
- apply a filter to a table based on all or part of a field;
- save a sort or a filter as a query;
- copy and delete a query;
- add, update and delete records in a query;
- use the Access Find feature.

New terms At the end of this section you should be able to explain the following terms:

Sort	An operation on a table that changes the order in which the records are displayed. Sorting does not change the content of records, only their location.
.Filter	An operation that restricts the display of a table to records that contain a particular value in a selected field.
Query	A query is a database operation that retrieves specific information from the database, based on criteria and sort orders that you specify.
Sort order	A particular way of ordering records based on field values. A sort order can be in ascending (1–9, A to Z) or descending (Z to A, 9–1) sequence.

Solving the information problem – or moving it?

At the beginning of this module you were promised that databases would help you find information quickly and easily. But until now you have learned only how to record information. Replacing a paper-based storage system with a computerized one only moves your information analysis problem rather than solves it.

You might be asking: why bother? You can use a word processor to keep lists of things, and if you want to put numbers, text and dates in neat columns, you can use a spreadsheet.

This lesson introduces you to three features that should convince you that a database is not just another kind of haystack, but is far better in terms of analysing stored information. These features are sorts, filters and queries.

Sorting: highlighting the relevant

You use *sorts* to highlight relevant table information. Whether you want to identify students who score the highest marks in tests, customers who purchase the most products, or regions that receive the heaviest rainfall, a sort rearranges the order of records in a table so that those you are interested in appear at the top.

Sort Ascending/ Sort Descending buttons

Sorting is easy to perform: you just click in the field you want to sort on, and then click the **Sort Ascending** or **Sort Descending** button on the Access toolbar.

Filtering: hiding the irrelevant

A sort presents you with an entire table, even when it's only a few of its records that currently interest you. *Filters* take data analysis a step further by displaying only the records of interest – and hiding the others from view.

Filter by Selection button

If, for example, you want to see only students who received a grade C in a test, you simply click in any field containing that grade, and click the **Filter by Selection** button. Access responds by showing only records from the table that contain a C grade. It's that simple.

Queries: saved sorts and filters

Save As Query button

If there are sorts or filters that you will want to apply regularly, you can make life easier for yourself by saving them as *queries*. That way they are always available with a double-click of the mouse. As you will learn in Lesson 5.8, queries can be more than merely saved sorts or filters.

One final search tool that you will find useful is the Find feature. As in other Microsoft Office applications, the Access Find feature helps you to locate a particular item of information quickly.

Open your Bookworm database

Open button

1 Launch Microsoft Access, click the **Open** button on the Access toolbar or choose **File | Open**.

2 Select the following database file and click **Open**:

Bookworm

You will use this sample database throughout this lesson.

Sort records in a table

Unless you tell it to do otherwise, Access arranges a table's records in order of their primary key field. If the field is an AutoNumber, this will also be the order in which the records were entered in the table: the ones entered first will be at the top of the table, and the most recently entered ones at the bottom.

Follow these steps to sort (rearrange) the records in the current table in a different order:

1 Click in any field of the column that you want to sort on.

Sort Ascending/ Sort Descending buttons

2 Click one of the two Sort buttons on the toolbar: **Sort Ascending** or **Sort Descending**. Each button applies a different *sort order*.

Each Sort button applies a particular sort order – a way of ordering records based on the values in one of their fields. A sort order can be ascending (1–9, A to Z) or descending (Z to A, 9–1).

The following table shows the effects of clicking in a text, number or date field, and then clicking the **Sort Ascending** button.

Text fields are sorted in alphabetic order	For number fields, the smallest numbers appear first	For date fields, the oldest fields appear first
City	**Unit Price**	**Birth Date**
Aachen	$2.50	19-Feb-1952
Anchorage	$3.60	04-Mar-1955
Barcelona	$3.60	09-Jan-1958
Berlin	$4.50	19-Sep-1958
Bruxelles	$5.60	29-May-1960
Buenos Aires	$5.60	02-Jul-1963
Caracas	$5.90	30-Aug-1963
Charleroi	$6.00	08-Dec-1968
Cork	$6.20	02-Jul-1969

The following table shows the effects of clicking in a text, number or date field, and then clicking the **Sort Descending** button.

Text fields are sorted in reverse alphabetic order	For number fields, the largest numbers appear first	For date fields, the most recent fields appear first

Z↓ A▼	Product		Z↓ A▼	Discount		Z↓ A▼	Order Date
	Zaanse koeken			25%			26-Jul-1996
	Wimmers			20%			25-Jul-1996
	Vegie-spread			20%			24-Jul-1996
	Tunnbröd			15%			23-Jul-1996
	Röd Kaviar			15%			22-Jul-1996
	Queso			10%			19-Jul-1996
	Pavlova			10%			19-Jul-1996
	Pâté chinois			6%			18-Jul-1996
	Mozzarella			5%			17-Jul-1996

Practise your record-sorting skills on your sample Books table. Click in any field of the following columns in turn, and then click the **Sort Ascending** button: AuthID, Title and Cost. The results of the three sort operations are shown below.

	ISBN	AuthID	Pages	Title	Copyright Year	Cost	PurchaseD:
▶ ⊞	010-9	1	302	Emma	1816	£4.99	30/11/2
⊞	414-2	16	450	The Name of the Rose	1983	£5.95	07/07/1
*		0					

	ISBN	AuthID	Pages	Title	Copyright Year	Cost	PurchaseD:
▶ ⊞	670-8	11	160	Animal Farm	1945	£6.99	03/04/1
⊞	242-4	12	289	The Shipping News	1993	£6.20	03/04/1
*		0					

	ISBN	AuthID	Pages	Title	Copyright Year	Cost	PurchaseD:
▶ ⊞	597-7	6	202	The BFG	1982	£3.99	01/05/2
⊞	439-2	10	254	The Return of the Naked Chef	2000	£24.80	23/10/2
*		0					

Let's practise some more. Click in any field of the following columns in turn, and then click the **Sort Descending** button: Pages, CopyrightYear and Cost. You can see the results of the three sort operations below.

	ISBN	AuthID	Pages	Title	Copyright Year	Cost	PurchaseD:
▶ ⊞	414-2	16	450	The Name of the Rose	1983	£5.95	07/07/1
⊞	670-8	11	160	Animal Farm	1945	£6.99	03/04/1
*		0					

	ISBN	AuthID	Pages	Title	Copyright Year	Cost	PurchaseD:
▶ ⊞	066-4	1	287	Mansfield Park	1814	£8.99	03/04/1
⊞	408-2	9	432	The History of the Kelly Gang	2000	£13.60	23/10/2
*		0					

	ISBN	AuthID	Pages	Title	Copyright Year	Cost	PurchaseD:
▶ ⊞	439-2	10	254	The Return of the Naked Chef	2000	£24.80	23/10/2
⊞	597-7	6	202	The BFG	1982	£3.99	01/05/2
*		0					

In Lesson 5.8 you will learn how to sort on multiple columns in a table.

Return to the unsorted order

If you have sorted a table to view records in a particular order, you can return to an unsorted view by sorting on the primary key field or by choosing **Records | Remove Filter/Sort**.

Save a sort as a query

If you want to repeat a particular sort, you can save it as a query. Here's how:

1 Display your table in Datasheet view.

2 Sort the table's records according to your requirements.

3 Choose **Records | Filter | Advanced Filter/Sort**.

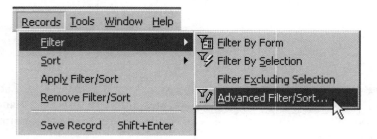

4 Access displays the rather complex-looking **Filter** dialog box. In the lower pane, the leftmost column should display the field on which you are sorting, followed by your chosen sort order. Some sample screens from the **Filter** dialog box are shown below.

Note: If any column of the **Filter** dialog box other than the leftmost column contains any data, delete that data. Otherwise your saved sort will not work correctly.

Save As Query button

5 When the **Filter** dialog box is displayed, a button named **Save As Query** appears on the Access toolbar. Click the button or choose **File | Save As Query**.

6 In the **Save As Query** dialog box, enter a name for your query, and click **OK**.

7 Close the **Filter** box by clicking the **Close** button at its top right corner. When you close your table, do not save it.

Your saved sort is now a query that Access lists on the **Queries** tab of the Database window.

Run a query

Follow these steps to open a query:

■ Display the **Queries** tab of the Database window, and double-click the query name.

Opening a query is sometimes called 'running' the query. You will see the table displayed according to your query's saved criteria – even after you have added or deleted table records, or changed the ones that are already there.

Save sorts as sample queries for your Books table

Let's practise by performing some sorts on your sample Books table, and then saving the results as queries. Display your Books table in Datasheet view. One after the other, click in the fields shown below, select the given sort order, and then save the sort with the suggested query names.

Sort field	Sort order	Toolbar button	Suggested query name
Title	Ascending	A↓Z	Books by Title Ascending
Cost	Descending	Z↓A	Books by Cost Descending
CopyrightYear	Ascending	A↓Z	Books by Copyright Year Ascending

Your saved queries appear on the **Queries** tab of the Database window.

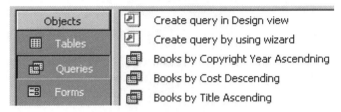

Filter records by selection in a table (whole field)

Filtering is for when you want to display only those records that share a common value in one field – for example, all records that contain a particular city (Manchester), exam grade (B), delivery date (24/10/03) or financial amount (£19.99).

A sort helps you focus on particular records in a table by bringing those records to the top of the table. A filter hides those you are not interested in.

Follow these steps to apply a filter:

1 Identify any record in your open table which has a field value that meets your particular requirements.

2 Click in that field.

Filter by Selection button

3 Click the **Filter by Selection** button in the toolbar.

Access now displays only records that contain your filtered value.

Let's try an example. Open your Books table in Datasheet view. Click a field of the CopyrightYear column where the value is 2000, and then click the **Filter by Selection** button. Watch what happens. Only records that also have a CopyrightYear of 2000 are visible on screen.

	ISBN	AuthID	Pages	Title	Copyright Year	Cost	PurchaseD:
▶ ⊞	624-X	4	230	Harry Potter and the Goblet of Fire	2000	£5.95	16/03/:
⊞	408-2	9	432	The History of the Kelly Gang	2000	£13.60	23/10/:
⊞	439-2	10	254	The Return of the Naked Chef	2000	£24.80	23/10/:
*		0					

You can filter already-filtered records, and continue filtering until you have refined your display to include only the record or records that you are interested in.

If you amend a field's content in any way and then click on another field or a toolbar button, Access saves the field change automatically: you are not prompted to save or discard the change. Be careful when clicking in a field to perform a filter operation that you do not accidentally change the field's value.

In particular, remember that clicking on a Yes/No checkbox field changes it, so you need to click a Yes/No field twice before you click on the **Filter by Selection** button.

Remove a filter

Filtering appears to remove records from the filtered table. But don't panic: the rest of your records are still in the table. They are just not displayed.

Remove Filter
button

- To remove a filter and display all a table's records again, click the **Remove Filter** button on the Access toolbar.

Access then reverts to displaying all the records in your table.

Filter records by selection in a table (partial field)

You don't need to select a whole field when filtering by selection. For example, if your table contained a large number of cookery books, you might want to display only those with the word 'Italian' in their title.

Let's try an example. Open your Books table in Datasheet view. In any field of the Title column that contains the word 'The' or 'the', drag across the word to select it.

Harry Potter and the Philosopher's Stone

Filter by Selection
button

Next, click the **Filter by Selection** button. All records that have that word anywhere in their Title are displayed, as shown below.

		ISBN	AuthID	Pages	Title	Copyright Year	Cost	PurchaseD:
▶	+	624-X	4	230	Harry Potter and the Goblet of Fire	2000	£5.95	16/03/2
	+	274-5	4	298	Harry Potter and the Philosopher's Stone	1997	£4.99	24/02/1
	+	629-0	4	340	Harry Potter and the Prisoner of Azkaban	1999	£7.50	19/04/2
	+	389-X	3	370	Love in the Time of Cholera	1985	£5.95	24/02/1
	+	597-7	6	202	The BFG	1982	£3.99	01/05/2
	+	408-2	9	432	The History of the Kelly Gang	2000	£13.60	23/10/2
	+	414-2	16	450	The Name of the Rose	1983	£5.95	07/07/1
	+	439-2	10	254	The Return of the Naked Chef	2000	£24.80	23/10/2
	+	242-4	12	289	The Shipping News	1993	£6.20	03/04/1
*			0					

Books : Table

Remove Filter
button

Remove the filter when finished by clicking the **Remove Filter** button on the Access toolbar.

The way that you select (drag across) the field value for filtering determines which records are displayed.

If you select the first letters or numbers in a field, Access displays all records in which the field begins with those letters or numbers.

If you select the last letters or numbers in a field, Access displays all records in which the field ends with those letters or numbers.

If you want to filter based on the entire first word or the entire last word in a field, include the first letter or the last letter only if you want to restrict the display to records that begin with or end with the selection. If you want all records that include the word anywhere in the field, select only part of the word.

Filter records in a table (multiple fields)

You can filter on values in more than one field. Two restrictions apply:

- The values you select must be in adjoining columns – if necessary move one of the columns.

- You must select the entire values in all the fields – selection of partial values is not permitted.

Here are the steps:

1 Click the value in the first field.

2 Hold down the **SHIFT** key.

3 Click the value(s) in the adjoining field(s). (Don't try to drag with the mouse. Just click in the fields.)

1999	£10.40
2000	£5.95
1855	£5.95

Filter by Selection button

4 Click the **Filter by Selection** button on the Access toolbar.

Access displays your filtered records. You can remove the filter in the usual way.

Save a filter as a query

As with sorts, you will probably want to repeat some filter operations regularly. And just as you can save a sort as a query, you can save a filter in a similar way. Here are the steps:

1 Display your table in Datasheet view.

2 Filter the table's records according to your requirements.

3 Choose **Records | Filter | Advanced Filter/Sort**.

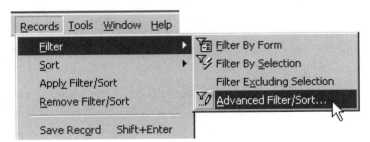

4 In the first two columns in the lower pane of the **Filter** dialog box, you can see the filter's sort details and then its filter details.

The left column shows the table's current sort field and sort order. You can amend this, if required. In the second column from the left are the filtered field (in the **Field** row) and the filtered value (in the **Criteria** row). Three sample screens from the **Filter** dialog box are shown below.

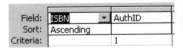

Note: If any columns of the **Filter** dialog box other than the first two contain any data, delete that data. Otherwise your saved filter will not work correctly.

Save As Query button

5 Click the **Save As Query** button on the Access toolbar or choose **File | Save as Query**.

6 In the **Save As Query** dialog box, enter a name for your query, and click **OK**.

7 Close the **Filter** box by clicking the **Close** button at its top right corner. You can close your table but do not save it.

Your saved filter is now a query that Access lists on the **Queries** tab of the Database window.

Why filters are also sorts, but sorts are not filters – and both are really queries
When you perform sorts and filters on a table, the two seem like very different operations. Sorts rearrange the order in which records appear. Filters, on the other hand, display only certain records and hide the remainder.
In Access, however, a filter is a kind of 'super sort' that filters and sorts. A sort, in contrast, is only a sort. If it was filtered too, it would no longer be a sort but a filter.
Both sorts and filters are examples of a common type of Access operation called a query: sort is the simplest type and filter is a slightly smarter one. This relationship is why you save both sorts and filters using the same command named **Advanced/Filter Sort**, why the dialog box displayed by this command is entitled **Filter**, and why the button you click to complete the save is called **Save As Query**.

Save a filter as a sample query for your Books table

Let's apply two successive filters to your sample Books table, then apply a sort, and finally save the result as a query. You will filter for books published in the twentieth century (the first filter), and then for recommended books only (the second filter).

1 Display the Books table in Datasheet view.

2 Locate any CopyrightYear field that contains a year in the twentieth century, and drag across the digits 19 to select them.

Filter by Selection button

3 Click the **Filter by Selection** button. Access now displays only twentieth century books.

4 Inspect your Recommended column. About half the books should be ticked. If not, tick every second book or so. You are now ready to filter on this column.

5 In any Recommended field where a box is ticked, click twice, and then click the **Filter by Selection** button again.

(You need to click the field twice, because the first click unticks the ticked box.)

Well done. Your Books table is now filtered twice: once on part of the CopyrightYear field, and a second time on the Recommended field. Next, you will sort the twice-filtered records by the date on which they were purchased.

Sort Ascending button

6 Click in any PurchaseDate field and click the **Sort Ascending** button on the toolbar. Depending on which books you ticked as Recommended, the table should look similar to that shown below.

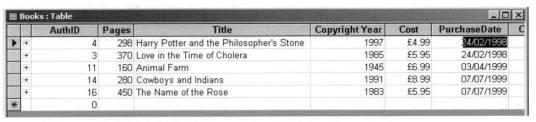

Your table has now been filtered twice, and then sorted. One step remains: saving the two filters and the sort as a query.

7 Choose **Records | Filter | Advanced Filter/Sort** to display the **Filter** dialog box. The lower pane of the dialog box should look as shown below.

In the first (left) column are the sort details, and in the second and third columns are the details of the two filters.

8 Click the **Save As Query** button on the toolbar or choose **File | Save As Query**. Name your query as follows, and click **OK**.

9 Click **OK** to close the **Filter** dialog box.

10 Click the **Close** button at the top right of the **Filter** box to close it. You can close your table without saving it.

You can open (run) your saved query at any time from the **Query** tab of the Database window.

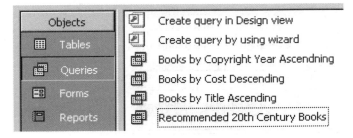

Add, update and delete records in a query

When you display a query in Datasheet view, can you insert, edit or delete records, just as you can in Datasheet view of a table? Yes, but with the following restriction:

■ The query must be based on a single table or on tables that are linked by a one-to-one relationship.

When these conditions apply, changes you make are implemented on the query's underlying table or tables.

Copy a query

Follow these steps to make a copy of a query within a database:

1 Display the **Queries** tab in the Database window.

2 Right-click the query and choose **Copy** from the pop-up menu.

3 Choose **Edit | Paste**.

4 Access prompts you to give the query a different name. Do so and click **OK**.

You might find it convenient to save copies of your queries before making changes to them.

Delete a query

Follow these steps to remove a query from a database:

1 Display the **Queries** tab in the Database window.

2 Right-click the query and choose **Delete** from the pop-up menu.

3 Click **Yes** when prompted to confirm that you want to delete the query.

Perform a quick find

Is there a quick way of finding a particular item of information among hundreds or thousands of records? Yes. Use the Access Find feature. Follow these steps to locate what you are looking for:

1 Open the relevant table in Datasheet view.

If you want to search through a particular column rather than the entire table, click in any field of that column.

Find button

2 Click the **Find** button on the Access toolbar, choose **Edit | Find**, or press the keyboard shortcut **Ctrl+f**. Access displays the **Find and Replace** dialog box.

3 On the **Find** tab, type the item that you are searching for.

4 Use the **Look In** pull-down list to indicate whether you want to search the entire table, or just the column in which the cursor is located.

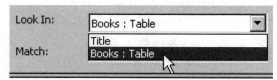

5 In the **Match** pull-down list, select one of the three possible match types: **Any Part Of Field** ("is" finds The History of the Kelly Gang and the Prisoner of Azkaban) **Whole Field** ("Harry Potter" finds nothing); or **Start Of Field** ("The" finds The Shipping News, The Name of the Rose, The Return of the Naked Chef, and The BFG, but not Harry Potter and the Prisoner of Azkaban).

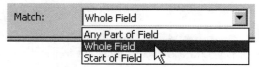

6 Click the **Find Next** button and Access should highlight the first occurrence of the searched-for item. You can continue finding matching items until Access indicates that there are no further matching records.

7 To close the **Find and Replace** dialog box, click the **Close** button.

Quit Access

You can close your Bookworm.mdb database and quit Access. You have now completed Lesson 5.7 of the ECDL Databases Module.

5.8

Building queries in Design view

Learning goals

At the end of this lesson you should be able to:

- display a query in Design view;
- modify a query in Design view;
- create a new query in Design view;
- use a query to perform a multi-column sort;
- include comparison and logical operators in a query;
- use Design view to reorder columns in a query.

New terms

At the end of this section you should be able to explain the following terms:

Design grid	The rows and columns that you use to design a query or filter in query Design view or in the Advanced Filter/Sort window.
Select query	A query that selects records from a table or tables based on criteria expressed as combinations of comparison operators, literals and logical operators.

In Lesson 5.7 you learned how to save sorts and filters as queries. But simple sorts and filters are only a foretaste of Access's ability to query databases. In this lesson you will meet Design view for queries – a view in which you can modify existing queries or create very powerful new ones.

As with Design view of a table, Design view of a query shows a split window, with an upper and a lower half. But there the similarity ends. At the top of the query Design view window are the tables from which the query can retrieve information. And beneath that is the so-called *design grid* of rows and columns.

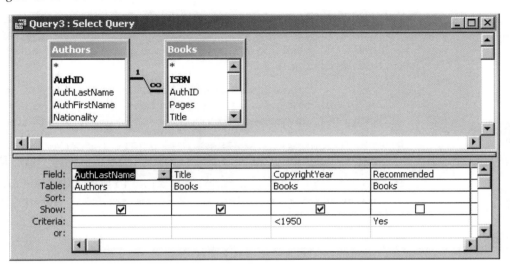

Mastering the design grid is the key to successful query building in Access. If you ever wondered what Access database experts do all day, the answer is they work with the design grid. This is where the power of Access lies.

The design grid presents five main rows, each of which plays a role in extracting only the information needed for a particular data analysis task.

You use the grid's top rows (Field and Table) for selecting the columns and tables that your query will draw information from, the third row (Sort) for specifying sort orders, and the fourth (Show) for including or excluding columns from the query results. You can sort on as many columns of the query as you choose. A column that provides information to the query need not itself appear as a column in the query.

On the fifth row (Criteria) you insert comparison operators, literals and logical operators that present tests which the values in records must pass in order to be retrieved by your query.

When you save a query, you save the query design, rather than its results. So when you make changes to the tables in your database, the results of the query also change.

Open your Bookworm database

Open button

1 Launch Microsoft Access, click the **Open** button on the Access toolbar or choose **File | Open**.

2 Select the following database file and click **Open**:

   Bookworm

   You will use this sample database throughout this lesson.

Switch between Datasheet and Design view of a query

Design View
button

**Datasheet
View** button

In Lesson 5.4 you discovered that there are two ways to view a table. In Datasheet view, a table is presented in familiar, easy-to-understand rows and columns. Design view, however, is rather more intimidating. It takes you 'behind the scenes' to where you can see and change the organizational structure of your table.

As with tables, so too with queries. You can switch between Datasheet and Design view of a query just as you can between the two views of a table: by clicking the relevant view button at the left of the Access toolbar.

- If your query is open in Datasheet view, switch to Design view by clicking the **Design View** button on the Access toolbar, or by choosing **View | Design View**.

- If your query is open in Design view, return to Datasheet view by clicking the **Datasheet View** button on the Access toolbar, or choosing **View | Datasheet View**.

An adjustable split bar divides the Design view of a query into two areas or panes:

- **Field list:** The upper pane shows the relevant table or tables and lists their fields. If fields in the tables are related, a relationship line appears between them.

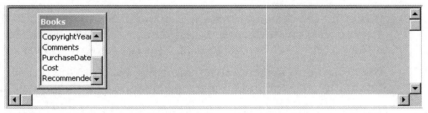

- **Design grid:** This provides a visual tool for building queries. You can specify the fields for display, the sort fields and their sort order, and the conditions that restrict which records are retrieved by the query.

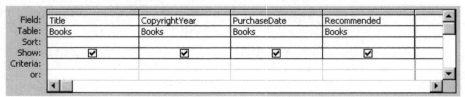

If the query is not currently open, you can open it in Design view by clicking it once to select it in the **Queries** tab of the Database window, and then clicking the **Design** button on the tab's toolbar.

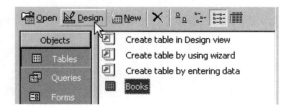

It's a good idea to maximize the query Design view window when working with it.

Display saved sort and filter queries in Design view

What does a sort or a filter, saved as a query, look like when you open that query and display it in Design view?

Find out for yourself by opening some of the queries that you created in Lesson 5.7 and switching to Design view to inspect them. You will discover that the Design view of a query looks very similar to the **Filter** dialog box displayed when, in Lesson 5.7, you chose the **Record | Filter | Advanced Filter/Sort** command to begin the procedure for saving a sort or a filter as a query.

Below are examples of a sort and a filter. Compare how they appear in the **Filter** dialog box and in query Design view.

A sort in the Filter dialog box

Field:	Pages ▾
Sort:	Ascending
Criteria:	
or:	

A saved sort in Design view

Field:	Pages
Table:	Books
Sort:	Ascending
Show:	☐
Criteria:	
or:	

A filter in the Filter dialog box

Field:	ISBN ▾	Cost
Sort:	Ascending	
Criteria:		5.95
or:		

A saved filter in Design view

Field:	ISBN	Cost
Table:	Books	Books
Sort:	Ascending	
Show:	☐	☐
Criteria:		5.95
or:		

Notice two additional rows in the Design view grid: a **Table** row and a **Show** row. The **Table** row enables you to base a query on more than a single table. The **Show** row with its tick boxes allows you to include or exclude individual fields from a query.

What queries can do that sorts and filters cannot

Sorts, filters, queries: each type of operation gives you progressively more choices about how you view the information in a database.

Sorts allow you to rearrange the order of displayed records. But you still see all the records and all their fields. This may be more information than you need.

Filters restrict the records that are displayed. But you still see every field of the filtered records. Again, not every field may be relevant to your information requirements.

Queries make it possible to restrict both the records and the fields displayed, helping you to focus only on the information that you are actually interested in. Is that all? No. A query, unlike a sort or filter, can draw on data from several tables. And filters in queries can include the kind of comparison and logical operators that you used in validation rules in Lesson 5.5.

Sorts, filters and queries are not alternatives to one another. Just as a filter can include a sort, a query can contain a sort and a filter. And a multi-table query can apply different sorts and filters to different tables.

Construct a new query: your three options

Access offers three ways to build a query:

- **Save a sort or a filter as a query:** In this approach, you first perform a sort or a filter, and then save it as a query with the **Record | Filter | Advanced Filter/Sort** command and the **Save As Query** toolbar button.

- **Use the Filter dialog box:** To create a query for a single table, choose **Record | Filter | Advanced Filter/Sort** without first performing a sort or a filter, enter the query details into the design grid, and then save the query with the **Save As Query** toolbar button.

- **Create the query in Design view:** To create a query for multiple tables, or any query that limits which fields are displayed in its results, choose the **Create query in Design view** option on the **Queries** tab of the Database window, select the relevant table(s), enter the details into the design grid, and then save and name your query.

Any query, however it is created, can be opened in query Design view, where you can amend any of its details or add some new ones.

Create a query that contains a multi-column sort

Sort Ascending/
Sort Descending
buttons

In Lesson 5.7 you learned how to sort a table on a single column by clicking any field in the relevant column, and then clicking the **Sort Ascending** or **Sort Descending** button on the Access toolbar. But what if you want to sort a table on multiple columns? For example, you might want to sort an employees table by surname and then, within surname, by date or birth.

Single-column sorts are sometimes called simple sorts and multi-column ones complex sorts. To sort a table on more than one column, you need to create a query that contains a multiple sort. Here are the steps:

1 Open your table in Datasheet view.

2 Choose **Records | Filter | Advanced Filter/Sort** to display the **Filter** dialog box.

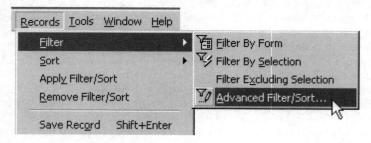

Because you are sorting (and not filtering), only the **Field** and **Sort** rows are relevant.

3 Access sorts on the leftmost column first, then on the next column to the right, and so on. So, in the leftmost column, select the first field you want to sort on, and then select its sort order.

You can continue selecting sort fields and sort orders in the second and third columns, and so on, until finished. Some sample design grids with multi-column sorts are shown below.

Field:	ISBN	AuthID	
Sort:	Ascending	Descending	
Criteria:			
or:			

Field:	ISBN	AuthID	CopyrightYear
Sort:	Ascending	Ascending	Descending
Criteria:			
or:			

Field:	AuthID	Pages	ISBN
Sort:	Ascending	Descending	Descending
Criteria:			
or:			

Save As Query button

4 Click the **Save As Query** button on the toolbar or choose **File | Save As Query**. Name your query when prompted and click **OK**.

5 Click the **Close** button at the top right of the **Filter** box to close it.

You can run the query by double-clicking its name on the **Query** tab of the Database window.

Create a query that contains comparison and logical operators

In Lesson 5.7 you learned how to filter a table by clicking in any field of a column, and then clicking the **Filter by Selection** button on the Access toolbar. Below you can see how a filter, created by clicking in an AuthID field that has a value of 1, appears in the design grid of the **Filter** dialog box.

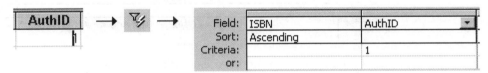

You can also filter on part of a field, as the following example shows. You can see that filtering on part of a field inserts the **Like** operator in the **Filter** dialog box.

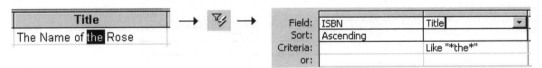

But what if you want to apply a filter other than 'equal to' or 'like'? With a query, you can create filters based on comparison operators (such as >), literals (such as 1900 and #26/11/02#) and logical operators (AND, OR). You met these in Lesson 5.5. Here are the steps:

1 Open your table in Datasheet view.

2 Choose **Records | Filter | Advanced Filter/Sort** to display the **Filter** dialog box.

3 You can use any column of the design grid for any purpose. But by convention the leftmost column is used only for sorting. Because we are focused here on filtering, ignore this column.

In the second and third columns (and further columns, if required), enter in the **Field** boxes the fields you want to filter on, and in the **Criteria** boxes your operators and literals. Some sample design grids with comparison operators and literals are shown overleaf.

Field:	ISBN	Pages	CopyrightYear
Sort:	Ascending		
Criteria:		>=200	<1900
or:			

Field:	ISBN	PurchaseDate	Cost
Sort:	Ascending		
Criteria:		<=#01/01/2000#	=6.99
or:			

Field:	ISBN	Cost	PurchaseDate
Sort:	Ascending		
Criteria:		<>5.95	>#31/12/2001#
or:			

And some sample design grids with comparison operators, literals and logical operators are shown below.

Field:	ISBN	Pages	AuthID
Sort:	Ascending		
Criteria:		>=100 And <=200	<>1 And <>5
or:			

Field:	ISBN	Pages	CopyrightYear
Sort:	Ascending		
Criteria:		=100 Or =200	>1889 And <2001
or:			

Field:	ISBN	PurchaseDate	
Sort:	Ascending		
Criteria:		>=#09/02/2001# And <=#26/11/2002#	
or:			

As you can see from the third example above, you can widen any column of the design grid if required. (Just click and drag the column header.) But it is not necessary. The condition will still apply even if it is not fully visible.

Also, it's not necessary to enter the equals operator (=) before a literal. The following two criteria have the same effect.

AuthID		AuthID
=12		12

Save As Query button

4 When finished, click the **Save As Query** button on the toolbar or choose **File | Save As Query**. Name your query when prompted and click **OK**.

5 Click the **Close** button at the top right of the **Filter** box to close it.

You can run the query by double-clicking its name on the **Query** tab of the Database window.

A query that contains comparison operators, perhaps joined by logical operators, is known as a *select query*. Why? Because it selects only certain information from a table and ignores the rest.

Create a query that includes only certain columns

By now you have learned how to build a query that retrieves from a table only the records you need to see. You can refine your information analyses even further by including only certain fields in the retrieved records, and excluding those you are not interested in. This is achieved by using the checkboxes in the **Show** row in a query's Design view.

Follow these steps to create a query that displays only specified fields in its results.

1   Display the **Queries** tab of the Database window, and double-click the **Create query in Design view** option.

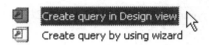

2   Access displays the **Tables** tab of the **Show Tables** dialog box. Click the table on which you want to base your query, click **Add** and then **Close**.

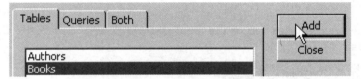

3   Perform the following actions in the Select Query window:

   ■ In the **Field** row of the design grid, select the fields from which you want your query to draw information.

   ■ In the **Sort** row, you can select a sort order for any field or fields.

   ■ In the **Show** row, untick any checkbox if you do not want that field to appear in your query's results. A query can sort or filter on a field without actually displaying that field.

   ■ In the **Criteria** row, enter any comparison operators, literals and logical and comparison operators. A sample is shown below.

Field:	ISBN	Pages	Title	CopyrightYear
Table:	Books	Books	Books	Books
Sort:				
Show:	☑	☐	☑	☐
Criteria:		>100 And <200		>=2000

4   When finished, click the **Close** button at the top right of the Select Query window, and save and name your query when prompted.

   You can run the query by double-clicking its name on the **Query** tab of the Database window.

Reorder columns in a query

Sometimes you may want to change the order in which columns appear in a query. For example, when you sort on multiple columns, Access works from left to right. If you want to sort first on what is currently the second or third column in the design grid, you could move that column to the left so that it becomes the new first column. Here are the steps:

1   Open the query in Design view.

2   Hold the cursor just above the column and click to select the entire column. The cursor changes shape to become a thick downward arrow.

Click and hold
with mouse to
select column

3 Click it again, but, this time, hold down the mouse button. Notice that that a dashed rectangle box appears on the tail of the mouse pointer.

4 Drag the column, left or right, to the new location. As you drag with the mouse over each column, Access displays a bold vertical line at the right of that column.

5 Access is asking you: is this where you want to place the column? If you have positioned the dragged column over your required new location, release the mouse button, and the column moves.

If not, keep dragging until the bold line appears at your required location, and release the mouse button

Try this a number of times until you are confident about it.

Create a multi-table query

You can use multi-table queries to bring together data from different tables. Follow these steps to create one:

1 Display the **Queries** tab of the Database window, and click the **Create query in Design view** option.

2 Access displays the **Tables** tab of the **Show Tables** dialog box. Hold down the **CTRL** key, click the tables you want to query, click **Add** and then **Close**.

3 Perform the following actions in the Select Query window:

■ In the **Table** row of the design grid, select the tables from whose fields you want use your query to draw information.

Table:	Customers	Customers	Products	Employees

■ In the **Field** row of the design grid, select the fields from which you want your query to draw information.

Field:	CustomerID	ContactName	ProductID	LastName
Table:	Customers	Customers	Products	Employees

■ In the **Sort** row, you can select a sort order for any field or fields.

Field:	CustomerID	ContactName	ProductID	LastName
Table:	Customers	Customers	Products	Employees
Sort:	Ascending	Descending		

■ In the **Show** row, untick any checkbox if you do not want that field to appear in your query's results. A query can sort or filter on a field without actually displaying that field.

■ In the **Criteria** row, enter any comparison operators, literals, and logical and comparison operators.

4 When finished, click the **Close** button at the top right of the Select Query window, and save and name your query when prompted.

You can run the query by double-clicking its name on the **Query** tab of the Database window.

Create a sample multi-table query

As practice, let's build a query that retrieves recommended books with a copyright year before 1950. This query draws data from both the Books table and the Authors table, and the results will be sorted in order of their author's last name.

1 Display the **Queries** tab of the Database window, and click the **Create query in Design view** option.

2 Access displays the **Tables** tab of the **Show Tables** dialog box. Hold down the **CTRL** key, click the Books and Authors tables, click **Add** and then **Close**.

3 Using the design grid, select or enter the details shown below.

Field:	AuthLastName	Title	Recommended	CopyrightYear
Table:	Authors	Books	Books	Books
Sort:	Ascending			
Show:	☑	☑	☐	☑
Criteria:			=Yes	<1950
or:				

All the books retrieved by the query will be 'recommended' books, so you do not need to display the Recommended column.

4 When finished, click the **Close** button at the top right of the Select Query window, and save and name your query when prompted.

Run the query by double-clicking its name on the **Query** tab of the Database window. The result should be similar to that shown below, depending on which books you have ticked as recommended in your Books table.

AuthLastName	Title	Copyright Year
Alcott	Little Women	1868
Austen	Sense and Sensibility	1876
Bronte	Northanger Abbey	1855
Bronte	Jane Eyre	1847
Orwell	Animal Farm	1945

Quit Access

You can close your Bookworm.mdb database and quit Access. You have now completed Lesson 5.8 of the ECDL Databases Module.

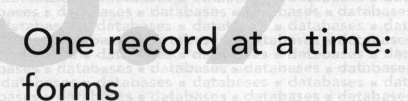

One record at a time: forms

Learning goals   At the end of this lesson you should be able to:

- use AutoForm to create a new form;
- use the Form Wizard to create a new form;
- view and navigate through table records with a form;
- use a form to sort and filter table records;
- use a form to create a new record;
- use a form to update a new record.

New term   At the end of this section you should be able to explain the following term:

Form   Forms enable table records to be viewed and updated one at a time. As forms are based on tables, you can create a form only after you have created a table.

Until now, you have been creating, updating and deleting table records in Datasheet view – they have been shown in rows, with a column for each field.

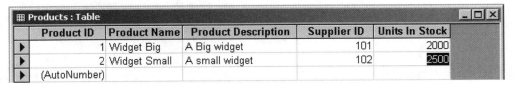

Datasheet view can make reading the information difficult, and it's annoying if the fields and records extend beyond the edges of your screen, so that you have to scroll left and right and up and down to see the items of interest.

About forms

Forms are better for those times when all you really want to see is information relating to a single record at one time, laid out in an attractive manner. Forms have the added advantage of being much easier to read, and you can design different, eye-pleasing forms for different purposes. As you will learn in this lesson, everything you can do in a datasheet you can also do in a form. You can:

- input new records;

- update existing records;

- sort the records into a different order;

- filter the records so that only ones that match your criteria are displayed.

Different views: same information

As forms are based on tables, you can create a form only after you have created a table. Both forms and the datasheet contain the same information: any change you make to data in a form is reflected immediately in the datasheet, and any change you make in a datasheet is reflected in the associated forms.

You can create forms quickly and easily with the Access Form Wizard. You simply select which fields from the table you want to include on your form, choose from a range of data layouts and decorative styles, and give your form a name.

Open your Bookworm database

Open button

1 Launch Microsoft Access, click the **Open** button on the Access toolbar or choose **File | Open**.

2 Select the following database file and click **Open**:

Bookworm

You will use this sample database throughout this lesson.

Use AutoForm to create a form

Access's AutoForm feature offers a fast and easy method of creating forms. AutoForm has one limitation, however:

- The form must include all fields from the underlying table or query.

Such a form is known as an all fields form. Follow these steps to create a form for the current database using the AutoForm feature:

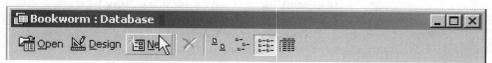

Forms tab

1 Display the **Forms** tab of the Database window.

2 Click the **New** button on the toolbar of the Database window – not on the toolbar of the main Access window.

3 In the **New Form** dialog box displayed, click the **AutoForm: Columnar** option. (It is unlikely that you would ever want to select any of the other AutoForm options.)

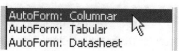

4 In the pull-down list select the table or query on which you want to base the form.

5 Click **OK**.

Access now displays your new form in a separate window. It's that simple.

As practice, use AutoForm to create all fields forms for your Books and Authors tables. They should look as shown below. Name them BooksAllFields and AuthorsAllFields.

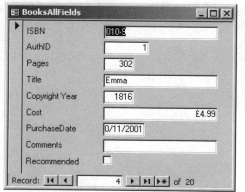

All forms that you create by whatever method are listed on the **Forms** tab of the Database window.

View records with a form

Displaying records from a table or query in a form is easy. Just:

1 Display the **Forms** tab of the Database window.

2 Double-click the form to open it.

To close a form, click the **Close** button at the top right of the form window.

Navigate records with a form

When you open a form to display records from the underlying table or query, you can move through the various records using the navigation buttons displayed at the lower-left of the form window.

Button	Description
⏮	Displays the very first record at the top of the table.
◀	Displays the previous record.
▶	Displays the next record.
⏭	Displays the very last record at the bottom of the table.

Record number box

You can also view a specific record by typing its record number directly and pressing **ENTER**.

Switch between Datasheet, Form and Design view

You now know three ways of looking at information in a table: Datasheet view, Design view and Form view.

- To switch between different views, click the arrow beside the **View** button on the Access toolbar, or choose the commands on the **View** menu.

Use a form to sort records

As in Datasheet view, you can sort records in Form view. Here are the steps:

1 In the form, click anywhere in the field that you want to sort on.

CopyrightYear | 1814

Sort Ascending/ Sort Descending buttons

2 Click the **Sort Ascending** or **Sort Descending** button on the Access toolbar.

Use a form to filter by selection

As in Datasheet view, you can filter records in Form view. Follow these steps:

1 Display a record that satisfies your filtering criterion.

CopyrightYear | 1847

2 Drag across the relevant field value (or part of a field value).

3 Click the **Filter by Selection** button on the Access toolbar.

Filter by Selection button

In the navigation area at the bottom left of the form window you can see the number of records that meet your criterion. If required, you can filter these records again to further refine your search. And, as in Datasheet view, you can save your filter criteria as a query.

Use a form to perform an advanced filter/sort

In Lesson 5.7 you learned how to use the design grid to perform a sort or filter. This option is also available for forms.

1 With a form open, choose **Records | Filter | Advanced Filter/Sort** to display the **Filter** dialog box.

2 Specify your criteria for the filter in the design grid, and click **OK**.

Filter by form

Filter by Form button

Apply Filter button

Remove Filter button

Yet another form option is called filter by form. Here is the procedure:

1 With a form open, click the **Filter by Form** button on the Access toolbar, or choose **Records | Filter | Filter By Form**.

2 In the displayed form, enter your criteria, or where fields show a pull-down list, select your criteria. Some fields may show default values for you to accept, amend or delete.

3 Click the **Apply Filter** button on the Access toolbar so that only those records that match your criteria will be viewable in the form.

4 Click the **Remove Filter** button on the Access toolbar, and all records in the underlying table or query again become viewable.

Use a form to create new records

Create New Record button

Forms are not just for viewing existing records. You can also add new ones:

■ To add a new record, click the **Create New Record** button in the navigation bar at the lower left of the form window. Access presents a new, blank form for you to fill in.

You can complete the fields in any order by clicking in the field and entering the information. The easiest way to complete the form, however, is as follows:

1 Complete the first field. Access automatically positions the cursor there when you open the form.

2 Proceed in order through the fields either by pressing **TAB** or by pressing **ENTER**.

3 When you have filled in the last field in the form, press **TAB** or **ENTER** to open up a new, blank form.

Practise your record-creation skills by adding a new record to the Authors table as follows:

1 Open your AuthorsAllFields Form.

2 In the navigation area at the bottom of the form window, click the **Create New Record** button.

3 Enter the details of Australian author Murray Ball as shown below.

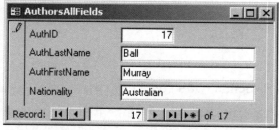

Access adds the AuthID field automatically. Remember: it's a primary key field of the AutoNumber data type.

4 Close the form window when finished.

Use a form to update records

Follow these steps to use the currently open form to modify the information:

1 Locate the record you are interested in, by navigation, sorting or filtering.

2 Click the field you want to change.

3 Delete, overwrite, or add a value.

4 To confirm the update, press **ENTER** or click in another field of the form.

Any changes you make to the information in a form are immediately reflected in the underlying table. Remember: the Datasheet and Form views are just two ways of looking at the same information.

Use the Form Wizard to create a form

The Form Wizard offers an alternative to AutoForm that does not have its limitations:

- Forms created can be based on multiple tables or queries.

- Forms need not include all fields.

- Forms can use a number of different styles.

In short, a form that you create with the Form Wizard can draw on a wider range of information, but can focus on a narrow area of interest. The Wizard presents four dialog boxes. Each is called 'Form Wizard', and contains a number of sub-steps.

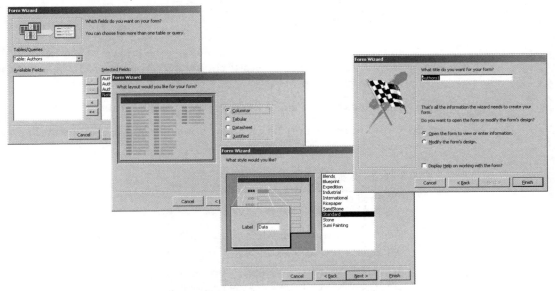

The following table summarizes each of the four **Form Wizard** dialog boxes.

Dialog box	Description
Form Wizard (1)	You select the table or query on which you want to base your new form, and the fields that you want to include in it.
Form Wizard (2)	You enter a columnar layout for your form. (It is unlikely that you would ever want to select any of the other layout types.)
Form Wizard (3)	You select a style for your form, and give it a name.
Form Wizard (4)	Finally, you tell Access what you want to do with your new form. Typically, you indicate that you want to open it to view or enter information.

Let's follow the Form Wizard procedure in more detail:

1 Display the **Forms** tab of the Database window, and double-click **Create form by using wizard**.

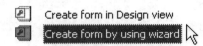
Create form in Design view
Create form by using wizard

2 Select the table or query that will be the basis for the form, and use the arrow buttons provided to move from the **Available Fields** list to the **Selected Fields** list those fields that you want included in your new form.

Button	Description
>	Includes the selected field in your new form.
>>	Includes all fields in your new form.
<	Removes the selected field from your new form.
<<	Removes all fields from your new form.

(You will recognize that the dialog box is very similar to the one presented by the Table Wizard from Lesson 5.2.). Click **Next** to continue the Form Wizard procedure.

3 In the second dialog box, Access offers you several possible layouts for your form. Typically, you will select the **Columnar** option. Click **Next** to continue the Form Wizard procedure.

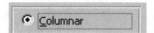
⦿ Columnar

4 In the third dialog box, Access offers you a choice of form styles. You can preview styles by selecting them in turn. Typically, you will select the **Standard** option.

Click **Next** to continue the Form Wizard procedure.

5 In the fourth dialog box, you accept or amend the suggested name for your form.

What title do you want for your form?
MyFirstForm|

Access also asks you what you want to do with your new form. Typically, you will select the option below.

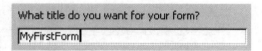
⦿ Open the form to view or enter information.

6 Click the **Finish** button to close the Form Wizard.

Well done. You can now use the form to browse through or update the records in its underlying table or query.

Practise your Form Wizardry by creating the following form for your Authors table.

1 Display the **Forms** tab of the Database window, and double-click the **Create form by using wizard** option.

2 Select the following fields for inclusion in your new form: AuthID, AuthLastName and AuthFirstName. Click **Next**.

3 Select the **Columnar** layout and click **Next**.

4 Select the **Standard** style and click **Next**.

5 Change the suggested form name to the following: Authors Form.

6 Select the **Open the form to view** or **Modify information** option, and click **Finish**.

A sample record displayed in your form should look as shown below. You can now close the form window.

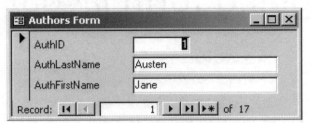

Quit Access

You can close your Bookworm.mdb database and quit Access. You have now completed Lesson 5.9 of the ECDL Databases Module.

5.10

Designing form layout

Learning goals At the end of this lesson you should be able to:

- display a form in Design view;
- create a form header and footer;
- change header and footer height;
- change the form width;
- hide a header or footer;
- set a header's or footer's background colour;
- insert a label container in a header or footer, and type and edit text;
- format label text;
- reposition a label container;
- resize a label container.

New term At the end of this lesson you should be able to explain the following term:

**Form
header/footer** An area at the top/bottom of a form that holds text or images which remain
the same regardless of which record is displayed in the form.

As you can see from the example below, taken from the sample Northwind database, forms need not be visually unexciting.

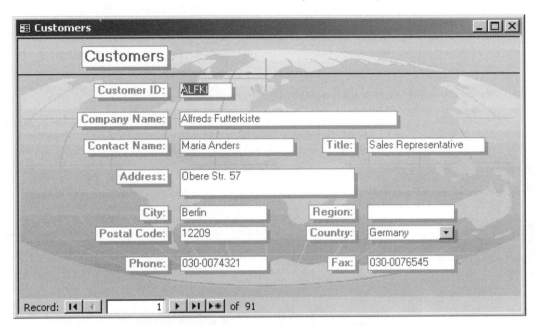

For most purposes, the Form Wizard does a fine job. By switching to Design view, however, you can 'go behind the scenes' of your form, and apply a wide range of formatting effects to brighten up a perhaps otherwise dull, grey form.

Form headers and footers

In addition to the main form area (called the details area) which holds the forms fields and their associated text labels, forms can also include a *header* and *footer* region. You can use the header and footer to display decorative or informative text, and take complete control over its appearance. For example, in Design view, you can:

- Change the position and alignment of text.
- Apply font formatting and colours.
- Set the background colour behind the text.

In this lesson you will explore the basics of these formatting features.

Open your Bookworm database

Open button

1 Launch Microsoft Access, click the **Open** button on the Access toolbar or choose **File | Open**.

2 Select the following database file and click **Open**:

Bookworm

You will use this sample database throughout this lesson.

Switch between Form view and Design view

**Design
View** button

Form View
button

You can switch between Form view and Design view of a form just as you can between the two views of a table: by clicking the relevant view button at the left of the Access toolbar.

- If your form is open in Form view, switch to Design view by clicking the **Design View** button on the Access toolbar, or by choosing **View | Design View**.

- If your form is open in Design view, return to Form view by clicking the **Form View** button on the Access toolbar, or by choosing **View | Datasheet View**.

Design view may look intimidating. It takes you 'behind the scenes' to where you can see and change the organizational structure of your form. Below is your all fields Authors form in Design view.

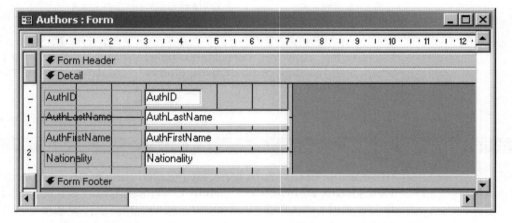

If a form is not currently open, you can open it in Design view by clicking it once to select it in the **Forms** tab of the Database window, and then clicking the **Design** button on the tab's toolbar.

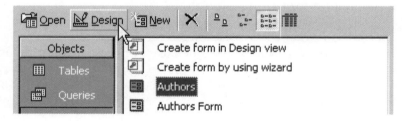

Work with the Formatting Toolbox

The toolbox

When you open a form in Design view, the associated toolbox should open automatically. If it does not, choose **View | Toolbox** to display it. The toolbox offers a number of useful options in addition to those available on the Access toolbar.

To discover a button's purpose in the toolbox, hold the mouse over it briefly – Access displays a brief description. Two of the more commonly used buttons are those for the **Line** and **Rectangle (Border)** drawing tools.

To hide the displayed toolbox, click **View | Toolbox** again.

Don't be afraid to experiment with the toolbar and toolbox options in Design view. If your formatting actions don't produce the results you had intended, use the **Undo** button to reverse your actions.

Create headers and footers on forms

Every form has a detail section that contains the form's field labels and text boxes:

AuthLastName

Field label

- **Field labels:** These are the items of text that describe the boxes which display values from the underlying table. By default, field labels have the same names as the table's columns.

13

Text box

- **Text boxes:** These are the rectangular boxes that display values from the underlying table.

In addition, a form can also include header and footer sections. Their two main features are as follows:

- Header and footer areas do not scroll when the rest of the form is scrolled.

- Header and footer areas display the information irrespective of which record is displayed in the form. For example, you could display a title for the form in the form header, and some instructions on form use in the footer.

In general, headers and footers can personalize a form, and make its purpose clearer to users. Here are the steps for inserting them:

1   Display your form in Design view. You can see that a form header and footer are present by default, but that their size is shrunk to zero.

2   Choose the **View** menu and look for the **Form Header/Footer** command. By default the command should be selected, as indicated by a check mark. If so, click it once to deselect it, and then a second time to reselect it. If it is not currently selected, click it now.

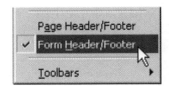

Your form in Design view should now look as shown overleaf. As you can see, the form headers and footers now occupy a larger area.

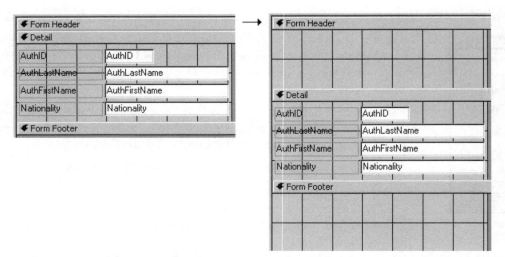

The new, expanded size of the header and footer areas is likely to be much too large for any practical form layout purpose. Switch from Design view to Form view to verify that this is so. You next need to learn how to change the vertical height of these two areas.

Change the header and footer vertical height

To change the size of a form header or footer area, hold the cursor over their dividing line, and then click, hold and drag.

For the form header, click on the dividing line just above the detail section, and drag up or down.

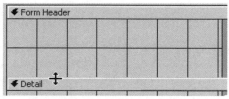 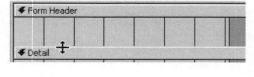

For the form footer, click on the bottom edge of the footer, and drag up or down.

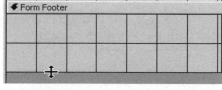 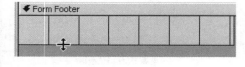

Hide a form header or footer

You can insert a header and footer only as a pair. If you want to hide one, do either of the following:

- Adjust its height until it has zero (i.e. no) height, or

- Right-click anywhere on the header or footer area, and choose **Properties** from the pop-up menu. In the **Format** tab of the Selection window, select a Visible option of **No**.

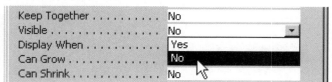

You can close the Selection window by clicking the **Close** button in its top right corner.

Change the form horizontal width

Changing the width of the form area

When you work with forms in Design view, you may find that the form background is not wide enough or, perhaps, too wide. (The background is the light grey area with black dots.)

- To change the width of the form background area, click its boundary (the cursor changes to a double-headed arrow), and then drag with the mouse.

You can resize the form background width as often as you wish in accordance with your design needs. The width of the header and footer areas is the same as that of the form background.

Set the header and footer fill (background) colours

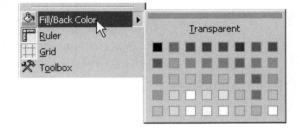

By default, headers and footers, like the detail section of a form, are shown with a grey background. But you are not limited to this colour. Follow these steps to change the background colour (Access calls it the fill color):

1 Right-click anywhere on the background area of a header or footer.

2 From the pop-up menu displayed, choose **Fill/Back Color**, and click a colour option of your choice.

Practise by changing the background colours in a form, and then switching to Form view to inspect the results of your colour changes.

Insert a label container in a header or footer and type text

Label button

Before you can type any text into a header or footer, you must first create a container to hold that text. Here are the steps to follow:

1 Click the **Label** button in the toolbox.

2 Move the cursor over the form header or footer area. Notice how the cursor changes shape to a letter A with a plus (+) sign.

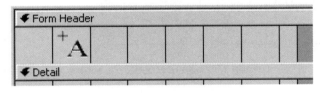

3 Click in the form header or footer, and drag to draw the container.

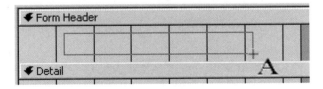

4 When finished drawing, release the mouse button.

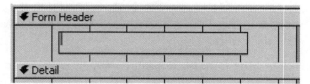

5 Access creates the container. Type text in it immediately.

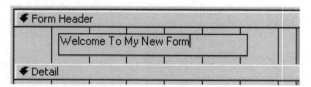

If you create a container, and then click anywhere else on the screen, Access deletes the empty container.

Edit label text

To amend previously typed text in a container, click in the container and edit text in the usual way. For example, you could amend the column heading 'Title' to 'Book Title'.

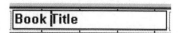

Format label text

You can use the buttons on the Access Formatting toolbar to change the font, font size, font colour or font style and other attributes of any header or footer text.

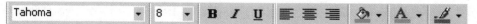

Just click anywhere in the text container to select the container, and then click the relevant toolbar button or option.

You cannot select and then format selected characters in a container, only the entire container.

Reposition a label container

Follow these steps to move a container to a different part of the header or footer area.

1 Click anywhere in the text container to select the container. Seven sizing handles and one move handle appear at the edges of the container. The move handle is the larger one at the top left of the container.

2 Click once on the move handle. The cursor changes to a pointing hand.

3 Drag with the mouse to move the container to its new location, and then release the mouse button.

Resize a label container

Follow these steps to change the size of a label container:

1 Click anywhere in the text container to select the container. Seven sizing handles and one move handle appear at the edges of the container. The move handle is the larger one at the top left of the container.

2 Click on any sizing handle. The cursor changes to a double-headed arrow.

3 Drag in the direction required, and release the mouse when finished.

Quit Access

You can close your Bookworm.mdb database and quit Access. You have now completed Lesson 5.10 of the ECDL Databases Module.

5.11

Printing and reports

Learning goals At the end of this lesson you should be able to:

- set page size, margins and orientation;
- preview a database object before you print it;
- use the options on the Print Preview window;
- print a table, form or query;
- create a report using the AutoReport feature;
- copy and delete a report.

New term At the end of this lesson you should be able to explain the following term:

Report A document (printed or on screen) that presents information in a structured way.

Print button

Like other Microsoft Office applications, Access offers you complete control over how information is printed.

The Access print options include a print preview feature and the ability, for tables and queries, to print selected rows only. You can change page size, margins and orientation with the **File | Page Setup** dialog box.

From screen prints to reports

Although you can print out any Access screen – such as the result of sorting or filtering records in Datasheet view – Access's built-in reporting features provide a wider range and greater depth of options for transferring your computerized database information to the printed page.

For example, you can highlight important information, group data into categories, and give totals and count information for each category, sub-category, and for the entire report.

Working with AutoReport

Access' AutoReport feature is the quickest and easiest way to produce a *report*. It offers two layout options:

- **Columnar:** Access prints each selected field on a separate line with the field name to its left.

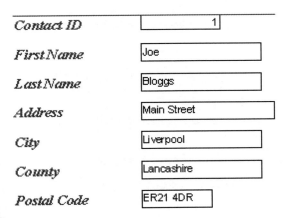

- **Tabular:** Access prints the fields of each record on a single line, and prints the field names once at the top of each page of the report.

Contact ID	First Name	Last Name	Address	City	County	Postal Code
1	Joe	Bloggs	Main Street	Liverpool	Lancashire	ER21 4DR

As a general rule, you use tabular layout for reports that have many records with small fields, and columnar layout for reports with larger fields and fewer records.

Set page size

You can specify the size of the page on which Access prints any database object.

1 Choose **File | Page Setup**, and click the **Page** tab.

2 Select an option from the **Size** pull-down list.

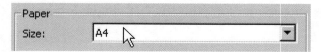

It is unlikely that you will want to change from the default of **A4**. This is the European standard paper size (21 cm wide and 29.7 cm high).

3 When finished, click **OK** to apply your page size settings and close the dialog box.

Set page orientation

Orientation is the direction in which the page is printed. To set page orientation:

1 Choose **File | Page Setup**, and click the **Page** tab.

2 Select an option from the **Orientation** area. Your options are **Portrait** ('standing up') and **Landscape** ('on its side').

3 When finished, click **OK** to apply your orientation setting and close the dialog box.

Set page margins

A margin is the distance of a page's printed content from the edge of the paper. You can set each of the page's four margins (top, bottom, left and right) independently as follows:

1 Choose **File | Page Setup**, and click the **Margins** tab.

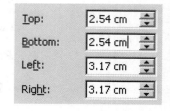

2 Amend the **Top**, **Bottom**, **Left** and **Right** margin values, as required.

The default margin values are: top and bottom, 2.54 cm (1 inch), left and right, 3.17 cm (1.25 inches).

3 When finished, click **OK** to apply your margin settings and close the dialog box.

Preview a printout

You can preview in a separate window on your screen how your printout will look before sending it to your printer.

Print Preview button

- To display a preview, click the **Print Preview** button on the Access toolbar or choose **File | Print**. Click **Close** to return to your document.

The upper portion of a sample Print Preview window is shown below.

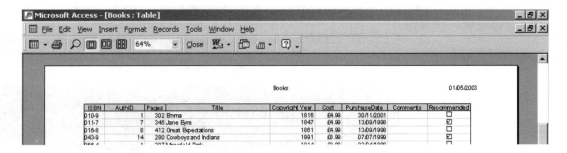

Work with the Print Preview window

When you display the Print Preview window, the main Access toolbar shows buttons that you can use to change how your previewed database object item is displayed.

Button	Description
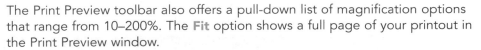	Click once to zoom in on your printout, and a second time to zoom out again.
	Click to display one page of your printout at a time.
	Click to display two pages of your printout at a time, side-by-side.
	Click to display up to six pages of your printout at a time.

Magnification options

The Print Preview toolbar also offers a pull-down list of magnification options that range from 10–200%. The **Fit** option shows a full page of your printout in the Print Preview window.

You can move around the currently previewed page using the scroll-bars. Use the navigation buttons at the lower left of the Print Preview window to move between pages.

Close button

To close the Print Preview window and return to your database object, click the **Close** button on the Print Preview toolbar. You can print the previewed database object by clicking the **Print** button on the Access toolbar or by choosing **File | Print**.

Print a table or query

Print button

To print the currently open table or query, choose **File | Print** to display the **Print** dialog box, select the page(s) that you want to print, and then click **Print**. Clicking the **Print** button on the Access toolbar does not show the **Print** dialog box. Before you print, ensure that you set the margins and page set-up to suit your requirements. Typically, you will want to print a table or query in landscape orientation.

To print only a selection of records from the currently open table or query:

1 Select the records from the table that you want to print.

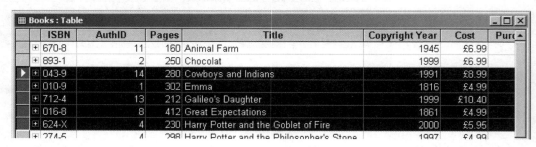

2 Choose **File | Print**.

3 Select the option on the right in the **Print** dialog box.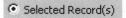

4 Click the **Print** button.

Print a form

To print the currently open form, choose **File | Print** to display the **Print** dialog box, select the page(s) you want to print, and then click **Print**. You cannot select individual records or ranges of records when printing a form.

A Print Preview window of a form printout is shown below. As you can see, Access places as many records as will fit on a single page. You will typically print forms in portrait orientation.

Clicking the **Print** button on the Access toolbar does not show the **Print** dialog box. Before you print, ensure that you set the margins and page set-up to suit your requirements.

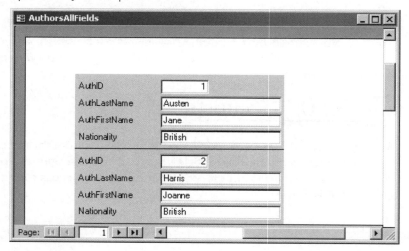

Explore the AutoReport feature

While you can directly print any currently open database object, Access's built-in reporting features provide a wider range and greater depth of options for transferring your computerized database information to the printed page.

The quickest, simplest way to produce a report in Access is to use the AutoReport feature. It offers two options:

■ **Columnar:** Access prints each field on a separate line, with field names in a column on the left and field values in a column on the right. Access does not split a record between pages. In most cases, therefore, each printed page will show only a single record.

■ **Tabular:** Access prints the fields of each record on a single line. Field names are printed once at the top of each page of the report. You can think of the tabular reporting option as a printed version of Datasheet view of a table.

Create a report with AutoReport: columnar

Let's practise using the AutoReport feature with the Books table of the Bookworm database.

Reports tab

1 Open the Bookworm database, display the **Reports** tab of the Database window, and click the **New** button on the toolbar.

2 In the upper part of the **New Report** dialog box, select the option shown below.

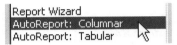

3 In the lower part of the **New Report** dialog box, select the Books table from the pull-down list of tables and queries, and click **OK**.

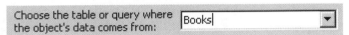

4 Access creates the report and displays it in a separate Print Preview window. It has the same name as the table that it is based on: Books.

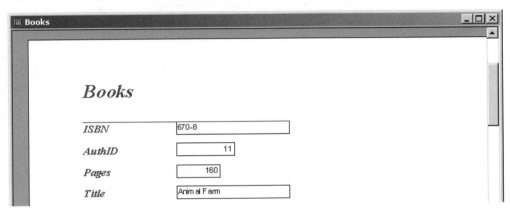

5 Close the Report window. You will be prompted to save it. Name it as shown below, and click **OK**.

Create a report with AutoReport: tabular

Next, let's try the second type of report that the AutoReport feature can produce, the tabular report.

1 With **Reports** tab of the Database window displayed, click the **New** button on the toolbar.

2 In the upper part of the **New Report** dialog box, select the option shown below.

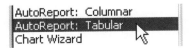

3 In the lower part of the **New Report** dialog box, select the **Recommended 20th Century Books** query that you created in Lesson 5.7. Click **OK**.

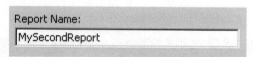

4 Access creates the report and displays it in a separate window. It has the same name as the query that it is based on.

5 Close the Report window. You will be prompted to save it. Name it as shown below, and click **OK**.

Report Name:

MySecondReport

AutoReports: some drawbacks

AutoReports are quick and easy to create, but they have limitations. These reports can be based only on a single table or query, and must include all the fields in that table or query. Moreover, in a tabular report, Access can sometimes trim the column headings and squeeze together the information in the columns.

A way around these issues is to first create a query that contains only the records and fields that you absolutely need in your report. Your query can, of course, draw information from more than one table. When finished building your query, you can then create an AutoReport based on that query.

Print a report

Print button

To print the currently open report, choose **File | Print** to display the **Print** dialog box, select the range of pages that you want to print, and click **Print**.

Clicking the **Print** button on the Access toolbar does not show the **Print** dialog box. Before you print, ensure sure that you set the margins and page set-up to suit your requirements.

Copy a report

Follow these steps to make a copy of a report within a database:

1 Display the **Reports** tab in the Database window.

2 Right-click the report and choose **Copy** from the pop-up menu.

3 Choose **Edit | Paste**.

4 Access prompts you to give the report a different name. Do so and click **OK**.

You might find it convenient to save copies of your reports before making changes to them.

Delete a report

Follow these steps to remove a report from a database:

1 Display the **Reports** tab in the Database window.

2 Right-click the report and choose **Delete** from the pop-up menu.

3 Click **Yes** when prompted to confirm that you want to delete the report.

Quit Access

You can close your Bookworm.mdb database and quit Access. You have now completed Lesson 5.11 of the ECDL Databases Module.

5.12

Reports: sorting, grouping, calculating

Learning goals

At the end of this lesson you should be able to:

- create a report using the Report Wizard;
- group records in a report;
- perform calculations on grouped data.

New terms

At the end of this lesson you should be able to explain the following terms:

Report Wizard   A feature that simplifies the process of creating a new report in a database.

Grouped report   A report in which information is divided into easy-to-read blocks, with data sorted within each block. Calculations may be performed on the data within each block.

About reports

In the previous lesson you learned how to use the AutoReports feature to produce good-looking reports quickly and easily. But to take full control of a report's content and format, you need to use the *Report Wizard*. The Wizard brings to the task of database reporting three very powerful features: sorting, groups and calculations.

Sorting your records

The current sort order of the records in a table (or query) you are reporting on may not be the order that you would like in your report. With the Report Wizard, you can apply single or multiple criteria sorts to the records you want to include in your report.

For example, if a business wanted to print a report on its customers, it could sort the information in order of (descending) sales value within (ascending) region name.

Grouping your sorted records

An elegant way of presenting sorted reports is to group the records within the sort criteria.

In the example of the customer report, Access would print the region name only once (and not on every line), and perhaps highlight the region name to make the report easier to read.

Performing calculations on groups

When you sort and then group your records, you can tell Access to perform calculations on the data within each group. Among the available calculation options are totals, averages, and maximum and minimum values.

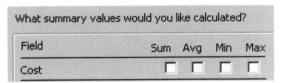

Layout and style options

Like AutoReports, the Report Wizard offers both columnar and tabular formats. But that is not all. You can also choose from a variety of formatting styles that range from the plain (adequate for most tasks) to the very decorative (for marketing purposes, perhaps).

Explore the Report Wizard

Access contains a *Report Wizard* that simplifies the process of creating a new report in a database. You start the Report Wizard by double-clicking the option below on the **Reports** tab of the Database window.

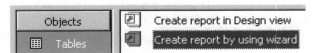

The Wizard presents six dialog boxes. Each is called 'Report Wizard', and contains a number of sub-steps. The following table summarizes their purpose.

Dialog box	Description
Report Wizard (1)	You select the table(s) and/or queries to report on, and choose the relevant fields.
	If your selected table(s) is/are part of a relationship, Access will further ask you how you want to view your report data.
Report Wizard (2)	You specify whether you want to group records within your report, and if so, how you want them grouped. Grouping a report makes it possible to perform calculations on the grouped data.
Report Wizard (3)	You specify single or multiple sort criteria for your report.
Report Wizard (4)	You select a layout from the range of formatting options provided by the Wizard, and set the page orientation.

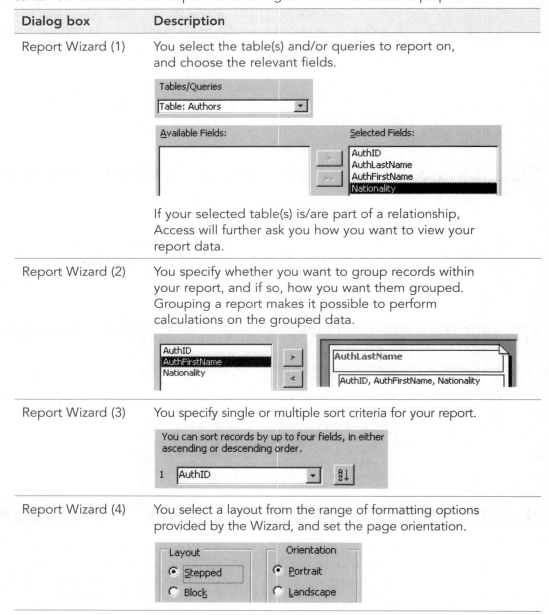

Report Wizard (5)	You select a style from the range of formatting options provided by the Wizard.

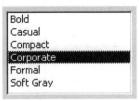

Report Wizard (6)	You name your report, and you tell Access what you want to do with it. Typically, you indicate that you want to view it in a Print Preview window.

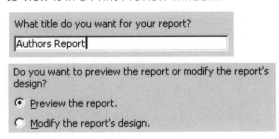

Produce an ungrouped report with the Report Wizard

The best way to learn about the Access Report Wizard is to use it. Let's create a report that does not include any groups or calculations on grouped data.

1 Display the **Reports** tab of the Database window, and double-click the **Create report by using wizard** option.

2 Recognize the next screen? Yes, it's similar to the one you used to create tables and forms.

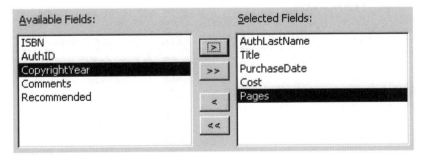

From the Authors table, select AuthLastName.

From the Books table, select Title, PurchaseDate, Cost and Pages.

When finished, click the **Next** button.

3 The Wizard checks for any natural relationships between the fields you have selected, and asks how you want to view your data. For example, because the Authors table has a one-to-many relationship with the Books table, it suggests grouping records by author.

For this exercise, choose **Books** and click **Next**.

4 Do you want to add any grouping levels? Grouping is a way of refining the way your report data is presented. For this exercise, just click **Next**.

5 How do you want Access to sort the records in your report? Sort on the following and click **Next**.

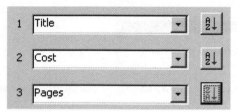

6 Select the layout for the report. As in previous Wizard exercises, you can get a good idea of what this final result will look like by selecting each in turn. Select the options as shown, and click the **Next** button.

7 Select the typographic style for the report. Again, see what they look like by selecting them in turn. For this exercise, select **Bold**, and click the **Next** button.

8 Finally, give the report a title: MyBooks. Select the **Preview** option, and click the **Finish** button.

After a few seconds, you then see your report in a Preview window on your screen. If it is exactly what you want, click the **Print** button on the toolbar, or choose **File | Print**.

Print button

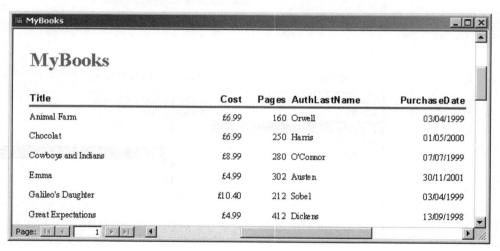

Produce a grouped report with the Report Wizard

The type of report that you produced with the Report Wizard in your first exercise is called a single-level report: each record is printed one after the other and they all look much the same. While applying one or more sort orders to a single-level report does make it a little easier to scan for information of interest, every record is still at the same level as every other record.

You can improve your report's readability by grouping the records in a logical order based on one or more fields. A monthly report of sales to customers, for example, might feature 50 sales transactions to the same customer named Smith. Instead of printing the word 'Smith' 50 times over, you could group the report on the customer surname field. The result would be that a sub-heading called 'Smith' would be printed just once, and under that would be all of Smith's individual transactions. This kind of report is called a multi-level report. Why? Because all the report lines are not of the same level: some are single records, but others are sub-headings.

Let's practise by creating a second report that is similar to your first one, but with one critical difference: the report will be grouped by author.

1   Repeat steps 1 to 3 of your first reporting exercise. The Report Wizard should now display the grouping options dialog box, the upper part of which is shown below.

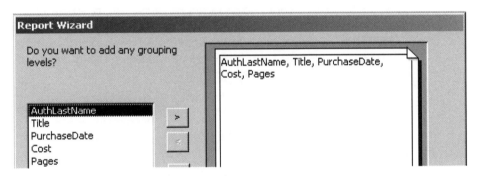

2   We want to group records in the report by author, so select AuthLastName.

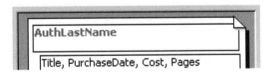

Click **Next**.

3   Repeat step 5 of the previous exercise.

4   Select the layout options as shown, and click the **Next** button.

5   Select the **Bold** style for the report, and click the **Next** button.

6 Name your report MyBooksGrouped. Select the **Preview** option, and click the **Finish** button.

After a few seconds, you then see your report in a Preview window on your screen. If it is exactly what you want, click the **Print** button on the toolbar, or choose **File | Print**.

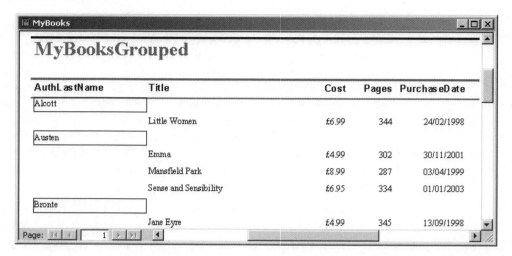

Perform calculations on grouped data within reports

Almost there. In your first reporting exercise you produced an attractive but single-level report. In your second, you created a grouped report. Now you are ready to move to stage three: perform calculations on grouped data in a report. Access offers the following calculation types (functions).

Function	Description	Example
Sum	Totals the field values in the group.	=Sum([Cost])
Min	Displays the minimum (or lowest) value for a field.	=Min([Cost])
Max	Displays the maximum (or highest) value for a field.	=Min([Cost])
Count	Counts the number of records in a group or in the overall report.	=Count([Title])

You insert one or more of these calculations on the sort dialog box of the Report wizard. Clicking the **Summary Options** button displays the relevant **Summary Options** dialog box. This button is available only if your report contains number fields, as these are the only type of field on which calculations may be performed.

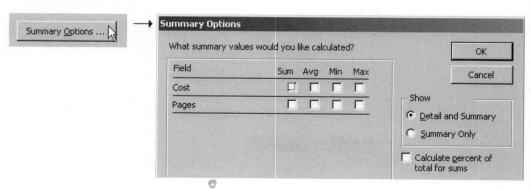

To apply an option, simply click the relevant checkbox, one of which is provided for each number field in your report. In most cases, you will accept the default setting: **Detail and Summary**. To see only grouped data in your report and no individual records, click **Summary Only** instead.

The third and independent option will, if selected, show on your report the percentage contribution of each record to the group total.

When finished with the **Summary Options** dialog box, click **OK** to return to the Sort Details dialog box of the Report Wizard.

As your third and final exercise in this lesson, let's build a report that includes summed group totals.

1   Repeat steps 1 to 3 of the your first reporting exercise. The Report Wizard should now display the grouping options dialog box.

2   We want to group the records in the report by author, so select AuthLastName as shown and click **Next**.

3   Sort the records on the same three fields and in the same three orders as your first two reports. But do not click the **Next** button yet.

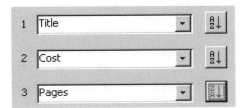

4   At the bottom of the Sort dialog box you can see the following button. Click it.

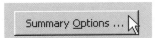

5   Access now displays the **Summary Details** dialog box. Select the options shown below and click **OK**.

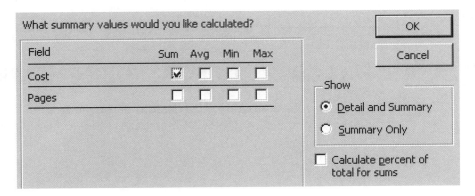

6 Access returns you to the Sort dialog box. Click **Next**.

7 As in your previous two reporting exercises, select the layout options and style shown below.

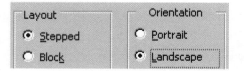

When prompted, name your report MyBooksGroupedandSummed. Select the **Preview** option, and click the **Finish** button.

You can see that Access has inserted group totals in your report.

MyBooksGroupedandSummed

AuthLastName	Title	Cost	Pages	PurchaseDate
Alcott				
	Little Women	£6.99	344	24/02/1998
Summary for 'AuthLastName' = Alcott (1 detail record)				
Sum		£6.99		
Austen				
	Emma	£4.99	302	30/11/2001
	Mansfield Park	£8.99	287	03/04/1999
	Sense and Sensibility	£6.95	334	01/01/2003
Summary for 'AuthLastName' = Austen (3 detail records)				
Sum		£20.93		
Bronte				
	Jane Eyre	£4.99	345	13/09/1998
	Northanger Abbey	£5.95	234	01/01/2003
Summary for 'AuthLastName' = Bronte (2 detail records)				
Sum		£10.94		
Carey				
	The History of the Kelly Gang	£13.60	432	23/10/2000
Summary for 'AuthLastName' = Carey (1 detail record)				
Sum		£13.60		
Dahl				
	The BFG	£3.99	202	01/05/2000
Summary for 'AuthLastName' = Dahl (1 detail record)				
Sum		£3.99		
Dickens				
	Great Expectations	£4.99	412	13/09/1998

Quit Access

You can close your Bookworm.mdb database and quit Access. You have now completed Lesson 5.12 of the ECDL Databases Module.

5.13

Designing a report layout

Learning goals At the end of this lesson you should be able to:

- switch between Print Preview and Design view of a report;
- edit header or footer text;
- resize a header or footer container;
- format header or footer text;
- set the header and footer fill (background) colours;
- reposition a header or footer;
- insert a new header or footer;
- remove a new header or footer.

Like Design views of other database objects that you have met in this module, the Design view of a report looks very different to the usual default view – and much more intimidating as well. Although AutoReports is a quick and effective tool, and the multi-option Report Wizard a very powerful one, you still need to be working in Design view to perform the kind of information analysis tasks that fall into the category of fine-tuning.

Moreover, it is only in Design view that you can add the visual gloss that transforms a merely competent database report into an eye-catching presentation.

The formatting options available for reports are very similar to those for forms, and, like forms, you will discover that reports are sub-divided into self-contained sections or bands that include various headers and footers in addition to the actual fields and their data values. The report below, from the sample Northwind database, provides a hint of the possibilities available.

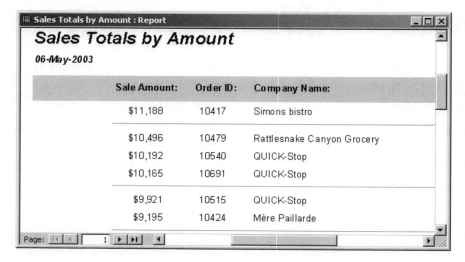

Switch between Print Preview and Design view

Design View button

Print Preview button

Just as the other database objects do, reports have a 'behind the scenes' Design view that allows you to inspect and amend the object's organizational structure.

- If your report is open in Print Preview, switch to Design view by clicking the **Design View** button on the Access toolbar, or by choosing **View | Design View**.

- If your report is open in Design view, return to Print Preview by clicking the **Print Preview** button on the Access toolbar, or choosing **View | Print Preview**.

(A third viewing option, Layout Preview, shows those parts of your report that do not include any calculations.)

If your report is not open, you can open it in Design view by clicking it once to select it in the **Reports** tab of the Database window, and clicking the **Design** button on the tab's toolbar.

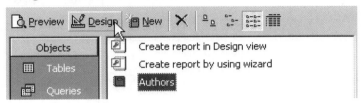

View the four bands of a report

An Access report can contain four main sections called bands. Three of these are headers or footers, and the fourth is the body of the report itself.

- To display the bands of the currently open report, switch to Design view.

In Design view, sections are represented as horizontal bands, and each section that the report contains is shown once.

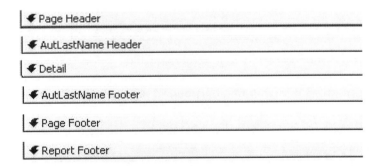

Let's look at each of these four bands in turn:

- **Report Headers and Footers:** Access prints these only once: at the start and at the end of the report respectively.

- **Page Headers and Footers:** Access prints these at the top and at the bottom of every page.

  If a report includes a report header, Access prints the report header first and then the page header after it on the report's first page. If a report includes a report footer, Access prints the report footer first and then the page footer after it at the bottom of the report's last page.

- **Report Detail:** This is the body of your report. It contains the information, drawn from a table or query, that you are reporting on.

- **Group Headers and Footers:** Groups can have their own headers and footers, which appear before and after the grouped data. Typically, the group header displays the values of the field that the group is defined on, and the group footer is used to create sub-totals of values within the group.

Inspect an ungrouped report in Design view

Display the first report that you created in Lesson 5.12, named MyBooks, in Design view. It should look as shown below.

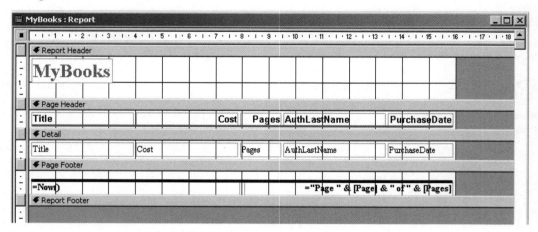

Let's examine the non-Detail bands of the report.

■ **Report Header:** This contains your report's name in large, coloured font.

■ **Page Header:** At the top of every page this report will print the following column headings: Title, Cost, Pages, AuthLastName and PurchaseDate. Notice that text fields are left-aligned but number fields are right-aligned.

■ **Page Footer:** At the left is =Now(), Access's code for today's date. At the right are the current page number and the total page number of the printout (="Page" & [Page] & "of" & [Pages]).

■ **Report Footer:** This is empty.

You can now close your report.

Inspect a grouped report in Design view

Display the second report that you created in Lesson 5.12, named MyBooksGrouped, in Design view. You can see that it contains an additional band not present in your first ungrouped report. This is AuthLastName, the header for the group that is based on the AuthLastName field. It appears before every occurrence of grouped data.

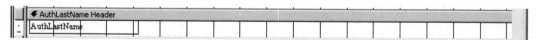

You can now close your report.

Inspect a grouped report with calculations in Design view

Your third report, MyBooksGroupedandSummed, contains grouped data that includes a calculation, and so in Design view you can see the additional areas shown below.

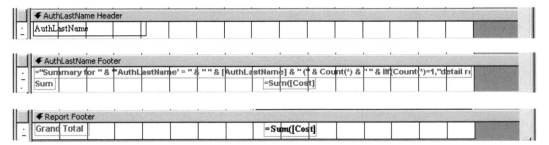

In addition to the AuthLastName Header there is the AuthLastName Footer that holds the actual group calculations and that appears after every occurrence of grouped data. There is also a Report Footer to contain, at the report's end, the total of the grouped sub-totals.

You can now close your report. In the next few sections you will discover ways of changing the appearance of your report's headers and footers.

Work with the Formatting toolbox

The toolbox

When you open a report in Design view, the associated toolbox should open automatically. If it does not, choose **View | Toolbox** to display it. The toolbox offers a number of useful options in addition to those available on the Access toolbar.

To discover a button's purpose in the toolbox, hold the mouse over it briefly and Access displays a brief description. Two of the more commonly used buttons are those for the **Line** and **Rectangle (Border)** drawing tools.

To hide the displayed toolbox, click **View | Toolbox** again.

Don't be afraid to experiment with the toolbar and toolbox options in Design view. If your formatting actions don't produce the results you had intended, use the **Undo** button to reverse your actions.

Edit header or footer text

To amend previously typed text in a box, click in its containing box, and edit the text in the usual way. For example, you could amend the column heading 'Title' to 'Book Title'.

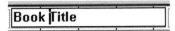

When you switch to Print Preview you can verify that the change has taken effect.

AuthLastName	Book Title	Cost	Pages	PurchaseDate

Resize a header or footer container

If you add or remove text in a header or footer, you may wish to resize the containing box. Here are the steps:

1 Click anywhere in the box to select it. Seven sizing handles and one move handle appear at its edges. The move handle is the larger one at the top left.

2 Click on any sizing handle. The cursor changes to a double-headed arrow.

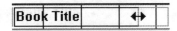

3 Drag in the direction required, and release the mouse when finished.

Format header or footer text

You can use the buttons on the Access Formatting toolbar to change the font, font size, colour or style, and any other attributes of the header or footer text.

Just click anywhere in the box to select it, and then click the relevant toolbar button or option.

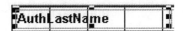

You cannot select and then format selected characters in a box, only the entire box. Try formatting some headers and footers in your sample reports, and then switching to Print Preview to inspect the results of your colour changes.

In the example below, the font of the page header from the Books table report has been changed from the default of Arial to Impact.

AuthLastName	Book Title		Cost	Pages	PurchaseDate

Set the header and footer fill (background) colours

Header and footer elements take their background colours from the options selected in the Report Wizard at the time the report was created.

But you are not limited to these preselected colours. Follow these steps to change the background colour of any header or footer (Access calls it the fill color):

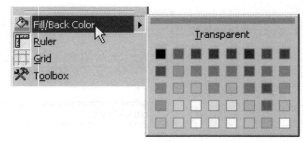

1 Right-click anywhere on the background area of a header or footer.

2 From the pop-up menu displayed, choose **Fill/Back Color**, and click a colour option of your choice.

Practise by changing the background colours of some headers and footers in your sample reports, and then switching to Print Preview to inspect the results of your colour changes.

In the example below you can see that the page header from the Books table report has been changed to a white font against a black background.

AuthLastName	Book Title		Cost	Pages	PurchaseDate

Reposition a header or footer

Follow these steps to move a header or footer element to a different part of its header or footer area.

1 Click anywhere in the text container to select the container. Seven sizing handles and one move handle appear at the edges of the container. The move handle is the larger one at the top left of the container.

2 Click once on the move handle. The cursor changes to a pointing hand.

3 Drag with the mouse to move the container to its new location, and then release the mouse button.

Hint: For small, precise adjustments, select the element, as above, but rather than dragging with the mouse, hold down the **CTRL** key and press an **ARROW** key.

In the example below you can see that the group header from the Books table report has been moved from the left of the page over to the centre.

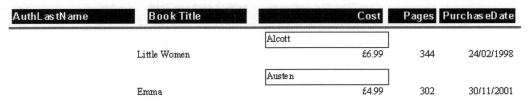

Notice that when you repositioned this header, you did not need to reposition any field. That is because the group header relates to a set of fields. However, when you move a header that refers to a single field, you also need to move that field.

In your sample Books report the Costs column comes before the Pages one. If you swap the page headers containing the words Costs and Pages, you need also to swap their related fields. Let's try it.

1 Open one of your sample reports in Design view.

2 Click on the Costs page header to select it, and then drag it by its move handle to the right.

3 Click on the Pages page header, and then drag it by its move handle to the left. The two page headers should now line up as shown below.

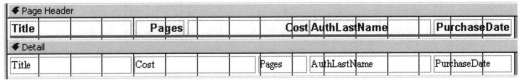

As you can see, the Pages header is above the Cost column, and vice versa.

4 Click on the Pages field, and then drag it by its move handle to the left. Click on the Costs field, and then drag it by its move handle to the right. The two page fields should now line up under the correct page headers as shown.

Page Header							
Title			Pages		Cost	AuthLastName	PurchaseDate
Detail							
Title			Pages	Cost		AuthLastName	PurchaseDate

5 Switch to Print Preview to inspect your work. Your column order should now look as follows.

Title	Pages	Cost	AuthLastName	PurchaseDate
Animal Farm	160	£6.99	Orwell	03/04/1999
Chocolat	250	£6.99	Harris	01/05/2000

Insert a new header or footer

You can insert new container boxes in any header or footer area, and enter and format the text in them. You may need to drag a band boundary to open up additional space to hold your inserted header or footer element. Let's try an example.

1 Open one of your sample reports in Design view.

2 Drag the upper boundary of the Report Footer band downward to create a new line of empty space within the Page Footer.

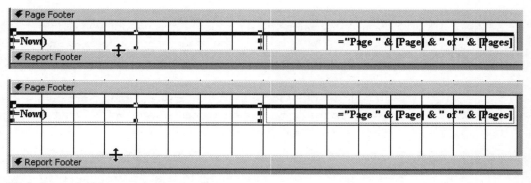

 Aa

Label button

3 Click the **Label** button in the toolbox.

4 Move the cursor over the page footer area. Notice how the cursor changes shape to a letter A with a plus (+) sign.

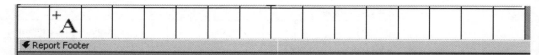

5 Click in the page footer area, and drag to draw the container.

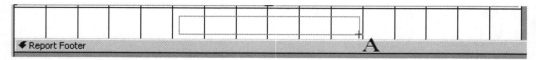

When finished drawing, release the mouse button.

6 Access creates the container. Type the following text in it immediately.

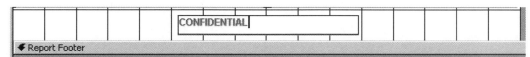

If you create a container, and then click anywhere else on the screen, Access deletes the empty container.

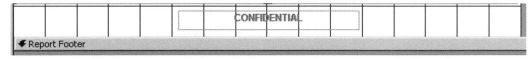

Center button

7 Click once on the inserted container, and click the **Center** alignment button on the Access Formatting toolbar. Your inserted footer should now look as shown.

Well done. You have followed all the steps for inserting, typing and formatting a new footer element in a report.

Remove a header or footer

To remove a header or footer element from a report (or a field), click once on it to select the element, and then click **Edit | Delete**. You can undo this removal action, if necessary.

Quit Access

You can close your Bookworm.mdb database and quit Access. Congratulations! You have now completed Module 5 of the ECDL, Databases. To remind yourself of the main features of Microsoft® Access, cut out the quick reference guide, called **database essentials**, at the back of the book and keep it beside your computer.

6

Presentations

Tomorrow you have two appointments: a visit to the dentist, and a presentation to an audience of strangers and friends. Which one fills you with greater terror? Whether it's to a group of potential customers, a national conference of fellow workers, or a local community group, delivering an address can be an intimidating prospect.

This is where presentation software such as Microsoft® PowerPoint comes in. By providing a range of easy-to-use but powerful tools for preparing impressive visual aids and printed handouts, PowerPoint can help your presentation succeed in its aim: better communication of your bright ideas.

Slides are the building blocks of a visual presentation. In this module you will learn how to create, manipulate and reorder slides, enter, edit and format text in them, apply coloured and patterned backgrounds, import pictures, and draw arrows, rectangles, circles and other simple graphics.

You will then move on to more advanced skills: creating transitions that control how one slide replaces another, adding sound effects, and applying animated effects in which the different elements of a slide are revealed gradually rather than all at once.

PowerPoint 2000 allows you to save your presentations in a file format other than its own. For example, you can convert a complete PowerPoint presentation into HTML format, so that it can be viewed in Internet Explorer or other a web browser. Think of this module as your chance to speak rather than be spoken to.

Your first steps in PowerPoint

Learning goals   At the end of this lesson you should be able to:

- start and quit PowerPoint;
- insert slides in a presentation;
- type, edit and delete text in slides;
- save, name, rename, open, create and close presentations;
- control the display of toolbars and toolbar buttons;
- change magnification views;
- undo, redo and repeat actions;
- use PowerPoint's online help.

New terms   At the end of this lesson you should be able to explain the following terms:

Presentation Software	Applications such as Microsoft PowerPoint that create visual aids and printed handouts for use when addressing an audience.
Slide	The basic building block of a visual presentation. It is equivalent to a page in a printed document. A slide typically contains text and graphics, and possibly sound, animations and video.
AutoLayout	One of 24 ready-made slide layouts. They typically include placeholders for text and other objects, such as images and charts.
Title Slide	A presentation's first slide. Typically, it has a different layout to the rest of the presentation.
Placeholder	A rectangular box within a slide for holding text or graphics.
PowerPoint Presentation	A file containing one or more slides. Presentation files end in .ppt.
Normal View	A PowerPoint view composed of a Normal pane (where you work with one slide at a time), an Outline pane (where you can work with the text of all slides) and a Notes pane (where you can work with additional text for the presenter).

Presentations and slides

A presentation is an address to an audience, accompanied by visual aids and possibly printed handouts for the audience. *Presentation software*, such as PowerPoint, helps you prepare these materials.

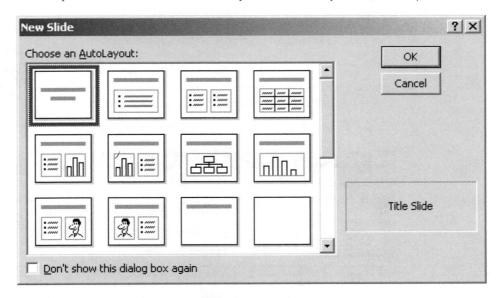

New slide button

Slides are the basic building blocks of a presentation. When you create a new presentation, PowerPoint automatically creates a single new slide. You can add a new slide to your presentation at any stage by clicking the **New Slide** button on the Standard toolbar.

PowerPoint always inserts a new slide after the currently displayed slide.

AutoLayouts

When you create a new presentation, or insert a new slide in an existing presentation, PowerPoint displays the New Slide dialog box, where you can choose you can choose from 24 ready-made slide layouts (*Auto Layouts*).

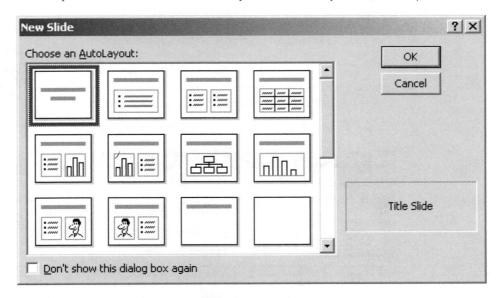

The *Title Slide* layout is designed for the first slide of a presentation.

Placeholders

Each slide layout contains one or more boxes called *placeholders*, within which you enter, edit and format text and graphics.

1 Click in the placeholder ...

2 PowerPoint removes the guide or 'dummy' text ...

3 Now type your own text.

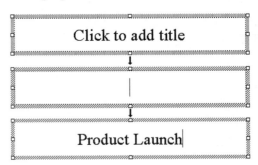

Launch Microsoft PowerPoint

PowerPoint

- Double-click the Microsoft PowerPoint icon or choose **Start | Programs | Microsoft PowerPoint**.

  PowerPoint may show a dialog box that offers a number of options, including the following.

  Leave the **Open an existing presentation** option selected. Next, select the checkbox shown below, and click **OK**.

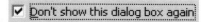

  On the next dialog box displayed, click **Cancel**. You can now work with PowerPoint's toolbar buttons and pull-down menus to create a new presentation or edit an existing one.

Create a new presentation

New button

- Click the **New** button on the Standard toolbar.

  Alternatively:

- Choose **File | New**. On the General tab of the dialog box, click the **Blank Presentation** option and click **OK.**

  You are shown the **New Slide** dialog box with a choice of *AutoLayouts*.

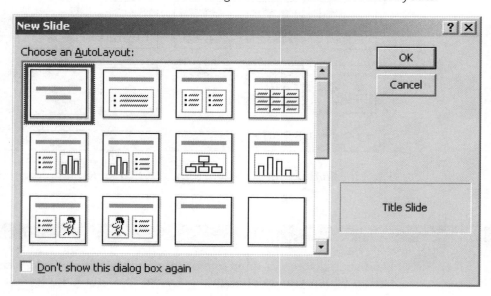

  Click once on a layout to see its name in the area at the right of the dialog box. To select a layout, double-click it, or click it once and then click **OK**. See below.

Enter text in a title slide

The first slide of a presentation is called the title slide. Like the first page of a book, it usually has a different layout from the rest of the presentation.

1 Click the first AutoLayout, which PowerPoint calls Title Slide, and then click OK. (Alternatively, double-click on the Title Slide AutoLayout.)

You are now shown a slide with *placeholders* surrounded by dotted lines.

2 Click in the top placeholder. PowerPoint changes its border, removes the 'dummy' text, and places a blinking text cursor inside it. You can now type text in the placeholder.

3 Type the following text in the top placeholder:

Product Launch

4 Click in the lower placeholder and type the following text:

Round Wheels

5 Click anywhere on the slide outside the lower placeholder to deselect it.

Congratulations! You have created your first slide in PowerPoint.

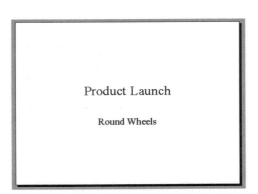

Edit text on a slide

Make a typing error? Correct your mistake with either of the following two keys:

■ **BACKSPACE:** Removes the character to the left of the cursor. You will find this key at the top-right of the keyboard, just above the **ENTER** key.

■ **DELETE:** Removes the character to the right of the cursor. Typically this key is in a group of six keys to the right of the **ENTER** key.

Add a second slide to a presentation

New Slide button

1 Click the **New Slide** button on the Standard toolbar or choose **Insert | New Slide**.

2 In the **New Slide** dialog box, double-click the AutoLayout named Bulleted List.

3 Click in the top placeholder and type the following:

Amazing Features

4 Click in the lower placeholder, type the following, and press **ENTER**:

Smooth Travelling for Passenger Comfort

Notice that PowerPoint places a bullet character (•) in front of your line of text.

5 Type the following text and press ENTER:

Reduced Fuel Consumption

6 Continue typing lines of text and pressing ENTER until your second slide looks as shown.

Do not press ENTER after your final line of text. If you do, PowerPoint will display another line beginning with a bullet. You can delete this by pressing the BACKSPACE key twice.

> ### Amazing Features
>
> - Smooth Travelling for Passenger Comfort
> - Reduced Fuel Consumption
> - Longer Engine Life
> - Multiple Uses in Transport Sector

Add a third slide to a presentation

New Slide button

1 Click the **New Slide** button on the Standard toolbar or choose **Insert | New Slide**.

2 In the **New Slide** dialog box, double-click the AutoLayout named 2 Column Text.

3 Click in the top placeholder and type the following text:

Choice of Colours

4 Click in the left placeholder, type the following two lines of text, pressing ENTER after the first line only:

Red

Green

5 Click in the right placeholder, type the following two lines of text, pressing ENTER after the first line only:

Blue

Grey

The third slide of your presentation should look as shown.

> ### Choice of Colours
>
> - Red   - Blue
> - Green   - Grey

Move between slides

When you have more than a single slide in your presentation, you will want to be able to view and work with a particular one:

- Press the **PAGE DOWN** key to move forward, one slide at a time.
- Press the **PAGE UP** key to move backwards through your presentation, one slide at a time.
- Press **HOME** to go to the very first slide.
- Press **END** to go to the last slide.

On a desktop PC, you will find these four keys in a group of six keys to the right of the ENTER key.

PowerPoint always inserts a new slide after the slide that is displayed when you click the **New Slide** button on the Standard toolbar or choose the **Insert | New Slide** command.

To insert a new slide at the end of your presentation, first display the final slide and then insert the new slide. To insert a new slide anywhere else within your presentation, first display the slide that will be located before your new slide, and then insert the new slide.

Change slide layout

You can change the AutoLayout that is currently applied to a slide, as the following example shows:

1 Display your second slide 'Amazing Features'.

2 Choose **Format | Slide Layout**. In the *Slide Layout* dialog box, select a different AutoLayout, for example the *Text & Clip Art* option. Click the **Apply** button to apply your new selected AutoLayout.

 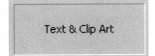

Notice the effect on your slide.

3 Change your slide back to its original layout by choosing **Format | Slide Layout** again, clicking the *Bulleted List* layout, and then clicking the **Apply** button.

Undo and redo actions

Undo button

Enter the wrong text? Press a wrong key? Don't panic. PowerPoint allows you to undo your most recent text entry or editing action if it has produced unwanted results.

Redo button

■ To undo an action, click the **Undo** button on the Standard toolbar or choose **Edit | Undo**. The **Redo** button replays the action.

■ Click **Undo** (or **Redo**) repeatedly to undo (or redo) your last series of actions.

■ To view a list of recent actions that you can undo or redo, click the arrow to the right of either button.

Practise using the Undo and Redo options by deleting text on your slides, and then reversing your deletions.

Repeat actions

To repeat your most recent action, choose **Edit | Repeat** or press **CTRL+y**.

If PowerPoint cannot repeat your last action, it changes the **Repeat** command to **Can't Repeat**.

Save and name your First-Steps presentation

Save button

1 Click the **Save** button on the Standard toolbar or choose **File | Save**.

2 In the **Save** dialog box, enter the following file name and click **Save**:

First-Steps

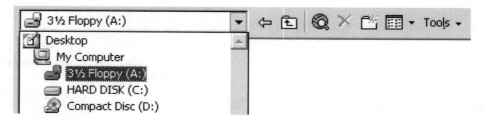

PowerPoint assumes that the file type is *Presentation*. You need not type the file name extension of ppt. PowerPoint adds it automatically.

Save a presentation with a different name to a diskette

It's a good idea to save a copy of your presentation to a diskette or other backup medium.

1 Insert a diskette in your computer's diskette drive.

2 Choose **File | Save As** and locate your A: drive.

PowerPoint suggests the current file name for you to accept or amend.

3 Type a different name in the **File Name** box, and click **Save**.

4 When finished, use **File | Save As** again to resave the presentation to its original location on your hard disk, and with its original name. (You will be asked if you want to replace the original file: click **OK**.)

If you do not resave your presentation to its original location, saving the file in future (by clicking the **Save** button on the Standard toolbar or choosing **File | Save**) will save the presentation to the diskette and not to your computer's disk drive.

Delete a slide

■ To remove a slide from a presentation, display the slide and choose **Edit | Delete Slide**.

As practice, display your third slide, choose **Edit | Delete Slide**, and then click the **Undo** button on the Standard toolbar to bring it back.

Close a presentation

■ Choose **File | Close** or click the **Close Presentation** button at the top-right of the presentation window.

If you have made changes to your presentation since you last saved it, you are prompted to save or discard them.

Close presentation

Open an existing presentation

Open button

1 Click the **Open** button on the Standard toolbar or choose **File | Open**.

2 Select the file you want from the **Open** dialog box, and click **Open**.

Switch between open presentations

■ If you have more than one presentation open, you can switch between them by clicking the presentations' names on the Windows Taskbar.

■ Alternatively, click the PowerPoint **Window** menu, and then click the presentation's name from the list at the bottom of the menu.

Display all commands on menus

By default, when you first choose a menu, PowerPoint displays only some of its commands. To see them all, you must click the double-arrow at the bottom of each menu. To view a complete list every time, follow these steps.

1 Choose **Tools | Customize** and click the **Options** tab.

2 Deselect the checkbox below, and choose **Close**.

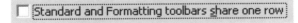

Display the standard and formatting toolbars on separate rows

By default PowerPoint displays the Standard and Formatting toolbars on a single row across the top of the screen. To display them as two, individual toolbars, follow these steps.

1 Choose **Tools | Customize** and click the **Options** tab.

2 Deselect the checkbox below, and choose **Close**.

☐ Standard and Formatting toolbars share one row

PowerPoint toolbars

Only three of PowerPoint's toolbars are relevant to this ECDL Module. The Standard toolbar includes buttons for managing files – that is, *PowerPoint presentations* – and for inserting new slides.

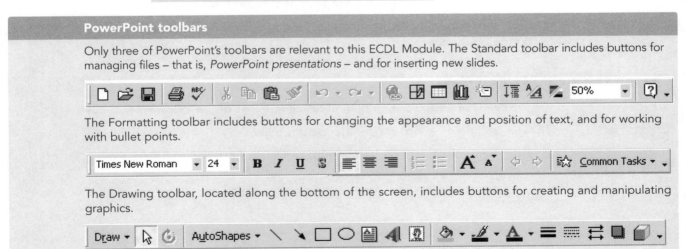

The Formatting toolbar includes buttons for changing the appearance and position of text, and for working with bullet points.

The Drawing toolbar, located along the bottom of the screen, includes buttons for creating and manipulating graphics.

Hide and display toolbars

1 Choose **View | Toolbars**.

2 Select or deselect the various toolbar options from the pull-down menu displayed.

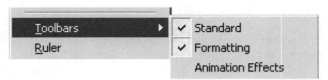

The check marks indicate which toolbars are already selected for display on screen.

Remove and redisplay toolbar buttons

Follow these steps to remove one or more buttons from a toolbar.

1 Display the toolbar that you want to change.

2 Hold down the **ALT** key, and drag the button off the toolbar.

PowerPoint removes the selected button. Want to bring it back again? Here's how.

1 Display the toolbar. Click the **More Buttons** button (at the very right of the toolbar) and then the **Add or Remove Buttons** button.

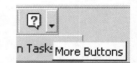

2 Click the button you want to display again.

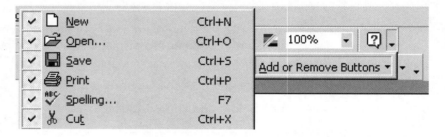

Buttons with a check mark beside their names are displayed on the toolbar.

3 Click anywhere outside the menu to close it. PowerPoint redisplays the button on the toolbar.

Change the magnification view

You can change the screen magnification in either of the following two ways.

Zoom box

1 Click in the **Zoom** box on the Standard toolbar.

2 Enter a number between 10 and 400, and press **ENTER**.

(You need not type the percent (%) symbol.)

Alternatively:

1 Choose **View | Zoom**.

2 Select a magnification option from the **Zoom** dialog box.

You can choose a preset option (25–200%), or select **Custom** and enter a number from 10 to 400. To return to normal view, select a magnification of 100%

Outline pane (text only of all slides)

Slide pane (text, graphics and other elements of a single slide)

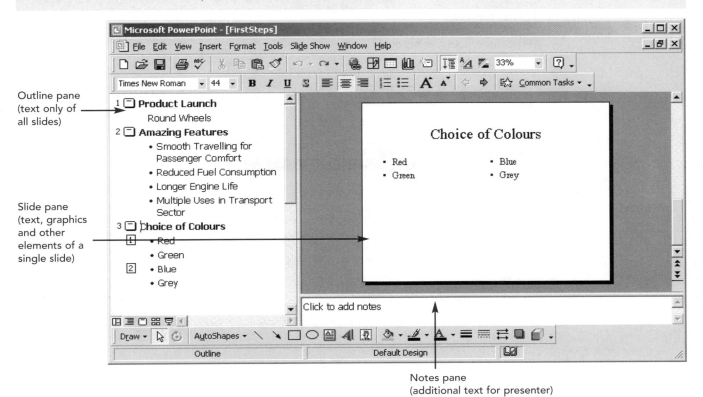

Notes pane (additional text for presenter)

Change pane size in normal view

You can adjust size of any of the three panes in Normal view.

add notes

add notes

- Move your cursor over a pane border. Notice how the cursor changes shape.
- Hold down the left mouse button, and move the mouse in any direction.
- Finally, release the mouse button.

Your can reverse your resizing action by dragging the pane border back to its original location.

Get online help from the Help menu

Help button

1 Choose **Help | Microsoft PowerPoint Help**, click the Microsoft PowerPoint **Help** button on the Standard toolbar, or press **F1**.

2 Word displays the Help window with the following three tabs:

- **Contents:** Here you will find descriptions of PowerPoint's main features. Where you see a heading with a book symbol, double-click it to view the related sub-headings. Double-click on a question mark symbol to read the online help text.

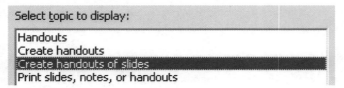

- **Answer Wizard:** Type your question in the box at the top-left of the dialog box, and click **Search**. PowerPoint displays a list of suggested help topics in the lower-left. Click a topic to display the associated text in the right pane.

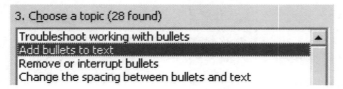

- **Index:** Type the word or phrase and click **Search**. PowerPoint displays all matches from the online help in the lower-left of the dialog box. Click on a topic to display the associated text.

You will see the following buttons, left to right, at the top of the online help window:

- **Hide/Show:** Hides or displays the left pane of the dialog box.
- **Back/Forward:** Moves you backwards and forwards through previously visited help topics.

Microsoft PowerPoint Help

- **Print:** Prints the currently displayed help topic.
- **Options:** Offers a number of display choices.

Take a few minutes to look through PowerPoint's online help system.

Get online help from a dialog box

1 Choose **File | Print** to display the **Print** dialog box.

2 Click on the question mark symbol near the top-right of the dialog box. PowerPoint displays a question mark to the right of the cursor.

3 Move the mouse down and left, and click anywhere in the **Name** box.

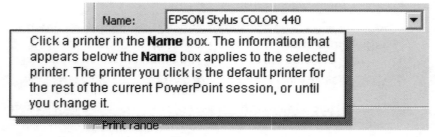

PowerPoint displays online help text that tells you about the selected option. Click **Cancel** to close the dialog box. Practise this exercise with other dialog boxes in PowerPoint.

To leave PowerPoint, choose **File | Exit** or click the **Close** button at the top-right of the PowerPoint window. You are prompted to save any open presentations containing unsaved work.

You can close your First-Steps.ppt presentation and quit PowerPoint. You have now completed Lesson 6.1 of the ECDL Presentations Module.

6.2

Bullet points and outlines

Learning goals	At the end of this lesson you should be able to:

- promote and demote slide text;
- increase or decrease line spacing between bullet points;
- change the horizontal alignment of bullet points;
- change the default bullet character;
- use a graphic as a bullet symbol;
- apply and change numbered bullets;
- enter and structure text in the Outline pane of Normal view;
- run a PowerPoint presentation in Slide Show view;
- hide and unhide individual slides in Slide Show view.

New terms	At the end of this lesson you should be able to explain the following terms:
Bullet Point	A bullet character (such as • or ▪) followed by one or a few words of text. Bullet points may be at different levels, indicated by their indentation, bullet character and font size.
Outline Pane	In Normal view, this shows the text of all your slides, so that you can judge how well your ideas and text flow from one slide to the next.
Slide Show View	The view you use for presenting your slides to your audience. PowerPoint's various menus and toolbars are not displayed in Slide Show view.

Bullet points and bullet levels

Except for the title slide, text on slides typically consists of *bullet points* – a bullet character followed by one or a few words of text.

Different bullet points may contain different categories or 'levels' of information. Different bullet levels are distinguished by different indents (distances from left slide edge), font sizes and bullet characters.

Locations

- United Kingdom
  - London, Cardiff, Edinburgh
- Germany
  - Berlin, Frankfurt, Hamburg
- Australia
  - Sydney, Melbourne, Adelaide

3 ECDL Modules

- Word Processing
  - ✓ Editing, Formatting, Tables, Templates
- Databases
  - ✓ Tables, Forms, Reports
- Internet
  - ✓ Web browsing, e-mail

Promoting and demoting bullets

Promote and **Demote** buttons

Use the **Promote** and **Demote** buttons on the Formatting toolbar to change the level of a selected bullet point or points with a single mouse click; PowerPoint alters the indents, font size and bullet characters for you.

Numbering bullets

Bullet characters can also be sequentially increasing numbers (1, 2, 3, ...) or letters (a, b, c, ...). Numbered lists are an appropriate choice when the order of reading is important, such as in directions and instructions.

Working in the outline pane

The *Outline pane* in Normal view offers a fast way to work with the text of your presentation because you don't need to switch forwards and backwards through individual slides.

In the Outline pane, text is positioned in such a way that you can identify text that is the title of a slide, and text that is a bullet point within a slide. PowerPoint creates a new slide for each slide title that you type in the Outline pane.

1 ☐ **ECDL: An Overview**
   ABC Training Corporation|

Open your First-Steps presentation

Open button

1 Launch PowerPoint, click the **Open** button on the Standard toolbar or choose **File | Open**.

2 Select the following file and click **Open**:

First-Steps

This is the three-slide presentation from Lesson 6.1. You will amend it during the first part of this lesson.

Promote and demote bullet points

PowerPoint enables you to change bullet point levels with a single mouse click: it alters the indents, font size and bullet characters for you. Follow the steps below to discover how.

1 Use the **PAGE DOWN** or **PAGE UP** key to display the second slide of the First-Steps presentation, and click at the end of the fourth bullet point.

> • Multiple Uses in Transport Sector|

2 Press **ENTER** to begin a new bullet point.

3 Type the following three words, pressing **ENTER** after the first and second words only:

> • Cars
> • Trucks
> • Bicycles|

4 Click at the start of the word Car, and drag down to select all three new bullet points.

> • Cars
> • Trucks
> • Bicycles

Promote button

Demote button

5 Click the **Demote** button on the Formatting toolbar. PowerPoint changes the display of the selected bullets points. Click anywhere else on the slide to deselect the three bullet points.

As practice, select the three bullet points again, click **Promote**, and view the result. When finished, and with the bullet points selected, click **Demote**. The bullet points are again demoted.

The three demoted bullet points are variously known as minor bullets, sub-bullets or level-two bullets. Avoid using more than two levels of bullets on a slide. You risk confusing your audience.

Change the bullet character

By default, PowerPoint uses the filled black circle (•) and the dash (–) as the bullet characters for the first two levels of bullet points. You can choose from a range of other bullet characters.

1 Display the second slide of your presentation, and click anywhere in the first bullet point.

- Smooth Travelling for Passenger Comfort

2 Choose **Format | Bullets and Numbering**. On the **Bulleted** tab of the dialog box, select the hollow circle bullet, and click **OK**.

3 Click anywhere in first bullet point.

- Reduced Fuel Consumption

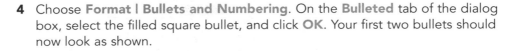

4 Choose **Format | Bullets and Numbering**. On the **Bulleted** tab of the dialog box, select the filled square bullet, and click **OK**. Your first two bullets should now look as shown.

o Smooth Travelling for Passenger Comfort
▪ Reduced Fuel Consumption

Change the bullet character colour

1 On the second slide of your presentation, click anywhere in the third bullet point.

- Longer Engine Life

2 Choose **Format | Bullets and Numbering**. On the **Bulleted** tab of the dialog box, click on the arrow to the right of the **Color** pull-down list.

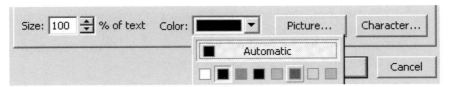

3 Click the colour blue, and click **OK**.

Use a graphic as a bullet character

Picture button

1 Click anywhere in the fourth bullet point.

- Multiple Uses in Transport Sector

2 Choose **Format | Bullets and Numbering**. On the **Bulleted** tab of the dialog box, click the **Picture** button. You are now shown PowerPoint's Picture Bullet gallery.

3 Select a bullet by right-clicking it, and then choosing **Insert** from the pop-up menu displayed.

PowerPoint closes the Picture Bullet gallery and replaces the default bullet character with your selected graphic bullet.

Use a special character for a bullet point

1 Drag over the three minor bullet points on the slide to select them.

2 Choose **Format | Bullets and Numbering**. On the **Bulleted** tab, click the **Character** button.

Character button

3 In the **Bullet** dialog box, select Wingdings in the **Bullets from** pull-down list, click any displayed character to select it, and then click **OK**.

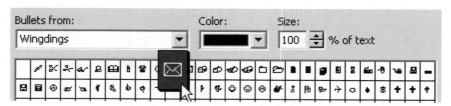

Your selected bullet character is now applied to the three minor bullet points.

Undo your bullet format actions

Undo button

Click the **Undo** button on the Standard toolbar a number of times until your second slide again contains the default black filled black circle (•) and dash (–) bullet characters.

Numbering bullet points

Numbering button

You can apply the numbered list format to selected bullet points by clicking the **Numbering** button on the Formatting toolbar or using options within the **Format | Bullets and Numbering** command. Let's add a new slide with numbered bullet points to your presentation.

New Slide button

1 Display your third slide and click the **New Slide** button on the Standard toolbar.

2 Double-click the **Bulleted List** AutoLayout, and type the following text in the top placeholder:

Marketing Plan

3 In the lower placeholder of your new slide, type the bullet points shown below.

Numbering button

4 Drag across the four bullet points that you typed in step 3 to select them. Click the **Numbering** button on the Formatting toolbar. PowerPoint applies its default numbering style.

• Develop pricing plan	• Develop pricing plan	1. Develop pricing plan
• Build distribution network →	• Build distribution network →	2. Build distribution network
• National launch	• National launch	3. National launch
• International launch	• International launch	4. International launch

Change the numbering style

You can amend the colour and starting value of the numbers in a numbered list, and change the size of the numbering character relative to the text of the line. Let's try it.

1   On your fourth slide, select the four numbered bullet points, and choose **Format | Bullets and Numbering**.

2   On the dialog box displayed, change the **Size % of text** to 120, the **Color** to green, and the **Start at** value to 2. Click **OK**. Notice the effect on your slide.

Undo button

3   Use the **Undo** button to return your slide to what it was at the beginning of step 1.

Change line spacing

PowerPoint allows you to 'space out' or 'squeeze' lines of text so that they fit the area of single slide.

1   Display the third slide of your presentation.

2   Select the two bullet points in the left placeholder, choose **Format | Line Spacing**, change the **Line spacing** value from 1 to 2 Lines, and click **OK**.

3   Repeat step 2 for the two bullet points in the right placeholder.

- Red   - Blue

- Green   - Grey

You can also use **Format | Line Spacing** to alter the spacing before and after selected lines.

Change text alignment

Alignment buttons

Alignment refers to the horizontal position (left, right or centre) of text on a slide. By default, PowerPoint centre-aligns slide titles and left-aligns bullet points. Aligning text is a two-step process: first select, then align. Let's try it.

1   Display your fourth slide and select all the bullet points in the lower placeholder.

2   Click the **Centre-align** button on the Formatting toolbar.

1. Develop pricing plan
2. Build distribution network
3. National launch
4. International launch

3 Your slide was easier to read before you centre-aligned the text. Select all the bullet points again, and click the **Left-Align** button on the Formatting toolbar.

The fourth alignment option of justified text is available only with the **Format | Alignment** command. Avoid justifying text on slides: it can be difficult for your audience to read justified text.

Save and close your First-Steps presentation

You have finished working with your First-Steps presentation.

1 Click the **Save** button on the Standard toolbar.

2 Choose **File | Close** to close the presentation.

Create and name your Training presentation

New button

1 Click the **New** button on the Standard toolbar to create a new presentation.

2 Click the **Save** button on the Standard toolbar. In the **Save** dialog box, enter the following file name and click **Save**.

Training

PowerPoint assumes that the file type is Presentation. You need not type the file name extension of .ppt.

Enter text in the Outline pane

1 On the **New Slide** dialog box, select the AutoLayout named **Title Slide**, and click **OK**.

You may want to increase the Outline pane size by dragging its border to the right.

2 Click anywhere in the Outline pane to select the pane. Type the following lines of text, pressing ENTER after each line except the final one:

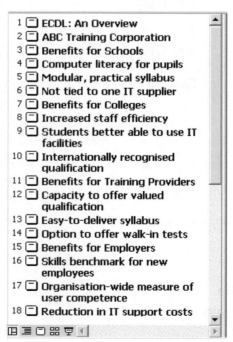

Notice that all the lines of text automatically take on the attributes of the first one: they all appear as slide titles. Notice too that PowerPoint numbers slide titles.

The Outline pane of Normal view displays the text of *all* slides in a presentation. It positions the text in such a way that you can identify text that is the title of a slide, and text that is a bullet point within a slide.

Slide titles are numbered, and bullet points are indented (moved in from the left slide edge) further than the text of the slide titles.

Structure presentation text in the Outline pane

After typing the entire text of your new presentation in the Outline pane, your next task is to structure the text by demoting the bullet points from slide titles.

Demote button

1 Click anywhere in your second line of text, and click the **Demote** button on the Formatting toolbar.

Your second line is now bullet point text within the first slide – and not a slide title.

1 ☐ **ECDL: An Overview**
ABC Training Corporation|

2 In turn, select the groups of text lines shown below, and click the **Demote** button to change each selected group of slide titles to bullet points.

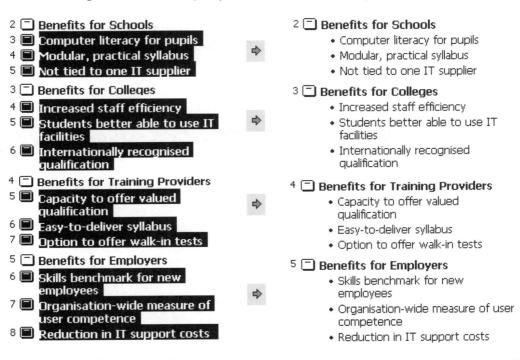

What is the relationship between the outline text and the content of individual slides?

PowerPoint creates a new slide for each slide title that you type in the Outline pane. PowerPoint inserts the demoted text lines in the Outline pane as bullet points on the associated slide.

Any text change you make in the Outline pane affects the individual slide, and any text change to a slide affects the Outline pane.

Run your PowerPoint presentation

You can preview how your slides look to your audience by choosing **View | Slide Show** or by clicking the Slide Show button at the lower left of your screen.

This shows your slides without any PowerPoint menus, toolbars or other screen elements that are displayed when you are creating or editing slides. To move between slides in *Slide Show view*:

- Press the **PAGE DOWN**, **PAGE UP**, **HOME** or **END** keys, as you would in Normal view, or

- Right-click anywhere on the screen, and choose a navigation option from the pop-up menu, or

- Click anywhere on the screen to move forward to the next slide.

To exit Slide Show view and return to your previous view, press the **ESC** key.

Hide and Redisplay slides

To hide a slide so that it displays in all views except Slide Show view, display the slide in Normal view and choose **Slide Show | Hide Slide**. To unhide a hidden slide, choose **Slide Show | Hide Slide** again. Practise this option by hiding a slide, running your presentation in Slide Show view, and then unhiding the slide.

Quit PowerPoint

You can close your Training.ppt presentation and quit PowerPoint. You have now completed Lesson 6.2 of the ECDL Presentations Module.

6.3

Copying, moving and reordering slides

Learning goals	At the end of this lesson you should be able to:

- copy, cut or paste entire slides within and between presentations;
- copy, cut or paste slide text within and between presentations;
- import text from non-PowerPoint sources;
- enter and edit speaker notes;
- print slides, handouts ands speaker notes.

New terms	At the end of this lesson you should be able to explain the following terms:
Slide Sorter View	A view where you can see all slides of a presentation at once.
Speaker Notes	A page that PowerPoint creates to accompany each slide. You can use it to record key points or additional details about your presentation.

Another view offered by PowerPoint is *Slide Sorter view*, where you can see miniatures of all slides of a presentation at once.

Slide Sorter view is also useful for:

- Checking that the appearance of slides is consistent.
- Changing the order of the slides in your presentation.
- Copying slides within and between presentations.

Copying and importing text

To copy or move text from one part of a slide to another, or between different slides of the same or different presentations: select the text by clicking and dragging; copy or cut the text; position your cursor where you want the text to appear; and paste the text.

You can also paste text into your slides from Word and other non-PowerPoint files.

Open your First-Steps and Training presentations

Open button

■ Launch PowerPoint, and open the following two presentations:

First-Steps (from Lessons 6.1 and 6.2)

Training (from Lesson 6.2)

You will work with these presentations throughout this lesson.

View an entire presentation in Slide Sorter view

To display your presentation in Slide Sorter view:

■ Choose **View | Slide Sorter** or click the **Slide Sorter view** button at the lower-right of your screen.

Display your First-Steps and Training presentations in Slide Sorter view. While the miniatures do provide you with an overview of your presentation, Slide Sorter is not a good view for reading text!

Reorder slides in Slide Sorter view

Slide Sorter view is useful for changing the order of slides. You can do this in two ways:

■ By dragging them with the mouse (better for small presentations).

■ By using cut-and-paste (better for larger presentations).

Follow the steps below to reorder slides in your First-Steps presentation by dragging.

1 In Slide Sorter view, click the title (first) slide to select it.

2 Drag the mouse until the cursor is over the third of the four slides.

PowerPoint places a vertical line at the point where it will position the slide when you release the mouse button.

3 Release the mouse button. PowerPoint has reordered your slides.

1   2   3   4

Change magnification in Slide Sorter view

Zoom box

- Use PowerPoint's Zoom feature to reduce or enlarge the display of Slide Sorter view. The default is 66%, allowing up to four slides to be displayed on a single row.

- To display the five slides of your Training presentation on a single row, reduce the Zoom value to 50% or less.

Move a slide in Slide Sorter view

You can copy and move slides within a presentation in Slide Sorter view. Let's move the title slide that you relocated in the previous exercise back to its original location.

1 Display your First-Steps presentation in Slide Sorter view.

2 Click the slide third slide (the title slide) to select it.

Cut button

3 Click the **Cut** button on the Standard toolbar, or choose **Edit | Cut**, or press **CTRL+x**.

4 Click the first slide (Amazing Features) to select it.

Paste button

5 Click the **Paste** button on the Standard toolbar, or choose **Edit | Paste**, or press **CTRL+v**.

PowerPoint positions the pasted slide after the slide you clicked on before you performed the paste action.

6 Click the second (title) slide, and drag it to the left so that it is again the first slide.

1   2   3   4

Copy a slide between presentations

You can copy or move (cut) slides between presentations as well as within them.

1 Display your Training presentation in Slide Sorter view.

Copy button

2 Click the title slide and press **CTRL+c**, or click the **Copy** button on the Standard toolbar, or choose **Edit | Copy**.

3 Switch to your First-Steps presentation, and display it in Slide Sorter view.

4 Click the second slide (Amazing Features) to select it.

1   2   3   4

5 Press **CTRL+v** to paste the copied slide as the new third slide of your First-Steps presentation.

       1   2   3   4   5

6 With the pasted slide still selected, press the **DELETE** key to remove it.

Copy and move text

To copy or move text from one part of a slide to another, or between different slides of the same or a different presentation, drag to select the text, copy or cut the text, position your cursor where you want the text to appear, and paste the text. Practise text copying with the following exercise.

1 In Normal view, display the third slide (Choice of Colours) of your First-Steps presentation.

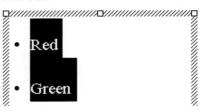

2 Select the two bullet points in the right placeholder.

3 Press **CTRL+x**. PowerPoint removes the selected text from the right placeholder.

4 Click in the left placeholder at the end of the second bullet point. Press **ENTER**. PowerPoint creates a new line beginning with a bullet character.

   • Grey| ⟶   • Grey

5 Press **CTRL+v** to paste the two bullet points.

If PowerPoint adds an additional bullet character on a new line after the two bullet points that you pasted, press the **BACKSPACE** key twice – once to remove the bullet character, and a second time to remove the new line.

6 Click anywhere in the right placeholder, and then click on its border. Press the **DELETE** key to remove the right placeholder.

- Blue
- Grey
- Red
- Green

7 Choose **Format | Slide Layout** to display a list of AutoLayouts. Click the option named Bulleted List, and then click **Apply**.

Your third slide should now show four bullet points in a single column.

Import text into PowerPoint

The simplest way to import text from another application into PowerPoint is to copy and paste it, as in the following exercise.

1 In Normal view, display the second slide (Amazing Features) of your First-Steps presentation.

2 Click the **New Slide** button on the Standard toolbar, select the Bulleted List AutoLayout, and click **OK**.

New Slide button

3 Click in the top placeholder and type the following text:

    Online Help Text

4 Choose **Help | Microsoft PowerPoint Help**. If it is not already displayed, click the Contents tab.

5 Select the heading text in the right pane of the online help window, and press **CTRL+c** to copy it.

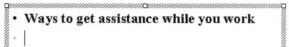

Ways to get assistance while you work

This topic provides reference information about:

Asking for Help from the Office Assistant

6 Switch back to PowerPoint. Ensure that the new slide that you created in step 2 is displayed. Click at the first bullet character, and press **CTRL+v** to paste the selected text.

• **Ways to get assistance while you work**
  •

PowerPoint creates a second bullet character beneath your pasted text because it assumes that you will want to add a second bullet point, either by typing or pasting text.

7 Copy and paste the following other headings from PowerPoint online help:

  Asking for Help from the Office Assistant
  Getting Help from the Help menu
  Getting Help from the Office Update Web site
  Finding out what's new in PowerPoint 2000

(Don't select from the list of hyperlinked headings near the top of the online help right-hand pane. Instead, select the headings as they appear down through the body of the text.)

After pasting the final bullet point, press the **BACKSPACE** key twice to remove the bullet character and new line that PowerPoint automatically inserted beneath it.

B

Bold button

8 The inserted text on your slide is in bold – as it was in online help. Select the five bullet points and click the **Bold** button on the Formatting toolbar to remove the bold effect. You can now close the Online Help window.

You can use the same method for copying to PowerPoint:

■ Text from a Word document.

■ A cell, cell range or chart from an Excel worksheet.

■ A picture (such as a scanned photograph) from a graphics application.

> Online Help Text
>
> • Ways to get assistance while you work
> • Asking for Help from the Office Assistant
> • Getting Help from the Help menu
> • Getting Help from the Office Update Web site
> • Finding out what's new in PowerPoint 2000

Add and edit speaker notes

PowerPoint creates what it calls a *speaker notes* page for each slide. You can access these pages to enter and edit text in either of two ways:

■ In Normal view, type or edit text directly in the Notes pane at the lower right of your screen. If required, you can enlarge the Notes pane by dragging its pane borders upwards or to the left.

■ Choose **View | Notes Page**, and then type or edit text for the currently selected slide. By default, PowerPoint displays speaker notes pages at about 38% of their full size. You may wish to increase this to nearer 100% when typing or editing.

Controlling page setup

You can control the way that PowerPoint prints slides on screen and on paper.

1 Choose **File | Page Setup** to display the **Page Setup** dialog box.

2 Select an option from the *Slides sized for* drop-down list. It is unlikely that you will want to select an option other than A4, the European standard. PowerPoint sets the values in the *Width* and *Height* boxes to provide 1.5 centimetre top and bottom margins.

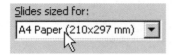

If you click *Custom*, you can enter values in the *Width* and *Height* boxes directly.

3 In the *Number slides from* drop-down list, select the starting number of the first slide that you want to print. The default is 1.

4 At the right of the dialog box, in the *Orientation* area, select your required options. The default for Slides is *Landscape* ('on its side'); the default for Notes, Handouts and Outline is *Portrait* ('standing up').

5 When finished, click **OK** to apply your page size settings and close the dialog box.

Create handout pages

You can, if you wish, simply print out your slides and distribute them to your audience. A better method is to produce handouts in which two, three, four, six, or nine slides are shown to a page. In the dialog box displayed by the **File | Print** command, select the **Handouts** option from the **Print what** list, and then select the number of slides per handout page.

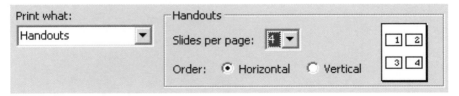

Print your presentation

You can print out a PowerPoint presentation in a variety of ways, depending on your requirements and on the hardware at your disposal:

Print button

■ First, choose **File | Print**, or click the **Print** button on the Standard toolbar.

■ Then, in the **Print what** pull-down box, you can choose to print slides, handouts, speaker notes or the outline.

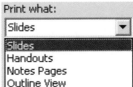

Whichever option you select, you can then specify, in the Print range area of the dialog box, whether you want to print all slides (or handouts, notes or the outline view), the current slide, or a selected range of slides.

To print a contiguous range, type the number of the first slide, a hyphen, and the number of the last slide. To print non-contiguous slides, type the individual slide numbers separated by commas.

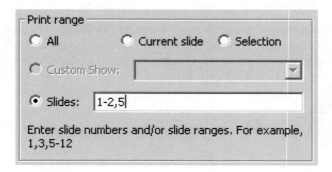

- If you wish to produce overhead projection foils (OHPs), you need to load your printer with blank foils before clicking **OK** on the **Print** dialog box.

- If you wish to produce 35mm slides, you need to have a special desktop film recorder connected to your computer.

- When you have made your choices, click **OK** to begin printing.

Quit PowerPoint

You can close your First-Steps.xls and Training.xls presentations, and quit PowerPoint. You have now completed Lesson 6.3 of the ECDL Presentations Module.

6.4

Presentation formatting

Learning goals At the end of this lesson you should be able to:

- apply text and background effects to individual slides;
- apply text and background effects to a presentation using the Slide Master;
- apply and customize a presentation colour scheme.

New terms At the end of this lesson you should be able to explain the following terms:

Colour Scheme A set of pre-selected co-ordinated colours that you can use to give your presentation an attractive and consistent appearance.

Slide Master This stores all the default attributes that you wish to apply to new slides, including text formatting and positioning, background and standard graphics (such as your company logo).

Your text formatting options include making text bold, putting it in italics, or placing a shadow behind it. You may also change the text font, size and colour with buttons on the Formatting toolbar.

Text formatting menu commands include Format | Replace Fonts and Format | Change Case.

Background formatting

Your two main background formatting options are:

■ Dark text against a light background (good for lighted rooms).

■ Light text against a dark background (good for darkened rooms).

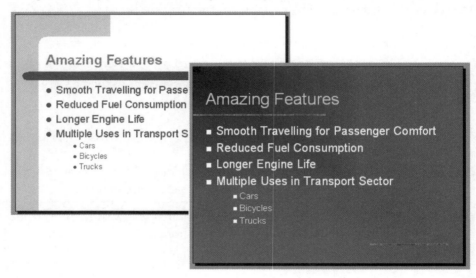

Backgrounds may consist of a solid, single colour or a decorative pattern.

Colour schemes

Colour schemes are bundles of professionally-designed preset text and background colours, which you can apply unchanged or customize to your requirements.

Slide Master

All slides take their default text formatting and positioning from the presentation's *Slide Master*. Anything that you insert on the Slide Master appears automatically on every slide of your presentation. You can override the defaults supplied by the Slide Master on any individual slide.

You can use both the Slide Master and colour schemes when formatting a presentation.

Open your First-Steps and Training presentations

Open button

- Launch PowerPoint, and open the following two presentations:

  First-Steps (from Lessons 6.1, 6.2 and 6.3)

  Training (from Lessons 6.2 and 6.3)

  You will use these presentations throughout this lesson.

Apply a colour scheme

PowerPoint comes supplied with a number of built-in colour schemes – professionally designed combinations of background and text colours. Let's apply one to your Training presentation.

1 Display your Training presentation in Slide Sorter view. In this view you will be better able to see how different colour schemes affect your presentation.

2 Choose **Format | Slide Color Scheme**. On the **Standard** tab, select the scheme with the yellow background, and click **Apply to All**.

   In Slide Sorter view, you can immediately see the impact on your presentation.

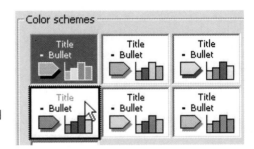

3 Choose **Format | Slide Colour Scheme** again. This time select the first (blue) background, and click **Apply to All**.

Customize a colour scheme

You can customize PowerPoint's preset colour schemes to suit your taste or needs.

1 Display your Training presentation in Slide Sorter view.

2 Choose **Format | Slide Color Scheme**. On the **Custom** tab, select **Title Text**, and click the **Change Color** button.

3 From the colours displayed, select a medium green, and click **OK**.

4 On the **Custom** tab, select **Text and Lines**, and click the **Change Color** button.

5 From the colours displayed, select a medium yellow, click **OK**, and then **Apply to All**.

6 Switch to Slide Show view and inspect your presentation.

Apply a decorative background

You can transform the appearance of your slides by changing their background, regardless of whether or not the slides already have a preset colour scheme already applied to them.

1 Display your First-Steps presentation in Slide Sorter view, and choose **Format | Background**.

2 Click on the pull-down list near the bottom of the dialog box, and click **Fill Effects**.

3 On the **Gradient** tab, click the **Preset** option, and select Daybreak from the pull-down list. Click **OK** and then **Apply to All**.

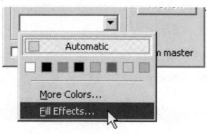

4 Switch to Slide Show view and inspect your presentation.

Change fonts on every slide

Most fonts fall into two families: serif fonts, so called because of their serifs (tails or squiggles), and sans serif fonts, which do not have serifs. In printed text, serif fonts such as Times New Roman are generally easier to read. For slides, however, sans serif fonts such as Arial are a better choice. PowerPoint's **Format | Replace Fonts** command enables you to change the fonts on every slide in a single action.

1 Display your First-Steps presentation in Normal view, and choose **Format | Replace Fonts**.

2 Select Times New Roman (PowerPoint's default font) in the **Replace** box, and Arial in the **With** box.

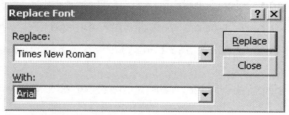

3 Click **Replace** and then **Close**.

4 Repeat this action with your Training presentation so that all its text is in the Arial font.

Change text font, font size and font style

You can apply most formatting options to selected text with the relevant pull-down lists and buttons on the Formatting toolbar.

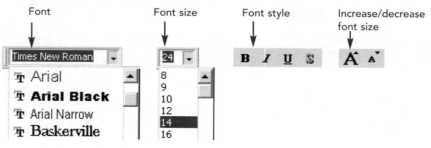

Change text to superscript or subscript

Two font effects not available from any toolbar are superscript and subscript. To apply either effect to selected text, you need to display the **Format | Font** dialog box.

- **Superscript:** This raises the selected text above the other text on the same line, and reduces its font size. Superscript is used most commonly for mathematical notation. For example: 2^2 or x^8.

- **Subscript:** This is text that is lowered beneath other text on the same line, and reduced in font size. Subscripts are commonly used in chemistry texts for formulas. For example: H_2SO_4.

Offset is the amount by which superscript or subscript text is positioned above (offset positive) or below (offset negative) the remainder of the text.

Change text colour

You can change the colour of selected text by clicking the arrow to the right of the **Font Color** button on the Drawing toolbar.

Don't see the colour you need? Click the **More Font Colors** button and select from the range available.

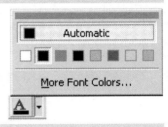

Change font case

You can change the case of a selected text with the **Format | Change Case** command.

The options are Lowercase, Uppercase, Title Case (initial capital for each word), Sentence Case (capitalizes the first letter of the first word in the selected text), and Toggle Case (changes the current case of all letters).

About the Slide Master

All slides take their default text formatting and positioning from the presentation's Slide Master. Moreover, any text or graphics inserted on the slide master appear automatically on every slide of the presentation. As you will discover in Lesson 6.5, this is useful for company logos or for recurring graphics such as lines and borders. A Slide Master consists of two main placeholders:

- **Title Placeholder:** This controls the format and positioning of text in every title placeholder in your presentation.
- **Object Placeholder:** This controls the format and positioning of text in every non-title placeholder.

Along the bottom of the Slide Master are three footer placeholders: for the date/time, footer text, and slide numbering. Your audience never sees the Slide Master; they see only its effects on the slides in your presentation. You can override the defaults supplied by the Slide Master on any individual slide.

Format a presentation from the Slide Master

1 In Normal view, display your First-Steps presentation, and choose **View | Master | Slide Master**.

2 Click anywhere in the title text in the top placeholder.

Text Shadow button

3 Click the **Text Shadow** button on the Formatting toolbar to apply a shadow effect.

4 With the cursor still positioned in the title placeholder, click the arrow to the right of the **Font Color** button on the Drawing toolbar, and then click the **More Font Colors** button

Font Colour button

5 On the **Standard** tab, select from the colour range, and click **OK**.

6 Switch to Slide Sorter view. Notice that PowerPoint has reformatted all your slides.

About slide numbers

When people in your audience ask questions, they may want to refer to a specific slide, so it is useful to identify each slide by number.

You insert slide numbers with the **View | Header and Footer** command. Use the **Notes and Handouts** tab of the same dialog box to include page numbers on your speaker notes and audience handouts. If you change the order of slides that contain slide numbers, PowerPoint automatically updates the slide numbers to reflect their new sequence.

Tip: To display a particular slide in Slide Show view, just type the slide number and press **ENTER**.

Add a slide footer

1 In Normal view, display your Training presentation, and choose **View | Header and Footer**.

2 In the Slide tab, leave the **Date and Time** checkbox selected, and select the **Update automatically** option. PowerPoint will refresh these details whenever you amend and resave the presentation.

3 Select the **Slide number** checkbox.

4 Leave the **Footer** checkbox selected, and type the following text in it:

ECDL Training

5 Typically, you will not want your title slide to show a footer. So select the **Don't show on title slide** checkbox.

6 Click **Apply to All**.

7 Page through your presentation to inspect the slide number and other footer details.

Format the slide footer

You can format the appearance of all slide footers in a presentation with the Slide Master.

1 In Normal view, display your Training presentation, and choose **View | Master | Slide Master**.

2 At the lower right of the Slide Master, click on the slide number symbol (#) to select it.

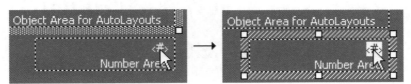

3 Using the Formatting toolbar, change the font to Arial Black and the font size to 16 points.

Font Colour button

4 Using the Drawing toolbar, change the font colour to white.

5 Change to Normal view to verify that your slide numbers have been reformatted.

When all slides are not the same

If your presentation deals with different topics, or if one or a few slides contain material that needs to stand out from the remainder, you can use the option within the **Format | Background** or **Format | Slide Color Scheme** dialog boxes named **Apply** (to current slide only). Even with the same background or colour scheme applied throughout a presentation, you can still emphasize particular slides by applying font effects directly to their text.

About presentation-wide formatting

In any presentation, you are not faced with the choice of using either a colour scheme or the Slide Master. You can use both. For example, you could begin by selecting a preset colour scheme, then customize some elements of the scheme, and finally use the Slide Master to apply various effects to every slide – such as font sizes, line spacing and special bullet characters.
(A third global formatting option, called design templates, is explained in Lesson 6.8.)

Quit PowerPoint

You can close your First-Steps.xls and Training.xls presentations, and quit PowerPoint. You have now completed Lesson 6.4 of the ECDL Presentations Module.

6.5

Working with graphics and pictures

Learning goals	At the end of this lesson you should be able to:
	■ draw simple graphics such as lines and boxes on a slide;
	■ draw AutoShapes on a slide;
	■ insert and use text boxes on a slide;
	■ insert Clip Art and other pictures on a slide;
	■ move, change the size and shape, rotate, group, and flip objects in a slide;
	■ apply line styles to lines and object borders, and fill colour and shadow effects on a slide;
	■ copy objects between slides.

New terms	At the end of this lesson you should be able to explain the following terms:
AutoShapes	Ready-made shapes, including lines, geometric shapes and flowchart elements, that you can use in your presentations.
Clip Art	Standard or 'stock' images that can be used and reused in presentations and other documents.

The graphics that you can draw on PowerPoint slides include simple shapes such as lines, arrows, rectangles, circles and ellipses. You can create these using the Drawing toolbar displayed along the bottom of your screen.

AutoShapes

AutoShapes are ready-made shapes that you can insert in your presentations. AutoShape categories include lines, basic shapes, flowchart elements, stars and banners, and callouts.

To select an AutoShape, click the **AutoShapes** button on the Drawing toolbar and choose from the options offered by the pop-up menu.

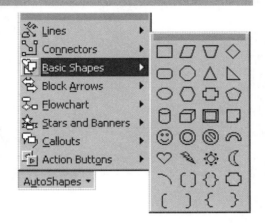

Text boxes

**Text Box
button**

A text box is a text placeholder that you insert directly on a slide. To draw a text box, click the **Text Box** button on the Drawing toolbar, click on the slide, drag the text box to the required size, and then type your text in it. PowerPoint does not show the content of text boxes in the Outline pane.

Pictures

You can illustrate slides by inserting pictures created in other software applications or scanned photographs. PowerPoint includes a gallery of *Clip Art* pictures.

Working with objects

Placeholders, lines, rectangles, ellipses, AutoShapes, text boxes and inserted pictures are all examples of what PowerPoint calls objects. There are a number of common operations – such as repositioning and resizing and rotating – that you can perform on objects regardless of their type.

Grouping and ungrouping objects

You can group objects so that you can work with them as if they were a single object. An object group can be ungrouped as required.

Open your First-Steps and Training presentations

Open button

- Launch PowerPoint, and open the First-Steps and Training presentations that you created in previous lessons.

You will use these presentations throughout this lesson.

Draw simple graphics

Displayed along the bottom of the PowerPoint window, the Drawing toolbar includes a number of tools for drawing lines, arrowed lines, rectangles, and ellipses.

To draw a line, click the **Line** button, place the cursor where you want the line to begin, click and drag to where you want the line to end, and release the mouse button.

To draw a line ending in an arrow, click on the **Arrow** button and draw it in the same way.

To draw a rectangle, click the **Rectangle** button, place the cursor where you want one corner of the rectangle, click and drag diagonally to where you want the opposite corner of the rectangle, and release the mouse button. You can draw a square by holding down the **SHIFT** key as you drag with the mouse.

To draw an oval (ellipse), click the **Ellipse** button, place the cursor where you want the shape to begin, click and drag until the shape is the size you want, and release the mouse button. You can draw a circle by holding down the **SHIFT** key as you drag.

If the Drawing toolbar is not currently visible in Normal view, choose **View | Toolbars | Drawing** to display it. Let's draw some simple graphics.

Line button

1 In Normal view, display your First-Steps presentation, and choose **View | Master | Slide Master**.

2 Click the **Line** button on the Drawing toolbar. Move the cursor over the slide, and draw a line along the bottom of your Slide Master's title placeholder as shown.

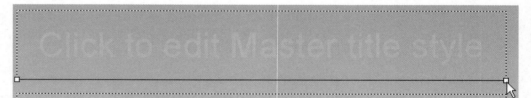

3 Switch to Normal view and display the title (first) slide.

4 Click the **Ellipse** button on the Drawing toolbar, and hold down the **SHIFT** key. This ensures that the shape you are about to draw will be a circle rather than an oval.

Ellipse button

5 Move the cursor over the slide and draw a small circle to the left of the words Round Wheels.

Don't worry too much about your circle's precise size or position, or its colour or border width. You will adjust these later in this lesson.

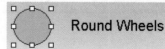

Change the width, style and colour of graphic lines

You can use the following buttons on the Drawing toolbar to modify properties of graphics.

	Use this button to change the interior colour of an oval, rectangle or other closed shape.
	Use this button to change the colour of a selected line or border.
	Use this to change the width (thickness) of a selected line or border.
	Use this to apply a dashed effect to a selected line or border.
	Use this to apply arrowheads to a selected line.

Let's amend some properties of the graphics that you have previously drawn.

1 In Normal view, display your First-Steps presentation, and choose **View | Master | Slide Master**.

Line Color button

2 Click the horizontal line along the bottom of the title placeholder, click the arrow to the right of the **Line Color** button, and change the line to the same orange colour as the title text.

Line Style button

3 With the horizontal line still selected, click the **Line Style** button, and select a line width of 3 pt.

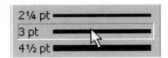

Arrow Style button

4 With the horizontal line still selected, click the **Arrow Style** button. Select a number of different arrow styles and view how they look. When finished, select Arrow Style 11.

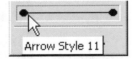

5 Switch to Normal view, display the title (first) slide, and click the circle to select it.

6 Click the **Dash Style** button, and click the Dash option from the pop-up menu.

Dash Style button

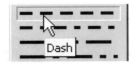

Fill Color button

7 With the circle still selected, click the arrow to the right of the **Fill Color** button, and change the circle interior to the same orange colour as the title text.

8 With the circle still selected, click the arrow to the right of the **Line Color** button, and change the circle border to dark grey.

Well done. You have learnt how to draw and amend simple graphics. You have finished working with your First-Steps presentation, and can save and close it if you wish. In the remainder of this lesson you will work with your Training presentation.

Insert an AutoShape

AutoShapes are ready-made shapes that you can include as supplied, or modify to your taste.

1 In Normal view, display your Training presentation, and choose **View | Master | Slide Master**.

2 Click the **AutoShapes** button, choose **Stars and Banners**, and select the 5-Point Star.

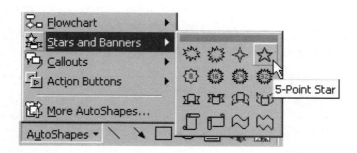

3 Hold down the **SHIFT** key, and draw the star in the lower right of the Object Area for AutoLayouts.

4 On the Standard toolbar, increase your magnification to 100%.

Fill Color button

5 With the star selected, use the **Fill Color** button on the Drawing toolbar to change its fill colour to the same yellow as the text.

Line Color button

6 With the star selected, use the **Line Color** button to change the star's border to yellow also.

Copy and paste graphics

You can copy and move (cut) AutoShapes and other graphics just as you can text: with buttons on the Standard toolbar, with commands on the **Edit** menu, and with keyboard shortcuts.

Use these methods to copy or move graphics within and between presentations.

1 With your yellow star selected, press **CTRL+c** to copy it.

2 Press **CTRL+v** twice to paste two copies of your yellow star.

Reposition graphics

To reposition a graphic within the same slide, first select it by clicking anywhere on it. Then drag the object to its new position. For small, precise movements, hold down the **CTRL** key and press the **ARROW** keys.

- Reposition your three yellow stars so that they are along a straight line.

Resize graphics

You can change the size and shape of a graphic by selecting it and clicking on any of its sizing handles. Next, drag the sizing handle until the object is the new shape that you require.

1 Using their corner sizing handles, change the size of the left and middle stars.

The first should be smaller than the second, and the second smaller than the third.

2 Switch to Slide Sorter view. Notice that each slide now has three stars in its lower right corner.

If your three stars overlap the text on any slide, switch back to the Slide Master, and reposition the three stars as necessary.

Align graphics

PowerPoint enables you to align a graphic in relation to the slide that contains it. Here's how:

1 Select the graphic or graphics that you want to align.

2 On the *Drawing* toolbar, click the **Draw** button, and, on the pop-up menu, click the **Align or Distribute** option.

3 Select the **Relative to Slide** option.

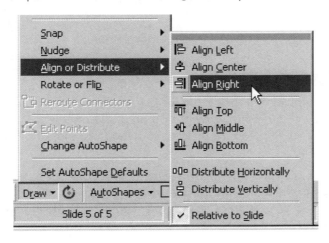

4 On the *Drawing* toolbar, again click the **Draw** button, and click the **Align or Distribute** option.

5 On the submenu displayed, select the alignment option that you require. PowerPoint offers three horizontal (Left, Centre, and Right) and three vertical (Top, Middle and Bottom) alignment options.

Insert a text box

Up to now, you have entered text on slides by selecting a placeholder and then typing text into it. You can also enter text by drawing a text box and then typing text into that.

You can format and align text in a text box in the same way as you would text in a placeholder. Note, however, that PowerPoint does not display in the Outline pane text entered in a text box.

1   In Normal view, display your Training presentation, and choose **View | Master | Slide Master**. If necessary, change the magnification so that you can see the whole slide in the slide pane.

Text Box button

2   Click the **Text Box** button, and draw a text box in the lower left corner of the slide.

3   Select the text box and type the following:

    Best Results

4   Select the text, and change it to Arial, bold, 24 points. If the text does not fit on a single line in your text box, click on a corner of the box and drag to make the box wider.

5   With the text selected, change its colour to the same medium green as the slide titles.

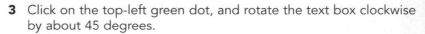

Rotate a text box or graphic

You can rotate a selected text box or graphic created in PowerPoint by clicking the **Free Rotate** button on the Drawing toolbar. Click on any of the green dots at the object's corners and drag the object to its new orientation. To flip (rotate by 180 degrees), click the **Draw** button on the Drawing toolbar, choose **Rotate or Flip**, and then **Flip Horizontal** or **Flip Vertical**. Let's try it.

1   Click your Best Results text box to select it.

2   Click the **Free Rotate** button on the Drawing toolbar. Notice how PowerPoint replaces the border of the text box by four green dots, one at each corner.

Free Rotate button

3   Click on the top-left green dot, and rotate the text box clockwise by about 45 degrees.

4   Press the **ESC** key to switch off the rotation feature.

Change the stack order of objects

If you have overlapping objects on a slide, you can change their stack order by clicking the **Draw** button on the Formatting toolbar, and choosing your required command from the **Order** submenu.

You can move graphics up or down within a stack one level at a time (**Bring Forward** or **Send Backward**), or you can move them to the top or bottom of a stack in a single action (**Bring to Front** or **Send to Back**).

You can illustrate your slides with pictures such as scanned photographs. PowerPoint includes a gallery of Clip Art pictures grouped in categories, ranging from Academic to Food and Transportation. You can include a picture in a slide in any of the following ways:

■ Create a new slide, and select either of the following two AutoLayouts:

 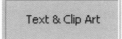 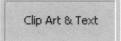

PowerPoint displays the Clip Art icon on your slide. Double-click the Clip Art icon, click on a picture category to view the individual pictures available, right-click on a picture, and choose **Insert** from the pop-up menu.

Alternatively:

Clip Art
button

■ Display an existing slide, and do either of the following: choose **Insert I Picture I Clip Art**, and select a picture from the range displayed; or, choose **Format I Slide Layout**, select either of the two AutoLayouts shown above, click **Apply**, double-click the Clip Art icon, and select the picture that you require.

You will practise working with pictures in the remainder of this lesson.

1   In Normal view, display the third slide (Benefits for Colleges) of your Training presentation.

2   Choose **Format I Slide Layout**, select the AutoLayout named Clip Art & Text, and click **Apply**. Notice how PowerPoint automatically reduces the font size of the bullet points.

3   Double-click the Clip Art icon to open the Clip Art Gallery, and click the Academic category.

Academic

Academic Clip Art gallery

4   Right-click the Graduation picture, and choose **Insert** from the pop-up menu displayed. PowerPoint inserts the picture in your slide.

5   Click on the lower-right handle of the inserted picture and reduce it in size by about 20%.

Your slide should look like that shown right.

Insert a second and third picture

Business Clip
Art gallery

1 In Normal view, display the fifth slide (Benefits for Employers) of your Training presentation.

2 Choose **Insert | Picture | Clip Art** and click the Business category to select it.

Right-click the Working Towards Goals picture, and choose **Insert** from the pop-up menu. Click the **Close** button at the top right of the Insert Clip Art window: it does not close automatically when you use the **Insert | Picture | Clip Art** command.

3 Reduce your inserted picture in size by about 40%, and move it to the centre of the lower part of your slide.

New Slide
button

4 With your fifth slide still displayed, click the **New Slide** button on the Standard toolbar.

5 Select the AutoLayout named Text & Clip Art, and click **OK**.

6 In the title placeholder of your new, sixth slide, type the following:

Benefits for Society

7 In the left text placeholder, type the following:

Participation for all in the Information Society

Home & family
Clip Art gallery

8 Double-click the Clip Art icon, and click on the Home & Family category.

Right-click on the Seniors picture, and choose **Insert** from the pop-up menu. PowerPoint inserts the picture in your slide.

9 Click on the lower right handle of the inserted picture and reduce it in size by about 20%. Drag the picture up until it is level with the bullet point text in the left placeholder.

Your two slides should look like that shown.

10 Choose **View | Slide Show**, or click the **Slide Show** button. Move forward and back through your presentation to see how it would look to the audience.

Insert non-Clip Art pictures

To insert an image of your own – your company logo, for example – on a slide, choose **Insert | Picture | From File**, select the required image file, and choose **Insert**. PowerPoint accepts images in most common image file formats.

Quit PowerPoint

You can close your First-Steps.xls and Training.xls presentations, and quit PowerPoint. You have now completed Lesson 6.5 of the ECDL Presentations Module.

6.6

Tables and charts

Learning goals At the end of this lesson you should be able to:

- create, enter text in, and format a table on a slide;
- create, enter text in, and format an organization chart on a slide;
- modify the structure of an organization chart;
- create bar, column and pie chart types for presenting quantitative information;
- reformat the appearance of a chart or selected chart elements;
- change a chart's type.

New term At the end of this lesson you should be able to explain the following term:

Organization Chart A diagram used to illustrate the people or units in an organization or system (represented by boxes) and their relationships (represented by lines).

You can create a table on a slide with a selected number of rows and columns, enter numbers and text headings, and apply formatting to it. As with text in a text box, PowerPoint does not display text in a table in the Outline pane of Normal view.

Organization charts

Organization charts are used to illustrate people's positions within an organization or the structure of components within a physical system or process. Such charts consist of boxes (for representing people or components) and lines (for representing their relationships). PowerPoint's organization chart tool provides a customizable chart template, with boxes arranged in a hierarchal structure.

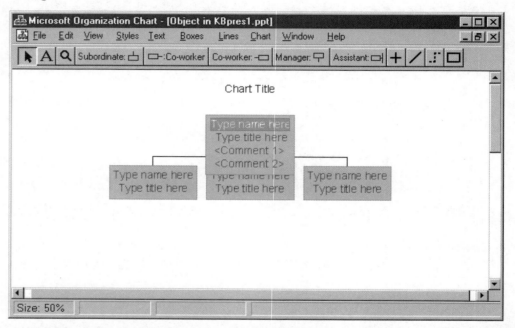

Working with charts

PowerPoint provides a variety of chart types that are useful for presenting quantitative information. The most commonly used types are the following:

- **Column Charts:** These are typically used to show figures that are measured at a particular time.

- **Bar Charts:** These are typically used to compare distances or speeds.

- **Pie Charts:** These are typically used to illustrate the breakdown of figures in a total. A pie chart is always based on a single column of numbers.

You can change the colour or format of any element in the chart by right-clicking on it. Among the chart elements that you can amend are the colours and patterns of bars, columns and pie chart slices, their identifying data labels, the chart legend and the type of details shown on the chart axes.

Open your Training presentation

Open button

- Launch PowerPoint, and open the Training presentation that you created in previous lessons.

You will use this presentation throughout this lesson.

Insert a table

You can create a table in PowerPoint in the following ways:

- **Existing Slide**: Click the **Insert Table** button on the Standard toolbar and drag to select the number of rows and columns you want. Alternatively, choose the **Insert | Table** command, select the number of rows and columns required, and click **OK**.

Alternatively:

Table icon

New Slide button

- **New Slide**: Create a new slide, select the AutoLayout named Table, double-click the table icon, select the number of rows and columns, and click **OK**.

Let's insert a table.

1   In Normal view, display the sixth slide (Benefits for Society) of your Training presentation.

2   Click the **New Slide** button on the Standard toolbar, select the AutoLayout named Table, and click **OK**.

3   Double-click the table icon, select 2 columns and 4 rows, and click **OK**. Type text in your slide until it looks as shown.

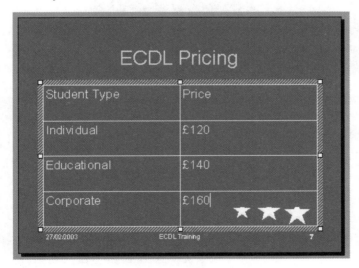

4   Select the top row of your table by dragging across the top two table cells with the mouse.

5   Click the **Bold** button and then the **Centre-Align** button on the Formatting toolbar.

6   With the top row still selected, use the **Fill Color** button on the Drawing toolbar to change its colour to the same medium green as the slide title text.

7 With the top row still selected, choose **View | Toolbars | Tables and Borders**. On the Toolbar, select the **Centre Vertically** option. Close the Tables and Borders toolbar.

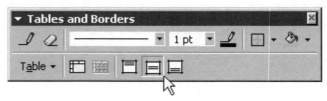

8 Select the three cells containing prices. Click the **Centre-Align** button on the Formatting toolbar.

9 With the table placeholder selected, click the centre sizing handle on the lower placeholder border. Your cursor changes to a double-headed arrow.

10 Drag the sizing handle upwards until the table placeholder no longer overlaps the three stars.

Click anywhere else on the slide to deselect the table placeholder. Your slide should look as shown.

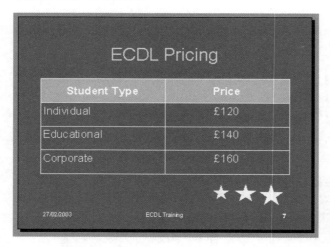

About organization charts

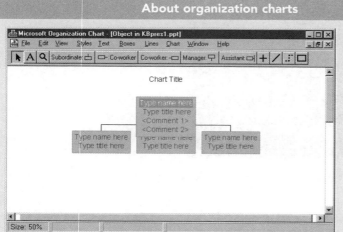

Organization charts are used to illustrate people's positions within an organization or the structure of components within a physical system or process. Such charts have two main components:

■ **Boxes:** These represent people in the organization or components within the system or process.
■ **Lines:** These represent relationships between people or units of the organization or system.

You could create organization charts using the drawing tools, but such charts are used so frequently that PowerPoint provides a template especially for producing them. The template offers a **Styles** menu that allows you to choose different chart types, and Text, Boxes and Lines for formatting the chart elements.

You can alter the template as you wish. Although the boxes have text labels in them, such as 'Type name here', you can enter any type of information in any box – the labels are for your guidance only.

Insert an organization chart

Let's insert a new slide containing an organization chart in your Training presentation.

1 In Normal view, display the seventh slide (ECDL Pricing).

New Slide button

2 Click the **New Slide** button, select the Organization Chart AutoLayout, and click **OK**.

3 Click in the title placeholder, and type:

ABC Sales Team

Organization Chart AutoLayout

4 Double-click the organization chart icon to open the Organization Chart window, and type text in the template as shown.

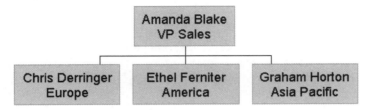

5 When you have finished working in the Organization Chart window, return to your slide by choosing **File | Exit and Return to**, and then clicking **Yes** on the dialog box displayed.

Within PowerPoint, you can move, resize or delete a chart as you would any graphic. To make any other changes to the chart, however, you must double-click the chart and make your changes in the Organization Chart window.

Work with the *Organization Chart* toolbar

By default the organization chart contains one 'manager' box and three 'subordinate' boxes. The toolbar displayed with the *Organization Chart* window provides buttons that enable you to create new boxes at different levels in the chart. In each case, you first click the toolbar button, and then click an existing box in the chart. PowerPoint inserts the new box relative to the box that you click.

Button	Description	Example
☐⊢:Co-worker Co-worker: ⊣☐	Click either button to insert a new box at the *same* level in the chart. The first button inserts the new box to the left of the selected box box. The second button inserts it to the right.	Graham Horton Asia Pacific ▮
Subordinate: ⛶	Click this button to insert a new box one level *lower* in the chart.	Graham Horton Asia Pacific ▮

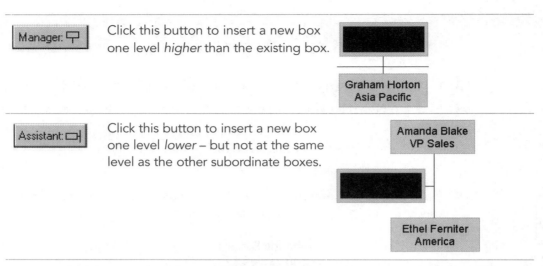

Click this button to insert a new box one level *higher* than the existing box.

Click this button to insert a new box one level *lower* – but not at the same level as the other subordinate boxes.

To delete any box from an organization chart, select it and then press the **DELETE** key. If you delete a box that has subordinate boxes under it, PowerPoint moves the subordinate boxes up one level in the chart.

Modify the structure of an organization chart

1 In Normal view, display the organization chart slide, and double-click the chart.

PowerPoint opens the chart in the Organization Chart window. The toolbar provides buttons for adding boxes (Subordinates, Co-workers, Managers, Assistants) and lines.

2 Let's begin by adding a co-worker. Click the second **Co-worker** button.

3 Click the box containing Graham Horton. A new box is created at its right, at the same level in the hierarchy. PowerPoint rearranges the other chart elements accordingly.

4 Click the new box, and enter text as shown below.

5 Close the Organization Chart window, and confirm that you want to update the chart in the presentation.

Reformat an organization chart

Shadow button

1 In Normal view, display the organization chart slide, and double-click the chart.

2 Click the **Shadow** button on the Drawing toolbar, and select Shadow Style 5.

3 With the chart still selected, click the **Shadow** button again. From the pop-up menu displayed, choose **Shadow Settings**. On the Shadow Settings toolbar, click the arrow to the right of the **Shadow Color** button, and select light blue as the shadow colour.

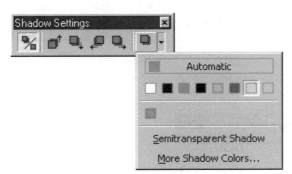

4 Close the Shadow Settings toolbar.

Be careful when choosing a colour for the shadow that you do not interfere with the legibility of your text.

About charts

When you insert a chart on a slide, PowerPoint displays the following:

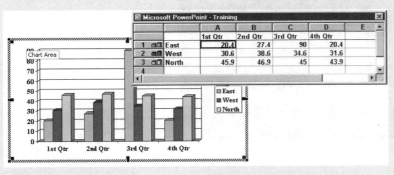

- **Datasheet:** A small spreadsheet that you can adapt by typing in your own text and numbers, over-writing those already present. You can add or delete rows or columns as you require. You can move the datasheet to a different part of your screen by dragging its title bar.
- **Chart:** This changes as you change the contents of the datasheet. You can change the colour or format of any element in the chart by double-clicking on it: you are presented with options that are relevant to that element.
- **Chart Menus:** Excel-like menus of charting commands appear at the top of the PowerPoint window.

You can close the datasheet window by clicking anywhere else on the PowerPoint screen. You can move, resize or delete a chart as you would any other object. To make changes to the data in the chart, however, you have to double-click on the chart and make your changes in the Datasheet window.

Insert a column chart

PowerPoint's default chart type is the column chart, which is typically used to show figures that are measured at a particular time. Let's insert a new slide containing a chart.

1 In Normal view, display the organization chart slide of your Training presentation.

New Slide button

2 Chose **Insert | New Slide** button, select the AutoLayout named Chart, and click **OK**.

3 Click in the title text placeholder and type the following text:

Sales Projections

Chart icon

4 Double-click the chart icon to open the Datasheet window.

5 Edit the text in the datasheet as shown. You can resize the Datasheet window at any stage by clicking on its lower-right corner and dragging.

		A	B	C	D	E
		1st Qtr	2nd Qtr	3rd Qtr	4th Qtr	
1	Europe	1000	1200	1300	1400	
2	North America	1200	1500	1400	1300	
3	Asia/Pacific	750	750	250	250	
4	Rest of World	750	750	750	750	
5						
6						

You will need to make the first column wider by clicking its boundary in the column header, and then dragging the boundary to the right.

6 When you have finished working in the datasheet window, close it. You are returned to your slide. Click anywhere else on your slide to deselect the chart placeholder. Your slide should look as shown.

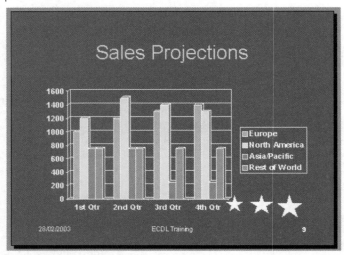

Reformat a chart

Let's change the colour of a chart column, and the colours of the chart axes and chart legend.

1 In Normal view, display the chart slide of the Training presentation.

2 Double-click the chart, and then right-click on any column of the chart. From the pop-up menu displayed, choose **Format Data Series**.

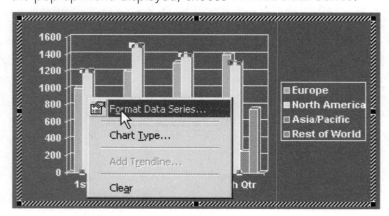

3 On the **Patterns** tab of the dialog box displayed, select a colour of white, and click **OK**.

Next, let's change the colour of the axes, axes text and legend text.

4 With the chart selected, right-click on the vertical axis and choose **Format Axis** from the pop-up menu.

5 On the **Font** tab of the dialog box displayed, click the arrow to the right of the **Color** box, select white, and click **OK**.

6 With the chart selected, repeat steps 4 and 5 for the chart's horizontal axis.

7 With the chart selected, right-click on the chart legend, choose **Format Legend**, and, on the **Font** tab, change the legend text colour to white.

Change chart type

If PowerPoint's default column chart type is not what you want, you can change the chart type.

1 In Normal view, display the chart slide, and double-click the chart to select it.

2 Click anywhere in the area surrounding the chart within the chart placeholder. From the pop-up menu displayed, choose **Chart Type**.

3 In the **Chart Type** dialog box, select **Bar** as the Chart type, click the first Chart sub-type, and click **OK**.

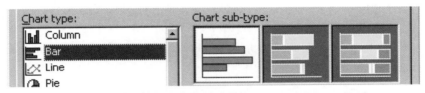

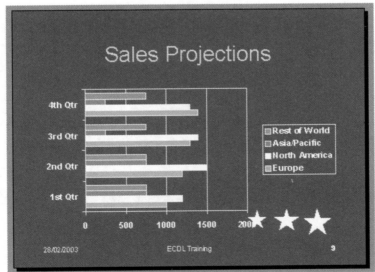

Insert a pie chart

Let's insert a new slide containing a pie chart. Pie charts can be based on a single column of numbers only.

1 In Normal view, display your bar chart slide.

New Slide
button

2 Click the **New Slide** button, select the AutoLayout named Chart, and click **OK**.

3 Click in the title text placeholder and type the following text:

Annual Sales Growth

4 Double-click the chart icon to open the Datasheet window, and edit the text as shown in the datasheet below.

Training - Datasheet		A	B	C	D	E
		1999	2000	2001	2002	
1 3-D Colum		12	15	19	21	
2 3-D Colum						
3 3-D Colum						
4						

To remove sample numbers and text that PowerPoint has placed in cells, click in each cell and press the **DELETE** key. When finished, close the datasheet and return to your slide.

5 Right-click on any column of your chart, choose **Chart Type** from the pop-up menu, select **Pie** as Chart type, select the first Chart sub-type, and click **OK**.

6 With the chart selected, right-click in the Plot Area – the area outside the pie shape but inside the chart area. From the pop-up menu displayed, choose **Format Plot Area**. On the dialog box displayed, select **None** for Border, and click **OK**.

7 With the chart selected, right-click on the chart legend, choose **Format Legend**, and, on the **Font** tab, change the legend text colour to white.

8 Right-click anywhere on the pie chart and choose **Format Data Series**. On the **Data Labels** tab, select **Show Value** and click **OK**. Click anywhere else on the slide to deselect the chart.

9 Switch to Slide Show view, and inspect your ten-slide presentation as it will be seen by your audience. Impressive, eh?

Quit PowerPoint

You can close your Training.xls presentations, and quit PowerPoint. You have now completed Lesson 6.6 of the ECDL Presentations Module.

6.7

Transitions and animations

Learning goals	At the end of this lesson you should be able to:

- apply manual, timed automatic and 'whichever comes first' slide advance methods;
- specify the nature and timing of transition effects;
- apply preset animations;
- customize animation effects so as to modify the order, direction, sound effect and dim effect of animations;
- include graphics and pictures in animations.

New terms	At the end of this lesson you should be able to explain the following terms:
Advance method	The way that PowerPoint displays the slides of a presentation: manually, automatically, or automatically with manual override. Automatic advance is often used for unaccompanied presentations.
Transition	A visual effect, such as a drop-down, box-out, dissolve, or fade, that controls how one slide in a presentation is replaced by another.
Animated Slide	A slide in which different elements are revealed at different times.

PowerPoint offers three slide *advance methods*:

■ Manual (operated by the presenter);

■ Automatic (after a specified time interval); or

■ 'Whichever comes first' (automatic with manual override).

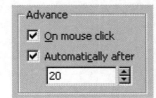

Automatic advance is often used in unaccompanied presentations that are left running in public areas.

Transitions

A *transition* is a graphic effect that controls how one slide replaces another – for example, the new slide could appear to drop down from the top of the screen. PowerPoint lets you select two aspects of a transition:

■ **Effect type:** The nature of the special effect with which PowerPoint introduces the slide.

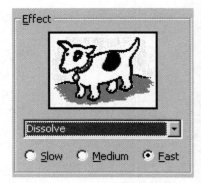

■ **Effect timing:** The speed with which PowerPoint runs the visual effect when introducing the slide.

Optionally, you can also link a sound to the transition between slides. Although you set the slide advance method and the slide transition effect in the same dialog box, the two effects are independent.

Animations

An *animated slide* is one on which the elements are revealed gradually rather than all at once. These can help the presenter focus the audience's attention on each point in turn. You can create animated slides using either of the following two methods:

■ **Preset animations:** A series of 13 ready-to-use animations, some with associated sound effects, which you can quickly apply to your slides.

■ **Custom animations:** These offer a wide range of dynamic effects and options.

The most common approach is to apply a present animation that is close to what you want, and then customize it where necessary.

Open your First-Steps and Training presentations

Open button

- Launch PowerPoint, and open the First-Steps and Training presentations that you created in previous lessons.

You will use these presentations throughout this lesson.

Apply an advance method to a presentation

The *advance method* is the way that PowerPoint displays the slides of a presentation: manually, automatically, or automatically with manual override. Let's apply the third method to your Training presentation.

1 In Normal view, display any slide of your Training presentation, and choose **Slide Show | Slide Transition**.

2 In the **Advance** area of the dialog box displayed, check **Automatically after**, and then type the number of seconds (for example, 15) that you want each slide to appear on screen. Ensure that the **On mouse click** checkbox is also selected. In the **Sound** pull-down list, select **Applause**.

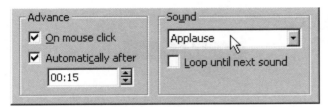

3 Click **Apply to All** to apply the automatic slide advance to your entire presentation. Save your presentation.

Switch to Slide Show view to see how your selected advance methods affect your presentation.

Apply a transition to a presentation

A transition is a visual effect that controls how one slide is replaced by another. Let's apply one.

1 In Normal view, display any slide of your Training presentation, and choose **Slide Show | Slide Transition**.

2 First explore the transition options on offer:

- **Effect**: Each time you click an option from the pull-down list, PowerPoint runs the effect in the sample picture. You can rerun the preview by clicking the picture.

- **Timing**: The options – Slow, Medium or Fast – set the speed at which the transition effect runs. Click an option and PowerPoint runs the effect with that timing in the sample picture.

For this example, select the effect named **Dissolve**, with **Fast** timing.

3 Click **Apply to All**.

You have the option of applying a different transition to each slide (by clicking **Apply**), but be careful: this option may have the effect of distracting or unsettling your audience.

Switch to Slide Show view to see how the transitions affect the presentation.

Apply a preset animation to a presentation

An *animated slide* is one on which the elements are revealed gradually rather than all at once. Let's apply one of PowerPoint's preset animations to your First-Steps presentation.

1 In Normal view, display your First-Steps presentation, and choose **View | Master | Slide Master**.

2 Click anywhere in the lower placeholder, where the bullet points are.

3 Choose **Slide Show | Preset Animation** and select the option called **Drive-In**.

4 Choose **View | Slide Show** and move through your slides to view the animation effect. Remember: you need to click the mouse (or press **PAGE DOWN** or **ENTER**) for each bullet point to appear.

Customize a preset animation

You can adapt a preset animation according to your taste or requirements.

1 In Normal view, display your First-Steps presentation, and choose **View | Master | Slide Master**.

2 Click anywhere in the lower placeholder, where the bullet points are.

3 Choose **Slide Show | Custom Animation**. The dialog box displayed shows the settings of the preset animation, and gives you the ability to change them.

On the **Effects** tab, replace the **From Right** setting with **From Left**, and the **Screeching Brakes** sound effect with **[No Sound]**.

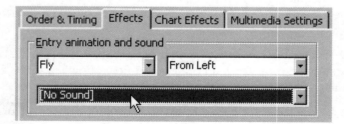

Next, in the **After animation** box, select medium green.

4 Click on the **Order & Timing** tab, select the **On mouse click** option, and click **OK**.

Switch to Slide Show view and move through your slides to view the animation effect.

Animate pictures and charts

By default, PowerPoint animates only those pictures and charts that are inserted within the appropriate slide layout (such as Text & Clip Art, Organization Chart or Chart). Also by default, PowerPoint does not animate tables.

Let's discover how PowerPoint gives you complete control over table, picture and chart animations. For example, the picture on the fifth slide of your Training presentation, which was included with the **Insert | Picture | Clip Art** command, and the pricing table.

1 In Normal view, display the Training presentation.

2 In Normal view, display the third slide (Benefits for Colleges), click anywhere on the slide, and choose **Slide Show | Custom Animation**.

On the **Order & Timing** tab, see how the picture, which PowerPoint calls Object 3, is included in the animation order.

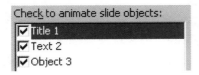

3 Repeat Step 2 for the following slides: Benefits for Society, ABC Sales Team, Sales Projections and Annual Sales Growth. In each case, you can see that the picture or chart is included in the animation order.

4 Display the Benefits for Employers slide, choose **Slide Show | Custom Animation**, and click the **Order & Timing** tab. Notice that the picture is not animated.

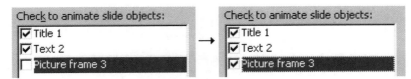

Click Picture frame 3 to select it, and click **OK** to close the dialog box.

5 Display the 'ECDL Pricing' slide and choose **Slide Show | Custom Animation**. On the **Order & Timing** tab, include the table in the animation order, and click **OK**.

6 Choose **View | Slide Show** and page through your presentation to see the effect on the Benefits for Employers and ECDL Pricing slides.

Quit PowerPoint

You can close your First-Steps.xls and Training.xls presentations, and quit PowerPoint. You have now completed Lesson 6.7 of the ECDL Presentations Module.

6.8

Proofing, templates and file formats

Learning goals At the end of this lesson you should be able to:

- use PowerPoint's spell-checker;
- save PowerPoint presentation files in the following file formats: PowerPoint slide shows, earlier versions of PowerPoint, HTML (web format) files, graphic (GIF or JPG) files, Rich Text Format (RTF) and PowerPoint design templates;
- create a presentation based on a design template, and apply a design template to an existing presentation;
- import cells and charts from Microsoft Excel into PowerPoint slides.

New term At the end of this lesson you should be able to explain the following term:

Design Template A PowerPoint file, containing a colour scheme and Slide Master with font settings and possibly built-in graphics and text, which can be applied to a presentation. Design template files end in .pot.

Spell-checking

Spelling mistakes really spoil a presentation: they make you look either careless or ignorant – and your effort to impress the audience may be wasted. While it is dangerous to rely totally on a spell-checker, it is also foolish not to use one at all.

Saving a presentation as a slide show

You can save a presentation as a slide show, so that it always opens as a ready-to-run slide show, whether you open it within PowerPoint or directly from the desktop. PowerPoint saves the file with the extension .pps. Your original presentation file is unaffected.

Other file formats

To help you share your files with others, PowerPoint 2000 allows you to save your presentations in a file format other than its own. The options include:

- **Earlier versions of Microsoft PowerPoint**: While you can generally use a later version of the software to open and work with a presentation that was created in an earlier version, the reverse is not necessarily true.

- **HTML (web page)**: You can convert a complete PowerPoint presentation, a single slide, or a range of slides into HTML format, so that they can be displayed in a web browser.

- **Graphics files**: You can save your slides in one of the two common graphic formats: JPEG or GIF.

- **Rich Text Format (RTF)**: To reuse an entire presentation in another application, the best option is to save the presentation in Rich Text Format (RTF).

Design templates

PowerPoint offers you the ability to save a presentation as a *design template*. You can then use the saved design template as a basis for quickly creating other, similar presentations.

PowerPoint comes with a range of professionally designed templates that you can use as supplied, or amend as required and save for later reuse.

Open your Training presentation

Open button

- Launch PowerPoint, and open the Training presentation that you created in previous lessons.

  You will use this presentation throughout this lesson.

Set your spell-check options

In PowerPoint, you can checking your spelling in two ways:

- As you type and edit text on slides (the automatic option). Wavy underlines indicate words with possible spelling errors. To correct the spelling, right-click a wavy line, and then choose the option you want from the pop-up menu displayed.

- Whenever you choose **Tools | Spelling**, press **F7** or click the **Spelling** button on the toolbar (the on-request option).

To turn automatic spell-checking on or off, select or deselect the **Check spelling as you type** checkbox on the **Spelling and Style** tab of the dialog box displayed by the **Tools | Options** command.

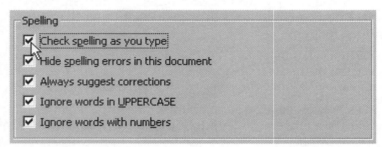

Perform a spell-check

When you run a spell-check, it identifies suspect words, and shows suggested alternatives. You can accept one of the suggestions, edit the word yourself, or leave the original unchanged.

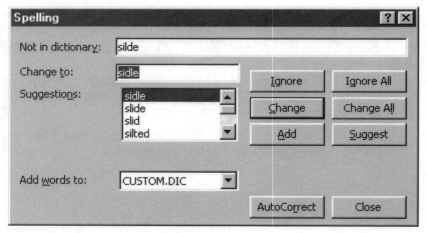

The spell-checker will not find incorrect spellings that are themselves valid words (such as 'form' instead of 'from').

Save a presentation as a slide show

You can save a presentation so that it always opens as a slide show, whether you open it within PowerPoint or directly from the desktop.

1 In Normal view, display your Training presentation.

2 Choose **File | Save As**, and select the folder where you want to save the file.

3 In the **Save as type** box, select **PowerPoint Show**, accept or change the current file name, and click **Save**.

PowerPoint saves the file with the extension .pps. Your original presentation file is unaffected.

4 Open Windows Explorer, and locate the folder where you saved your slide show. Double-click the slide show. PowerPoint responds by running the slide show on your screen.

When finished, close the slide show, but leave the presentation open.

Work with earlier versions of PowerPoint

While you can generally use a later version of the software to open and work with a presentation that was created in an earlier version, the reverse is not necessarily true. You can save your PowerPoint 2000 presentations in the file formats of previous versions of PowerPoint. You have three main options:

- PowerPoint 97-2000 & 95 Presentation.

- PowerPoint 95 Presentation.

- PowerPoint 4.0.

Work with HTML (web) format

You can convert a complete PowerPoint presentation, a single slide, or a range of slides into HTML format, so that they can be displayed in a web browser. PowerPoint offers a range of options when converting a presentation to HTML. Let's try it.

1 In Normal view, display your Training presentation.

2 Choose **File | Save As Web Page** and select the folder where you want to save.

To change the web page title (the text that appears in the title bar of the web browser), click **Change Title**, type the new title in the **Page title** box, and then click **OK**. When finished, click **Publish**.

3 On the **Publish as Web Page** dialog box display, select the values as shown overleaf.

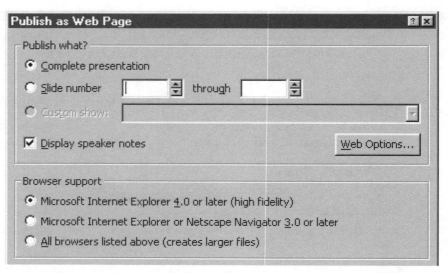

To see how the web version of your presentation looks in a web browser, select the checkbox at the bottom of the dialog box.

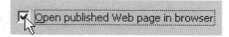

When finished, click **Publish**.

4 After a few seconds, PowerPoint will perform the file conversion, and open the first page of your presentation in the web browser. Click the slide titles on the left of the screen to navigate through the web-based version of your presentation. A sample page is shown below. You can close the file when finished.

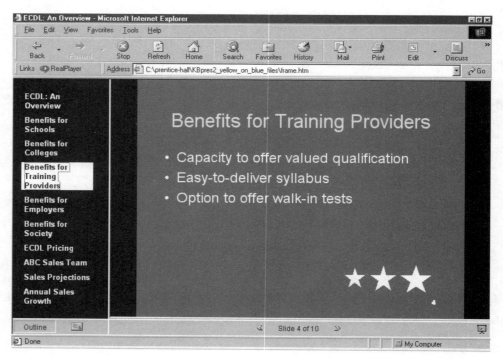

Set HTML options

PowerPoint offers a range of options when converting a presentation to HTML. To view the choices available for an open presentation:

- Choose **File | Save As Web Page** and select the folder where you want to save the file.

- Click **Publish** to display the **Publish as Web Page** dialog box, and click **Web Options** to display a dialog box with four tabs.

Your main options are as follows:

- **Slide navigation controls**: The default is white text against a black background.

- **Location of files**: Where do you want the supporting files located? The default is in a separate sub-folder.

- **Screen size**: The default is 800 x 600.

Save slides as graphics

If you want to use your slides in other graphic programs, or within web pages, you can save them in one of the two common graphic formats: JPEG or GIF. To save an open presentation as a graphic:

- Choose **File | Save As**.

- Select the folder where you want to save the file, and accept or amend the suggested file name.

- Click on the arrow to the right of the **Save as type** box.

- Select **GIF Graphics Interchange Format (*.gif)** or **JPEG File Interchange Format (*.jpg)**, and click **Save**.

- PowerPoint asks if you want to convert the entire presentation or just the current slide. Respond as appropriate.

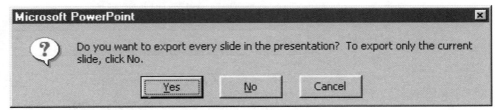

- If you have selected all slides, you are shown another dialog box, similar to the one below.

PowerPoint saves the file(s) with the extension .gif or .jpg. Your original presentation file is unaffected.

Use PowerPoint slides in other applications

To use text and/or graphics from a single slide in a Microsoft Word document, copy the items in PowerPoint (select them and press **CTRL+c**), and paste them in Word (position the cursor and press **CTRL+v**).

To reuse an entire presentation in another application, the best option is to choose **File | Save As** and select **Outline (*.rtf)**. This is Rich Text Format, a format common to all Microsoft Office applications.

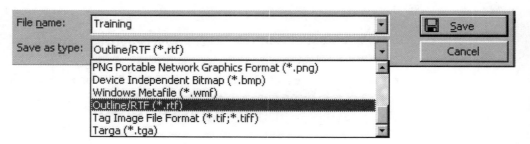

PowerPoint saves the file with the extension .rtf. Your original presentation file is unaffected.

Save a presentation as a template

PowerPoint offers you the ability to save a presentation as a design template. You can then use the saved design template as a basis for quickly creating other, similar presentations. To save an open presentation as a design template:

■ Choose **File | Save As**.

■ Select the folder where you want to save the file, and accept or amend the suggested file name. Typically, PowerPoint suggests that you save your design templates in the following folder:

C:\Program Files\Microsoft Office\Templates\Presentation Designs

■ Click on the arrow to the right of the **Save as type:** box.

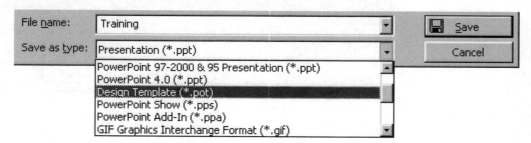

■ Select the Design Template option, and click **Save**.

PowerPoint saves the design template with the extension .pot. Your original presentation file is unaffected. The next time you want to create a presentation, you can start with that saved design template and all the slides will take on its characteristics.

Apply a design template to a presentation

You can apply a design template to a presentation in either of two ways:

- **New presentation**: Create the presentation using the **File | New** command, and select the required design template from the list displayed.

- **Existing presentation**: Choose **Format | Apply Design Template**, and select the required design template from the list displayed.

When you apply a design template to an existing presentation, the Slide Master and colour scheme of the new template replace any Slide Master and colour scheme contained in the presentation. Let's try it.

1   In Normal view, display your Training presentation.

2   Choose **Format | Apply Design Template** to display the template choices available.

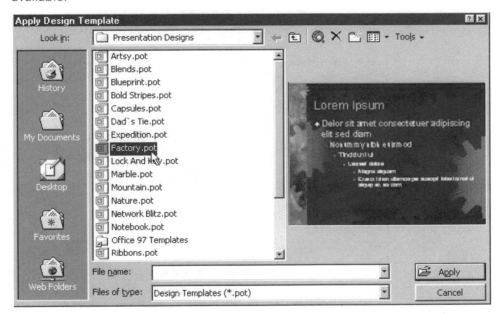

3   Select the Factory.pot template, and click **Apply**.

4   Switch to Slide Show view to see the result. Pretty cool, eh?

5   Switch back to Normal view, and experiment further with other design templates.

When finished, choose **File | Save As**, and save the presentation with a name that indicates that it is a design template. Do not close PowerPoint.

About design templates

In addition to design templates that you may create yourself, PowerPoint comes with a wide range of professionally designed templates. You can use the design templates as supplied, or amend them according to your particular needs or taste, or to your company identity scheme, and save them for later reuse. To view PowerPoint's presupplied design templates, choose **File | New**, and click the **Design Templates** tab on the **New Presentation** dialog box.

Import spreadsheets

PowerPoint allows you to import numerical data from spreadsheets. Let's create a new presentation and import data from an Excel worksheet to it.

1 Open Microsoft Excel. In a new workbook, enter the information shown.

	A	B	C
	River	**Length (km)**	**Location**
1			
2	Nile	6693	North/East Africa
3	Amazon	6436	South America
4	Yangtze	6378	China
5	Huang He	5463	China
6	Ob-Irtysh	5410	Russia

rivers.xls

Save the workbook with the file name rivers.xls.

2 Switch to PowerPoint, choose **File I New**, select the design template called Bold Stripes, and click **OK**.

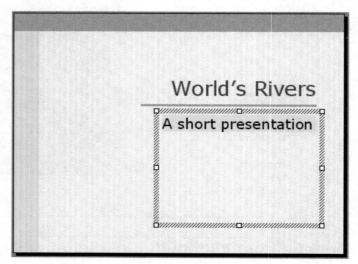

3 On the AutoLayout dialog box shown, select Title Slide, click **OK**, and type the text as shown.

4 Insert a second slide by clicking the **New Slide** button on the toolbar, selecting the AutoLayout named Title Only, and clicking **OK**.

5 In the top placeholder of your second slide, enter the following text:

Longest Rivers

Click anywhere outside the top placeholder to deselect it.

6 Choose **Insert I Object**. On the dialog box shown, select the Create from file checkbox, and click **Browse**.

○ Create new
◉ Create from file

7 On the next dialog box, navigate to the folder where you saved the rivers.xls Excel file, select the file, and click **OK**. You are returned to the previous dialog box.

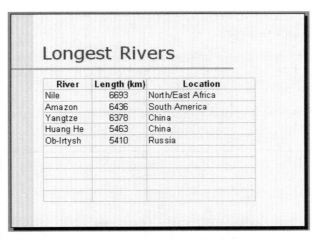

Longest Rivers

River	Length (km)	Location
Nile	6693	North/East Africa
Amazon	6436	South America
Yangtze	6378	China
Huang He	5463	China
Ob-Irtysh	5410	Russia

8 Click **OK** to close the first dialog box. The Excel worksheet is inserted on your slide. Reposition and resize the imported worksheet until your slide looks as shown above. Save your presentation with an appropriate name.

About imported worksheets

You can work with an imported worksheet as you would any imported picture. For example, you can place a border or shadow around it, and copy it to other slides or the Slide Master. A worksheet included on the Slide Master appears on every slide of the presentation.

To change the content or appearance of the worksheet, double-click it, and use the Excel menus and toolbars displayed. To deselect the worksheet, click anywhere on the slide outside it.

Import an Excel chart

You can also import spreadsheet charts into PowerPoint.

1 Display your rivers.xls Excel worksheet, select the cell range A1:B6, and click the **Chart Wizard** button on the toolbar.

rivers.xls

	A	B	C
1	**River**	**Length (km)**	**Location**
2	Nile	6693	North/East Africa
3	Amazon	6436	South America
4	Yangtze	6378	China
5	Huang He	5463	China
6	Ob-Irtysh	5410	Russia

2 On the first **Chart Wizard** dialog box, select a chart type of bar chart, and click **Next**. On the second and third **Chart Wizard** dialog boxes, accept the default values and click **Next**. On the fourth dialog box, click **Finish**. Excel creates the chart on your worksheet.

3 With the chart selected, copy it to the Clipboard, click the **New** button on the Excel Standard toolbar, and paste the chart in the new workbook. Save the workbook as rivers_chart.xls. You can now close Excel.

4 Switch to PowerPoint, and display the rivers presentation that you created in the previous exercise in Normal view.

5 Insert a third slide by clicking the **New Slide** button, selecting the AutoLayout named Blank, and clicking **OK**.

6 Choose **Insert | Object**. On the dialog box shown, select the **Create from file** checkbox, and click **Browse**.

7 On the next dialog box, navigate to the folder where you saved the rivers_chart.xls Excel file, select the file, and click **OK**. You are returned to the previous dialog box.

8 Click **OK** to close the first dialog box. The Excel chart is inserted on your slide. Reposition and resize the imported chart until your slide looks as shown.

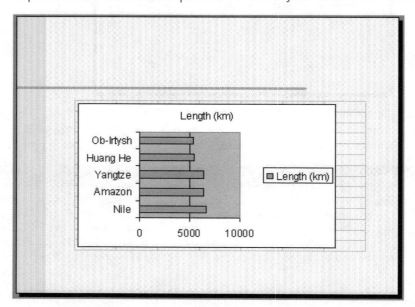

Quit PowerPoint

You can close all your files and quit PowerPoint. Congratulations! You have now completed Module 6 of the ECDL, Presentations. To remind yourself of the main features of PowerPoint, cut out the quick reference guide, called **presentation essentials**, at the back of the book and keep it beside your computer.

7

Information and communication

'The Internet is like a library.' You will hear this kind of statement a lot from people who know little about either.

If the Internet is a library, it's a strange one indeed. For starters, there is no indexing system. At any rate, the books are not arranged on numbered shelves but scattered on the floor. A lot of what is in the books is untrue, even in the non-fiction ones. There is no librarian, and no information desk. Did we mention also that the lights are turned off?

What's more, you can make as much noise as you like when using the Internet, while at the same time collecting facts and figures (and fiction and music and video and software and pictures and travel information and sports results and stock prices and weather reports and recipes and …) from all around the world. This module will arm you with the knowledge and skills that will enable you to find your way easily and effectively around this mass of information.

In fact, the principal use of the Internet is for e-mail – a way of sending messages from your computer to someone else's computer, whether they are in the next room or in a different hemisphere.

Think of this module as your chance to borrow knowledge and skills you won't ever be asked to return, and to become part of an online electronic community.

71

Exploring the web

Learning goals At the end of this lesson you should be able to:

- start Internet Explorer and visit a website;
- explore a website by scrolling down pages and clicking on hyperlinks;
- move backwards and forwards through previously visited web pages;
- open several windows at once in Internet Explorer;
- access and use Internet Explorer's online help.

New terms At the end of this lesson you should be able to explain the following terms:

Home Page	The first or front page of a website. Typically, it presents a series of links that you can follow to view the site's other pages.
Address Bar	An area above the main window that shows the address (preceded by 'http://') of the currently displayed web page. You can also use the Address bar to enter a web address. (You need not type 'http://'.)

Surf the Web

Prepare to take your first steps in exploring the World Wide Web, or 'web' as it is popularly known. In this lesson you will visit and explore websites operated by national newspapers based in Australia, France, Germany and Italy, and by Microsoft.

Your start web page

Internet Explorer typically takes you to a particular web page – called the start page – whenever you start the application. If you obtained your copy of Internet Explorer from your ISP, the start page is probably the *home page* of your ISP's website. A home page is the first or front page of a website.

Web pages typically contain hyperlinks – items of text (or graphics) that, if clicked on, open another web page, or take you to different part of the page that you are on.

Visiting websites

Every web page has a unique web address, which you must enter in Internet Explorer when you want to visit that web page. You can enter a web address in two main ways.

One is to choose the **File | Open** command (or press **CTRL+o**) to display the **Open** dialog box, type the required address and then click **OK**.

A second method is to enter the required web address in the *Address bar* near the top of the Internet Explorer window, and click the **Go** button or press **ENTER**.

Using the Standard toolbar

Along the top of the Internet Explorer window is the Standard toolbar, which provides convenient, one-click access to commonly-used actions.

Online help

Internet Explorer offers an online help system. You can search through and read online help in two ways: from the **Help** menu, or by clicking the question-mark button in dialog boxes and then clicking the item you want explained.

Start Internet Explorer

Internet
Explorer

Start the Microsoft Internet Explorer application as follows:

■ Double-click the Internet Explorer icon or choose **Start | Programs | Internet Explorer**.

If your computer has a permanent Internet connection, you are ready to surf the web.

If you have a dial-up connection, you must first dial your Internet Service Provider (ISP). Internet Explorer may be set up to do this automatically. If not, you will need to dial your ISP separately.

Enter your user name and password (if Internet Explorer has not recorded them from the last time that you dialled your ISP), and click the **Connect** button.

View your start web page

Typically, Internet Explorer is set up so that it takes you to a particular web page (the start page) whenever you start the application.

If you obtained Internet Explorer from your ISP, this start page is probably the home page of the ISP's website.

A sample ISP home page is shown above.

Visit a website

Let's visit the website of *The Age*, a newspaper published in Melbourne, Australia.

1 Choose **File | Open** or press **CTRL+o**. (Hold down the **CTRL** key and press the letter **o**.)

2 In the **Open** dialog box displayed, type the web address shown below, and click **OK**.

Internet Explorer displays the home page of *The Age* website. Leave the web page open.

Explore a Website

▸ national
▸ world
▸ features
▸ opinion
▸ business
▸ technology
▸ sport
▸ realfooty
▸ entertainment
▸ multimedia

1 Along the left of *The Age's* home page you can see a list of the newspaper's main sections.

Each section name is a hyperlink – if clicked, it opens another web page, or moves you to different part of the same page.

2 Click the hyperlink named Technology. Internet Explorer now displays a new web page, the Technology page.

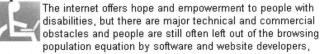

Here you can see summaries of the newspaper's technology stories. Each summary ends with a hyperlink named More.

ICON COVER STORY
Equal access
The internet offers hope and empowerment to people with disabilities, but there are major technical and commercial obstacles and people are still often left out of the browsing population equation by software and website developers, writes Amanda Morgan. more

Screen shots reproduced with the permission of *The Age*.

3 Click any More hyperlink to display a web page containing an individual technology story.

Leave the news story page open on your screen.

Explore the Standard toolbar

Across the top of the main window is the Standard toolbar. To hide and redisplay it, choose **View | Toolbars**, deselect and reselect the **Standard Buttons** option.

Button	Description
⇐ Back	Returns you to the previously displayed web page.
⇒ Forward	Reverses the effect of pressing the **Back** button.
⊗ Stop	Halts the retrieval of the web page from the website. Click this button if the web page you are trying to view is taking too long to display.
↻ Refresh	Click this button to re-request the current web page from the website if, for example, it displays incorrectly or incompletely.
⌂ Home	Displays your selected start web page. See Lesson 7.5.
Search	Displays Internet Explorer's built-in web search facility at the left of the main window. See Lesson 7.4.
Favorites	Displays a list of your saved web addresses at the left of the main window. See Lesson 7.5.
History	Displays a list of the web pages that you visited at the left of the main window. See Lesson 7.5.
Print	Prints the current web page without displaying the **Print** dialog box. Use the **File	Print** command instead when you want to amend the default print settings. See Lesson 7.2.

Move forwards and backwards through a series of web pages

Let's practise using the **Back** and **Forward** buttons at the left of the toolbar to return to the web pages that you visited earlier, and then move forward again to the ones you visited most recently.

1   With a technology news story displayed from *The Age* newspaper, click the **Back** button. This returns you to the web page you visited most recently – the summary of technology stories.

2   Click the **Back** button again to return to the second-last web page that you visited – *The Age's* home page.

3   Click the **Forward** button. This moves you forward, one page at a time, retracing your original movement through the website.

4   Click the **Forward** button a second time. This brings you forward to the web page from which you originally began to move backwards – the individual technology news story page.

Enter an address in the Address bar

When you visit a web page, its web address is displayed in the so-called *Address bar* near the top of the Internet Explorer window. You can also use the Address bar to enter a web address. Although the Address bar always displays 'http://' before a web address, you need not type 'http://' when entering an address in the bar.

If the Address bar is not shown on your screen, choose **View | Toolbars | Address Bar** to display it.

1   Click anywhere in the Address bar. This selects the currently displayed web address, which is then shown in reverse (white-on-black).

2   Use the **BACKSPACE** or **DELETE** key to remove the currently displayed web address. The Address bar is now empty. Type the following web address, and click **Go** or press the **ENTER** key.

Internet Explorer now displays the front page of Canada's *Toronto Star* newspaper.

Practise your web browsing skills by clicking on hyperlinks to display pages within the Toronto newspaper, and using the **PAGE DOWN** and **PAGE UP** keys to scroll through each displayed web page.

Open multiple web pages

You are not limited to opening a single web page at one time, as the following example shows.

1 Visit the website of the French newspaper *Le Monde* at www.lemonde.fr

2 Open a new, second window by choosing **File | New | Window** or pressing **CTRL+n**. By default, the new window displays whatever web page is shown in the previous one – in this case, the home page of *Le Monde*.

3 Press **CTRL+o** and enter the following web address: www.welt.de

Your second window now displays the home page of the German newspaper, *Die Welt*.

4 Open a third window, and enter the following web address: www.lastampa.it. This is the home page of the Italian newspaper, *La Stampa*.

Well done. You have now opened three windows in Internet Explorer You can switch between open windows by clicking them or by clicking their icons in the Windows Taskbar.

Close an Internet Explorer window

When you have multiple windows open in Internet Explorer, you can close any one window by clicking the **Close** button at the top right of the window or by choosing **File | Close**.

If you have just a single window open, closing that window closes the Internet Explorer application.

Open a framed web page

A framed web page is composed of several, independent sub-windows called frames. Let's visit one.

1 Visit the Microsoft Developers Network website at the following address:

http://msdn.microsoft.com/library/

2 Scroll down through the left frame, and then scroll down through the right frame. Notice that each frame acts like it is a window in its own right.

3 Click any hyperlink in the left window. When you do, Internet Explorer displays different content in the right frame.

In this example the web page is divided into two horizontal (left/right) frames. Sometimes framed web pages are split vertically (top/bottom), or both vertically and horizontally.

Like Word, Excel and other Microsoft applications, Internet Explorer contains a searchable online help system. Let's explore the options available.

1 Choose **Help | Contents and Index** or press **F1**.

2 Internet Explorer displays the **Help** window with the following main tabs:

■ **Contents**: Here you will find descriptions of Internet Explorer's main features. Where you see a heading with a book symbol, double-click it to view the related sub-headings. Double-click on a question-mark symbol to read the online help text.

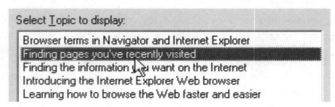

■ **Index**: Type your question in the box at the top-left of the dialog box, and click **Display**. Internet Explorer displays a list of suggested help topics in the lower-left. Click a topic to display the associated text in the right pane.

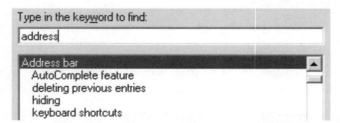

■ **Search**: Type the word or phrase and click **List Topics**. Internet Explorer displays all matches from the online help in the lower left of the dialog box. Click on a topic to display the associated text.

You will see the following buttons, left to right, at the top of the online help window:

■ **Hide/Show**: Hides or displays the left pane of the dialog box.

■ **Back/Forward**: Moves you backwards and forwards through previously visited help topics.

■ **Options**: Offers a number of display choices, and enables you to print the currently displayed online help text.

■ **Web Help**: Takes you to Microsoft's web-based support site for Internet Explorer

Take a few minutes to look through Internet Explorer's online help system.

Use help from dialog boxes

You can access online help directly from a dialog box, as this example shows.

1 Choose **Tools | Internet Options**, and click the **General** tab of the Internet Options dialog box.

2 Click the question-mark symbol near the top right of the dialog box. Internet Explorer displays a question mark to the right of the cursor. Click anywhere in the **Address** box to display help text telling you about this item.

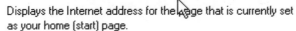

> Displays the Internet address for the page that is currently set as your home (start) page.
>
> The home page is the page you see each time you start Internet Explorer. You can return to the home page at any time by clicking the **Home** button on the toolbar.

3 Click anywhere else on the screen to close the help text window.

Practise this exercise with other dialog boxes in Internet Explorer.

Quit Internet Explorer

You can close Internet Explorer by clicking the **Close** button or choosing **File | Close**. You have now completed Lesson 7.1 of the ECDL Information and Communication Module.

7.2

Saving, downloading, printing

Learning goals At the end of this lesson you should be able to:

- save text, images and web addresses from the web;
- download images, video and sound files, software and complete web pages from the web;
- print web pages, and use the page setup and print options.

Selecting and copying from the web

If you see something on the web that you like, you can obtain it in two ways: select the item, and then copy-and-paste it to a file on your computer, or download the item as a file in its own right.

You select text by dragging across it, and copy it to the clipboard with the **Edit | Copy** command. You select an image or web address by right-clicking it, and choosing the **Copy** command from the pop-up menu.

You can then paste the copied text, image or web address from the clipboard to a Word document or other file.

Downloading from the web

To download an item means to transfer a copy of it from a web page to your computer. The original item remains on the web page.

Among the items that you can download are the following: images, video files, sound files, the text of a web page, and a software program. In each case Internet Explorer displays a dialog box indicating the progress of your download. You can halt the download at any stage.

```
Saving:
...WindowsMediaPlayer600K.wmv from download.microsoft.com
■
Estimated time left:  23 min 20 sec (44.5 KB of 6.88 MB copied)
Download to:          C:\D...\WindowsMediaPlayer600K.wmv
Transfer rate:        5.90 KB/Sec
```

You can also download an entire web page – including its text, graphics and other components. When you download an entire web page, Internet Explorer responds by performing two actions:

■ Saving the web page as a single file.

■ Creating a folder of the same name as the web page in which it places images and other files related to the saved web page. The folder is stored in the same location as the saved web page.

Downloading files and viruses

Be careful when choosing a file to download to your PC from the World Wide Web. The file may contain a virus that could damage your PC. Virus-infected files fall into two main categories:

■ Files that appear to be sound, video or other regular files, but are really viruses in disguise.

■ Microsoft Office files, such as Word documents or Excel workbooks, that contain types of viruses known as macro viruses. As their name suggests, macro viruses exploit the macro capabilities within Microsoft Office files to host malicious programs.

Respecting copyright

The Internet, in the words of one cynical commentator, 'is about the free exchange of other people's ideas and work'.

As you will learn, it's not difficult to copy and download items from the web to your computer. But it may not always be legal. If you intend reproducing copyright material that you obtained from the web, ask for permission first.

Select and copy text from a web page

Follow these steps to copy text from a web page to a Microsoft Word document on your computer.

1 Visit the following web address to display a copy of George A. Miller's classic essay, *The Magical Number Seven, Plus or Minus Two: Some Limits on Our Capacity for Processing Information*:

   www.well.com/user/smalin/miller.html

2 When the web page has loaded fully, scroll down to the end of the page. (A quick way of moving to the bottom of a page is to press **CTRL+END**.)

3 Press **PAGE UP** two or three times until Internet Explorer displays the last paragraph of the essay, which begins with the words 'And finally'.

4 Click at the start of the paragraph and drag the mouse down and right until you have selected the entire paragraph. The selected text should look as shown.

And finally, what about the magical number seven? What about the seven wonders of the world, the seven seas, the seven deadly sins, the seven daughters of Atlas in the Pleiades, the seven ages of man, the seven levels of hell, the seven primary colors, the seven notes of the musical scale, and the seven days of the week? What about the seven-point rating scale, the seven categories for absolute judgment, the seven objects in the span of attention, and the seven digits in the span of immediate memory? For the present I propose to withhold judgment. Perhaps there is something deep and profound behind all these sevens, something just calling out for us to discover it. But I suspect that it is only a pernicious, Pythagorean coincidence.

5 Choose **Edit | Copy** or press **CTRL+c** to copy the text to the clipboard.

6 Launch Microsoft Word, open a new document, and choose **Edit | Paste** or press **CTRL+v** to paste the selected text into Word.

   When finished, you can close the Word document without saving it, and close Word.

   To save all the text from a web page, choose **Edit | Select All**, and then copy the text to the clipboard. Note that text pasted into another application from a web page may lose its formatting.

Select and copy a web address from a web page

Follow these steps to copy a web address from a web page to a Microsoft Word document on your computer.

1 Visit the Pearson Education website at the following web address:

   www.pearson-books.com

2 Right-click the link named Computing at the left of the home page, and choose **Copy Shortcut** to copy the web address to the clipboard.

   Careers & Personal Development
   Computing
   Engineering

3 Launch Microsoft Word, open a new document, and choose **Edit | Paste** or press **CTRL+v** to paste the web address text into Word. It should look as shown below.

   http://www.pearsoned.co.uk/Bookshop/subject.asp?item=2¶

   When finished, you can close the Word document without saving it, and close Word.

Select and copy an image from a web page

Follow these steps to copy an image from a web page to a Word document on your computer.

1 Visit the Billy's Best Bottles wine guidance website at the following web address:

www.billysbestbottles.com

2 Click the link named HOW I SEE WINE.

3 Wait for the web page to load fully, and right-click on Billy's picture at the right of the page.

Billy Munnelly

4 Choose **Copy** from the pop-up menu displayed to copy the selected image to the clipboard.

5 Open Microsoft Word, open a new document, and choose **Edit | Paste** or press **CTRL+v** to paste the image into Word.

6 In Word, right-click the pasted image, and choose **Format Picture** from the pop-up menu.

7 Click the **Layout** tab, click the **In line with text** option, and click **OK**.

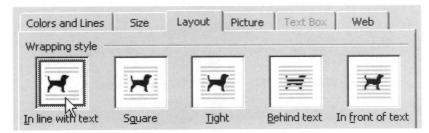

When finished, you can close the Word document without saving it, and close Word.

Download images from a web page

Follow these steps to download an image file from a web page to your computer.

1 Visit the Pearson Education website at the following web address:

www.pearson-books.com

2 Wait for the web page to load fully, and then right-click on any book cover image.

3 Choose **Save Picture As** from the pop-up menu displayed.

4 In the **Save As** dialog box then displayed, accept or change the image's file name, select the location you want to save the file to, and click **Save**.

Most image files on the Web are in either gif (pronounced with a hard 'g', as in gift) or in jpg (pronounced jay-peg) format.

Download video files from a web page

Follow these steps to download a video file from a web page to your computer.

1 Visit the following web page of the Microsoft Office XP website:

www.microsoft.com/windowsxp/windowsmediaplayer/default.asp

2 At the right of the web page, click the link named Videos & Demos.

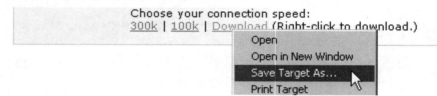

3 On the new web page displayed, right-click any link named Download, and choose **Save Target As** from the pop-up menu displayed.

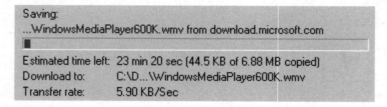

4 In the **Save As** dialog box then displayed, accept or change the video's file name, select the location you want to save the file to, and click **Save**.

Internet Explorer now displays a dialog box indicating the progress of your video file download.

Saving:
...\WindowsMediaPlayer600K.wmv from download.microsoft.com
▊
Estimated time left: 23 min 20 sec (44.5 KB of 6.88 MB copied)
Download to: C:\D...\WindowsMediaPlayer600K.wmv
Transfer rate: 5.90 KB/Sec

You can click the **Cancel** button at any stage to end the video file download.

Download sound files from a web page

Follow these steps to download sound files from a website to your computer.

1 Visit the Microsoft Multimedia website at the following address:

www.windowsmedia.com

2 In the search box at the top of the home page, type:
download samples

Click the **Search** button.

3 On the next page displayed, right-click any of the items found by your search.

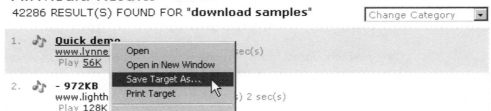

4 In the **Save As** dialog box then displayed, accept or change the file name, select the location you want to save the file to, and click **Save**.

Internet Explorer now displays a dialog box indicating the progress of your sound file download.

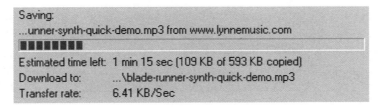

You can click the **Cancel** button at any stage to end the sound file download.

Download software from a web page

Follow these steps to download software from a website to your computer.

1 Visit the downloads page of software developer Adobe at the following address:

www.adobe.com/products/acrobat/readstep2.html

2 Select your required language (the default is English) and the platform (for example, Windows 98 or Windows ME).

3 At the bottom of the web page click the **Download** button.

4 In the **File Download** dialog box shown select the following option and click **OK**.

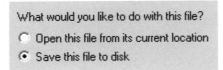

5 In the **Save As** dialog box displayed, select the location on your computer that you want to save to, accept or change the default file name, and click **Save**.

Internet Explorer now displays a dialog box indicating the progress of your software download. You can click the **Cancel** button at any stage to end the file download.

Save the text of a web page

Follow these steps to download all the text from a web page:

- Choose **File | Save As** and select the following option.

- Select the location on your computer that you want to save to, accept or change the default file name, and click **Save**.

Download a web page

Follow these steps to save an entire web page – including text, graphics and other components.

1 Visit the website of the Leader to Leader Institute, Peter Drucker's non-profit management organization, at www.pfdf.org.

2 Choose **File | Save As**, and select the following **Save as type** option.

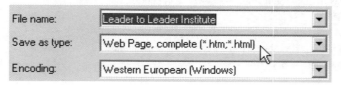

3 Select the location on your computer that you want to save to, accept or change the default file name, and click **Save**.

You can use My Computer or Windows Explorer to view your saved web page and related files.

Set up print options

Before printing a web page, choose **File | Page Setup** to check that the current print options are the ones you want. Internet Explorer's **Print Setup** dialog box offers you the following options:

- **Paper Size**: A4 is the European paper size standard.

- **Header and Footer**: You can include or exclude the following in the header and footer areas of the printed web pages: Page title, Web page address, Page number in printout, Total number of pages in printout, and Date of printing.

  These header and footer options are indicated by symbols such as &P and &d. To see a list of symbols and their purpose, refer to Internet Explorer's online help.

- **Orientation**: Portrait ('standing up') or Landscape ('on its side').

- **Margins**: The distance of the page's printed content (text and graphics) from the edge of the paper. You can set each of the four margins (top, bottom, left and right) independently.

  When finished, click **OK** to save your print settings and close the dialog box.

Display and print header and footer online help

1. Choose **File | Page Setup** and click the question-mark symbol near the top right of the dialog box. Internet Explorer displays a question mark to the right of the cursor.

2. Click anywhere in the **Header** box for Internet Explorer to display help text telling you about the various header codes. (The footer codes are exactly the same.)

Provides a space for you to type header text that will appear at the top of the page, or footer text that will appear at the bottom of the page.

To print specific information as part of the header or footer, include the following characters as part of the text.

Type this	To print this
&w	Window title
&u	Page address (URL)
&d	Date in short format (as specified by Re ⁓ ˉ ⁓tings in C⁓ˉ
&b&b	The text immediately following the first "&b" as centered, and the text following the second "&b" as right-justified.

---

3. Right-click anywhere on the yellow help text, and choose **Print** from the pop-up menu to obtain a printed list of the header codes. Then click anywhere else on the screen to close the help text window.

   Retain your printout for future reference.

Print a web page

To print your currently displayed web page, choose **File | Print** and then click **OK** on the Print dialog box. Alternatively, click the **Print** button on the Standard toolbar. Clicking this **Print** button does not display the **Print** dialog box. The **General** tab of the **Print** dialog box offers the following options:

- **Page Range**: Your options are: all pages, a specified range of pages, or the part of the page that you have selected by dragging over it with the mouse.

- **Number of Copies**: If you select any number greater than one, you can specify whether you want the copies collated or not.

- **Frames**: If the page you want to print contains frames, click the **Options** tab on the **Print** dialog box to view your choices.

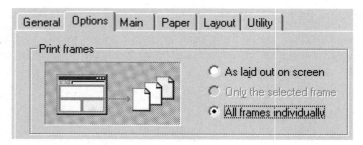

You can opt to print the frames as they are arranged on screen, or one frame after the other.

When finished, click **Print** to output the page(s) to the currently selected printer.

Preview a printed web page

To see how your currently displayed web page will look when it is printed using the current page setup and print options, choose **File | Print Preview**.

When finished, click the **Close** button to close the **Print Preview** window.

Quit Internet Explorer

You can close Internet Explorer by clicking the **Close** button or choosing **File | Close**. You have now completed Lesson 7.2 of the ECDL Information and Communication Module.

7.3

Finding information within websites

Learning goals	At the end of this lesson you should be able to:
	■ find a word or phrase on a web page;
	■ use a site index to locate information within a website;
	■ use a search engine to find information within a website;
	■ use an interactive form to find information within a website.

New terms	At the end of this lesson you should be able to explain the following terms:
Navigation Bar	A horizontal or vertical list of hyperlinks to the main components of a website, such as Home (the front page), Site Index (or Site Map or Guide), Company Profile, Products, Services and Staff Contacts.
Site Index	Also known as a site map or site guide, this is a web page that lists the main contents of a website.
Website Search Engine	A program that searches a specific website for keywords entered by the user. It displays or 'returns' a list of web pages within the site on which it found occurrences of the entered word or words.
Keyword	Text or other keyboard characters entered to a search engine. The engine then displays or 'returns' a list of documents containing the entered text. Typically, the returned list provides links to the individual pages, and displays a summary description of each page.
Interactive Form	A series of fields on a web page that you use to request a specific item of information, or a product or service. You can also use a form to submit information, such as your name and credit card number.

Finding text within a web page

To help you find a particular word or phrase within the text on a web page, Internet Explorer provides the **Edit | Find (on this Page)** command.

Finding information within a website

Websites typically display a *navigation bar* or navbar – a horizontal or vertical list of hyperlinks to the main components of a website – along the top or down the left of each page.

Larger websites help users to navigate by providing one, two or all three of the following features: site index, search engine and forms.

Using a site index

A *site index*, sometimes known as a site map or site guide, is a web page that lists the main contents of a website. It is similar in purpose to the contents page of a printed book.

Using a website search engine

A *website search engine* is a program that searches for occurrences of text (words, numbers or other keyboard characters, known collectively as *keywords*) that you enter, and displays (*returns*) a list of all web pages that contain such text, together with a summary description of each listed page.

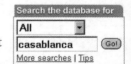

Using an interactive form

An *interactive form* is a series of fields on a web page that you use to request a specific item of information, or a product or service. You will commonly find forms on travel and holiday websites, and on websites that sell highly configurable products (such as computers).

You can also use a form to submit information, such as your name and credit card number.

Find text within a web page

You can use the **Edit | Find (on this Page)** command to locate a particular word or phrase on a web page. Words that are displayed within images are ignored. Wait until a page is fully retrieved and the word Done is shown in the Status bar before using the command.

Let's try the command on a lengthy, text-intensive web page.

1 Open Internet Explorer and visit the web page containing George A. Miller's classic essay, *The Magical Number Seven, Plus or Minus Two*. The address is:

www.well.com/user/smalin/miller.html

2 Choose **Edit | Find (on this Page)**, enter the following word in the **Find what** box, and click **Find Next**.

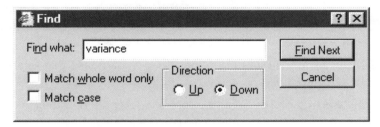

3 Internet Explorer takes you to the first occurrence of the word on the web page. The dialog box stays open on your screen.

4 To find further occurrences, click **Find Next** again. When finished, click **Cancel**.

Use a website index page

Let's practice finding information within three websites, that of a film database (IMDB), a media corporation (Pearson) and an Australian newspaper (*The Age*), using the index page of each site. In each case, click on a number of links from the index web page to explore the particular website and, when finished, click the **Back** button to retrace your steps to the web site's home page.

1 Visit the website of the Internet Movie Database at www.imdb.com.

2 At the bottom of the home page click the hyperlink named Index.

Home | Search | Now Playing | News | My Movies | Games | Boards | Help | US Movie Showtimes | Top 250 | Register | Recommendations | Box Office | Index | Trailers | IMDbPro.com - Free Trial | IMDb Publicity Photos

This brings you to the IMDB's index page, which lists of the website's contents.

3 Visit the website of the Pearson media corporation at www.pearson.com.

4 At the bottom of the home page click the hyperlink named Site Map.

About us | Investors | Media | People | Community | Site map
Contact us | Legal statement | Copyright © 2002 Pearson plc

This brings you to the site map page of the website.

5 Visit the website of *The Age*, a newspaper published in Melbourne, Australia, at www.theage.com.au.

6 At the left of the home page you can see a link named site guide. Click it to display the contents of the *The Age's* website.

Some websites display their main links across the top of every page; others list them down one side of the page. A list of the main website links is called a *navigation bar* or navbar. A navbar may be made up of text or graphics.

Use a website search engine

Many websites offer a search engine to help you find one or a few specific items. Let's practice using search engines within three websites: a film information site (Internet Movie Database), a magazine archive (*The Scout Report*), and an online dictionary of computer terminology (PC Webopedia).

1 Visit the Internet Movie Database at www.imdb.com.

2 In the **Search** box near the top left of the home page, enter a film title – for example, *Casablanca* – and click the **Go!** button.

The IMDB responds by listing pages from its database that relate to your selected film.

3 Visit the website of *The Scout Report*, a weekly online publication that identifies and reviews Internet resources of interest to researchers and educators. Its address is:

www.scout.cs.wisc.edu/report

4 In the **Search** box near the top right of the home page, enter a subject in which you are interested – for example, botany – and click **Search**.

The Scout Report responds by listing articles that relate to your entered topic.

5 Visit the PC webopedia website at www.pcwebopedia.com.

6 In the **Search** box near the top of the home page, enter a term you would like explained – for example, modem – and click **Go!**.

PC Webopedia responds by displaying a page containing an explanation of your entered word.

In Lesson 7.4 you will learn about search engines that enable you to search the web and not just an individual website. You will also learn how to perform searches with multiple keywords.

Use an interactive form to request a map

Forms are a way for websites to provide very specific information. Let's try two forms: one to request a map, and a second to specify a PC and calculate its price.

1 Visit the Microsoft MapPoint website at www.mappoint.com.

2 On the home page, beneath the heading *Find a Map*, click the **Address in** option. (It should be selected by default.)

3 Click in the dropdown list box at the right of the **Address in** option button, and select Portugal.

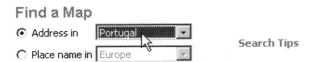

4 In the *City* box, type the name *Oporto*, and then click the **Get Map** button.

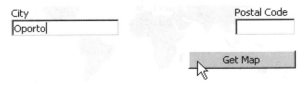

The website responds by displaying a map that matches your entered requirements. To practise, try some other locations.

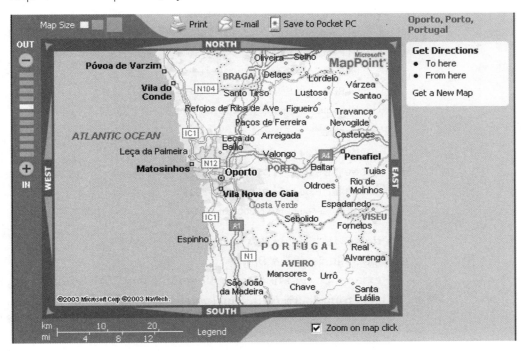

Use an interactive form to specify and price a new PC

Almost all PC manufacturers now sell their products online. Note that the links and link names in the website chosen – Dell UK – may change over time. And relax: this is just an exercise; you are not about to order a new PC!

SHOP ONLINE

Desktops

Workstations

1 Visit Dell's British website at www.dell.co.uk.

2 Click the link named Home & Home Office.

3 On the new page displayed, click the link for Desktops.

You should now see a new page listing a number of different models of PC.

Online Shopping and Services

▶ **Home & Home Office**
Latest deals on PCs and accessories for the family and working from home

▶ **Small Business**
Special offers and services for smaller businesses

4 Beneath any PC model click the link named Customise & Buy.

Dimension 2350	Dimension 4550	Dimension 8250
From £499	**From £599**	**From £670**
Price inc. VAT & Del	Price inc. VAT & Del	Price inc. VAT & Del
or **£17**/Mth over 36 months	or **£20**/Mth over 36 months	or **£23**/Mth over 36 months
▶ Customise & Buy	▶ Customise & Buy	▶ Customise & Buy
▶ Product Details	▶ Product Details	▶ Product Details

5 You should now see a form that lists several options for PC components, such as Memory, Monitor, Hard Drive, and so on.

Processor Upgrade ❓ Learn More

○ Intel Celeron Processor 1.8GHz

○ Intel Celeron Processor 2.0GHz (+£20)

○ Intel Celeron Processor 2.2GHz - DELL RECOMMENDS! (+£40)

○ Intel Pentium 4 Processor 2.0GHz (+£60)

○ Intel Pentium 4 Processor 2.4GHz (+£70)

○ Intel Pentium 4 Processor 2.50GHz (+£90)

○ Intel Pentium 4 Processor 2.60GHz (+£110)

Hard Drive ❓ Learn More

○ 30GB IDE Hard Drive (5400 rpm)

○ 30GB IDE Hard Drive (7200 rpm) (+£10)

○ 60GB IDE Hard Drive (7200 rpm) (+£30)

○ 120GB IDE Hard Drive (7200 rpm) (+£70)

Price £445.46 (excl. VAT) ▶ Add to Basket

£580.99(incl. VAT & Del)

Personal Loan: £16.41 over 48 months incl. VAT & Del ⦿ 48 ○ 36 Months

Rates from 13.9% APR. Our Typical Rate is 17.9% APR More Information...

Delivery included - based on one unit purchased. Click add to basket to see a price breakdown.

© Dell Computer Corporation 2001

6 Make and change a number of selections. Notice that as you select different PC options, the price of the PC, as displayed at the bottom of the web page, changes accordingly.

7 When finished experimenting with the form, click the **Back** button on the toolbar repeatedly to revisit Dell's home page.

Quit Internet Explorer

You can close Internet Explorer. You have now completed Lesson 7.3 of the ECDL Information and Communication Module.

7.4

Finding information on the web

Learning goals

At the end of this lesson you should be able to:

- locate information on the web by navigating through the categories of a directory site;
- locate information on the web by entering keywords into search engines and meta search engines;
- perform phrase searches using quotation symbols;
- perform multiple keyword searches using the plus (+) and minus (-) logical operators.

New terms

At the end of this lesson you should be able to explain the following terms:

Directory Site	A website that lists and categorizes other sites on the web according to their subject matter. Typically, it offers several hierarchical layers, with a listing of website addresses at the lowest level.
Search Engine	A website that enables you to search for material on the web by entering a word or phrase. The search engine returns a list of sites where the specified words were found.
Phrase Search	A query to a search engine that is placed inside quotes. Only web pages containing all the entered words, in the order entered, are found.
Logical Search	A web search that uses logical operators, such as the plus and/or minus symbols, to include and/or exclude specified words or phrases from the results.

So much information, so little time

Faced with the huge amount of information on the web, how can web surfers hope to locate individual items of interest to them? It's not as difficult as it may sound – once you learn the techniques.

Directory websites

These websites catalogue information on the web according to subject matter. You can locate information on the web by navigating through the various category levels.

The original and biggest *directory site* is Yahoo! where you can browse information by category, sub-category, and, usually, sub-sub-category.

Search engines and meta search engines

A *search engine* allows you to enter a word or phrase, searches for instances of it, and then displays (returns) a list of web pages that match your entered word or phrase. A popular search engine is www.google.com.

Meta search engines are websites that submit keywords to several search engines. In effect, they allow you to use multiple search engines at once. An example is www.dogpile.com.

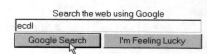

Phrase searches

When searching for a phrase – a sequence of words in a particular order – enclose the phrase within double quotes. For example: "Manchester United" or "Edgar Allan Poe".

This ensures that you will find only pages that contain all the words of your query, and that contain them in the order in which you type them.

Logical searches

You can include the plus (+) and/or minus (-) symbols to include and/or exclude specified words or phrases from the search results. For example to find information on the post-Beatles career of John Lennon, you could enter:

"John Lennon" -Beatles

Use the Yahoo! web directory site

1 Launch Internet Explorer and visit the Yahoo! website at www.yahoo.com.

2 In the right-hand category column under the Science heading, click the link named Astronomy.

Entertainment
Movies, Humor, Music...

Arts & Humanities
Photography, History, Literature...

Recreation & Sports
Sports, Travel, Autos, Outdoors...

Science
Animals, Astronomy, Engineering...

Health
Diseases, Drugs, Fitness...

Social Science
Languages, Archaeology, Psychology...

3 You are now shown a new web page. It lists astronomy sub-categories in alphabetic order. Click the link named Planetaria.

- **Astrophysics** *(127)*
- **Auroras@**
- **Comets, Meteors, and Asteroids@**
- **Companies@**
- **Conferences and Events@**

- **Organizations** *(22)*
- **Pictures** *(78)*
- **Planetaria** *(66)*
- **Radio Astronomy** *(82)*
- **Research** *(260)*

4 You are shown a third web page. This one lists the websites of some 50 planetaria, including Armagh (at www.armagh-planetarium.co.uk). Click on Armagh Planetarium to visit its web page.

- American Museum of Natural History - Frederick Phineas and Sandra Priest Rose Center for Earth and Space - featuring the Hayden Planetarium.
- Armagh Planetarium
- Audubon Louisiana Nature Center - Louise W. Freeman Planetarium - offers public shows, school programs, and laser shows.

Screen shots reproduced with permission of Yahoo! Inc. © 2003 by Yahoo! Inc. YAHOO! and the YAHOO! logo are trademarks of Yahoo! Inc.

You have now completed the exercise. There are country-specific versions of Yahoo! available for a wide range of nations including the UK, Ireland, France, Germany, Italy, Australia and New Zealand. You can link to them from the main site at www.yahoo.com. Another popular *web directory site* is About.com. Most directory sites also offer a search engine facility.

Search the web with the Google search engine

1 Visit the Google *search engine* at www.google.com.

2 Type the keyword ECDL and click the **Google Search** button.

Google responds by displaying a list of web pages that contain your entered keyword.

When your query returns more than a single page of results, search engines provide links at the bottom of each page to allow you to move forwards and backwards through the pages of results.

To print the result of a web search, simply print the results page(s) as you would any other web page.

Use Internet Explorer's default search engine

Clicking the **Search** button on Internet Explorer's toolbar opens a new area called the Search bar at the left of the screen.

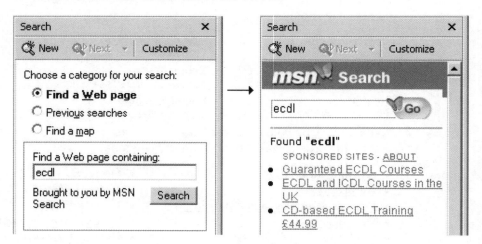

You can type your query in the box provided, click the **Search** button, and view your results.

Clicking the **Search** button again on the toolbar closes the Search bar.

Perform a phrase search

When searching for a phrase, a sequence of words in a particular order, enclose the phrase within double quotes. *Phrase searches* are commonly used to find information on people and organizations – even song lyrics. Let's try a few examples.

1 Visit the following search engine website: www.alltheweb.com

2 In the search box provided, enter the following queries, one after the other, and click the **Search** button after each one.

> "Manchester United"

> "Edgar Allan Poe"

> "Ministry of Defence"

> "Pleasant Valley Sunday"

Practise your searching skills by entering your full name, within quotes, to www.google.com.

Use the plus (+) and minus (-) search operators

To search for web pages containing multiple words when the words are not necessarily beside one another, use the plus (+) operator. To learn the rules of the card game solitaire, you could enter:

> solitaire +rules

To find web pages about the solo career of singer Geri Halliwell, without being overwhelmed by pages relating to her former group, the Spice Girls, you could enter:

> "Geri Halliwell" -"Spice Girls"

As you can see, you can combine the plus and minus operators with phrases inside double quotes. Here are four sample *logical search* queries and search engines to practise them on.

www.altavisita.com	www.excite.com
"James Bond" +"Sean Connery"	Bizet +Carmen +"Placido Domingo"
Your results should include web pages about James Bond films that starred actor Sean Connery.	Your results should include web pages that refer to performances of Bizet's opera Carmen that feature singer Placido Domingo.

www.go.com	www.looksmart.com
"John Lennon" -Beatles	Microsoft +Windows -95 -XP -NT -2000
Your results should provide details on the post-Beatles career of John Lennon.	Your search results should provide information on Windows 98 only.

Use a meta search engine

A meta search engine is a search engine that searches search engines. Just enter your word or phrase and the meta search engine submits it to a range of individual search engines, and returns the matching results. Let's try it.

1 Visit the meta search engine at www.dogpile.com.

2 Enter the following and click the **Fetch** button.

Access +XP +sort

Your results will include web pages, found by a range of individual search engines, that describe sort operations in the Microsoft Access XP database application.

Other popular meta search engines include www.mamma.com and www.metacrawler.com.

Use a natural language search engine

The Ask Jeeves website is an example of a search engine that accepts questions in plain English.

1 Visit the Ask Jeeves website at www.aj.com.

2 Type the following question and click the **Ask** button:

How do I find an e-mail address

You don't need to end your question with a question mark (?).

Ask Jeeves displays its one or more interpretations of your question. Click on any of these links to be taken to the relevant web pages.

Here are some sample queries that you could enter to Ask Jeeves:

Who is the secretary general of the UN

Who invented plastic

Who wrote Catch 22

What is the currency in Portugal

What is the temperature in Florence

A version of the search engine that returns web pages suitable for younger web surfers, Ask Jeeves for Kids, is at www.ajkids.com.

You can close Internet Explorer. You have now completed Lesson 7.4 of the ECDL Information and Communication Module.

7.5

Mastering Internet Explorer

Learning goals   At the end of this lesson you should be able to:

- save web addresses as Favorites and organize them into folders;
- revisit saved web addresses and delete Favorites;
- display and hide Internet Explorer's Address, Search, Favorites and History bars;
- change Internet Explorer's start page;
- switch on and off the display of images on web pages;
- adjust the text size of displayed web pages;
- change history settings;
- empty Internet Explorer's cache.

New term   At the end of this lesson you should be able to explain the following term:

Favorites   A list of website addresses stored in Internet Explorer. Favorites remove the need to remember or retype the URLs of frequently visited websites.

Working with Favorites

As you browse the web, you will discover pages that you would like to return to at a later stage. You can tell Internet Explorer to store a web page's address by using the *Favorites* feature. This saves you having to remember (or write down) that page's web address.

To revisit such a page, you simply click its name from your list of saved Favorites – so much easier than retyping its address each time you want to visit it. Favorites are sometimes called bookmarks.

Controlling display elements

You can switch on or off the various screen elements of Internet Explorer to suit your working needs and personal taste. You can also change your start page, vary the size of web page text, and browse the web more quickly by switching off the display of images on web pages.

About the History list and cache

Unless you tell it otherwise, Internet Explorer keeps a record in its History list of every web address that you visit. You can specify the length of time that visited addresses are retained, and delete the list contents completely.

In addition to the addresses of visited web pages, Internet Explorer also stores images and other elements from those pages in a so-called cache. This speeds up the loading of the web pages when you revisit them. You can empty Internet Explorer's cache at any stage.

About cookies

By default, Internet Explorer accepts so-called cookies from certain websites that generate them. These are small text files that can identify you to the website operator. You can set up Internet Explorer to reject such cookies, to always accept them or to prompt you each time a cookie is presented.

Save a web address in Favorites

**Favorites
button**

Add button

Follow these steps to add a web page to your list of *Favorites* so that you don't need to remember (or write down) that page's web address.

1 Launch Internet Explorer and visit the web page whose web address you want to save. For example: www.yahoo.com

2 Is the Favorites bar displayed to the left of Explorer's main window? If not, click the **Favorites** button on the Standard toolbar to display it.

3 At the top of the Favorites bar, click the **Add** button.

You are now shown the **Add Favorite** dialog box. Accept or change the name of the web page whose address you are saving (in this case, Yahoo!). When finished, click **OK**.

Internet Explorer adds the name of the currently displayed page to your **Favorites** menu.

Delete a Favorite

To remove a saved web address from your Favorites, follow these steps:

■ Is the Favorites bar displayed to the left of Explorer's main window? If not, click the **Favorites** button on the Standard toolbar to display it.

■ Right-click on the Favorite that you want to remove, and choose **Delete**.

Create a folder for your Favorites

**Favorites
button**

Organize button

You can group Favorites in folders, so making them easier to find. Let's create a folder to store addresses of search engine websites. In the next exercise you will add web addresses to the folder.

1 Is the Favorites bar displayed to the left of Internet Explorer's main window? If not, click the **Favorites** button on the Standard toolbar to display it.

2 At the top of the Favorites bar, click the **Organize** button to display the **Organize Favorites** dialog box.

3 You are shown a new dialog box with four main buttons. Click the **Create Folder** button.

4 At the lower right of the dialog box an empty space opens for you to enter the name of your new folder. Type the following name: Search Engines.

5 Click the **Close** button to close the dialog box. You have now created an empty folder.

Add a new Favorite to a Favorites folder

Let's add a few web addresses to the folder named Search Engines that you created in the previous exercise.

1 Visit the following website: www.altavista.com

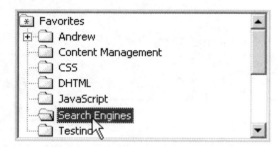

Favorites button

Create in <<
button

2 Is the Favorites bar displayed to the left of Internet Explorer's main window? If not, click the **Favorites** button on the Standard toolbar.

3 At the top of the Favorites area, click the **Add** button. (Alternatively, choose **Favorites | Add to Favorites**.)

4 Can you see a list of folders in the lower part of the dialog box? If not, click the **Create in <<** button.

Scroll down the **Create In** list until you see the Search Engines folder that you created previously.

Click the folder to select it.

5 With the folder selected, click the **OK** button.

6 Repeat the above steps for each of the following other search engine websites:

www.northernlight.com	www.alltheweb.com
www.hotbot.com	www.google.com

Well done. You have created a folder of saved web addresses.

Revisit a saved web address

📁 PHP
📁 JavaScript
📁 Search Engines
📁 Testing

To revisit a saved web address, click its name from your list of saved Favorites. Let's try it.

1 Is the Favorites bar displayed to the left of Internet Explorer's main window? If not, click the **Favorites** button on the Standard toolbar.

2 Scroll down the list of Favorites until you see your Search Engines folder. Click it.

3 Click a saved web address from the Search Engines folder for Internet Explorer to display the associated web page.

Alternatively, click the **Favorites** menu at the top of the Internet Explorer window, click the Search Engines folder from the menu displayed, and then click your required search engine website.

Change your start page

Your start page (which Internet Explorer calls the home page) is the web page that the program visits and displays when you open Internet Explorer. You can change it any time you choose.

1 Go to the page you want to display whenever you start Internet Explorer. For example: www.munnelly.com.

2 Choose **Tools | Internet Options** and select the **General** tab.

3 In the Home page area of the dialog box, click the **Use Current** button, and then click **OK**.

Home

Home button

You can restore your original start page – the one set up when Internet Explorer was installed – by clicking the **Use Default** button in the **Internet Options** dialog box. To specify a blank start page – that is, no start page – click the **Use Blank** button.

To display (that is, visit) your start page at any stage, click the **Home** button on the Standard toolbar.

Control text size display

You can change the default size in which Internet Explorer displays text – a very useful feature if you have poor or limited vision.

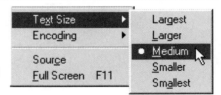

■ Choose **View | Text Size**, and select the size of text that you want.

You can revert to the default text size of **Medium** at any stage.

You can maximize the size of Internet Explorer's main window by choosing **View | Full Screen**. To revert to normal display, click the **Restore** button at the top-right of the screen.

Some web pages – such as home pages at www.adobe.com and www.zdnet.com – are designed with fixed-sized fonts, so using the **View | Text Size** options does not change how they display.

Switch web page images off and on

Internet Explorer allows you to switch off images, so that you see only the text of visited web pages, together with a small icon indicating the location of each non-displayed image. Here's how.

Icon indicates non-displayed image

1 Choose **Tools | Internet Options**, and click the **Advanced** tab.

2 Scroll down to the Multimedia category.

3 In the multimedia category, deselect the **Show pictures** option, and click **OK**.

When images are switched off, you can view an individual image by right-clicking its icon and choosing **Show Picture**. To redisplay images on all web pages, simply reverse the steps above.

Switch the Address bar on/off

Beneath the Standard toolbar is the Address bar. This shows the address of the currently displayed web page. You can also use it to enter a web address: you type in the required address and then click the **Go** button or press the **ENTER** key.

- To hide and redisplay the Address bar, choose **View | Toolbars**, then deselect and reselect the **Address Bar** option.

Switch the Favorites, Search and History bars on/off

At any one time, you can display one of the three bars to the left of the main window:

- **Favorites bar**: To view this bar, click the **Favorites** button on the Standard toolbar. You can then view your list of saved web addresses.

- **Search bar**: To view this bar, click the **Search** button on the Standard toolbar. See Lesson 7.4.

- **History bar**: To view this bar, click the **History** button on the Standard toolbar.

The History bar shows the web addresses that you visited in previous days and weeks. To revisit a web page in the History bar, click a week or day, click a website folder to display individual pages, and then click the page icon to display the web page.

You can sort your History details by clicking the arrow next to the **View** button at the top of the History bar.

Change your History settings

To change the number of days that Internet Explorer keeps track of your visited pages, or to delete the list completely, choose **Tools | Internet Options**, and click the **General** tab.

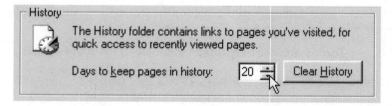

In the History section of the dialog box, make your required changes. To remove the currently saved history details, click the **Clear History** button. When finished, click **OK** to close the dialog box.

Empty Internet Explorer's cache

Internet Explorer stores elements from every visited web page in a cache. This speeds up the loading of the web pages when you revisit them. Follow these steps to delete the cache's contents.

1 Choose **Tools | Internet Options**, and click the **General** tab.

2 In the Temporary Internet files area, click the **Delete Files** button. You are now shown the **Delete Files** dialog box. Select the **Delete all offline content** checkbox, and click **OK**.

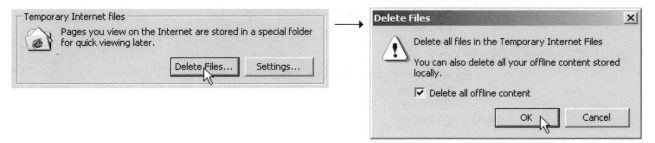

3 Click the **OK** to close the **Internet Options** dialog box.

Follow these steps to empty the cache automatically every time Internet Explorer is closed.

1 Choose **Tools | Internet Options**, and click the **Advanced** tab.

2 Scroll down the **Settings** list until you see the **Security** section. Select the option shown below.

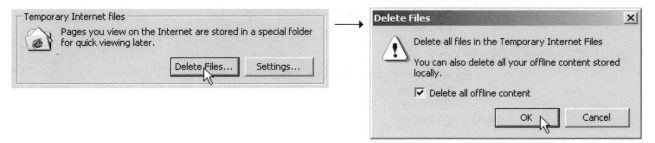

3 Click **OK** to close the **Internet Options** dialog box.

About cookies

A cookie is a small text file that is written to your computer by a website, and which can be read only by the website that placed it there. Ever returned to a website and seen your name displayed on the screen? It is because on a previous visit you gave your name to the website, and it was stored in a cookie on your computer. When you returned, the website read the cookie and greeted you with a personal message.

Cookies are of two types: permanent cookies that are written to the Cookies folder on your hard disk drive, and temporary or so-called session cookies that are stored only in the memory of Internet Explorer, and that are deleted when you leave the website.

Cookies cannot run programs, cannot access other files on your hard drive, and cannot deliver viruses.

Enable and disable cookies

Follow these steps to specify how Internet Explorer is to handle cookies.

1 Choose **Tools | Internet Options**, and click the **Security** tab.

2 Click the **Custom Level** button to display the **Security Settings** dialog box.

3 Scroll down until you see the **Cookies** section, and select your required options for stored and session cookies.

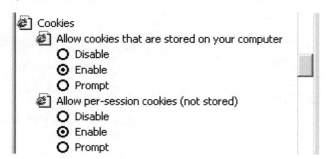

4 Click **OK** to close the **Security Settings** dialog box, and click **OK** again to close the **Internet Options** dialog box.

Display and delete your cookies

Follow these steps to display any cookies currently stored on your computer's hard disk drive.

1 Choose **Tools | Internet Options**, and click the **General** tab.

2 In the Temporary Internet files area, click the **Settings** button. In the **Settings** dialog box click the **View Files** button to list any cookies on your hard disk drive.

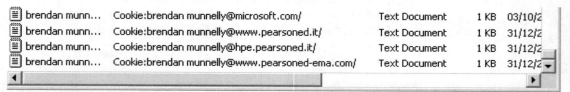

To delete any one cookie, right-click it and choose **Delete** from the pop-up menu.

To delete all cookies, choose **Edit | Select All**, and press the **DELETE** key.

When prompted to confirm that you want to delete the cookie(s), click **Yes**.

3 Close the cookie list by clicking the **Close** button at the top-right of the window, and then click **Cancel** to close the dialog boxes.

Quit Internet Explorer

You can close Internet Explorer. You have now completed Lesson 7.5 of the ECDL Information and Communication Module.

7.6

Web fundamentals

Learning goals At the end of this lesson you should be able to:

- connect to an IP address;
- reveal the IP address of a domain name;
- display your computer's IP address;
- analyse the protocol, server name, folder name and file name in a URL;
- register at a password-protected website;
- use an encrypted connection to a website;
- download files from FTP sites;
- participate in newsgroups.

New terms At the end of this lesson you should be able to explain the following terms:

Web Server	A computer on an Internet-connected network that stores files and delivers them over the Internet in response to requests from web browsers.
Web Browser	An application such as Microsoft Internet Explorer that enables a user to request files from a web server over the Internet, and displays the requested files on the user's computer.
IP Address	A unique identifier of every computer attached to the Internet. IP addresses are written as four numbers in the range 0–255, separated by full stops.
DNS	The Domain Name System. A network within the Internet that translates domain names, entered in web browsers, to IP addresses.
SSL	The Secure Sockets Layer protocol that uses encryption to protect data in transit between web browsers and web servers.
URL	An Internet address that specifies the protocol used to access the web page or file, contains the name of the web server on which the page resides, and includes (or implies) the name of a particular document or file.
Firewall	A firewall prevents unauthorized access to or from a computer or network. All communications passing through the firewall are examined and suspect ones are blocked.

Web servers and web browsers

A *web server* is a computer that stores files of a particular format, and makes them available ('serves them up') over the Internet to computer users who have a software application called a web browser.

A *web browser* is a software application that sends requests to a web server for files, and then displays the files on the user's screen. Microsoft Internet Explorer is the most widely used web browser application. Others include Netscape Navigator and Opera.

Protocols: the rules of communication

For computers to communicate with one another over any network, they must follow common rules of communication or protocols. Protocols specify such matters as how the sending computer will indicate that it has finished sending a message, and how the receiving computer will indicate that a message has been received.

The interaction between web servers and web browsers is based on the HyperText Transfer Protocol or HTTP. Other Internet protocols include the file transfer protocol (FTP) and the network news transfer protocol (NNTP).

The Internet and the web

Don't confuse the term 'World Wide Web' with the term 'Internet'. They mean different things. The Internet is a computer network: it's a very large, international network that is made up of millions of smaller networks, but it's still just a network. The Internet is based on the protocol named TCP/IP, which enables different types, models, ages and sizes of computers to communicate with one another. (The 'I' in TCP/IP stands for Internet.)

The web, however, is a service that operates over the Internet. It consists of millions of pages that are stored on computers around the world. You can think of the Internet as a railway track, and the web as a train that runs along it. The web uses the additional HTTP protocol that operates on top of TCP/IP. The purpose of HTTP is to enable web clients to communicate with web servers and vice versa. The Internet was created before the web, but the web could not exist without the Internet to support it.

In summary, the term World Wide Web or web describes a client–server, file sharing service based on the HTTP protocol that operates over the Internet.

The role of the Internet Service Provider (ISP)

The Internet is a network of networks, not a network of individual computers such as ordinary PCs. You cannot simply 'connect' your PC to the Internet. Instead, you must connect your PC to a network that is connected to the Internet.

Most Net users connect to the Net through an Internet Service Provider or ISP. An ISP is an organization that operates a network of the type that can connect to the Internet. Typically, ISPs do not charge for their services, so that the only cost of Internet access is that of making a local telephone call to your ISP.

IP addresses and domain names

Just as every telephone has a unique number, every computer on the Internet has a unique, numeric *IP address*. IP addresses (such as 216.71.158.220) are translated into easier-to-remember domain names (such as munnelly.com) by the Domain Name System (*DNS*), a network within the Internet.

A single domain name may represent more than one IP address. Very busy domains may be backed by over a dozen web server computers, each with its own IP address.

Protection against hackers: passwords and encryption

A hacker can mean someone who seeks to access IT systems to cause damage (by deleting files, for example), to eavesdrop on private information (such as health records), or to steal commercially valuable information (such as credit card numbers or product specifications).

Confidential passwords can protect web pages and files held on web servers, and encryption can 'scramble' information as it travels across the Internet so that it is unreadable without the required 'key'. A widely used encryption system is a protocol named *SSL* (Secure Sockets Layer) that protects information in transit between web browsers and web servers.

Connect to an IP address

Just as every telephone has a unique, identifying number, every *web server* on the Internet has a unique *IP address*. IP addresses are written as four numbers in the range 0–255 separated by full stops. Let's practice entering IP addresses in a web browser.

- Launch Internet Explorer and enter the following IP address:

  216.71.158.220

Your browser should display the home page of the website www.munnelly.com.

Because they contain numbers, IP addresses are sometimes known as numeric IP addresses.

Reveal the IP address of a domain name

Easier to remember than numeric IP addresses (such as 216.71.158.220) are alphabetic domain names (such as www.munnelly.com). Another difference is that a single domain name may represent more than one IP address. Very busy domains may be backed by over a dozen web server computers, each with its own IP address.

The translation of domain names, entered in web browsers, to IP addresses is performed by the Domain Name System (*DNS*), a network within the Internet.

1 Visit the following web address:

www.webreference.com/services/dns/

2 Click the hyperlink named nslookup.

nslookup search

A Web-based nslookup search, that finds the numeric IP address of the domain entered.

3 Type the following web address in the box and click the **Submit Query** button:

redact.ie

4 You should see the results shown below.

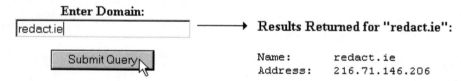

Nslookup Gateway

Enter Domain:

| redact.ie | ⟶ | **Results Returned for "redact.ie":** |

Submit Query

```
Name:      redact.ie
Address:   216.71.146.206
```

Discover your computer's IP address

Depending on how your Internet connection is set up, your IP address is either static (a permanent address that never changes) or dynamic (a temporary address that is allocated by your ISP each time you connect). Here's how to discover the IP address currently assigned to your computer:

▪ Enter the following web address:

www.whatismyipaddress.com

You don't need to enter any further details. The web page responds as shown below.

What is my IP Address?

Your IP Address:
194.125.205.148

Visit US-registered domains

Domain names have at least two parts, separated by a dot (.). In a US-registered web address, the last part of the address – the so-called suffix – indicates the type of organization. Commercial businesses are assigned the suffix of .com, educational institutions are .edu, not-for-profit organizations are .org, and government agencies are .gov. Practice visiting the following US-registered domains.

www.latimes.com	www.princeton.edu
www.slashdot.org	www.cia.gov

Visit non-US domains

Some countries such as Germany (.de), France (.fr), Italy (.it), Netherlands (.nl) and Ireland (.ie) use a suffix to indicates only the country of registration. Try visiting some of the following examples.

www.yahoo.it	www.meteo.fr	www.mut.de
www.juventus.it	www.renault.fr	www.bmw.de
www.ferrari.it	www.louvre.fr	www.berlinonline.de

Other countries use two suffixes: one to categorize the web address by type, and the second to indicate the country. In the UK, commercial sites end in .co.uk, academic sites in .ac.uk or sch.uk, and government sites in .gov.uk. Below are a few UK examples to try.

www.harrods.co.uk	www.mcc.ac.uk
www.thisislondon.co.uk	www.ox.ac.uk
www.itn.co.uk	www.bcs.org.uk
www.chelseafc.co.uk	www.amnesty.org.uk

Australia and South Africa also categorize web addresses by organization type. Try some of these.

www.smh.com.au	www.icdl.co.za
www.ntu.edu.au	www.unisa.ac.za
www.ics.org.au	www.cssa.org.za
www.thesource.gov.au	www.durban.gov.za

Analyse a URL

To use a web browser to request a web page or other file, you need to know two things:

- The name of the web server – the Internet-connected computer on which the particular web page or file is located.

- The name of the web page or other file on the web server.

Add these two items together, and precede them by a third (the HTTP protocol), and what you get is called a Uniform Resource Locator or *URL*. Try this example:

www.botany.com/leaf.htm

Notice how a forward slash (/) separates the web server name from the web page name. When you do not specify a page or file name, the browser displays the default page, usually called index.htm, index.html or default.asp. For example:

www.wit.ie/index.html

On web servers, as on other computers, files are organized into folders. For example:

www.cravero-cheese.it/ing/01/01cravero.html

www.interact.co.nz/interact/links/accq.html

A forward slash (/) separates folder names and page names. Sometimes a URL contains just the web server and folder name – but not the name of the page or file within the folder. In such cases, your web browser displays the default web page within that folder. For example:

www.tcd.ie/drama/

is really:

www.tcd.ie/drama/index.html

Register at a password-protected website

Website operators can restrict access to particular web pages and files on their websites by means of confidential passwords. For example, to view computer book samples at the author of this book's website, you must first complete an online registration form. In return, you receive by e-mail a password that enables you to access the protected areas of the website. Let's try it.

1   Visit the author's website at www.munnelly.com, and click the hyperlink named Sign In To.

SIGN IN TO:

▸ Request printed book samples

2   On the next web page displayed, enter the requested details, and click the **Continue** button.

3 On the next web page, click the **Submit Details** button. You are now shown another page that displays your entered details. You will then receive a password by e-mail.

4 On receiving your password, enter it and your e-mail address on the home page of www.munnelly.com, and click the **Go** button.

About SSL and SSL digital certificates

The presence of 'https' in the Address bar indicates that communication between your web browser and the web server is managed by a protocol called the Secure Sockets Layer (*SSL*). SSL protects only the link between the browser and server; it does not protect data when it is held on the web server.

E-commerce, e-banking and other websites that offer SSL connections to web browsers possess SSL digital certificates that verify their authenticity. They are issued by Certification Authorities within a legal policy and technical framework known as Public Key Infrastructure (PKI).

Use an encrypted connection to a website

You will know that you are using a secure encrypted Internet connection to a website when the letters 'https' rather than 'http' appear in Internet Explorer's Address bar. Let's try it.

1 Visit the Pearson Education website at the following web address:

www.pearson-books.com.

2 At the right of any book on the home page click the link named BUY.

 ECDL 4
The Complete Coursebook for Office XP
Brendan Munnelly, Paul Holden
0130399175, August 2003
£18.99

3 On the next web page displayed, click the button shown below.

Proceed to Checkout (using secure server) >>

4 You are now shown a web age with 'https' in the Address Bar and a closed lock symbol in the Status Bar.

Address https://secure.pearsoneducationbooks.com/Checkout/CheckoutLogin.asp

Done 🔒 Internet

You can exit the website's book purchase page by clicking the toolbar **Back** button.

About firewall protection

While surfing the web you may meet web pages that hide programs that attempt to write new files to your computer, amend existing files, or collect information from your hard disk drive. Variously known as adware or spyware, such intrusive or malicious programs can be blocked by another kind of software: a *firewall*.

A firewall prevents unauthorized access to or from a computer or network. All communications passing through the firewall are examined and suspect ones are blocked.

Deal with web access failures

There will be times when you are frustrated! Perhaps the website you are looking for no longer exists. Perhaps it's a private website accessible only by authorized users within a company. Perhaps there's a technical problem with the server that hosts the website. Or, more commonly, perhaps you have entered an incorrect URL. In certain cases, you will be asked if you intended a similar web address, as in the example below, where the user mistyped railtrack as ralitrack.

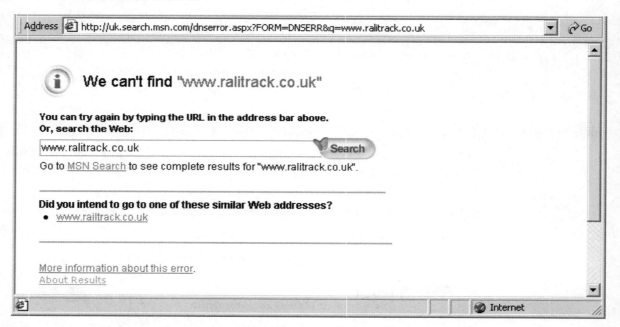

Download a file from an FTP site

File Transfer Protocol or FTP is an Internet protocol designed specifically for transferring files between two types of computer: a file server, and a client. You can use Internet Explorer as an FTP client for downloading files from a file server to your computer. You will know that you are connected to a file server and not a web server when the letters 'ftp' rather than 'http' appear in Internet Explorer's Address bar.

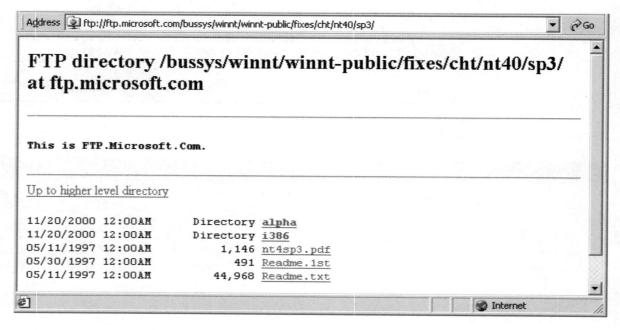

You can use FTP to transfer files from your client computer to a server on the Internet, a process known as uploading. You cannot upload with Internet Explorer or other web browser; you must use an FTP client application such as WS_FTP (available from www.ipswitch.com) or BulletProof FTP (from www.bpftp.com).

HTTP and FTP: how they differ

FTP is a two-way protocol that allows files to transferred between server and client computers. HTTP, in contrast, is a one-way protocol that enables files to be transferred in one direction only: from the server to the client.

Moreover, under HTTP a file is transferred into the memory of the client computer, and not to its hard disk. With FTP, the reverse is true: files are moved between the hard disk drives of the two computers, and are not copied to the memory of either.

Participate in newsgroups

A newsgroup is an Internet-based discussion group based on the Network News Transfer Protocol or NNTP. There are thousands of newsgroups covering every imaginable topic of interest. Newsgroups and the protocol that supports them are known collectively as Usenet. A number of websites offer access to newsgroups through the HTTP protocol, with the result that you can view and write (post) messages to newsgroups with a web browser such as Internet Explorer. Let's explore what they have to offer.

1 Visit the following website: groups.google.com

Post and read comments in Usenet discussion forums.

alt. Any conceivable topic.	**news.** Info about Usenet News...
biz. Business products, services, reviews...	**rec.** Games, hobbies, sports...
comp. Hardware, software, consumer info...	**sci.** Applied science, social science...
humanities. Fine art, literature, philosophy...	**soc.** Social issues, culture...
misc. Employment, health, and much more...	**talk.** Current issues and debates...
	Browse complete list of groups...

2 Click any link to browse through the contributions. A typical series of messages (called a thread) begins with a question to the newsgroup seeking information, clarification or advice.

Contributors to the thread then add their own comments, and gradually the thread grows, often becoming quite large. You can follow the complete thread of the discussion that follows by clicking on the links to the individual messages.

Design your own web page

Web pages are formatted in a language called HyperText Mark-up Language (HTML). To see what HTML looks like:

■ Display any web page in your browser.

■ Choose **View | Source**.

An example is shown below. Choose **File | Exit** to close the HTML and return to normal view.

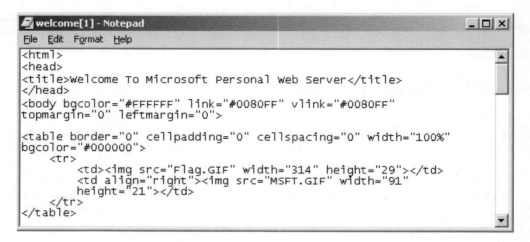

Writing directly in HTML is quite difficult. Fortunately, a wide range of editing and designing applications such as Microsoft FrontPage and Macromedia Dreamweaver are available to make the task easier. The best web designs bring together a range of skills including writing and editing, graphic design and layout, information design, programming and technology skills. Perhaps the best way to start is to take inspiration from sites that you like or are impressed by.

Quit Internet Explorer

You can close Internet Explorer. You have now completed Lesson 7.6 of the ECDL Information and Communication Module.

7.7

E-mail with Outlook Express

Learning goals   At the end of this lesson you should be able to:

- start and quit Microsoft Outlook Express;
- display the following four screen elements: Folders List, Message List, Preview Pane and toolbar;
- display an e-mail in the Preview Pane or a separate window;
- print and delete an e-mail;
- set up incoming and outgoing e-mail options;
- hide and display toolbars;
- change display text size, font, colour and style;
- access and use the Outlook Express online help system.

New terms   At the end of this lesson you should be able to explain the following terms:

Folders List	The part of Outlook Express where e-mails are stored and grouped according to type: received (Inbox), waiting to be sent (Outbox), already sent (Sent Items), marked for deletion (Deleted Items), and stored for later editing (Drafts). Users can create additional folders and sub-folders for further organizing their e-mails.
Message List	A list of the e-mails contained in the currently selected Outlook Express folder. Outlook Express displays a summary of information about each one.
Preview Pane	An area of the Outlook Express screen that shows the content of the e-mail that is currently selected in the Message List.
E-mail Collection	The action of transferring e-mails from the Internet to your computer. You must be connected to the Internet to collect e-mail, but you can read your collected e-mails whether you are online or not.

Question: what do most people use the Internet for? Answer: e-mail. It's fast becoming the preferred method of communication in business, and – because it is so inexpensive to use – it is also used by friends and family as a way of staying in contact.

This lesson introduces you to Outlook Express, Microsoft's free e-mail application.

Folders List, Message List and Preview Pane

The three main screen elements of Outlook Express are: *Folders List*, *Message List* and *Preview Pane*.

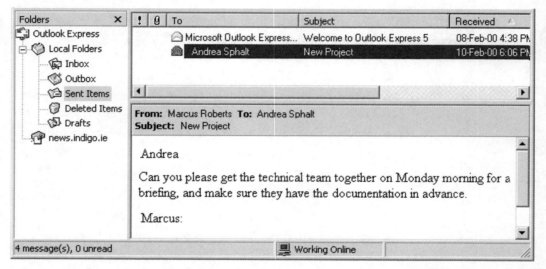

- **Folders List**: Shown on the top left of the main window, this shows five folders. When a folder contains an unread e-mail, Outlook Express shows the folder name in bold, and, in brackets, the number of unread e-mails in that folder.

- **Message List**: When you click any folder in the Folders List, Outlook Express displays the folder's contents in the Message List on the top right of the screen. For each e-mail, Outlook Express shows the sender or recipient, the subject, and the date and time it was sent or received.

- **Preview Pane**: When you click an e-mail in your Message List, Outlook Express displays the e-mail's contents in an area beneath the Message List called the Preview Pane. To display a different e-mail, simply click on a different e-mail in the Message List. If you double-click an e-mail in the Message List, Outlook Express displays the e-mail in a separate window.

Start Outlook Express

Outlook
Express

Start the Microsoft Outlook Express application as follows:

■ Double-click the Outlook Express icon or choose **Start | Programs | Outlook Express**.

If your computer has a permanent Internet connection, you are ready to send and receive e-mail messages.

If you have a dial-up connection, you must dial your Internet Service Provider (ISP). Outlook Express may be set up to do this automatically. Enter your user name and password (if Outlook Express has not recorded them from the last time that you dialled your ISP), and click the **Connect** button.

If your computer is used by a number of people, you may have to identify yourself, so that you get your own e-mail and not someone else's. To do this, choose **File | Switch Identity**, select your name from the list, and click **OK**.

Set display elements

You can control the screen layout so that only the features you use most often are shown.

1 Click on any folder shown at the left of the Outlook Express window, for example, Inbox.

2 Choose **View | Layout** to display a list of layout options, with a checkbox beside each one.

3 In the upper area of the dialog box, select only the options shown.

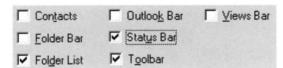

4 In the lower area of the dialog box, select only the options shown.

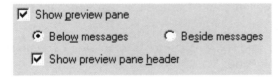

5 Click **OK**. Your screen layout should look similar to that shown below.

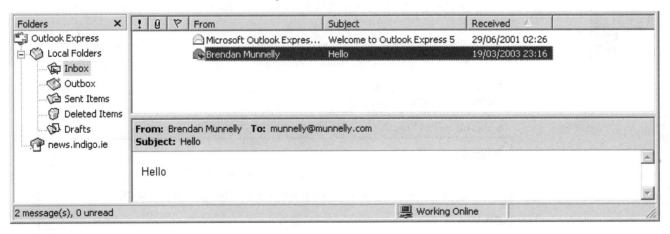

Explore your Folders List

At the left of the screen your can see the *Folders List*, which contains at least five folders.

- **Inbox**: Your incoming e-mails (those sent to you by other people).

- **Outbox**: Your outgoing e-mails (those you have composed) until you send them.

- **Sent Items**: Copies of all the e-mails you have sent to others.

- **Deleted Items**: All e-mails (both incoming and outgoing) you no longer want to keep.

- **Drafts**: Any e-mails you have not finished composing.

 Inbox (1)

When a folder contains an unread e-mail, the folder name is shown in bold, and, in brackets, you can see the number of unread e-mails in that folder.

Open an e-mail folder

Click any folder in the Folders List to view in the *Message List* (top right of screen) details of the e-mails that the folder contains: its sender or recipient, subject, and the date and time sent or received. Further information is provided by the following symbols:

A read e-mail, displayed in light type.

An unread e-mail, displayed in bold type.

An e-mail, whether read or unread, with one or more files attached to it.

An e-mail marked as high priority by its sender.

In addition to the five e-mail folders provided with Outlook Express, you can create folders and sub-folders of your own, and move e-mails in and out of them. See Lesson 7.9.

Read an e-mail: Preview Pane or separate window

When you see an e-mail in your Message List that you want to read, you can display it in two ways:

- Click the e-mail once to display its contents in an area beneath the Message List called the *Preview Pane*.

- Double-click an e-mail to read it in a separate window. You can minimize the e-mail's separate window (so that you can come back to it later), or maximize it (so that it fills the screen).

When finished with the separate window, close it by clicking the **Close** button at its top right. This closes only the e-mail's separate window – not Outlook Express.

The **Close** button

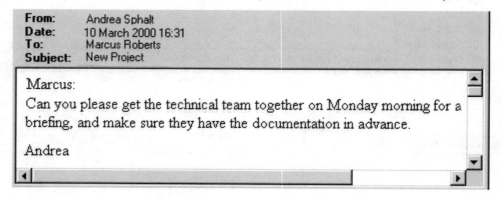

From: Andrea Sphalt
Date: 10 March 2000 16:31
To: Marcus Roberts
Subject: New Project

Marcus:

Can you please get the technical team together on Monday morning for a briefing, and make sure they have the documentation in advance.

Andrea

Switch between open e-mails

When you open several e-mails in separate windows, you can switch between the different windows by clicking the e-mails' names on the Windows Taskbar.

Resize screen elements

You can resize the Folders List, Preview Pane and Message List by clicking on the border between them, holding down the mouse button, and dragging.

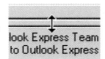

Don't be afraid to resize and arrange the screen elements to suit your taste.

Manage your outgoing e-mail: dial-up connection

If you have a dial-up Internet connection, you will typically want to be able to write (compose) your e-mails offline – that is, without being connected to the Internet. That way you can take as long as you need to edit and spell-check your e-mails without worrying about your telephone costs.

You dial your ISP only when you are ready to send your e-mails, and then send several of them (even hundreds of e-mails, to all over the world) in a single, short phone call. To set up this option:

1 Choose **Tools | Options**, and click the **Send** tab.

2 Deselect the **Send messages immediately** option, and click **OK**.

> ☐ Send messages immediately

Your e-mails will be stored in your Outbox folder until you decide to send them.

Manage your incoming e-mails: permanent Internet connection

If you have a permanent Internet connection, you will probably want to send your e-mails as soon as you have finished composing them. Why wait? To set this option:

1 Choose **Tools | Options**, and click the **Send** tab.

2 Select the **Send messages immediately** option, and click **OK**.

Store copies of outgoing e-mails in your Sent Items folder

Outlook Express can place a copy of all outgoing e-mails in your Sent Items folder, so that you have a copy of them for future reference. It's a good practice to set this option:

1 Choose **Tools | Options**, and click the **Send** tab.

2 Select the **Save copy of sent messages in the 'Sent Items' folder** option, and click **OK**.

> ☑ Save copy of sent messages in the 'Sent Items' folder

Manage your incoming e-mail: dial-up connection

If you have a dial-up Internet connection, you will generally not want Outlook Express to dial your ISP every time that you launch the application. Here's how to switch off this automatic dial-up option:

1   Choose **Tools | Options**, and click the **General** tab.

2   Deselect the options as shown below, and click **OK**.

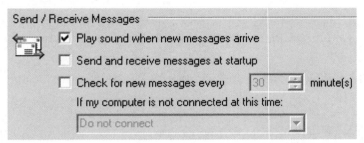

Manage your incoming e-mail: permanent connection

If you have a permanent Internet connection, you can set up Outlook Express to collect your e-mails from the Internet automatically at specified intervals.

1   Choose **Tools | Options**, and click the **General** tab.

2   Select the options as shown below, and click OK.

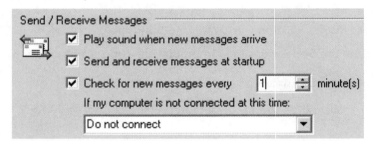

Send and collect your e-mail: dial up connection

If you have a dial-up connection, you can collect incoming e-mails and send outgoing ones in a single phone call. Your workflow would typically be as follows:

1   Use Outlook Express offline to read through e-mails you have received, and to compose new e-mails for sending to others.

2   Dial your ISP to connect to the Internet.

Send/Recv
button

3   Click the **Send/Recv** button on the Outlook Express toolbar or choose **Tools | Send and Receive | Send and Receive All**.

This last step collects any e-mails that are waiting for you on your ISP's mail server computer, and sends any e-mails in your Outbox folder to their recipients over the Internet.

Composing and sending, collecting and reading

Don't confuse the action of *collecting* e-mails with the action of reading them. If you have a dial-up Internet connection, you can read your e-mail whether you are online or not. You need to go online only to collect your e-mail from the Internet.

Similarly, you don't need to go online to compose a new e-mail. You need connect to your ISP only to send it. You can collect and send e-mails in a single phone call.

Print an e-mail

Print button

To print the currently open e-mail, click the **Print** button on the Outlook Express toolbar or choose **File | Print**.

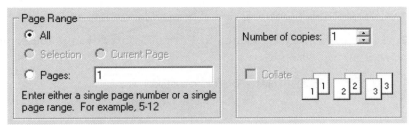

The **Print** dialog box (which is displayed only if you choose the **File | Print** command and not when you click the **Print** toolbar button) gives you the following options:

- **All**: Prints every page of the e-mail.

- **Selection**: Prints only the currently selected text of the e-mail.

- **Pages**: To print a group of continuous pages, enter the first and last page number of the group separated by a dash.

Other options on the **Print** dialog box allow you to specify how many copies you want to print of your selected pages, indicate whether you want multiple copies collated, and whether you want to print to a file rather than a printer.

Delete an e-mail

Delete button

Irrespective of whether an e-mail is in your Inbox, Outbox, Sent Items or Drafts folder, you can delete it as follows:

1 Click the e-mail in the Message List to select it.

2 Click the **Delete** button on the toolbar or choose **Edit | Delete**.

Restore a deleted e-mail

Is a deleted e-mail really deleted? No. Outlook Express places it in the Deleted Items folder. To retrieve the e-mail:

1 Click the Deleted Items folder in the Folders List to display deleted e-mails in your Message List.

2 Click the e-mail in the Message List to select it.

3 Hold down the mouse button and drag the e-mail from the Message List to the Inbox or other folder in the Folders List.

Empty the deleted items folder

You can remove all deleted e-mails by emptying the Deleted Items folder.

1 Click the Deleted Items folder in the Folders List to select it.

2 Choose **Edit | Empty 'Deleted Items', Folder**, and click **Yes** when prompted.

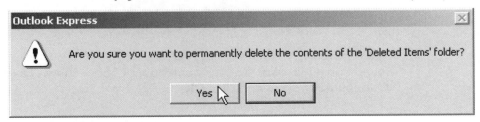

Set up automatic e-mail deletion

Don't want your e-mails saved in the Deleted Items folder when you quit Outlook Express? Follow these steps:

1 Choose **Tools | Options,** and click the **Maintenance** tab

2 Select the **Empty messages from the 'Deleted Items' folder on exit** option, and click **OK.**

Display and hide the three main toolbars

Across the top of the main window is the Outlook Express toolbar. To hide and redisplay it, choose **View | Layout,** deselect and reselect the **Toolbar** option, and click **OK.**

A second toolbar you will meet is the Read Message toolbar. This is displayed across the top of the separate window displayed when you double-click an e-mail in the Message List.

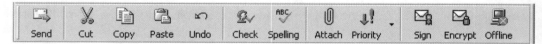

A third toolbar is the New Message toolbar. This is displayed across the top of the separate window displayed when you compose a new e-mail. For more details see Lesson 7.9.

To hide the second or third toolbar, right-click on it and choose **Toolbar** from the pop-up menu. To redisplay it, right-click on the menu bar and choose **Toolbar.** For more details see Lesson 7.8.

Hide and display the Views toolbar

As your e-mails increase in number over time, you may want to switch on the Views bar. This displays a pull-down list above the Message List that allows you to select which e-mails are displayed.

Views	Show All Messages ▼		
	Hide Read Messages		
Folders	Hide Read or Ignored Messages	Subject	Received △
Outlook Express	Show All Messages	Microsoft Outlook Expres... Welcome to Outlook Express 5	29/06/2001 02:26

To hide and redisplay it, choose **View | Layout,** deselect and reselect the **Views Bar** option, and click **OK.**

Display and hide Outlook-style icons

You can display, at the left of the Folders List, a list of icons similar to those found in the Microsoft Outlook application. Choose **View | Layout,** select the **Outlook Bar** option, and click **OK.**

Change text size display

You can change the default size in which Outlook Express displays text – a very useful feature if you have poor or limited vision.

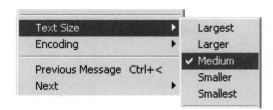

- With a folder or e-mail selected, choose **View | Text Size**, and select the size of text that you want.

You can revert to the default text size of Medium at any stage.

Set screen fonts and styles

You can change the default font that Outlook uses to display the text of e-mails as follows:

1 Choose **Tools | Options**, and click the **Read** tab.

2 Click the **Fonts** button, change the settings, and click **OK** and **OK.**

Format the text of e-mails

You can change the default font that Outlook uses for e-mails as follows:

1 Choose **Tools | Options**, and click the **Compose** tab.

2 Click the **Font Settings** button, change the settings, and click **OK** and **OK**.

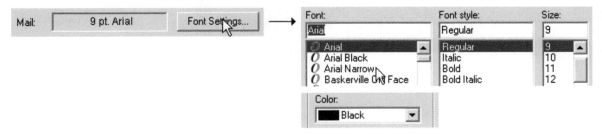

Get online help from the Help menu

Like Word, Excel and other Microsoft applications, Outlook Express contains a searchable online help system. Let's explore the options available.

1 Choose **Help | Contents and Index** or press **F1**.

2 Internet Explorer displays the **Help** window with the following main tabs:

- **Contents:** Here you will find descriptions of the application's main features. Where you see a heading with a book symbol, double-click it to view the related sub-headings. Double-click on a question-mark symbol to read the online help text.

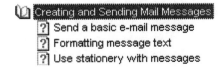

- **Index:** Type your question in the box at the top-left of the dialog box, and click **Display**. Internet Explorer displays a list of suggested help topics in the lower-left. Click a topic to display the associated text in the right pane.

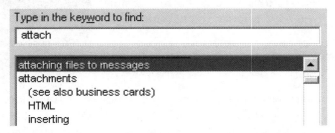

- **Search:** Type a word or phrase and click **List Topics**. Internet Explorer displays all matches from the online help in the lower left of the dialog box. Click on a topric to display the associated text.

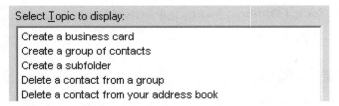

You will see the following buttons, left to right, at the top of the online help window:

- **Hide/Show:** Hides or displays the left pane of the dialog box.

- **Back/Forward:** Moves you backwards and forwards through previously visited help topics.

- **Options:** Offers a number of display choices, and enables you to print the currently displayed online help text.

- **Web Help:** Takes you to Microsoft's web-based support site for Outlook Express.

Take a few minutes to look through Outlook Express's online help system.

Get online help from dialog boxes

You can access online help directly from a dialog box, as this example shows.

1 Choose **Tools | Options**, and click the **General** tab.

2 Click the question-mark symbol near the top-right of the dialog box. Outlook Express displays a question mark to the right of the cursor.

3 Click the option named **Play sound when new messages arrive**.

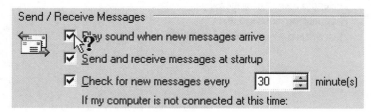

Outlook Express displays help text telling you about the option.

> Specifies whether your computer plays a sound when new messages arrive. If you clear this check box, you do not hear any sound, but the Outlook Express status bar and message list will indicate that you have unread messages.

Practice with other dialog boxes in Outlook Express.

E-mail advantages

- **Convenient and unobtrusive:** You can read and send e-mail at any time that you choose, independently of time zones and business hours. Unlike phone calls, the arrival of e-mail does not interrupt your work routine. Depending on your e-mail software, you may be able to check your e-mail box from anywhere in the world.
- **Fast and economical:** E-mails are typically delivered within minutes to anywhere in the world, much faster than the postal system or snail mail as Internet users refer to it. It's also much cheaper to send an e-mail than post a letter or make a long-distance telephone call.
- **High reliability:** While not perfect, e-mail is very reliable. Undeliverable e-mail is automatically returned to the sender, and for critical messages, the sender can request a receipt of delivery from the recipient.
- **Text reusability:** If text that you want to include in a message already exists in a Word document or other file, you can simply copy and paste it in your e-mail. Why type it twice?
- **Group communication:** E-mail applications enable you to send the same message to many – even many hundreds – of individuals in a single, simple action – and for the cost of a single phone call.
- **Wide range of handling options:** Incoming e-mails can be printed, saved to disk, replied to, forwarded to others, or deleted. No other mode of communication offers such a wide range of manipulation options.
- **Address Books:** E-mail applications provide electronic Address Books for recording your contacts' e-mail addresses, together with their personal or business details.
- **Privacy protection with encryption:** You can prevent unauthorized persons reading your e-mails by encrypting them so that they are unreadable without the proper key.
- **An educational tool:** E-mail can enable classes to 'visit' each other anywhere in the world, and share information, practice foreign languages, exchange school news, learn about new cultures – and enquire about the weather.

Quit Outlook Express

You can close Outlook Express. You have now completed Lesson 7.7 of the ECDL Information and Communication Module.

7.8 Composing and sending e-mail

Learning goals At the end of this lesson you should be able to:

- compose and send e-mails;
- copy text into an e-mail;
- spell-check an e-mail;
- send the same e-mail to several recipients;
- attach a file to an outgoing e-mail;
- set the priority of an outgoing e-mail;
- add a signature to outgoing e-mails;
- explain why an e-mail may 'bounce', and know what to do about it.

New terms At the end of this lesson you should be able to explain the following terms:

Bounced E-mail	An e-mail that, for whatever reason, fails to reach its recipient, and is returned to its sender with a message to that effect.
Cc: (Carbon Copy)	A field in an e-mail header where you can enter the addresses of people to whom you want to send a copy of the e-mail.
Bcc: (Blind Carbon Copy)	A field in an e-mail header that enables you to copy an e-mail to other recipients. Bcc: recipients can view addresses in the To: and Cc: fields, but not addresses in the Bcc: field. To: and Cc: recipients cannot view any addresses in the Bcc: field.
Signature (sig) File	An appendage at the end of e-mails. Typical contents include the sender's full name, occupation or position, phone and fax numbers, and e-mail and website addresses.
File Attachment	A file, typically a formatted file such as a Word document, that is appended to and sent with an e-mail.
Message Priority	An indication to an e-mail recipient of a message's urgency. The priority of an e-mail has no impact on the speed with which it travels.

Composing an e-mail

To write (compose) a new e-mail, click the **New Mail** button on the Outlook Express toolbar, enter the e-mail's subject and recipient, type the text, and click the **Send** button on the New Message toolbar.

You can copy text from a word processor or other application to an e-mail in Outlook Express, and spell-check your e-mail messages as you would a document in Microsoft Word.

Sending an e-mail

Outlook Express can transfer your new e-mail directly to the Internet – or store it in your Outbox folder for sending later. If you have a dial-up connection you would generally choose to hold all your outgoing messages in your Outbox until you are ready. That way, you can view and type e-mail messages without being connected to the Internet.

The Drafts folder of Outlook is where you can store messages that you are not yet ready to send. A *bounced e-mail* is an e-mail that, for whatever reason, fails to reach its recipient, and is returned to its sender with a message to that effect.

Multiple recipients

You can address an outgoing e-mail to multiple recipients in three ways: as equal recipients (To:), as *carbon copied* recipients (Cc:), or as *blind carbon copy* recipients (Bcc:).

When sending an e-mail to several people, separate each e-mail address by a comma or semi-colon. You can optionally include a space after each comma or semi-colon, to make the addresses easier to read.

To:	joe@bloggs.com, wallace@preston.com.au, grommit@sean.co.za

Signature files

You can append a *signature file* to your outgoing messages, and choose a different signature file for different audiences. Typical signature contents include full name, occupation or position, phone and fax numbers, and e-mail and website addresses. Some people also include a favourite quote, company slogan or short personal statement.

File attachments

You can *attach* formatted files – such as pictures, spreadsheets and word-processor documents – to your e-mails.

Compose and send an e-mail

Create Mail

Create Mail button

Let's go through the steps of writing (composing) and sending an e-mail in Outlook Express.

1 Click the **Create Mail** button on the Outlook Express toolbar or choose **File | New | Mail Message**.

Your e-mail address (for example, marcus@redact.ie) is displayed in the **From** box.

2 Click in the **To** box, and type the address of the person to whom you are sending the e-mail.

3 Click in the **Subject** box, and type a brief description of your e-mail.

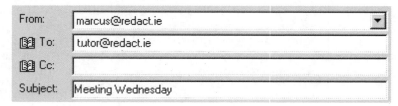

4 Click in the main text box, and type the text of your e-mail.

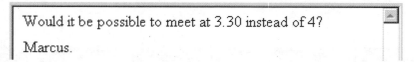

Send

Send button

5 To delete text from your e-mail, drag across the text to select it, and do any of the following: choose **Edit | Cut**, press **CTRL+x**, or press the **DELETE** key.

6 When finished typing, click the **Send** button on the New Message toolbar or choose **File | Send Message**. Congratulations! You have now composed and sent your first e-mail.

If you have a permanent Internet connection, your e-mail is typically sent to its recipient immediately. If you have a dial-up connection, your e-mail typically waits in your Outbox folder until you next click the **Send/Recv** button on the Outlook Express toolbar. See Lesson 7.7.

Copy text into an e-mail

Typing text directly into Outlook Express is just one way of composing an e-mail. Another is to reuse previously typed text by copying it from another e-mail (whether received or sent), and then pasting it into the new one. As the following example shows, you can also copy text into an outgoing e-mail from another file such as a Microsoft Word document.

1 Start Microsoft Word and, in a new document, type the text you want to use in your e-mail.

2 Drag across the text to select it, and choose **Edit | Copy** or press **CTRL+c** to copy it to the Clipboard.

1.0···Overview¶

¶

Many·Internet·service·providers·and·online·services·require·you·to·manually·enter·information,·such·as·your·user·name·and·password,·to·establish·a·connection.·With·Scripting·support·for·Dial-Up·Networking,·you·can·write·a·script·to·automate·this·process.¶

¶

3 In Outlook Express, open the e-mail you want to paste the text into, or compose a new e-mail.

4 Position the cursor where you want the pasted text to appear, and choose **Edit | Paste** or press **CTRL+v**.

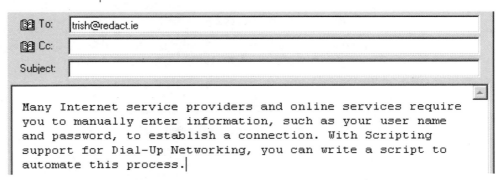

Format text in individual e-mails

Follow these steps to apply formatting to the text of an individual e-mail that you are composing:

1 Drag across the e-mail text to select it. (To format an entire e-mail, choose **Edit | Select All**.)

2 On the Formatting toolbar, click the buttons for the options you want.

If you have trouble formatting, click the **Format | Rich Text (HTML)** in a New Message window. A dot appears beside the command when it is selected.

Ensure e-mail compatibility

Some e-mail applications can send or receive e-mail only with the text-only POP3 protocol, which is increasingly giving way to the new, more fully-featured IMAP4 protocol. Even though you can send e-mails containing fonts, tables and images similar to those that can be created by word-processing applications, some e-mail users may not be able to view your e-mail properly.

You therefore have a choice:

■ Make use of sophisticated HTML formatting options by choosing the **Format | Rich Text** command in the **New Messages** window.

■ Ensure the widest possible readership for your e-mails by choosing **Format | Plain Text**.

Check your spelling

Outlook Express can check your spelling and suggest corrections to errors in two ways:

- **Automatically:** When you click the **Send** button on the New Message toolbar or choose **File | Send Message**.

  To set up automatic spell-checking, choose **Tools | Options**, click the **Spelling** tab, select the following two options, confirm your language setting, and click **OK**.

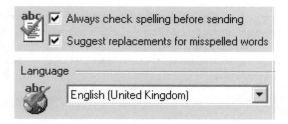

Spelling

Spelling button

- **On-request:** When you click the **Spelling** button on the New Message toolbar or chose the **Tools | Spelling** command.

  Subsequently, when you send an e-mail, you will be alerted to any word in your e-mail that Outlook Express does not recognize, and offered some alternatives. (Not all unusual spellings are wrong, however, and not all usual spellings are right.)

  You can **Ignore** the alert, **Change** the problem word to the alternative highlighted, or **Add** the word that caused the problem to the dictionary, so that it does not cause any further alerts.

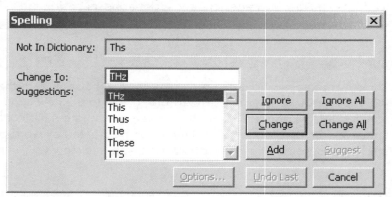

Outlook Express uses the same spelling dictionary as Word and other Microsoft Office applications. If you do not have any of these installed, spell-checking is unavailable in Outlook Express.

About e-mail addresses and bounced messages

You must address an e-mail message correctly for it to be delivered to the intended recipient. E-mail addresses consist of a username, followed by the @ sign, followed by the domain name. For example, marysmith@xyz.co.uk. An e-mail address never contains any spaces, and a dot (.) separates the parts after the @ sign.

For more information on Internet domains, see Lesson 7.6.

If you send an e-mail to someone and, for whatever reason, it cannot be delivered, you usually receive a message to that effect. Such e-mails are said to 'bounce' – you send them out; they bounce right back.

The most likely reason for an e-mail bouncing is that you have typed an incorrect address: did you spell it right? Did you put in all the right punctuation? Did you put in a hyphen (-) instead of an underscore (_)? Occasionally, your e-mail fails to get through and you don't get any message to that effect. While this is rare, it does happen.

Request an e-mail receipt

Don't assume that because you sent an e-mail, the recipient definitely received it. If it's that important, ask them to acknowledge receipt, either in your e-mail, or automatically.

1 Compose a new e-mail in the normal way.

2 Choose **Tools | Request Read Receipt**.

3 Send the e-mail as normal.

When the e-mail is received and opened by its recipients, they are informed that you have requested confirmation.

They can choose to send the confirmation or not, but they don't have to do any work – they just click **Yes**.

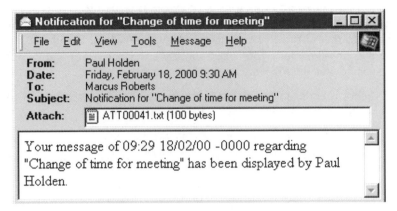

You then get an e-mail like the one above.

Finding e-mail addresses

There are five main sources of e-mail addresses: business cards, incoming e-mails, websites, the Find People option, and the Internet Explorer Address Book:

- **Business cards:** Most people in business today include their e-mail address on their business cards. (Some include only their e-mail address – they don't want to be contacted any other way!)

- **Incoming e-mails:** Many of the people you want to send e-mail to have already been in contact with you. Simply go to your Inbox, find an e-mail from the right person, copy their address to the clipboard and paste it into your e-mail.

- **Websites:** If you know the organization to which the person belongs, find its website. Many of them (particularly colleges and government agencies) include e-mail directories.

- **Find People option:** Choose **Tools | Address Book**, select the **Edit | Find People** button, select a directory service from the **Look In** pull-down list, type the name of the person you are looking for, and click **Find Now**.

- **Address Book:** An Outlook Express feature that enables you to record e-mail addresses for easy reference. See Lesson 7.10.

E-mail multiple recipients equally

To send an e-mail to several people, enter each of their e-mail addresses in the **To** box, separated by a comma or semi-colon.

To make a string of multiple addresses easier to read, include a space after each comma or semi-colon.

E-mail one main recipient, with copy to another

To send a copy of the e-mail to another person, enter their e-mail address in the **Cc** (Carbon copy) box.

To:	joe@bloggs.com
Cc:	wallace@preston.com.au, lauren@porridge.ca

Generally, you use the **Cc** box to enter the e-mail address of other recipients you think should see this e-mail as a matter of courtesy or organizational procedure.

E-mail with blind carbon copies

With blind copying, you send a copy of an e-mail to one or more other persons – without the main recipient knowing about it. Before doing this, you need to reveal the **Bcc** box by choosing **View | All Headers**. The **Bcc** box is shown on all e-mails you subsequently compose, until you turn it off (by choosing **View | All Headers** again).

You simply enter in the **Bcc** box the e-mail addresses of anyone you want to blind-copy the e-mail to:

- The Bcc recipients know the names of the To and Cc recipients.
- The To and Cc recipients do not know the names of the Bcc recipients.
- The Bcc recipients do not know each other's names.

To:	trish@redact.ie
Cc:	
Bcc:	peter@redact.ie

You can enter as many e-mail addresses as you wish in the **To** box and in the **Bcc** box, and you can include both Cc and Bcc recipients in the same e-mail.

Mass e-mail and blind carbon copying

A common use (abuse?) of the Bcc field is for the sending of mass e-mails that advertise products or services.

The sender places all the recipients' addresses in the Bcc field, so that no one recipient knows who else also received the e-mail. Should the e-mail fall into the hands of a competing company, they are unable to view the sender's list of clients and prospects. In the To field, the sender types his or her own e-mail address.

Every e-mail you send must have at least one address in the To box; otherwise, it will 'bounce' back to you.

Attaching files to e-mails

E-mails are generally short text messages. But suppose you want to send a family photograph to your uncle, a spreadsheet to your accountant, a PowerPoint presentation to head office, or a beautifully formatted word-processed document to your tutor? Easy: you send it as an *attachment* to your e-mail message.

Send an e-mail with an attachment

Attach

Attach button

1 Compose your e-mail in the normal way.

2 Click the **Attach** button on the New Message toolbar or choose **Insert | File Attachment**.

3 In the **Insert Attachment** dialog box, locate the file you want to attach to your e-mail, and click **Attach**.

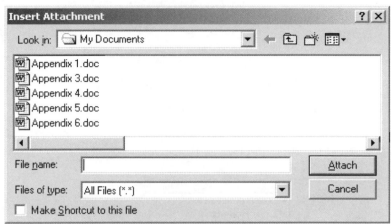

Outlook Express adds a line in the e-mail header to show the attachment file name and file size. To attach multiple files, repeat steps 2 and 3 above.

4 Click the **Send** button on the New Message toolbar or choose **File | Send Message** to send the e-mail with its attachment.

Remember that the person who receives your attached file can work with it only if they have the appropriate software application.

Delete an attachment from an outgoing e-mail

If you decide against sending an attachment with an e-mail, right-click the file name in the **Attach** box of the e-mail header, and choose **Remove** from the pop-up menu.

Outlook Express removes the attachment immediately from the e-mail.

Set e-mail priority

All e-mails you send are important, right? But some may be more important than others, and you will want to ensure your recipients know it. Here's how to mark an outgoing e-mail as high-priority.

1 Compose the e-mail in the usual way.

2 Choose **Message | Set Priority | High**.

3 Click the **Send** button or choose **File | Send Message**.

High-priority e-mails (incoming or outgoing) are identified by a red exclamation mark. Use the high-priority setting sparingly. If every e-mail you send is high priority, they will all be treated in the same way. The priority of an e-mail does not affect the speed with which it is transmitted over the Internet or an internal e-mail network.

You can also change the priority of e-mails you have received. This is a useful way of highlighting e-mails that you want to come back to at a later stage.

When you compose an e-mail, you may want to finish it off with a small block of text as a signature. The easiest and most efficient way to do this is to create a *signature* (sometimes known as a signature file or a sig file). Outlook Express will append this to your outgoing e-mails – either automatically to all e-mails or only to ones that you select.

Most people include their name and contact details. Some add an advertising slogan, a short message, or a link to their website. You can also create different signature files for different purposes.

Create your signature file

Follow these steps to learn how to create an e-mail signature file.

1 Choose **Tools | Options**, and click the **Signatures** tab.

2 Click the **New** button, and then select the **Text** option.

3 In the **Edit Signature** text box enter your name, address, telephone number and other contact details.

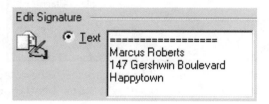

4 Select the **Add signatures to all outgoing messages** checkbox, but do not select the **Don't add signatures to Replies and Forwards** checkbox.

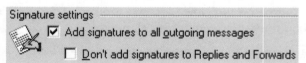

5 Click **OK**.

Outlook Express automatically appends your signature to all subsequent e-mails you compose and send.

If you want to be more selective, do not select the **Add signatures to all outgoing messages** checkbox, as in step 4 above. Instead, when you have composed the e-mail, position the cursor at the point in the e-mail where you want the signature to appear and choose **Insert | Signature**.

Create multiple signature files

To create a second (or a third ...) signature file, choose **Tools | Options**, and select the Signatures tab. Then click **New**, and proceed exactly as when you created your first signature file.

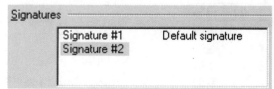

Choose which of your signatures you want to be the default by clicking it and selecting **Set as Default**. Finally, click **OK**.

If you have created more than one signature file, and you subsequently choose **Insert | Signature**, you are offered a choice from those available.

Rename your signature files

You can rename your signature files, so that it is easier to identify the right one for the circumstances. You might have a signature file called Business, one called Personal, and one called Family, for example.

To do this, choose **Tools | Options**, and select the **Signatures** tab. Next, click the signature file you want to rename, and select **Rename**. Then enter the new name for the file. Do the same for the other files you want to rename. When finished, click **OK**.

Edit your signature file

To edit your signature file, choose **Tools | Options**, and select the **Signatures** tab.

Your signature files are listed. Select the one you want to change by clicking it. Then make whatever changes you want, by adding, deleting or overwriting the existing information. When finished, click **OK**.

About the Drafts folder

If your e-mails are held in your Outbox folder until you click the **Send/Recv** button, you have the luxury of being able to change your mind. Think of the Drafts folder as the place where you keep your half-finished thoughts, your letters of resignation and your job applications, until you are sure that they are right and you want to send them.

You can delete an e-mail in the Outbox in the same way as any other e-mail. You select it in the Message List, and do any of the following: click the **Delete** button on the toolbar, choose **Edit | Delete**, or press the **DELETE** key. Alternatively, you might want to move the e-mail into the Drafts folder while you think about it some more.

Save an e-mail to the Drafts folder

To put a new e-mail into the Drafts folder, compose the e-mail as normal and choose **File | Save**. To revisit an e-mail in the Drafts folder, open the folder, select the e-mail in the Message List, and double-click it to open it. You can then make any changes or additions, and either save it again to the Drafts folder, or send it.

You can also move an e-mail directly from the Drafts folder to the Outbox by dragging it from the Message List to the Outbox in the Folders List.

Rules of netiquette

Netiquette is short for network etiquette: the do's and don'ts of online communication. It encompasses both common courtesy online and the informal 'rules of the road' of the Internet. Here is a summary of Netiquette's main points:

■ **Virus protection:** Use an anti-virus program to check your incoming e-mails, because some viruses use your Address Book to send themselves to everyone you know, and so infect their computers. See Lesson 2.4.

■ **Relevant subject line:** Always include a subject header that reflects the content of your e-mail. Your recipients should not have to read your e-mail to discover what you are on about.

■ **Spell-checking:** Use the spell-checker to correct your outgoing e-mails. Nobdoy wnats ot raed rbbush.

■ **Talk, don't shout:** Type your e-mail in mixed case letters. UPPER CASE LOOKS AS IF YOU'RE SHOUTING!

■ **Respect others' privacy:** Never include contact or personal details of others in your e-mails without their permission.

■ **Respect others' content:** Some people could be very hurt if you copy their content and use it in your e-mails without permission. And if you are forwarding another's e-mail, don't change the original wording.

■ **Keep it to the point:** Try to achieve a balance between being too brief (which can cause offence in certain cultures) and being too long-winded (people have only limited time to deal with their e-mail Inbox).

- **File attachments:** Never send very large (more than 100KB) file attachments to people without first asking their permission. Larger files can take a long time for the recipient to download.
- **Avoid flame wars:** Do not send abusive or heated messages (flames). If you receive a flame, it is best to ignore it.
- **Heed company e-mail policies:** If your Internet access is through a corporate account, check with your employer about their policy regarding private e-mail. Be careful about sending messages to friends at their work e-mail addresses. The next message they receive might be a dismissal notice!

Quit Outlook Express

You can close Outlook Express. You have now completed Lesson 7.8 of the ECDL Information and Communication Module.

7.9

Responding to received e-mail

Learning goals	At the end of this lesson you should be able to:

- forward a received e-mail to another person;
- reply only to the sender of an e-mail;
- reply to all the recipients of the original e-mail;
- copy text between e-mails, and from an e-mail to another application;
- open, save and delete file attachments;
- create and delete mail folders;
- transfer e-mails between mail folders;
- search in your mail folders for a particular e-mail.

New terms	At the end of this lesson you should be able to explain the following terms:
Forwarding	The act of passing to another person an e-mail that you have received. You typically include some comments of your own in the forwarded e-mail.
Reply to Sender Only	The act of replying to a received e-mail. Only the person who sent you the e-mail gets your reply. The reply typically includes some or all of the text of the original e-mail.
Reply All	The act of replying to a received e-mail. Everyone who received the original e-mail also gets your reply. The reply typically includes some or all of the text of the original e-mail.

You can perform various actions on a received e-mail. In summary, you can:

- *Forward* the e-mail to someone else, typically accompanied by some comments of your own which you enter in the text area above the original e-mail.

- *Reply to the sender only*, so that just the originator of the e-mail sees your reply.

- *Reply to all* recipients of the original e-mail.

- Copy-and-paste text from it to another e-mail, or to a Microsoft Word document or other file.

File attachments

Outlook Express indicates that an incoming e-mail has a file attachment by displaying a paper-clip icon.

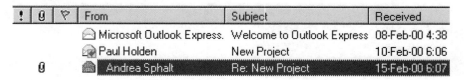

You can open, save and delete attachments. File attachments may contain viruses, and you should use a reliable virus protection application to scan them.

Mail folders

You can create your own mail folders in addition to those supplied with Outlook Express, such as the Inbox and Sent Items folder.

You can copy or move e-mails between different folders, delete folders that you no longer want, sort the e-mails within folders in different ways, and search through your mail folders for specific e-mails by sender, receiver, subject or date.

Forward an e-mail

Forward button

If you receive an e-mail that you want to pass on to someone else, the simplest way is to *forward* it. Follow these steps to discover how.

1 Open the e-mail you want to forward by clicking it once or twice in your Message List.

2 Click the **Forward** button on the Read Message toolbar or choose **Message | Forward** to open what looks like a New Message window – but with two differences:

■ The **Subject** box shows the subject of the original e-mail, preceded by the abbreviation Fw:.

■ The original e-mail is shown and identified.

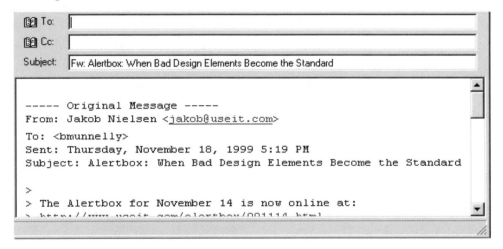

3 In the **To** box, type the address of the person to whom you want to forward the e-mail.

4 In the message area, add text of your own. (It is helpful to the recipient if you clearly distinguish your own comments from the original message.)

5 Click the **Send** button on the New Message Toolbar or choose **File | Send Message**.

Reply to sender only

Reply button

When you receive an e-mail message, you can send a reply either to the person who sent it to you (only), or to all the people who received the original e-mail (including the sender). Most often, you will want to reply to the person who sent you the e-mail.

1 Open the e-mail you want to reply to by clicking it once or twice in your Message List.

2 Click the **Reply** button on the Read Message toolbar or choose **Message | Reply to Sender** to open what looks like a New Message window – but with two differences:

■ The **To** box and the **Subject** box are already completed.

■ The original e-mail message is shown and identified.

📇 To:	Jakob Nielsen
📇 Cc:	
Subject:	Re: Alertbox: When Bad Design Elements Become the Standard

```
----- Original Message -----
From: Jakob Nielsen <jakob@useit.com>

To: <bmunnelly>
Sent: Thursday, November 18, 1999 5:19 PM
Subject: Alertbox: When Bad Design Elements Become the Standard


>
> The Alertbox for November 14 is now online at:
> http://www.useit.com/alertbox/991114.html
```

You can edit the **Subject** box if you wish. You can also remove all or part of the original e-mail to which you are replying.

3 Enter the text of your reply in the Message box, above the words 'Original Message'.

4 Click the **Send** button on the New Message toolbar or choose **File | Send Message**.

Remember, it's not very helpful to get a single word reply to an e-mail ('Yes', or '4.30'). The person who reads it could have sent hundreds of e-mails, and could be reading your reply several days later. That's why including the original message with your reply is a good idea.

However, if the original message is very long, and your answer is 'yes', it is helpful to cut out those parts of the original message that do not require a response, so that it becomes very obvious what you are agreeing to.

Reply to all recipients

The *Reply All* option enables you to reply to an e-mail, with your reply going to everyone who received the original message. You use it in exactly the same way as the Reply (to sender only) function.

You will find this feature particularly useful when working with a number of people on a project (drawing up a contract, for example), or discussing something that requires unanimous agreement (to schedule a meeting, for example). To use this option with a received e-mail:

Reply All

Reply All button

- Click the **Reply All** button on the Read Message toolbar or choose **Message | Reply to All**.

- Proceed as in Reply to sender only, above.

Copy and move the text of an e-mail

You can reuse the text of one e-mail in another e-mail, or in another application such as Microsoft Word. And you can move text around within the same message. Practice your text-moving skills with this example.

1 Open an e-mail, or compose a new one.

2 Drag across the text you want to copy to select it.

3 Choose **Edit | Copy** or press **CTRL+c**.

4 Go to where you want to insert the copied text: a location within the same e-mail, another e-mail or another file such as a Word document.

5 Position the cursor where you want the copied text to appear, and choose **Edit | Paste**, or press **CTRL+v**.

Block an e-mail sender

Outlook Express enables you to block e-mail from a specified e-mail address (such as sales@xyz.com) or from all address at a specified domain (such as any e-mail that ends in @xyz.com). E-mails from blocked senders or domains go not to your Inbox but to your Deleted Items folder. You will find this feature useful when dealing with spam.

Follow these steps to block e-mails:

1 In your Message List, click an e-mail from the sender whose messages you want to block.

2 Choose **Message | Block Sender**. You are prompted as follows.

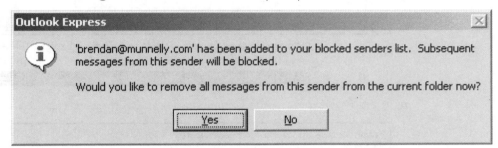

3 Respond as required.

Blocking a sender applies to text-only POP e-mail. It does not apply to HTTP e-mail or IMAP messages that can contain images. See the next topic to block all e-mails from a domain.

Manage your blocked senders list

You can use the so-called blocked senders list to add or remove blocked addresses, and to extend the blocking to all usernames at a particular domain.

1 Choose **Tools | Message Rules | Block Senders List** to display the **Blocked Senders** tab of the **Message Rules** dialog box.

2 To remove a sender or domain from the list, click the name to select it, click the **Remove** button, and then click **Yes** when prompted.

To change a sender's name or domain on the list, select the name, click **Modify**, make your changes in the dialog box, and click **OK**.

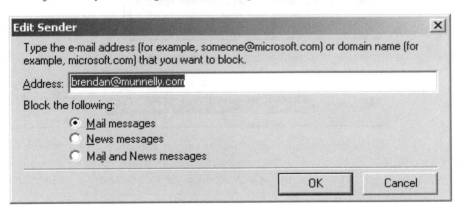

To add a new sender or domain to the list, click **Add**, enter the details, and click **OK**.

3 When finished, click **OK** to close the dialog box and apply the amended blocking rules.

Identify incoming e-mails with file attachments

You can identify an e-mail with a file attachment in the following ways:

■ In the Message List, the e-mail is shown with a paper-clip icon.

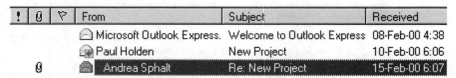

■ In the Preview Pane, the e-mail header shows a paper-clip icon.

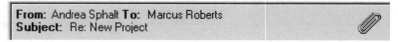

■ If displayed in a separate window, the e-mail header shows an **Attach** box, with the name and size of the file.

Open an e-mail attachment

You can open an attached file in either of two ways:

■ If viewing the e-mail in the Preview Pane, click the paper-clip icon in the e-mail header to display the file name, and then select the file name from the pop-up menu.

■ If viewing the e-mail in a separate window, double-click the file name in the **Attach** box.

You can open a file attachment only if you have an application that is capable of opening it. If someone sends you an attachment that was created in an application that is not installed on your computer (or even a different version of a program that is installed), you may be unable to open it.

Save an e-mail attachment

You can save an attached file in any of the following ways:

- Choose **File | Save Attachments**. (This command is available whether you are viewing the e-mail in the Preview Pane or in a separate window.)

- In the Preview Pane, click the paper-clip icon in the e-mail header and choose **Save Attachments**.

- In a separate e-mail window, right-click the file name in the **Attach** box and choose **Save As** from the pop-up menu.

  In each case, you specify where on your computer you want to save the file, accept or change the file name, and click **Save**.

- If you open an attachment and do not save it, you can subsequently open it only from within Outlook Express. If you save it, you can subsequently open it from within Outlook Express and from the relevant application.

- If you save an attachment and subsequently delete it, you will not be able to open it either from within Outlook Express or from within the application. And if you delete the e-mail without first saving the attachment, the attachment is also deleted.

Using e-mail folders

Once you start using e-mail, you'll probably get a lot of it. Some of it is important at the time, but has a short shelf-life ('Meet you for lunch' 'OK'). Some of it you need to keep for reference (the minutes of the project meetings). Some of it is simply junk mail. How do you keep it organized so that you can find what you want, when you want it? You create mail folders, that's how!

Create a new mail folder

1 Choose **File | New | Folder**, and in the **Folder Name** box type your new folder's title.

2 Click the folder in which you want your new folder to be located, and click **OK**.

- If you want it to be at the same level as the Inbox, Outbox and other main folders of Outlook Express, click Local Folders.

- If you want it to be a sub-folder of an existing folder such as your Inbox, click that folder.

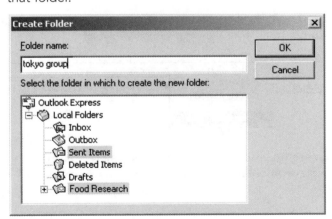

Transfer e-mails between folders

Follow these steps to transfer an e-mail from one folder to another.

1 Open the folder that contains the e-mail that you want to transfer.

2 In the Message List, click the e-mail you want to move to select it.

3 Choose **Edit | Move to Folder**.

4 In the Folders List, click the folder into which you want to move the e-mail.

5 Click **OK**.

Alternatively, click the e-mail in the Message List, and drag it to the folder in the Folder List on the left of the screen. You can transfer unwanted e-mails to the Deleted Items folder in this way.

If you choose **Edit | Copy to Folder**, the e-mail will be copied to the second folder – it will appear in both folders.

Delete a mail folder

Be careful. It is possible to delete a mail folder, but you can't change your mind. The folder and all its contents will disappear forever. Follow these steps to discover how.

1 In the Folders List, click to select the folder you want to delete.

2 Choose **File | Folder | Delete** or click the **Delete** button on the Outlook Express toolbar.

3 When prompted to confirm the folder deletion, click **Yes**.

Add and remove e-mail headings in mail folders

In any mail folder you can change the way that Outlook Express displays column headings. By default, Outlook Express displays the following headings: Priority, Attachment, Flag, From or To, Subject, and (date) Received or Sent. In the Outgoing, Sent and Drafts folders, the heading named (mail) Account is also shown by default.

Follow these steps to hide a currently displayed heading or to display a currently hidden one:

1 Open the mail folder whose headings you want to change.

2 Right-click anywhere on the row of headings across the top of the folder, and choose **Columns** from the pop-up menu displayed.

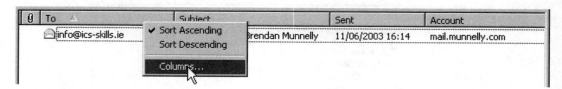

Outlook Express now displays the *Columns* dialog box. Headings that are currently displayed contain a tick mark in the checkbox at their left.

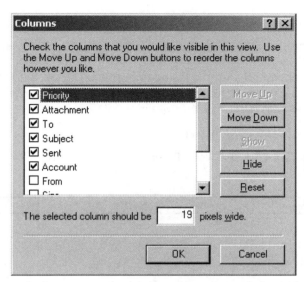

3 To hide a currently displayed heading, click its checkbox to deselect it. To display a currently hidden heading, click its checkbox to select it.

4 When finished selecting and deselecting headings, click the **OK** button to apply your changes and close the dialog box.

Marking an e-mail as read or unread

You can mark an individual e-mail as read or unread, regardless of whether you have previously opened it or not. Here's how:

1 Open the mail folder containing the relevant e-mail.

2 Right-click the e-mail and choose the **Mark as Unread** or **Mark as Read** command from the pop-up menu displayed.

If you have previously opened the selected e-mail, you are offered the first command. If not, you are offered the second one.

Search for specific e-mails

Find

Find button

Follow these steps to find a specific e-mail.

1 Click the **Find** button on the Outlook Express toolbar or choose **Edit | Find | Message**.

2 If you know which folder the message is in, click the **Browse** button and select that folder for the **Look in** box. If you're not sure where it is, choose **Local Folders** and select the **Include subfolders** checkbox.

3 Fill in whatever you know about the e-mail – who it was from (or, if you sent it, who it was to), the subject, or some word or phrase in the text of the   e-mail. You don't have to use full words: even a single letter is enough. You can also specify a range of dates.

4 Click the **Find Now** button. Outlook Express displays a list of e-mails that satisfy your criteria.

When you see the one you want, double-click it to open it.

Sort e-mails in a folder

An alternative way of finding a particular e-mail is to sort the items in the folder. If you sort your Inbox alphabetically by the name of the sender (the **From** field), you can find all the messages from a particular person, for example. Or you can find your most recently received messages by sorting it on the **Received** field. Let's try sorting a mail folder.

1 Click your Inbox in the Folders List.

2 In the Message List, click the word **From** in the header. Outlook Express sorts your messages alphabetically by the name of the sender.

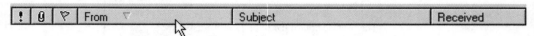

3 Click the word **From** again. Outlook Express re-sorts the messages into reverse alphabetic order.

4 Click the **Received** field in the header. Outlook Express sorts your messages into the order in which they were received. As before, you can reverse the order by clicking **Received** again.

Compress your e-mail folders

As more e-mails gather in your various mail folders, you may wish to compress the folders to reduce the amount of space they occupy on your hard disk drive. Here is the procedure:

1 Click the folder in the Folders List to select it.

2 Choose **File | Folder | Compact** to compress the selected folder.

Alternatively, choose **File | Folder | Compact All Folders**.

Your folder's physical size is reduced, but it continues to look and work just as before in Outlook Express.

Quit Outlook Express

You can close Outlook Express. You have now completed Lesson 7.9 of the ECDL Information and Communication Module.

7.10

Mail contacts and security

Learning goals

At the end of this lesson you should be able to:

- add, change and delete contacts in your Address Book;
- create and delete contact groups;
- add, edit and remove contacts;
- e-mail the members of a contact group;
- explain digital ID, encryption and digital signature.

New terms

At the end of this lesson you should be able to explain the following terms:

Contact	A person or organization whose details (such as name and e-mail address) you have recorded in the Address Book of your e-mail application.
Nickname (Alias)	A shortened form of an e-mail address that you can enter in the To field of an e-mail as an alternative to typing the contact's e-mail address in full.
Address Book	A feature of an e-mail application that enables you to record details about your e-mail contacts for easy reference.
Mailing List/Contact Group	A list of e-mail addresses to which you can send a message in a single operation by entering the list's name in the To field of the e-mail.

Recording your e-mail contacts

First:	Robert	Middle:		Last:	Ward

Title:		Display:	Robert Ward ▼	Nickname:	rw

An *e-mail contact* is a person or organization whose details (such as name and e-mail address) you have recorded in your e-mail application software. Outlook Express allows you to record a wide variety of information about your contacts, spread over seven tabs in a dialog box.

As a minimum, each contact must contain a first name, a last name and a display name. The first two you enter; the third is supplied, by default, by Outlook Express. An e-mail *nickname* or *alias* is a shortened form of an e-mail address that you can enter in the To box of an e-mail as an alternative to typing the contact's e-mail address in full.

Managing your e-mail Address Book

An *Address Book* is that part of your e-mail application where your contacts are stored for easy reference. You can type contact information into your Address Book directly, or you can add contact details to the Address Book from outgoing or incoming messages.

Outlook Express allows you to edit contact details, and to sort contacts according to such headings as last name and phone number.

About contact groups/mailing lists

A *mailing list* or a *contact group* is a list of e-mail addresses to which you can send a message in a single operation by entering the list's name in the To field of the message. A contact group may contain the names of other contact groups. You can change the composition of a contact group by adding or removing members. An individual may be a member of more than one group.

Digital IDs: envelopes and signatures

A digital ID has two roles: it ensures privacy by encrypting the message, and it ensures authenticity by preventing forgery and content tampering.

You can think of a digital ID as an electronic version of both a sealed envelope and a handwritten signature. There are different classes of digital IDs, each offering different levels of security and trustworthiness. Digital IDs are provided by independent certification authorities, and are installed in the Address Book of Outlook Express.

Explore your Address Book

**Addresses
button**

To explore the variety of information that you can record about your contacts, click the **Addresses** button on the Outlook Express toolbar or choose **Tools | Address Book** to open the **Address Book** dialog box.

Next, click the **New** button on the Address Book toolbar, and then choose the **New Contact** command.

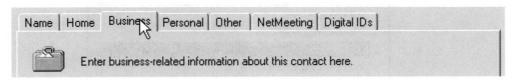

Click successively on the seven tabs of the dialog box, view the various fields available, and, when finished, click **Cancel**.

Add a contact to your Address Book

Let's add a contact to your Address Book.

1 Open your Address Book by clicking the **Addresses** button. Click the **New** button on the Address Book toolbar, and then choose the **New Contact** command.

2 In the **Name** tab of the **Properties** dialog box, type the First Name, Last Name and E-mail Address of a contact.

3 In the **Nickname** box, type a short, easy-to-remember version of the contact's name (even a single letter). Do not enter any spaces in the Nickname. When finished, click **OK**.

When sending e-mails, you can enter the Nickname in the **To** field instead of the recipient's full e-mail address. Nicknames are sometimes called aliases.

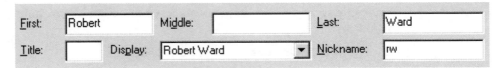

To create several new contacts in one operation, click **Add** after you type the details of each one. The **Add** button adds new contacts without closing the dialog box. The **OK** button adds the most recently entered contact – and closes the dialog box.

Contacts: the minimum details

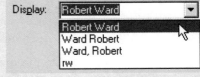

At a minimum, each contact in your Address Book must contain a First Name, a Last Name and a Display Name. All other contact details are optional. The first two you enter; the third is supplied, by default, by Outlook Express.

The Display Name is the name that appears in the To field of e-mails that you send to that contact, and in the From field of e-mails you receive from that contact.

You can change the default Display name by typing in a different name or by selecting an alternative from the pull-down list. The pull-down list contains variations of the First/Middle/Last name, as well as anything you typed in the **Nickname** box or the **Company** box of the **Business** tab.

Edit your contacts

You can change the details of a contact or add further details at any time as follows:

1 Open your Address Book by clicking the **Addresses** button.

2 Double-click the relevant contact to select it.

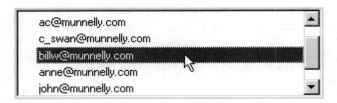

3 Edit the current details, and click **OK** when finished.

Delete a contact

To delete a contact, open your Address Book, select the relevant contact, and do any of the following: click the **Delete** button on the Address Book toolbar, press the DELETE key, or choose **File | Delete**.

Add contact details directly from e-mails

You can add a new contact by opening your Address Book, and entering and saving the relevant details as above. Two other methods are also available:

■ Display the Inbox or Outbox Message List, right-click on an e-mail, and choose **Add Sender to Address Book** from the pop-up menu.

■ When replying to an e-mail, right-click the name in the **To** field, and choose **Add to Address Book** from the pop-up menu.

You can also add all reply recipients to your Address Book automatically as follows:

1 Choose **Tools | Options**, and click the **Send** tab.

2 Select the option shown below, and click **OK**.

☑ Automatically put people I reply to in my Address Book

Sort your Address Book contacts

You can sort your contacts in your Address Book by headings such as name and telephone number. Let's try it.

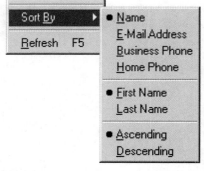

1 Open your Address Book by clicking the **Addresses** button on the Outlook Express toolbar.

2 On the menubar of the Address Book, choose **View | Sort By**.

3 Select the **Name**, **First Name**, and **Ascending** options. You may have to repeat step 2 to achieve this. You can then easily find a person by their first name by scrolling through the list.

Let's practice sorting by telephone number.

1 Click the words **Business Phone** in the header row.

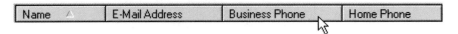

2 Click on the same words a second time.

Note that the order changes with each click, from ascending to descending to ascending again. You can now find the name you want by scrolling to the telephone number you recognize.

About contacts groups/mailing lists

If you regularly use e-mail to stay in touch with your football team, your research group, or your extended family, then you already know that you can send the same message to them by including all their names in the **To** or **Cc** box. (Remember to separate them with semi-colons, and to have at least one name in the **To** box!)

However, after a while, all that typing can get a bit tedious. What do you do? You set up what is generally known as a distribution or mailing list, but which Outlook Express calls a contact group.

Create a contact group

Follow these steps to set up a new contact group:

1 Open your Address Book by clicking the **Addresses** button on the Outlook Express toolbar.

2 Click the **New** button on the Address Book toolbar, and then choose the **New Group** command.

3 Give the new group a name – preferably a short, easy-to-remember name.

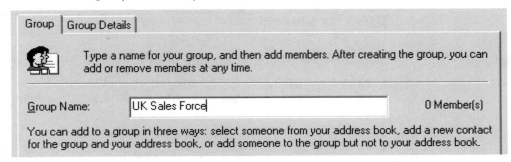

4 If a person is already in your Address Book, click **Select Members** to view a new dialog box that lists your e-mail contacts. For each contact you want to include, click their name and then click **Select ->**.

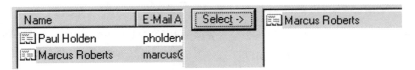

When finished, click **OK** to return to the main contact group dialog box. Now, go to step 5.

If the people you want to include are not in your Address Book, and you don't want them to be (because you never want to address them as individuals), type their name and e-mail address and click **Add**.

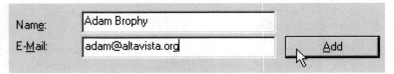

Continue typing names and e-mail addresses and clicking the **Add** button until you have entered the persons who are not in your Address Book.

5 When you have finished, click **OK**.

Once you have set up the group, you simply insert its name in the To field of the e-mail. Outlook Express sends the e-mail to everyone in the group.

A contact group may contain the names of other contact groups. For example, your Global Sales group might consist of three groups – the Europe Sales group, the US Sales group, and the ROW Sales group. An individual may be a member of more than one group. At any time you can change the composition of your group by adding new members or removing existing ones.

Send an e-mail to a contact group

Create Mail

Create Mail button

Send

Send button

Follow this procedure to send an e-mail to everyone in a contact group:

1 Click the **Create Mail** button on the Outlook Express toolbar or choose **File | New | Mail Message**.

2 In the **To** box of the e-mail header enter the name of the contact group.

3 Fill in the **Subject** field with an appropriate content, and type your e-mail.

4 When finished typing, click the **Send** button on the New Message toolbar or choose **File | Send Message**. Your e-mail will be sent to everyone in the contact group.

Remove members from a contact group

1 Open your Address Book by clicking the **Addresses** button on the Outlook Express toolbar.

2 Open your contact group by double-clicking its name at the left of the Address Book dialog box.

3 Click the name of the person you want to remove, and click **Remove**.

4 When finished, click **OK**.

If you remove a name from a group, they still remain in your Address Book, and in any other group of which they are a member. However, if you delete (or change) a name in your Address Book, it is deleted (or changed) in every group of which it is a member.

Sending an e-mail over the Internet is like sending a postcard: it is easy to intercept and read as it travels to its destination. To ensure confidential messages stay confidential, you can protect them with a so-called digital ID. This has two roles:

- It ensures privacy by encrypting the message – translating it into a form that is unreadable without the correct decoding keys.

- It ensures authenticity by preventing forgery or content tampering. Recipients are assured that the e-mail really came from you.

You can think of a digital ID as an electronic version of both a sealed envelope and a handwritten signature. There are different classes of digital IDs, each offering different levels of security and trustworthiness.

Obtaining and installing a digital ID

You can purchase a digital ID online from websites operated by independent certification authorities such as RSA and Verisign, and then download and install the ID within your e-mail software application. Outlook Express simplifies this process. Simply choose **Tools | Options**, click the **Security** tab, click the **Get Digital ID** button, and follow the online instructions to install the digital ID on your Address Book.

Three components of a digital ID

A digital ID has three components:

- A public key and a private key: These two keys, working together, enable an e-mail to be encrypted on your computer, and then decrypted back to a readable form on the recipient's computer. Your public key is available to anyone who requests it. Only you have access to your private key.

- A digital signature: When send an e-mail using your digital ID, you are adding your digital signature and public key to the message. The combination of a digital signature and public key is called a digital certificate.

How e-mails with digital IDs are exchanged

To send a secure e-mail to a recipient, you use your digital signature to identify yourself, and their public key to encrypt the message. When the recipient gets the secure e-mail, they use their private key to decrypt the message for reading. When you receive a secure message, you use your private key to decrypt it, and their digital signature to verify its authenticity.

Quit Outlook Express

You can close Outlook Express. Congratulations! You have now completed Module 7 of the ECDL, Information and Communication. To remind yourself of the main features of Internet Explorer and Outlook Express, cut out the quick reference guide, called **information and communication essentials** at the back of the book and keep it beside your computer.

IT essentials

Uses of computers

In our *Information Society* wealth and incomes depend increasingly on the ability to create, process and distribute information in all its various forms. Computers are widely used in government, business, financial services, manufacturing, healthcare and education.

While computers can store large amounts of information, retrieve selected information easily, and perform complex calculation quickly, those tasks that require *human judgement* are better left to humans to perform.

Keeping your information safe

Protect your valuable and *irreplaceable* data files by:

- Saving frequently (from RAM to hard disk)

- Making regular backup copies (to removable storage media), and storing backups offsite.

- Applying *usernames* and *confidential passwords*. The best passwords include both numbers and letters.

- Assigning access *rights* to network users so that they can use only the appropriate commands and view only relevant information.

- Protecting against viruses by installing anti-virus software. Viruses are spread through files downloaded from the Internet, through files attached to e-mails, and through the exchange of infected diskettes or CDs.

Data protection

The *EU Data Protection Directive* imposes specific responsibilities on anyone who maintains databases of personal information.

Health and safety

Take sensible precautions to avoid the main hazards associated with computer usage:

- Repetitive strain injury: Take a break every 15–20 minutes to allow your muscles to rest and recuperate.

- Eyestrain: Look away from your screen frequently, ensure the surrounding lighting is roughly equal to that of your screen, and position your screen so that any light sources are not behind or in front of you. An *anti-glare filter* can reduce reflected light from windows, light bulbs or other sources.

- Posture problems: Ensure your desk supports your screen at the correct eye level, and use a chair that provides adequate lumbar (lower back) support.

- Cabling, electrical overload: Ensure that cables are kept tidy, secure, and out of the way, and don't overload electricity sockets.

You can reduce the *environmental impact* of computer usage by choosing energy-efficient monitors, by saving and recycling paper, and by recycling printer ink cartridges.

Computers and information

Information is the result of counting, measuring, drawing and photographing things. Computers store and process information. Information is measured in terms of how much storage space it occupies.

A bit is the smallest unit. Eight bits make one byte. A kilobyte (KB) is a thousand bytes, a megabyte (MB) is a million, and a gigabyte is one thousand million (GB). Hardware includes the physical components of a computer. Software is the instructions that tell the hardware how to behave. A computer is hardware, but it does software.

Key hardware components

A modern computer contains three critical elements of hardware:

- Central Processing Unit (CPU): The brains of the computer. A typical CPU has a speed of about 2GHz.

- Random Access Memory (RAM): The volatile (temporary) storage area where the computer holds the software and information that it is currently working on. Common RAM sizes are in the range 64–512 MB (million bytes).

- Hard Disk Drive: A permanent and very large storage area. Sizes are typically in the 10–100GB range.

Computer hardware

A basic PC consists of a system unit, a screen, a keyboard, and a mouse or other pointing device. Other common items include a printer, a modem for connecting the computer to the telephone network, loudspeakers and microphones. A scanner or digital camera enables the capture of images, drawings or photo-graphs for inclusion in reports, newsletters or e-mails.

A personal digital assistant (PDA) is a hand-held device that combines the functions of a computer, mobile phone, fax sender, Web browser, e-mail client, and personal organizer.

Computer software

Software falls into two main categories:

- Application Software: Programs such as word processors that perform useful tasks.

- System Software: Also known as the operating system, this is software that controls the computer itself.

Licensed software must be purchased and used only under specified conditions. Software is developed by systems analysts and programmers in a process that involves research, analysis and development. Testing is almost never comprehensive, so bugs (errors and problems) sometimes occur.

Computer networks

Networking enables computer users to share hardware, applications, and data files, and to exchange e-mails. Networks may cover a small area (LANs) or a larger region (WANs).

PSTN and ISDN refer to two very different types of physical cables and the exchanges that connect them. PSTN (Public Switched Telephone Network) is the older-style, human-voice carrying system. ISDN (Integrated Services Digital Network) is the newer digital system, created specifically to carry computer-style digital signals.

ASDL (Asymmetric Digital Subscriber Line) refers to a method of transferring data at very high speeds through the traditional PSTN telephone system.

The Internet

The Internet is a worldwide network of networks. It is the most common medium for e-mail, and provides the infrastructure for the World Wide Web – a vast array of files that that can be accessed with a web browser.

Web pages are in a format called HTML. A search engine is a web page that allows you to locate files that contain information of interest. An intranet is like a private Internet within a company or department, and is not publicly accessible.

E-commerce

This is the use of the Internet for business purposes. You can shop 365 days a year, 24 hours a day, buy from anywhere in the world, and communicate with other buyers to get their views.

However, you can't touch and feel the goods, and there are issues surrounding security of personal details and credit card numbers, and of returns of unsatisfactory or incorrect goods.

Teleworking

The Net makes it possible for people to work from home or from locations other than the conventional workplace.

Teleworkers don't have to commute, and can set their schedules to suit home life better. Some people, however, find teleworking isolating, and they miss the interaction with colleagues.

Windows essentials

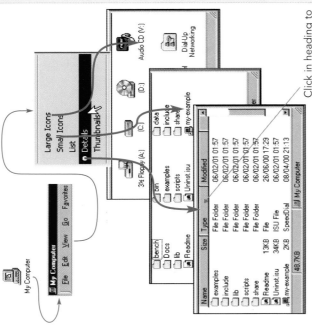

Windows vocabulary

Powering up/ Booting	Starting a computer. You don't 'switch on' a computer; you 'power it up' or 'boot' it.
Clicking	Pressing the left mouse button.
Clipboard	A temporary storage area to which you can copy or cut folders or files. You can paste from the clipboard to any location within the same or a different drive.
Cursor/ Pointer	A symbol that you move around the computer screen by moving the mouse around your (physical) desktop.
Double-clicking	Pressing the left mouse button twice in quick succession.
Dragging	Moving a selected item across the screen by clicking on it with the left mouse button, and holding down the button as you move the mouse.
Drive	A physical storage device for holding files and folders. Typically, A: is the floppy diskette drive, C: is the hard disk, and D: is the CD-ROM drive.
Pull-down menu	A list of options that appears (pulls down or drops down) when you click on a menu name.
File	The computer's basic unit of information storage. Everything on a computer is stored in a file of one type or another.
File name extension	A three-letter addition to a file name that indicates the type of information stored in the file. The extension is separated from the file name by a full-stop (dot).
Folder	A container for files or other folders. Files grouped into folders are easier to find and work with.
Menu	A list of items from which you can choose. The options typically allow you to direct the application, modify a file, or get more information.
Multi-tasking	The ability of Windows to open several applications and files at one time.
My Computer	A desktop feature that enables you to view all the folders and files on your computer.
Recycle Bin	A storage area where Windows holds deleted files until emptied.
Right-clicking	Pressing the right mouse button.
Screen saver	A program that takes over the computer's display screen if there are no keystrokes or mouse movements for a specified amount of time.
Sub-folder	A folder located within another folder.
Taskbar	A horizontal bar across the bottom of the Windows desktop that displays the Start button and the names of any open applications.
Toolbar	A collection of buttons that enable you to execute a sequence of actions with a single mouse-click.
Virus	A program that is loaded on to a computer without the user's knowledge and that damages software or data files in some way.
Windows Explorer	A program for viewing the folders and files on your computer, and for performing such actions as renaming, moving and deleting.
Windows Find	A feature that enables you to locate folders or files wherever they are on your computer.

My Computer essentials

My Computer

File Edit View Go Favorites

Large Icons
Small Icons
List
Details
Thumbnails

3½ Floppy (A:) (C:) (D:) Audio CD (V:)
Dial-Up Networking

bench, Docs, lib, Readme
bin, examples, scripts, Uninst.isu
data, include, share, my-example

Name	Size	Type	Modified
examples		File Folder	06/02/01 01:57
include		File Folder	06/02/01 01:57
lib		File Folder	06/02/01 01:57
scripts		File Folder	06/02/01 01:57
share		File Folder	06/02/01 01:57
Readme	13KB	File	26/06/00 17:29
Uninst.isu	34KB	ISU File	06/02/01 01:57
my-example	2KB	SpeedDial	08/04/00 21:13
48.7KB			My Computer

Click in heading to sort by name, size, type or date modified (2.3)

Common file types	extension (2.3)
Word	.doc
Excel	.xls
PowerPoint	.ppt
Access	.mdb
Plain text	.txt
Help	.hlp
Web	.htm, .html
Temporary	.tmp
Compressed	.zip
Image	.jpg, .gif, .tif, .bmp, .pcx, .psp, .ai
Music	.mp3, .wav
Video	.avi

If all else fails ... (2.1)

If you can get no response from an application, press the following three keys simultaneously: CTRL, ALT and DELETE.

Shortcuts (2.5)

CTRL + x	Cut
CTRL + c	Copy
CTRL + v	Paste
CTRL + z	Undo
F1	Help

Windows essentials

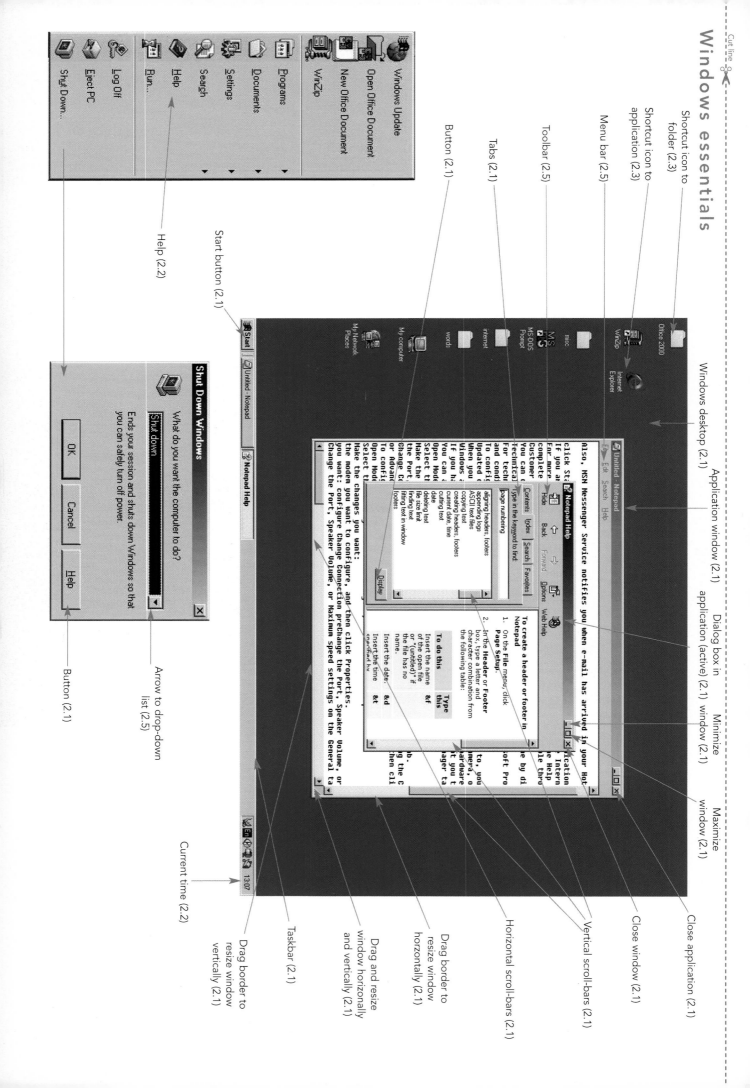

Shortcut icon to folder (2.3)

Shortcut icon to application (2.3)

Menu bar (2.5)

Toolbar (2.5)

Tabs (2.1)

Button (2.1)

Help (2.2)

Start button (2.1)

Windows Update

Open Office Document

New Office Document

WinZip

Programs

Documents

Settings

Search

Help

Run...

Log Off

Eject PC

Shut Down...

Windows desktop (2.1)

Application window (2.1)

Dialog box in application (active) (2.1)

Minimize window (2.1)

Maximize window (2.1)

Close application (2.1)

Close window (2.1)

Vertical scroll-bars (2.1)

Horizontal scroll-bars (2.1)

Drag border to resize window horizontally (2.1)

Drag and resize window horizontally and vertically (2.1)

Drag border to resize window vertically (2.1)

Taskbar (2.1)

Arrow to drop-down list (2.5)

Button (2.1)

Current time (2.2)

Shut Down Windows

What do you want the computer to do?

Shut down

Ends your session and shuts down Windows so that you can safely turn off power.

OK   Cancel   Help

word processing essentials

Word 2000

---

word processing vocabulary

Term	Definition
Alignment	The horizontal positioning of lines in a paragraph. They can share a common centre-point, begin at the same point on the left, end at the same point on the right, or begin and end at the same points.
Bulleted and numbered lists	A list of items that are bulleted (preceded by a dot or other symbol) or numbered (preceded by a sequentially increasing number).
Clipboard	A temporary storage area to which you can copy text (or graphics). You can paste to any location within the same or different documents.
Data source	A file containing information (such as names and addresses) that will be different in each copy of a form letter.
First line indent	The positioning of the first line of a paragraph a greater distance in from the left margin than the remaining lines of the same paragraph.
Font	A typeface: a particular style of text. The two main font families are serif and sans serif.
Form letter	A Word document containing information (text, spaces, punctuation and graphics) that remains the same in each copy of the merged letter.
Hanging indent	The positioning of the first line of a paragraph closer to the left margin than the remaining lines of the same paragraph.
Headers and footers	Standard text and graphics that are printed in the top and bottom margins of every page of a document.
Indent	The positioning of a paragraph of text a specified distance in from the left and/or right margin.
Inter-line spacing	The vertical space between lines within a paragraph of text. Word's default is single line spacing.
Inter-paragraph spacing	The spacing between successive paragraphs of text.
Margin	The distance of the text and graphics from the edge of the printed page. Word lets you specify separate top, bottom, left and right margins.
Merge field	An instruction to Word to insert a particular type of information, such as a job title or a line of an address, in a specified location on a form letter.
Non-printing characters	Symbols that Word displays on the screen to help you type and edit your document, but that are not printed.
Normal View	A view of a Word document that displays only the text.
Outline View	A view of a Word document that displays the structure of a document, with text indented progressively to reflect its level of importance.
Paragraph mark	A symbol shown on the screen (but not printed) to indicate the end of a paragraph (¶).
Print Layout View	A view of a Word document that displays it exactly as it will appear when you print it.
Table	An array of cells arranged in rows and columns that can hold text and graphics.
Tabs	Predefined horizontal locations between the left and right page margins that determine where typed text is positioned. Using tabs on successive lines gives the effect of side-by-side columns of text.
Word document	A Microsoft Word file containing text and sometimes graphics too. For example, a letter or a report.
Word template	A file that can contain ready-made text, formatting and page settings, and interface controls. Every Word document is based on, and takes its characteristics from, a template of one kind or another.

---

keyboard shortcuts

Shortcut	Action
CTRL+c	Copy selected text
CTRL+v	Insert text from clipboard
CTRL+x	Delete selected text
CTRL+y	Redo or repeat last action
CTRL+z	Undo last action
CTRL+b	Bold
CTRL+i	Italic
CTRL+l	Left align
CTRL+r	Right align
CTRL+j	Justify
CTRL+ENTER	Page break
CTRL+s	Save
CTRL+a	Select all
CTRL+u	Underline
ALT+CTRL+1	Apply Heading 1
ALT+CTRL+2	Apply Heading 2
ALT+CTRL+3	Apply Heading 3
END	Move to end of line
CTRL+END	Move to end of document
ALT+CTRL+z	Go back
HOME	Go to start of line
CRTL+HOME	Go to start of document
ALT+F4	Close or Exit
ALT+SHIFT+d	Insert current date
CTRL+f	Find
CTRL+h	Replace
CTRL+o	Open
CTRL+n	New
CTRL+p	Print

word processing essentials

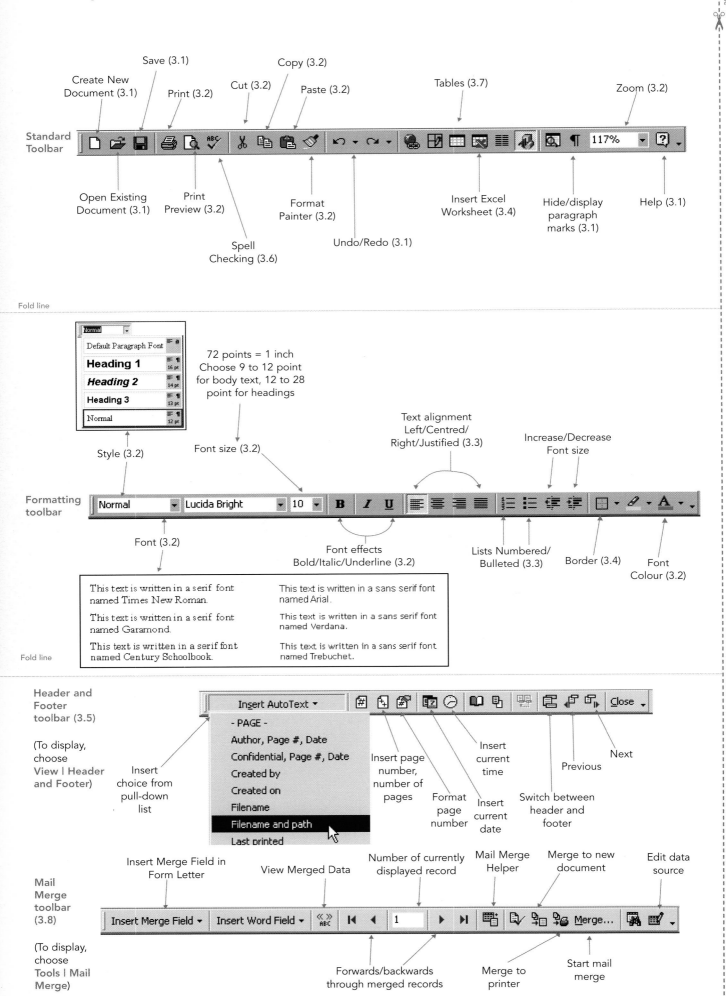

Standard Toolbar

Create New Document (3.1)
Save (3.1)
Print (3.2)
Cut (3.2)
Copy (3.2)
Paste (3.2)
Tables (3.7)
Zoom (3.2)

Open Existing Document (3.1)
Print Preview (3.2)
Spell Checking (3.6)
Format Painter (3.2)
Undo/Redo (3.1)
Insert Excel Worksheet (3.4)
Hide/display paragraph marks (3.1)
Help (3.1)

Fold line

72 points = 1 inch
Choose 9 to 12 point for body text, 12 to 28 point for headings

Text alignment Left/Centred/Right/Justified (3.3)

Increase/Decrease Font size

Style (3.2)
Font size (3.2)

Formatting toolbar

Font (3.2)
Font effects Bold/Italic/Underline (3.2)
Lists Numbered/Bulleted (3.3)
Border (3.4)
Font Colour (3.2)

This text is written in a serif font named Times New Roman.

This text is written in a serif font named Garamond.

This text is written in a serif font named Century Schoolbook.

This text is written in a sans serif font named Arial.

This text is written in a sans serif font named Verdana.

This text is written in a sans serif font named Trebuchet.

Fold line

Header and Footer toolbar (3.5)

(To display, choose **View | Header and Footer**)

Insert choice from pull-down list

Insert page number, number of pages

Insert current time

Next

Previous

Format page number

Insert current date

Switch between header and footer

Mail Merge toolbar (3.8)

(To display, choose **Tools | Mail Merge**)

Insert Merge Field in Form Letter

View Merged Data

Number of currently displayed record

Mail Merge Helper

Merge to new document

Edit data source

Forwards/backwards through merged records

Merge to printer

Start mail merge

Cut line

spreadsheet essentials

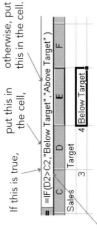
Microsoft Excel

---

spreadsheet vocabulary

Term	Definition
Absolute cell reference	A reference to a cell or cell range in the format $A$1, A$1 or A$1. Excel does not adjust an absolute cell reference when you copy or move a calculation containing such a reference.
Argument	The inputs to a calculation that generate the result.
AutoFill	An Excel tool for quickly copying or incrementing the entries in a cell or range.
Bar chart	A 'sideways' column chart that shows items vertically and values horizontally.
Cell range	A group of cells on a worksheet.
Cell reference	The location or 'address' of a cell on a worksheet.
Chart area	The margin area inside the chart boundaries but outside the actual plotted chart. It typically holds labels identifiying the chart axes.
Column chart	Excel's default chart type, in which items are shown horizontally and values vertically.
Comma separated Values (CSV) text file	A text file format in which data items are separated horizontally by commas and vertically by paragraph breaks.
Data point	An item being measured and its measured value.
Data series	A group of related data points.
Excel Chart	A graphic or diagram based on the numbers, text and calculations that are located in the rows and columns of an Excel worksheet.
Formula	An equation that performs operations such as addition, subtraction, multiplication or division on data that is stored in a worksheet.
Function	A predefined formula built in to Excel and used for a specific purpose.
Label	A piece of text in a worksheet cell that provides information about the number in an accompanying cell, usually either below it or to its right.
Marquee	A flashing rectangle that Excel uses to surround a cell, or cell range, that you have copied to the Clipboard.
Name box	The rectangular area above the top-left corner of a worksheet in which Excel displays the cell reference of the active cell.
Number style	The way in which Excel displays a number on screen and on printouts. Number format affects only the appearance and not the value of numbers.
Operators	Symbols that specify the type of calculation you want to perform on the arguments of a formula. Excel's four main arithmetic operators are +, -, * and /.
Pie chart	These are typically used to illustrate the breakdown of figures in a total. A pie chart is always based on a single data series.
Plot area	The area containing the actual plot. It is bounded by the two chart axes and is enclosed within the chart area.
Relative cell reference	A reference to a cell or cell range in the format A1. Excel changes a relative cell reference when you copy or move a formula or function containing such a reference to a new location.
Sorting	Rearranging columns of cells based on the values in the cells. Sorting does not change the content of cells, only their location.
Tab-delimited text file	A text file format in which data items are separated horizontally by tabs and vertically by paragraph breaks.
Worksheet	A page that is made up of little boxes (cells) arranged in rows and columns. Relationships can be created between the cells so that changing the contents of one cell affects the contents of the related cells.
Workbook	A file containing worksheets.

---

what goes in a cell?

Relative cell reference (4.5)   Absolute cell reference (4.5)

=I4+D1*$E$1

Constant (4.2)

	C	D	E
		3	2
	20		

Operators (4.2)
- / Division
- * Multiplication
- + Addition
- − Subtraction

Note: Calculated in that order!

Cell range(s) (4.2)

=SUM(C1:D1,D2:E2,C3)

	C	D	E
	3	4	2
	6	7	1
	5	9	**20**

Function (4.3)

In the specified cell range(s):
SUM Gives the total value
AVERAGE Gives the average value
MAX Gives the maximum value
MIN Gives the minimum value
COUNT Gives the number of non-blank cells

If this is true,   put this in the cell,   otherwise, put this in the cell.

=IF(D2>C2,"Below Target","Above Target")

	C	D	E	F
	Sales	Target		
	3	3	4	Below Target

- < Is less than
- > Is greater than
- >= Is greater than or equal to
- <= Is less than or equal to

spreadsheet essentials

Cut line

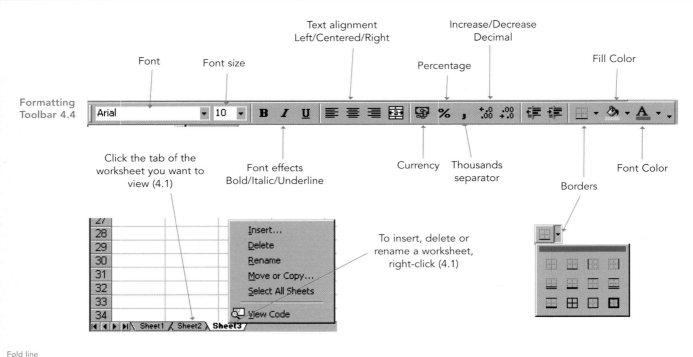

Standard Toolbar

- Open existing workbook (4.1)
- Print options (4.6)
- Cut (4.5)
- Undo/Redo (4.1)
- Charts (4.7, 4.8)
- Zoom (4.1)
- Create new workbook (4.1)
- Spell checking (4.6)
- Paste (4.5)
- AutoSum (4.3)
- Sort Ascending/Descending (4.5)
- Help (4.1)
- Save (4.1)
- Copy (4.5)

Fold line

Formatting Toolbar 4.4

- Text alignment Left/Centered/Right
- Increase/Decrease Decimal
- Font
- Font size
- Percentage
- Fill Color
- Click the tab of the worksheet you want to view (4.1)
- Font effects Bold/Italic/Underline
- Currency
- Thousands separator
- Borders
- Font Color

Insert...
Delete
Rename
Move or Copy...
Select All Sheets
View Code

To insert, delete or rename a worksheet, right-click (4.1)

Sheet1 Sheet2 **Sheet3**

Fold line

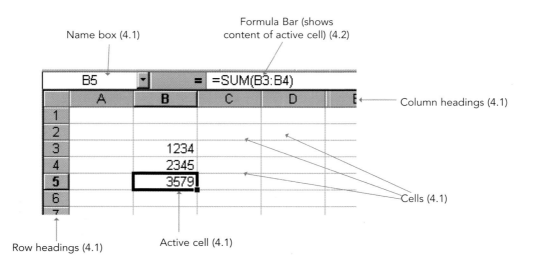

- Name box (4.1)
- Formula Bar (shows content of active cell) (4.2)
- Column headings (4.1)
- Cells (4.1)
- Row headings (4.1)
- Active cell (4.1)

B5   =   =SUM(B3:B4)

	A	B	C	D	E
1					
2					
3		1234			
4		2345			
5		3579			
6					
7					

database essentials

Microsoft Access

---

database vocabulary

Database Management System (DBMS)	An application such as Microsoft Access that enables you to collect information on a computer, organize it in different ways, sort and select pieces of information of interest to you, and produce reports.
Data type	This determines the kind of data that can be entered in a field, and how Access treats that data.
Field properties	The set of characteristics that you can apply to a field, such as its maximum size or default value. Most field properties depend on the field's data type.
Form	Forms enable table records to be viewed and updated one at a time. As forms are based on tables, you can create a form only after you have created a table.
Indexed field	A field that a table can use to find and sort records. Access automatically makes primary key fields indexed fields. You can index other fields if required.
Literal	A literal value, such as a specific number (12), date (26/11/04) or text (Yes).
One-to-many relationship	A record in the first table can have many matching records in the second table. But a record in the second table can have only one matching record in the first table.
One-to-one relationship	A record in the first table has no more than one matching record in the second table. Typically, the two tables have the same primary key.
Primary key	A field in a table that is used to identify each record in the table uniquely.
Relational integrity	A system of rules enforced automatically by Access that prevents the insertion, deletion or changing of data that threatens or breaks a relationship.
Relationship window	A window that displays existing links between tables, and that provides a visual method for working with links.
Select query	A query that selects only records from a table or tables based on criteria expressed as combinations of comparison operators, literals and logical operators.
Sort	An operation on a table that changes the order in which the records are displayed. Sorting does not change the content of records, only their location.
Table relationship	A link between records in different tables of the same database.
Validation rule	This sets limits or conditions on the values that may be entered into a field. When a user enters data into a field, Access checks the data to ensure that it complies with the validation rule.

Design view

Design view: A view in which you can display and change the organizational structure of your table.

Primary Key Indicator (5.2)

Books : Table

Field Name	Data Type
ISBN	Text
Title	Text
Pages	Number
CopyrightYear	Number

Data type	Used for (5.5)
Text	Alphabetic or numeric data up to 255 characters. Cannot be used in calculations.
Memo	Alphabetic or numeric data up to 64,000 characters. Cannot be used in calculations.
Number	Numeric data that may be used in calculations.
Date/Time	Date or time data.
Currency	Money values or other numeric data used in calculations where the number of decimal places does not exceed four.
AutoNumber	A number assigned to each new record automatically, starting with 1.
Yes/No	Fields that can have simple yes/no, true/false, or on/off values only.

General	Lookup
Field Size	50
Format	
Input Mask	
Caption	
Default Value	
Validation Rule	
Validation Text	

Validation rules	Only accepted values
>=10 AND <=100	Numbers in the range 10 to 100 inclusive.
>10 And <100	Numbers in the range 10 to 100 exclusive.
>=#01/01/03# AND <=#31/12/03#	Dates in the year 2003.
>=Date() and #<=31/12/06#	Dates from today up to the end of 2006.
>=#01/01/90# AND =<Date()	Dates from the beginning of 1990 up to and including today.
<10 Or >100	Numbers less than 10 and numbers greater than 100.
#25/12/03# or =#25/12/04#	Christmas Day 2003 or Christmas Day 2004.
="Small" OR ="Medium" OR ="Large"	One of the words Small, Medium or Large.
IN("Mr", "Ms", "Mrs", "Dr")	Any one of the quoted character strings.

database essentials

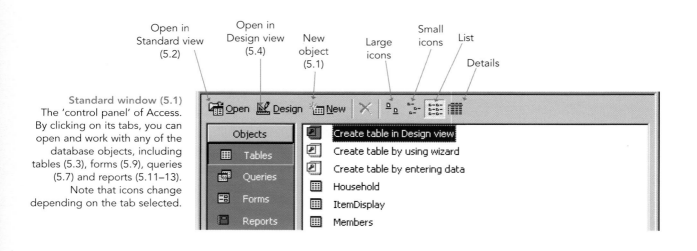

Open in Standard view (5.2)
Open in Design view (5.4)
New object (5.1)
Large icons
Small icons
List
Details

Standard window (5.1)
The 'control panel' of Access. By clicking on its tabs, you can open and work with any of the database objects, including tables (5.3), forms (5.9), queries (5.7) and reports (5.11–13). Note that icons change depending on the tab selected.

Fold line

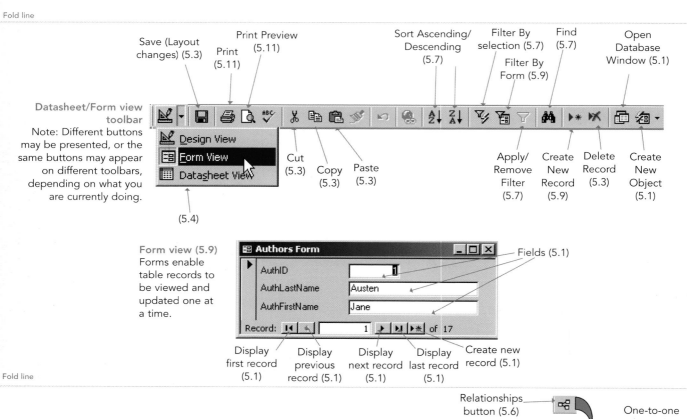

Datasheet/Form view toolbar
Note: Different buttons may be presented, or the same buttons may appear on different toolbars, depending on what you are currently doing.

Save (Layout changes) (5.3)
Print (5.11)
Print Preview (5.11)
Sort Ascending/ Descending (5.7)
Filter By selection (5.7)
Filter By Form (5.9)
Find (5.7)
Open Database Window (5.1)

(5.4)
Cut (5.3)
Copy (5.3)
Paste (5.3)
Apply/ Remove Filter (5.7)
Create New Record (5.9)
Delete Record (5.3)
Create New Object (5.1)

Form view (5.9)
Forms enable table records to be viewed and updated one at a time.

Fields (5.1)

Display first record (5.1)
Display previous record (5.1)
Display next record (5.1)
Display last record (5.1)
Create new record (5.1)

Fold line

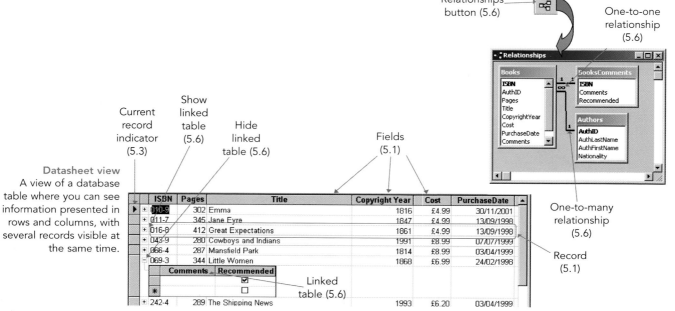

Relationships button (5.6)
One-to-one relationship (5.6)

Current record indicator (5.3)
Show linked table (5.6)
Hide linked table (5.6)
Fields (5.1)

Datasheet view
A view of a database table where you can see information presented in rows and columns, with several records visible at the same time.

One-to-many relationship (5.6)
Record (5.1)
Linked table (5.6)

presentation essentials

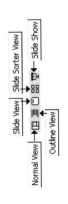

PowerPoint

presentation vocabulary

Advance method	The way that PowerPoint displays the slides of a presentation: manually, automatically, or automatically with manual override. Automatic advance is often used for unaccompanied presentations.
Animated slide	A slide in which different elements are revealed at different times.
AutoLayout	One of 24 ready-made slide layouts. They typically include placeholders for text and other objects, such as images and charts.
AutoShapes	Ready-made shapes, including lines, geometric shapes and flowchart elements, that you can use in your presentations.
Bullet point	A bullet character (such as • or ■) followed by one or a few words of text. Bullet points may be at different levels, indicated by their indentation, bullet character and font size.
Clip Art	Standard or 'stock' images that can be used and reused in presentations and other documents.
Colour scheme	A set of pre-selected co-ordinated colours that you can use to give your presentation an attractive and consistent appearance.
Design template	A PowerPoint file, containing a colour scheme and Slide Master with font settings and possibly built-in graphics and text, which can be applied to a presentation. Design template files end in .pot.
Normal view	A PowerPoint view composed of a Normal pane (where you work with one slide at a time), an Outline pane (where you see work with the text of all slides) and a Notes pane (where you can work with additional text for the presenter).
Organization chart	A diagram used to illustrate the people or units in an organisation or system (represented by boxes) and their relationships (represented by lines).
Outline pane	In Normal view, this shows the text of all your slides, so that you can judge how well your ideas and text flow from one slide to the next.
Placeholder	A rectangular box within a slide for holding text or graphics.
PowerPoint presentation	A file containing one or more slides. Presentation files end in .ppt.
Slide	The basic building block of a visual presentation. It is equivalent to a page in a printed document. A slide typically contains text and graphics, and possibly sound, animations and video.
Slide Master	This stores all the default attributes that you wish to apply new slides, including text formatting and positioning, background and standard graphics (such as your company logo).
Slide Show view	A view you use for presenting your slides to your audience. PowerPoint's various menus and toolbars are not displayed in Slide Show view.
Slide Sorter view	A view where you can see all slides of a presentation at once.
Speaker notes	A page that PowerPoint creates to accompany each slide. You can use it to record key points or additional details about your presentation.
Title slide	A presentation's first slide. Typically, it has a different layout to the rest of the presentation.
Transition	A visual effect, such as a drop-down, box-out, dissolve, or fade, that controls how one slide in a presentation is replaced by another.

views

Normal View → Slide View Slide Sorter View Slide Show
→ Outline View

Normal view

Slide pane (text, graphics and other elements of a single slide)

Outline pane (text only of all sides)

Notes pane (additional text for presenter)

Slide Sorter view

Copy, Move and Reorder slides using drag-and-drop

Slide Show view

No editing possible. Press Esc key to return to edit mode.

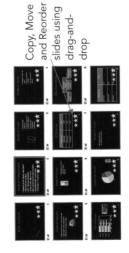

Sales Projections

presentation essentials

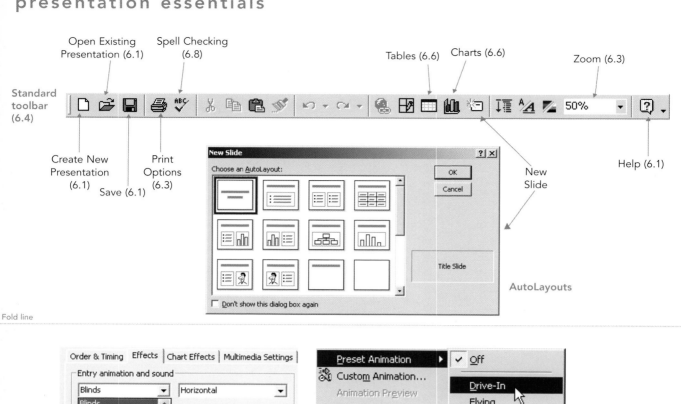

Standard toolbar (6.4)

- Open Existing Presentation (6.1)
- Spell Checking (6.8)
- Tables (6.6)
- Charts (6.6)
- Zoom (6.3)
- Create New Presentation (6.1)
- Save (6.1)
- Print Options (6.3)
- New Slide
- Help (6.1)
- AutoLayouts

Fold line

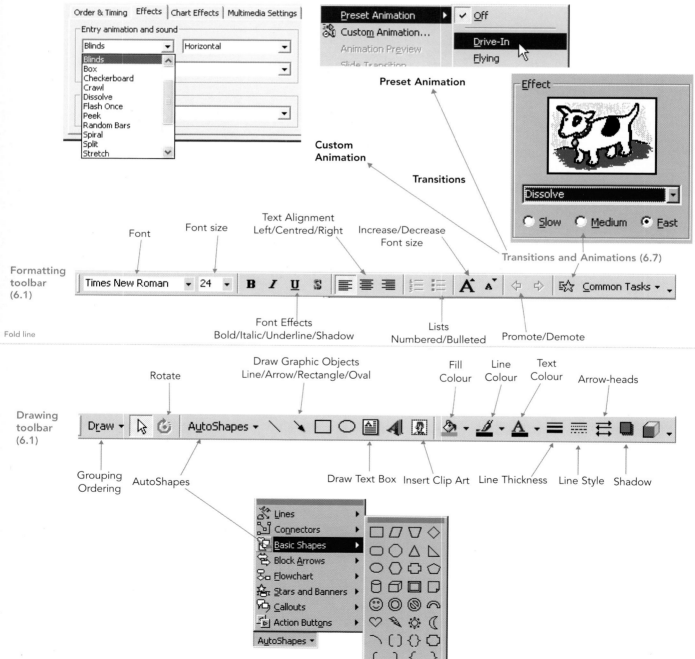

Preset Animation

Custom Animation

Transitions

Transitions and Animations (6.7)

Formatting toolbar (6.1)

- Font
- Font size
- Text Alignment Left/Centred/Right
- Increase/Decrease Font size
- Font Effects Bold/Italic/Underline/Shadow
- Lists Numbered/Bulleted
- Promote/Demote

Fold line

Drawing toolbar (6.1)

- Rotate
- Draw Graphic Objects Line/Arrow/Rectangle/Oval
- Fill Colour
- Line Colour
- Text Colour
- Arrow-heads
- Grouping Ordering
- AutoShapes
- Draw Text Box
- Insert Clip Art
- Line Thickness
- Line Style
- Shadow

Cut line

information and communication essentials

Internet Explorer Outlook Express

internet vocabulary

Term	Definition
Address bar	An area above the main window that shows the address (preceded by 'http://') of the currently displayed web page.
Directory site	A website that lists and categorizes other sites on the web according to their subject matter.
DNS	The Domain Name System. A network within the Internet that translates domain names, entered in web browsers, to IP addresses.
Favorites	A list of website addresses stored in Internet Explorer. Favorites remove the need to remember or retype the URLs of frequently visited websites.
Firewall	A firewall prevents unauthorized access to or from a computer or network. All communications passing through the firewall are examined, and suspect ones are blocked.
Home page	The first or front page of a website. Typically, it presents a series of links that you can follow to view the site's other pages.
Interactive form	A series of fields on a web page that you use to request a specific item of information, or a product or service. You can also use a form to submit information, such as your name and credit card number.
IP address	A unique identifier of every computer attached to the Internet. IP addresses are written as four numbers in the range 0-255, separated by full stops.
Keyword	Text or other keyboard characters entered to a search engine. The engine then displays or 'returns' a list of documents containing the entered text.
Logical search	A web search that uses logical operators, such as the plus and/or minus symbols, to include and/or exclude specified words or phrases from the results.
Navigation bar	A horizontal or vertical list of hyperlinks to the main components of a website, such as Home (the front page), Site Index (or Site Map or Guide), Company Profile, Products, Services and Staff Contacts.
Phrase search	A query to a search engine that is placed inside quotes. Only web pages containing all the entered words, in the order entered, are found.
Search engine	A program that searches for keywords entered by the user. It displays or 'returns' a list of web pages on which it found occurrences of the entered word or words.
Site index	Also known as a site map or site guide, this is a web page that lists the main contents of a website
SSL	The Secure Sockets Layer protocol that uses encryption to protect data in transit between web browsers and web servers.
URL	An Internet address that specifies the protocol used to access a web page or file contains the name of the web server on which the page resides, and includes (or implies) the name of a particular document or file.
Web browser	An application such as Microsoft Internet Explorer that enables a user to request files from a web server over the Internet, and displays the requested files on the user's computer.
Web server	A computer on an Internet-connected network that stores files and delivers them over the Internet in response to requests from web browsers.

e-mail vocabulary

Term	Definition
Address Book	A feature of an e-mail application that enables you to record details about your e-mail contacts for easy reference.
Bcc: (Blind Carbon Copy)	A field in an e-mail header that enables you to copy an e-mail to other recipients. Bcc recipients can view addresses in the To: and Cc fields, but not addresses in the Bcc field. To and Cc recipients cannot view any addresses in the Bcc field.
Bounced e-mail	An e-mail that, for whatever reason, fails to reach its recipient, and is returned to its sender with a message to that effect.
Cc: (Carbon Copy)	A field in an e-mail header where you can enter the addresses of people to whom you want to send a copy of the e-mail.
Contact	A person or organization whose details (such as name and e-mail address) you have recorded in the Address Book of your e-mail application.
E-mail collection	The action of transferring e-mails from the Internet to your computer. You must be online to collect e-mail, but you can read collected e-mails offline.
File attachment	A file, typically a formatted file such as a Word document, that is appended to and sent with an e-mail.
Folders List	The part of Outlook Express where e-mails are stored and grouped according to type: received (Inbox), waiting to be sent (Outbox), already sent (Sent Items), marked for deletion (Deleted Items), and stored for later editing (Drafts). You can create additional folders and sub-folders for further organizing your e-mails.
Forwarding	The act of passing to another person an e-mail that you have received. You typically include some comments of your own in the forwarded e-mail.
Mailing List/Contact Group	A list of e-mail addresses to which you can send a message in a single operation by entering the list's name in the To field of the e-mail.
Message List	A list of the e-mails contained in the currently selected Outlook Express folder. Outlook Express displays a summary of information about each one.
Message priority	An indication to an e-mail recipient of a message's urgency. The priority of an e-mail has no impact on the speed with which it travels.
Nickname (alias)	A shortened form of an e-mail address that you can enter in the To field of an e-mail as an alternative to typing the contact's e-mail address in full.
Preview Pane	An area of the Outlook Express screen that shows the content of the e-mail that is currently selected in the Message List.
Reply All	The act of replying to a received e-mail. Everyone who received the original e-mail also gets your reply. The reply typically includes some or all of the text of the original e-mail.
Reply to Sender Only	The act of replying to a received e-mail. Only the person who sent you the e-mail gets your reply. The reply typically includes some or all of the text of the original e-mail.
Signature (sig) file	An appendage at the end of e-mails. Typical contents include the sender's full name, occupation or position, phone and fax numbers, and e-mail and website addresses.

Go back one page in the sequence of web pages visited in this session (7.1)

Halts the retrieval of a web page (7.1)

Returns to the start web page you specified (7.1, 7.5)

Displays a list of your saved web addresses (7.5)

Prints the current web page (7.2)

Internet Explorer Standard toolbar

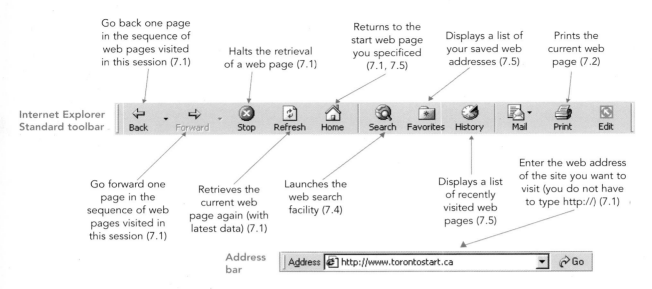

Go forward one page in the sequence of web pages visited in this session (7.1)

Retrieves the current web page again (with latest data) (7.1)

Launches the web search facility (7.4)

Displays a list of recently visited web pages (7.5)

Enter the web address of the site you want to visit (you do not have to type http://) (7.1)

Address bar

Fold line

Write a new e-mail (7.8)

Reply to all recipients of current e-mail (7.9)

Print current e-mail (7.7)

Send queued e-mails and collect waiting e-mails (dial-up connection) (7.7)

Search for e-mails satisfying specified criteria (7.9)

Outlook Express Standard toolbar

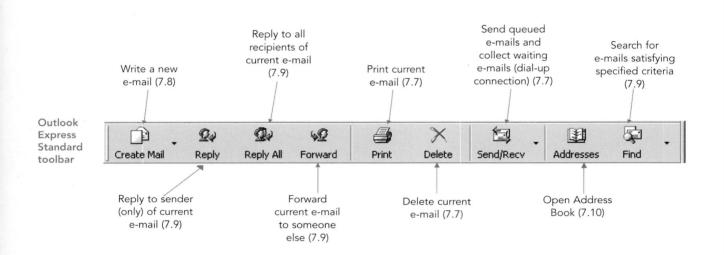

Reply to sender (only) of current e-mail (7.9)

Forward current e-mail to someone else (7.9)

Delete current e-mail (7.7)

Open Address Book (7.10)

Fold line

Send e-mail (7.8)

Copy selected text to the clipboard (7.8)

Attach a file (7.8)

Outlook Express New Message toolbar

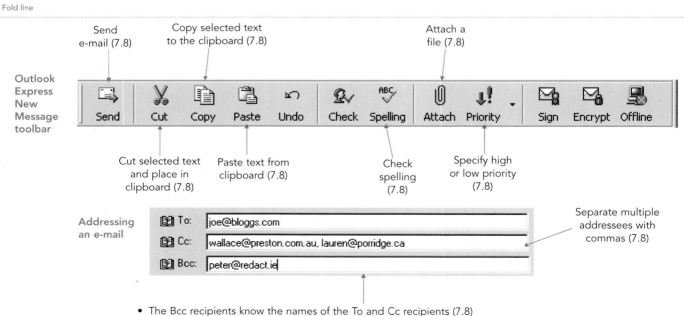

Cut selected text and place in clipboard (7.8)

Paste text from clipboard (7.8)

Check spelling (7.8)

Specify high or low priority (7.8)

Addressing an e-mail

Separate multiple addressees with commas (7.8)

- The Bcc recipients know the names of the To and Cc recipients (7.8)
- The To and Cc recipients know each others' names, but do not the names of the Bcc recipients
- The Bcc recipients do not know each other's names.